Social Support, Well-being, and Teacher Development

"The main theme of the book—social support, fits well to the present society for the needs of promoting well-being and healthy life style among people. The book presents an interdisciplinary investigation while it is a reader-friendly text for the general public."

—Dr. POON Wai Kit, *Medical practitioner*

"Wonderful conceptualization of teachers as social support givers. Great contribution to the field of teacher development. Fantastic resource for those interested in how social support enhances the well-being of learners and educators."

—Dr. Alfredo Bautista, *National Institute of Education (Singapore)*

"Lam argued in this book that teachers' role remain very important—teachers are encouraged to continue to give social support to students, to enhance the well-being of students; and, in return, teachers will be rewarded with emotional satisfaction."

—Mr. TANG Wai Chung, *Solicitor*

Bick-har LAM

Social Support, Well-being, and Teacher Development

Springer

Bick-har LAM
The Education University of Hong Kong
Hong Kong, Hong Kong

ISBN 978-981-13-3575-4   ISBN 978-981-13-3577-8   (eBook)
https://doi.org/10.1007/978-981-13-3577-8

Library of Congress Control Number: 2018964009

© Springer Nature Singapore Pte Ltd. 2019, corrected publication 2019
This work is subject to copyright. All rights are reserved by the Publisher, whether the whole or part of the material is concerned, specifically the rights of translation, reprinting, reuse of illustrations, recitation, broadcasting, reproduction on microfilms or in any other physical way, and transmission or information storage and retrieval, electronic adaptation, computer software, or by similar or dissimilar methodology now known or hereafter developed.
The use of general descriptive names, registered names, trademarks, service marks, etc. in this publication does not imply, even in the absence of a specific statement, that such names are exempt from the relevant protective laws and regulations and therefore free for general use.
The publisher, the authors and the editors are safe to assume that the advice and information in this book are believed to be true and accurate at the date of publication. Neither the publisher nor the authors or the editors give a warranty, express or implied, with respect to the material contained herein or for any errors or omissions that may have been made. The publisher remains neutral with regard to jurisdictional claims in published maps and institutional affiliations.

This Springer imprint is published by the registered company Springer Nature Singapore Pte Ltd.
The registered company address is: 152 Beach Road, #21-01/04 Gateway East, Singapore 189721, Singapore

Foreword I

Humans are first a social species, and though we might often not be very sociable, we rely on others in almost all that we do. Our social behaviour is embedded within both our biological and our cultural systems: biological in that we form pair bonds to reproduce and the resulting families mostly stay together; cultural, in that the different group processes within and between families vary by place and time. The family, whether the recent nuclear form or the traditional extended form, provides a context from within which the person emerges. This emergence takes place by way of the interactions a child has with others around her and the physical environment that she encounters. Within this environment, she is equipped with the roles and skills she is expected to need. If she is fortunate, she will be sent to school as part of this process. School acts as an agent of the family's expectations for what development is required. All too often this is anticipated to be a knowledge acquisition process within which a teacher transfers knowledge and the skills to use such to a receptacle that will absorb them. Woe betide the child who does not, or cannot take this stuff and hold it in their heads. Woe too, the teacher whose charges look out of the window rather than to the lesson of the hour.

According to the twentieth-century Soviet psychologist, Lev Vygotsky, a higher psychological function first appears between people, before it appears in the child as an intrapsychical category. This reflects a tight link between the social organisation of behaviour and individual organisation of thinking, implying culture-driven learning requires social space to build intellectual space, and mostly, these social spaces are scripted for them by adults and later, by more capable peers.

Vygotsky was adamant that a child learns by encountering situations where they must learn to take control of the 'space' between external and internal control of mastery—the zone of proximal development. This zone is the difference between 'a child's actual development as determined by independent problem-solving' and the 'potential development as determined through problem-solving under adult guidance or more capable peers': meaning-making is transferred from adult control to child control. The teacher must explicitly support the child's adoption of the control over learning and in doing this teaches yet more implicitly about the process of learning; persistence, effort and eventually self-efficacy in the process, and thereby extends the zone further. Or at least that's the theory. All too often today teaching is outcome focused to the extent that it dominates teaching to the test to achieve occupational goals that increasingly seems to be futile to many students. The incongruence students face between having to pursue paths that seem only to privilege career success or failure at their ends and the impact this has for their emotional development can be crippling, as the growing rates of student self-harm and suicide reveal.

That teaching is a social enterprise is self-evident. But it is more than the speaking of facts and the guidance thereto. Vygotsky's work points directly to the critical role of the supportive function of the social exchange that is teaching. This is as important for the teacher's well-being as it is for that of the student.

This book focuses directly on that social function. In particular, it addresses the emotional side of the learning process, and the importance of this both in building learning efficacy as well as topic mastery and in the resultant confidence of the child. This requires, in today's ubiquitous market parlance, that the student sees value in what they are doing and that value has an emotional as well as intellectual valance. This has powerful implications for the health of children and young people.

The growing problem of student disengagement is perhaps symptomatic of the failure to address the social function of teaching. With this exciting new addition to the literature, let's hope it is the beginning of a much greater return of focus to supportive aspects of the teacher–student relationship as the core vehicle for effective learning, in the same way that focus has been brought to the centrality of the doctor–patient relationship as a core vehicle for healing. If we fail to accommodate and develop these critical social functions, we cannot expect outcomes to improve.

Hong Kong
September 2018

Richard Fielding
Honorary Professor of
Medical Psychology in Public Health
The University of Hong Kong

Foreword II

One of my first acquaintances with some of the concepts covered in this book—and indeed with Bick-har herself as an active and ardent researcher—was at a departmental annual research conference. The Department of Curriculum and Instruction—of which I had recently become head in the mid-2010s—holds an annual internal conference, where a number of colleagues present some of their ongoing research to the Department at large. Colleagues have a standard (limited) amount of time to present some aspect of their research to the rest of the Department, after which fruitful discussion usually ensues. While colleagues do of course discuss research issues in the corridors and canteens of the University, it is at the annual research conference, however, where they have the opportunity to really see in depth what a number of their contemporaries are up to.

It was against this backdrop of the 2015 annual conference that I became rather more aware of what Bick-har was up to, but equally of the scale of what she was involved in. Bick-har was presenting something that was very dear to her. This was, I now realise, what formed the basis for Chap. 5—the study exploring the attitudes and support behaviour of four exemplary teachers.

I recall that Bick-har had a tonne of—very interesting—data in her presentation pertaining to both qualitative and quantitative perspectives. There were slides full of statistical output and (dense) participants' quotes up on the screen. As I recall, each colleague was supposed to have 20 min to present, followed by 5 min of questioning. Bick-har was still in full flow after 45 min and appeared to be nowhere near the time for questions ☺. When I went up to her afterwards and talked to her about what she hadn't had time to cover, the scale of the project became apparent to me and how its intricacies and complexities appeared to represent rather more than would be appropriate for a single academic article. I suggested that she consider taking a step back, consider the bigger picture and perhaps try and put this web of related issues together in a book.

And so, 3 years later, here we are. I know it has been something of a labour of love for Bick-har. I am very impressed by the scale and scope of it all, and I am convinced that it will be well received by a wide range of stakeholders. All I can say is: Congratulations, Bick-har! You done good! I am sure it will all be worth it.

Hong Kong
November 2018

David Coniam
Head of Department and
Chair Professor of Curriculum and Assessment
Department of Curriculum and Instruction
The Education University of Hong Kong

Preface

This book relates social support to the discussion of learning and teaching. It aims to provide sufficient information for researchers and teachers in the education profession to recognise the theories and practice of social support that could be applied to research and classroom practice, which will have an impact upon the learning outcomes of students and teachers' professional development.

Human beings feel contented when they perceive the environment as supportive; they feel competent and rewarded when they are engaged in altruistic helping behaviours. These psychological processes are found to benefit well-being and physical health. They are studied in health psychology as a key research component known as social support. In simple words, social support refers to the care and assistance available to individuals from another person.

Social support is strongly reminiscent of teachers' support to students in the school environment, with students as support receivers and teachers as support givers during classroom instruction. It is well known that teachers' emotional support for students can enhance educational outcomes and teachers' intrinsic interest in learners often yields satisfaction to teachers to make them more engaged in their career; yet these benefits are under-theorised and are not well documented in the literature.

In fact, the affective dimension of teachers' work, such as teacher emotional support and affective outcomes of student learning, continues to excite considerable interest among practitioners. There are also more theoretical concerns over learner-centred pedagogies and the distinction between the practice of a caring mentor of teaching and a simple imparter of knowledge; nevertheless, teachers may find teachers' emotional work in the classroom not much recognised as increasing demands on academic achievement become more dominant in schools in the twenty-first century where the value of education is focused on examination results. The impetus for the book was prompted by the above issues. The book attempts to provide key answers to inform whether and how social support of teachers benefits students and teachers themselves, and what the forms of social support-related practice are in the education literature. The book will add to practitioners' knowledge and to their professional 'toolbox' regarding learning and teaching, and teacher development.

Social Support, Well-being, and Teacher Development is the title of the book. As the name suggests, social support is the main theme of the book. Well-being is the object of social support, i.e. the goals to achieve social support. Teacher development is the area that the results of the investigation of the book serve. Social support behaviour of teachers is found to benefit both teachers and students—social support being incorporated in teaching to develop high-level teaching expertise that supports student learning with rewarding educational outcomes. It can be assumed that only if teachers are trained and developed to acquire the knowledge, traits and skills to perform the role of supporting students in the classroom should it be possible to realise the benefits of incorporating social support in the practice of teaching in the classroom. Substantial recommendations in the book are therefore made regarding teacher training and professional development, guided by the vision of promoting a supportive educational environment in schools.

The book is written with the background of an increasingly competitive global economy. People in twenty-first-century societies are becoming more disconnected to one another as the values of individualism and consumerism prevail. The overall declining mental health of school-aged children and teachers worldwide also shines a warning light for policymakers at this time. This book is a bid to recommend social support as a norm that may help improve the social environment and provide a perspective from which to view education that can guide practitioners' work and to stimulate further research in the area. The book contains 7 chapters; a preview of the book content and each chapter is introduced in Chap. 1.

Clearly, the project could not have been successfully completed without the contributions of a number of individuals.

I would like to express my deep and sincere thanks to Prof. Richard Fielding for writing the Foreword I for the book; his foreword gives insights to guide readers to approach the book. I cannot thank him enough for his support to write for me as he knows me only at a distance. A very special thanks should go to Prof. Dave Coniam for writing the other Foreword II and his valuable guidance to me during the course of writing this monograph. I have found this project more rewarding than I could have ever imagined as I learned under his mentorship. I would like to deeply thank Prof. Richard Ryan for writing the recommendation for the book and his encouragement. Thanks should also go to Dr. Alfredo Bautista, Dr. Poon Wai Kit and Mr. Tang Wai Chung for writing the short commentaries. Their point of views in the positions of a prolific academic researcher, medical doctor and solicitor help readers to understand the book from different angles. Thanks for their kindness to write out of their very busy work schedule. I would like to thank Prof. Peter Falvey for his valuable advice on the linguistic (or language) aspects of the book; his scaffolding support has made the final revision process of the book enjoyable and meaningful for me. Thanks to him! I would like to extend my appreciation to Winkie Li and Yuanyuan Guan for their high quality research assistance support and to Cecilia Hiu See Tang for reading of the manuscript from a student's perspective.

The book has been partially funded by an Internal Research Grant and credit should go to the Education University of Hong Kong for recognising research scholarship.

Hong Kong   Bick-har LAM

Contents

1 Introduction 1
    What Is Social Support 1
    How Social Support Is Related to the Education Profession 2
        The Context—A Quest for Improvement in the Education
        Environment 3
    Audience of the Book 6
    Social Support, Well-being and Teacher Development 6
    Preview of Book Content 7
        Social Support in the Health Psychology Discipline 7
        Social Support in the Context of Learning and Teaching 12
        Social Support Givers and Teacher Development 16
    Overall Conclusion 19
    References 21

2 Understanding Social Support 29
    Why Study Social Support? 29
    What Is Social Support? 31
    Major Conceptions of Social Support 32
        Stress Buffering, Coping and Adjustment 33
        The Social Constructionist and Interactionalist Approaches 38
        Social Capital Strengthens Social Resources 43
        Supportive Relationships and Social Integration 44
        Support Giving and Support Givers 46
    Social Support Research—Methods and Studies 49
        Considering the Research Approaches to Be Taken
        and the Instruments to Be Used 49
        Complications When Measuring Social Networks 52
        Relating Social Support to Well-being Measures 54
        Quantitative or Qualitative Approach to Studying
        Social Support 55

xiii

Potential Confound	55
Limitations of the Current Scales for Studying Social Support	56
Implications to Study Social Support in Education	56
Satisfying Social Ties Enhance Human Development	57
Conclusion and Limitations of the Chapter	59
References	73

3 Well-being, Psychological Adjustments and Effective Social Support Giving ... 85

Well-being as an Outcome Measure of Social Support	86
Determinants and Constituents of Well-being	86
Self-actualisation and Life-Span Theory of Development	89
Socio-emotional Development and Well-being	90
Who Needs Social Support?	91
Poor Health Conditions	92
Adjustment and Adaptation	93
Social Support Is not Always Welcomed	96
Support Offered by Similar Others Are More Effective	99
Relationships Determine the Effectiveness of Social Support	101
Help at the Right Time by the Right Person	102
The Dual Effect of Online Network	104
Culture and Social Support	106
Personality May Limit the Amount of Social Support We Get	109
Gender Differences in the Perception and Utilisation of Social Support	112
The Facilitative and Inhibitive Conditions of Social Support	116
Recommendations	116
Well-being as the Long-Term Goal of School Education	116
Social Support as a Topic of Study for Teachers	119
Conclusion	120
References	122

4 Social Support, Student Outcomes and Teaching Strategies ... 135

Background	136
The Theoretical Reasons of Social Support on Students	138
Attachment Theory	138
Broaden-and-Build Theory	140
Social Exchange Theory	141
Social Constructionist Learning Theory	142
Affective Learning Versus Cognitive Learning	144
The Meta-Theory Derived to Guide Learning and Teaching	146
Social Support Behaviours and the Corresponding Learning Outcomes	147
Emotional Support Enhances Self-esteem, Socio-emotional Competence and Academic Functioning	147

Contents   xv

Positive Relationships Protect Students from Negative Outcomes.... 151
Types of Social Support Teachers Give in Teaching 153
Teacher and Student Expectations Shapes Students' Path
to Success 154
School and Classroom Environment Characteristics as Social
Support 157
Teaching Strategies that Utilise Social Support 160
Pedagogies Emphasises Emotional Support, Feeling and Thinking ... 160
Cooperative Learning Utilises Social Support 161
Feedback Strategies as Support to Drive Learning Motivation 165
Strategies to Support Students with Special Educational Needs 168
Implications and Recommendations 172
A Theoretical Framework that Guides Learning and Teaching 173
Teacher Professionalism Regarding Commitment, Traits and
Knowledge 173
A Social Support Approach to Education Planning and Teaching ... 174
Designing Pedagogies to Promote Change Noting the Cultural
Context 176
Further Research and Limitations 177
References 178

**5 Expert Teachers' Social Support Behaviours—A Humanised
Classroom Characterised by Productive Learning** 193
Background of Studying Teacher Behaviours 194
Studying Teacher Cognition and Teaching Expertise............ 194
Democratic Classroom Management 196
Autonomy-Supportive Teaching Styles....................... 198
Productive Classroom Discourse and Monitoring Student
Learning.. 199
Caring, Empathetic and Virtuous Personality Traits Underlie
Teacher Behaviours....................................... 200
Four Expert Teachers' Teaching Behaviours in the Classroom 202
The Study Background 202
Methods.. 203
Analysis of Teacher Behaviour and Student Motivation 204
Discussion of Findings 207
Teacher Behaviours....................................... 207
The Key Instructional Formats Adopted by Expert Teachers 208
Building the Positive Classroom Climate—Positive Affect,
Relatedness, and Autonomous Motivation 216
Classroom Management Features: Self-discipline,
Learning-Focused and Respectfulness 221

Contextual Influences on Teaching Styles	223
Student Motivation	224
Conceptualisation of the Results	225
Good Teachers Humanise Students	225
Affective-and-Cognitive Scaffoldings as an Area of Teaching Expertise	227
Implications and Recommendations	228
The Triad of Teaching Expertise for Learning to Teach	228
Specifying Social Support as the Rationale of Learner-Centred Education	230
Conclusion, Major Limitations and Future Studies	231
References	233

6 Social Support Giving and Teacher Development 241

The Nature of the Teaching Profession and Self-generating Rewards of Teaching	242
Teachers' Declining Mental Health and Dissatisfactions with the Teaching Profession	243
Social Support Giving Benefits Teacher Development	245
Teacher's Satisfaction in Teaching—The Psychic Rewards of Teaching	245
Social Support Giving Benefits Teacher—Satisfaction, Reduced Distress, Positive Development	246
Surviving the Demands and Becoming a Competent Teacher	248
Teaching as 'Emotional Work' Versus 'Emotional Labour'	249
Emotional Work at the Organisational Level Constructs Teachers' Self and Agency	252
Personality Traits and Knowledge of Teacher Emotions that Facilitate Teaching	255
The Performativity Culture Risks the Caring Profession and Turns Teachers Away	258
Recommendations: Preparing and Supporting Teacher Development	261
Emotional Knowledge as Essential Knowledge for Teachers	261
Strengthening Socio-emotional Capacity and Skills for Reflection	262
Building Support Networks and Setting Shared Goals to Promote Meaningful Teaching	264
Promoting Opportunities to Enhance Teacher Self-efficacy	265
Organisational Support to Promote Teacher Well-being	266
Further Research	267
Conclusion	268
References	270

Contents   xvii

**7 Constructing a Supportive Environment
  for Student Learning and Teacher Development** 279
  Social Support—Human's Innate Ability to Connect.............. 280
  Societal Background and Problems in the Education Environment..... 281
  Synthesis of the Investigation Results 283
    Social Support Research and Implications 284
    Social Support Assumptions, Its Practice and Educational
    Outcomes... 286
    Effective Social Support and Variables of Studying Social
    Support in Education 289
    The Practice of Social Support Teaching and the Triad
    of Teaching Expertise 290
    Teachers as Support Givers—Teacher Commitment Drives
    Career Development 292
  Recommendations for School and Classroom Environment 295
  Recommendations for Teacher Development 297
  Contributions of the Book................................. 299
  Further Research Directions 303
  Overall Conclusion...................................... 305
  References 305

**Correction to: Social Support, Well-being, and Teacher
Development**... C1

Chapter 1
Introduction

Abstract This chapter provides a preview of the content of the book to help readers understand the structure of the book and the concepts discussed in each chapter. It introduces what social support is and why it is selected as the topic of investigation, how social support is related to education, who the target audience is, what the key concepts addressed in the content of the book are, and the background to writing the book. The other six chapters are reviewed at the end of the chapter to highlight the issues addressed in each subsequent chapter while providing an understanding of each chapter to the whole.

What Is Social Support

The definition of social support can be comprehensively captured in the short description suggested by Albrecht and Adelman (1987). It refers to 'verbal and non-verbal communication between recipients and providers that reduces uncertainty about the situation, the self, the other, or the relationship, and functions to enhance a perception of personal control in one's life experience' (p. 19). In real life, this kind of human support has been found to exert a potent influence on people, contributing to physical and mental health. It can create psychological conditions in which people can feel safe, respected, self-valued and competent, enabling people to enjoy greater autonomy in mastering his or her own life, to improve one's own disadvantaged conditions and to bring one's potential into full play, thus contributing the best to the society. As for support providers, helping behaviours promote their feelings of being recognised, important and competent (Caprara & Steca, 2005). Engaging in altruistic behaviour can also reduce stress. Hence, social support has been formulated as an important research component in health psychology since the 1970s.

The original version of this chapter was revised: Belated corrections have been incorporated. The correction to this chapter is available at https://doi.org/10.1007/978-981-13-3577-8_8

© Springer Nature Singapore Pte Ltd. 2019
B. LAM, *Social Support, Well-being, and Teacher Development*,
https://doi.org/10.1007/978-981-13-3577-8_1

How Social Support Is Related to the Education Profession

Psychologists have discovered that human beings have a tendency to form strong and stable interpersonal bonds with other persons (Reis, Sheldon, Gable, Roscoe, & Ryan, 2000). 'The need to belong' is an innate psychological process which is found to play a central role in human motivation (Baumeister & Leary, 1995). Furthermore, the role of teachers from whom students can expect nurturance also indicates the role relationships play in education. For instance, monitoring individual students and adjusting lessons to individual needs are the skills that expert teachers possess (Borko & Livingston, 1989). Teachers with high-level teaching expertise are found to show a higher level of respect towards students (Hattie, 2003), and they tend to provide a guiding process of learning for students in teaching (Hattie, 2003). Furthermore, care (Teven & Hanson, 2004), empathy (Nickerson, Butler, & Carlin, 2009) and virtuous personality traits (Richardson & Fallona, 2001) are essential for earning trust from students, resulting in enhanced motivation (Teven & Hanson, 2004) and a positive learning environment (Asad & Hassan, 2013). More recently, teachers' autonomy-supportive teaching has been promoted by researchers as it has been found to improve educational outcomes (Reeve, Deci, & Ryan, 2004). This teaching style seeks to encourage students to act on their own locus of control, behaviours such as 'asking what students want' and 'allowing time for students to work in their own way' are recommended (Ryan & Deci, 2017). While the teacher is the figure from whom nurturance is expected, student–peer relationships are also valued as an important source of support for student learning. Researchers agree that 'relatedness' is one of the traits (Ryan & Deci, 2001) that are essential for human flourishing (Seligman, 2011). Relatedness pertains to the feeling that one is close and connected to significant others, and has been trialled in various educational intervention programmes to target improving students' well-being (Niemiec & Ryan, 2009). The discussion above suggests, the concerns for social bonds and the benefits of social support have been considered an important foundation for teaching in the scholarship of education.

The emotional aspect of teaching is not, however, explicitly taught in teacher education programme nor has it acquired a proper place in education. Working in schools, teachers may often consider how they could support learners with diverse needs. Beginning teachers might not be sure what kind of help could be effective for students, and what relationship status they should maintain with learners is (Emmer & Stough, 2001). More experienced teachers may struggle whether they should approach students with more consideration and emotional support; some might feel the competition of time and would want to minimise emotional work because of the heavy syllabus they have to cover in class (Lam, 2011a, 2011b). In fact, teachers may need knowledge that can guide them to play the combined role of an academic advisor and a life coach. Moreover, the educational benefits of the emotional aspect of teaching should also be clarified and promoted so that the school environment can support teachers in playing this role in their teaching.

It appears that, since the beginning of the twenty-first century, researchers and practitioners have started to investigate ways to deal with the problem of student disengagement (Fredricks, Blumenfeld, Friedel, & Paris, 2005), focusing attention on leaners' needs and the facilitation of learners in social–psychological development processes instead of imposing external standards and controls on students. With this new vision in mind, education is considered with reference to human development that is based upon human virtues, to develop ways to support school students to achieve life satisfaction and give them strength (Feeney and Collins, 2015), so that they can fully participate in opportunities offered in school and society for exploration, growth and development. Social support, which is strongly reminiscent of the intricate relationship between students and teachers, and among students in the classroom, stands out as a relevant topic that has the potential to contribute in the current educational context. It is a topic that can relevantly contribute to the currently growing literature that revolves around learner-centred education.

While the potentials of social support in education are indicated in the works of researchers in the field of education (e.g. Ahmed, Minnaert, van der Werf, & Kuyper, 2010; Hargreaves, 1999; Wentzel, 1994; Wilcox, Winn, & Fyvie-Gauld, 2005; Woods & Jeffrey, 1996), efforts to bridge the fields of education and health psychology on this topic have not yet been seen. This book, *Social Support, Well-being, and Teacher Development* is an attempt to investigate social support in the learning and teaching context to close this gap.

The Context—A Quest for Improvement in the Education Environment

As mentioned above, the affective dimension of teachers' work has continued to excite considerable interest in education, partly because older approaches to education are being far too narrowly defined on individual success (Cheng, 1999), causing school education to become an extraordinary burden in school which is not meaningful to students. The contextual background of twenty-century society also prompts more attention to young people regarding the development of social relationships and social bonds. The incentive for me to pursue a book on social support and its application in the field of education dates back to 2015 with the loss of a student I was close to who committed suicide in the university hostel because of academic pressure. At the same time, figures that were released between September 2015 and April 2016, showed there were more than 30 cases of Hong Kong students' suicide (Cheung & Chiu, 2016), showing an alarming frequency of students committing suicide since 2015. The worsening problems of academic pressure have also been reflected in other parts of the world. In Asian-Pacific countries especially, it is not uncommon to find students who see themselves as losers (Bray, 2017). Academic pressure is the main cause of student suicides in many countries (Arun & Chavan,

2009; Lam, 2017; Liu & Tein, 2005) and it has been shown to be on a rising trend (Centers for Disease Control, 2013; World Health Organization, 2017, 2014).

While student problems alert different stakeholders in societies, teacher suicides and mental health problems have also emerged as common worldwide. In countries such as U.S.A. (Steinhardt, Smith Jaggars, Faulk, & Gloria, 2011), Spain (Betoret, 2006), Singapore (Chan, Lai, Ko, & Boey, 2000), Australia and Asia Pacific countries (Martin, Collie, & Frydenberg, 2017a, 2017b), teacher mental health problems have suggested a marked increase over the past decades. Cases of teacher suicides are also alarming. A growing number of teachers are having suicidal thoughts, and ending their own lives as a solution to end the confusion they encounter in teaching. In Hong Kong, despite the relatively high salary in the teaching profession, teaching seems to be losing its appeal (Lai, Chan, Ko, & So, 2005; HKFEW, 2015) because of its heavy workload and job demands (e.g. managing student diversity). Decreasing job security (HKFEW, 2015) also intensifies pressure on teachers (Choi & Tang, 2009; Hong Kong Primary Education Research Association, & Education Convergence, 2006). The overall declining mental health of school-aged children (Polanczyk, Salum, Sugaya, Caye, & Rohde, 2015; Storrie, Ahern, & Tuckett, 2010) and teachers worldwide (Education Support Partnership, 2015; King, Caleon, Tan, & Ye, 2016) has alerted policymakers to the emerging problems in school and education.

Sociologist David Émile Durkheim (1897−1951) discussed suicide in societies. He mentioned that suicide is a social phenomenon, which is inevitable in any given society (Durkheim, 2013). A society is made up of people with distinct types of characters and personalities, where each suicide victim has his or her own reasons pushing them to end their lives. It is this uniqueness that makes it hard for any government or anti-suicide institution to effectively prevent these tragedies from happening. According to Durkheim (2013), these people prefer to end their lives because of disintegration in the social environment. Nevertheless, an upward trend of suicide cases in a specific entity, be it a country, a timeframe, an age group, an establishment or even an ethnicity, duly indicates that certain social issues must have arisen (Kushner & Sterk, 2005). This very situation is now happening in different corners of the world—an increasing rate of student and teacher suicides, which probably indicates some potential 'bombs' and sheds some light on the dilemmas in societies in the twenty-first century.

Researchers commonly argue that the wave of changes in education systems since the 2000s which have been aimed at preparing students for the increasingly knowledge-based economy of societies has been made out of good intentions (Cheung & Wong, 2012; McNeil, 2002). The result, however, is that education in schools creates a great deal of tension for both the students and teachers (Chiu, 2017; Lam, 2014, 2015). Academic pressure is an immediate cause of depression for school students. In schools, assessment and academic achievements have been the key agendas (Feld & Shusterman, 2015). Student results are not only compared between individuals in the class, but also among schools and across countries internationally. More standardised examinations have been developed to assess competencies for ensuring the abilities of future citizens to fit a more competitive twenty-first-century society for supporting the knowledge-based economy (Hong Kong Institute of Asia-

Pacific Studies, 2016), and the results are being used to indicate education success. These often give rise to keen competition for students and create pressure for both students and teachers. And because of the urge for achievement, governments, policymakers and school managers have high expectations of educational outcomes, and teachers are charged with heavy responsibilities for achieving a high outcome standard, spending additional time in giving additional instructions and training to students in order to boost their results (HKFEW, 2015).

School-aged children and adolescents are also faced with challenges typical for a twenty-first-century, globalised society. They face huge uncertainties due to the intensified competition and internationalised labour market (Blossfeld, Klijzing, Mills, & Kurz, 2005), with downward occupation mobility and less stable and less favoured terms of employment affecting the planning of their adult life (Mills, Blossfeld, & Klijzing, 2005). Another significant feature is the flavour of individualism based in a consumerism culture. Due to the worldwide shared values of lifestyle and tastes, it is not uncommon to find that people all over the world nowadays aspire to consumption and ownership of brand names (Larson et al., 2002), for gaining a sense of self-worth. Unfortunately, the ownership of material goods cannot fulfill the higher order needs of human beings. They can only be fulfilled through the pursuit of intrinsic goals in life (Arnett, 2002). Furthermore, the tendency towards upward comparison and the dismissal of traditional cultural values in a society makes people increasingly disconnected from one another, changing the traditional social support system in their neighbourhoods (Sharma & Sharma, 2010).

In Hong Kong, negative mental states are constantly displayed in other strata of our society. A recent study has reported that Hong Kong secondary students exhibit a relatively low index in the area of spiritual health (physically, mentally and socially speaking) (Sun & Shek, 2010). Another survey reflects the low life satisfaction index of the youngsters, proclaiming their disappointment about their general livelihood in aspects including disparity between the rich and the poor and ever-changing education policies (Li, Chan, Chung, & Chui, 2010). There are instances of youngsters attempting to fight back through some radical means in order to vent their accumulated distress and anger (Cheung & Chiu, 2016). Furthermore, the behaviour of young people has also come into question. Driven by the wish for 'becoming the dragon' (Chinese idiom) which prevails in Chinese societies, as a result of the degenerated Confucian heritage culture (Lam, 2011a, 2011b), many parents in Hong Kong train their children to pay attention exclusively to academic study and take over the routine jobs that children should learn to do since they are too young to become independent adults. As a result, many kids, teenagers and university-aged young adults have been found to lack self-management skills and rely heavily on parents in their daily management routines including the completion of homework (The Hong Kong Institute of Family Education, 2013).

As individual achievement is the goal for almost everyone, people's social engagement has generally decreased (Vohs, Mead, & Goode, 2006). And because the materialistic and consumerist values prevail in the larger social environment, people have a lower sense of personal responsibility; they become more hesitant to give help (Bauer, Wilkie, Kim, & Bodenhausen, 2012). As young people tend to behave in a more isolated and detached manner from social ties, they lack social support and personal skills to cope with stress properly (Cheung & Chiu, 2016). This social environment also creates a similar situation for mature adults such as teachers, whose tension comes from a heavy workload, accountability demands and the overwhelming challenges from teaching the younger generation, hence leading them to embark upon a journey of self-destruction.

The book is timely to rekindle social support at the background of a competitive, globalised twenty-first-century environment. The book explains learning and teaching in relation to human's genuine need for social support (such as developing satisfying social ties and social relationships), which suggests a unique theme in exploring education with insights. The book also highlights the importance of human belongingness and self-esteem as important conditions for supporting academic functioning, underscores the full character of teachers and emphasises the teacher's role as a caring mentor of teaching. The investigative results provide theoretical and practical implications to justify that teacher commitment, motivation and interest in learners are the prerequisites to support teacher development, in the path of becoming satisfying and outstanding teachers.

Audience of the Book

The primary readers of the book are academics in the field of education, who can gain a solid understanding of the research and practice of social support and apply the knowledge in their own research, teaching and programme development. Academics from the psychology and health psychology disciplines will also be interested in this book as it provides an updated review of research related to social support, well-being and theories of education psychology. Students at the postgraduate levels and academic researchers who are keen to explore topics such as teacher development, learning and teaching, well-being and mental health, will also find the book as a useful reading tool and benefit from the scholarship of the book. The book also fits undergraduate students who will serve as teachers, counsellors, education psychologists and community programme developers at the bachelor degree level, in areas including education, psychology and related disciplines.

Social Support, Well-being and Teacher Development

As the title shows, the book is portrayed with three broad labels, i.e. *social support, well-being* and *teacher development*, illustrating the meaning and content of the book.

Social Support is the main theme that links the whole book; *Well-being* is the idea of conceptualising the benefits of social support, which means the goals to achieve social support. In the book, the two constructs will be explored to give the theoretical background of and indicate the directions for discussing social support in the context of education. The book then moves on to investigate social support in teachers' instructional practice and the school environment, and the results suggest findings of the positive educational outcomes that social support behaviours and instructional practice contribute to students' well-being. The investigation is further extended to social support providers, i.e. teachers, the result of which addresses the important idea that teachers' social support giving benefits their own professional development and career advancement. As the results illustrate the positive impacts of social support on students (as support receivers) as well as the benefits of social support on teachers (as support givers), *Teacher Development* is, therefore, the area that the results of the investigation of the book serve. It is assumed that teachers should be developed to acquire the knowledge, traits and skills of carrying out social support practice in the classroom should it be possible for realising the benefits to teachers in the path of teachers' professional learning. Therefore, a substantial part of the book discusses the results on teacher education and development, in preparing teachers to carry out social support practice in teaching, as a key focus. Hence, the book is titled 'Social Support, Well-being, and Teacher Development'.

While each of the book chapters can be read as an individual and complete piece on a comprehensive investigation of a topic as named in the title of each chapter, the content of the book is integrated to address the key concepts of social support and well-being in the contexts of health care and education, and to provide a set of converging and coherent concepts that guides practitioners' research and practice in the field of education.

Preview of Book Content

Social Support in the Health Psychology Discipline

The next two chapters, Chaps. 2 and 3, are foundations of the book in clarifying the meaning of social support and well-being, with the latter being the outcome of the former in order to explore the construct of social support and its research approaches mainly in health psychology.

In Chap. 2, the meaning, research approaches and research outcomes of social support generated mainly from health psychology are explored. It seeks to understand the following:

- What does the concept 'social support' entail?
- What are the theoretical assumptions of social support?
- What are the methodological issues of studying social support research?
- What are the implications of social support for education?
- What potential links does social support imply for education for further study in the book?

The definition of social support is a daunting task for researchers as 'social' support involves a series of interactions and processes. It can be studied with different approaches. A general definition is adopted in Chap. 1 to illustrate the general meaning, suggesting 'support accessible to an individual through social ties to other individuals, groups, and the larger community' (Lin, Ensel, Simeone, & Kuo, 1979, p. 109)—essential to physical and psychological health. The chapter explains further about the assumptions of social support and the variables for research to provide a frame of reference for readers to understand this construct more comprehensively.

Based on a review of theoretical and empirical literature as well as meta-analysis of studies of social support, five assumptions of social support are suggested to explain the meaning of social support, with one of them describing social support from the position of support providers. A large amount of literature is drawn to construct the current framework of analysis to explain the main approaches of social support from the position of recipient, including the work of Barrera and Ainlay (1983), Cohen (2004), Cohen and McKay (1984), Coleman (1990), Feeney and Collins (2015), Goldsmith (2004), Guay et al. (2006), Lakey and Cohen (2000a, 2000b), Lazarus and Folkman (1984), López and Cooper (2011), Lin (1999; 2017), Sarason, Sarason, and Pierce (1990a, 1990b), Sarason, Sarason, Shearin, and Pierce (1987), Sherbourne and Stewart (1991), Taylor (2007), Uchino (2009) and Uchino. Bowen, Carlisle, and Birmingham (2012).

The first assumption is 'stress buffering and coping', which proposes that support action and perceived support can help individuals to buffer stress and improve coping performance in a stressful situation, making people feeling less stressed. The second assumption is constructed upon the theoretical models of 'social constructionist and interactionalist'. It proposes that people's stable beliefs about the supportiveness of others affect one's social cognition in perceiving a more supportive or less supportive environment around them. It suggests that a person's interaction with others in the social environment matters when it comes to defining social support. As people act in relation to others, the interaction gives people meaning and a sense of self. The sense of self creates an identity for individuals and implies how individuals should take part in the social environment. Perception of low support is detrimental because it may affect people's self-worth and create anxiety. 'Social capital' is the third assumption which explains social support; it conceptualises social support as the benefits a person receives from their social relationship. It explains a person's gain from both their 'close ties' and 'weak ties' in their social network and network sites, leading to greater control of situations and beneficial outcomes in different types of events. The fourth assumption is known as 'quality of relationships', which assumes that good quality experience in different relationships affects a person's life experience positively, as people may perceive support positively and receive effective support. The final assumption, which is a separate factor from the above assumptions, describes social support giving. It discusses the motives of support givers in giving support such as one's empathic concerns about others, reducing support givers' own distress and feelings of competence through giving support to others. Among the different assumptions, social support is found to have a positive effect on health and well-being, in the situations of support receiving and giving.

As a whole, the literature suggests that social support does not only work when people have encountered problems; rather, it forms a person's beliefs and expectations of whether they are being supported. If the beliefs and expectations are positive, it has a positive effect on human psychological functioning via mechanisms such as 'self-esteem', 'self-efficacy' and 'self-concept', that benefit the person's work and living. Social support, as defined by the perception of being cared for, affects a person's health and well-being. Therefore, knowing about social support is helpful to professionals whose job involves service and the provision of expert knowledge and advice to other parties, such as teachers who are responsible to help students acquire knowledge and also guide their students' development.

The impact of social support is also discussed in Chap. 2. The main effect of social support supposes that social support lasts and it works on people's development in their lifetime, versus the 'stress buffering effect' which refers to the relief of aversive effects of a stressor at a particular time in life. The review of literature in Chap. 2 identifies that research on support givers appears to be an under-researched topic. The preliminary evidence discussed in the chapter regarding the motive of support giving suggests that the giving of social support generally comes from social support givers' intrinsic interest in helping others, that support givers can equally benefit from social support as it can enhance their sense of self-worth, self-esteem and can relieve one's own stress. These findings have important implications for studying teachers—if teachers' interest in learner development is crucial to creating a sense of satisfaction, the type of satisfaction that can drive their work and their personal development in the profession. The topic of studying teachers as social support givers is, therefore, included as one of the important components of the book, i.e. in Chap. 6.

Chapter 2 reports that social support is often measured with reference to higher order concepts such as self-esteem and self-efficacy (comprising a person's perceptions of his/her own ability and self-worth), subject to Bandura's (1986) social cognitive theory. Other variables such as mastery, belonging and social influence (Thiots, 2011) are also used to address the importance of personal control in one's life and social relationships. The latter part of the chapter discusses the methodological issues of studying social support. It makes suggestions on the directions of research on social support which is still a developing field of interest, and this research topic also shows the potential contribution to other academic disciplines and professional areas. The chapter makes a number of implications regarding the relevance of applying social support to the context of learning and teaching, such as redefining the core value of education and teachers' moral role in the classroom, providing ideas to further elaborate the prevailing concept of 'learner-centred' in the educational literature and suggesting principles of practice to carry out learner-centred pedagogies. These implications provide insights that can help practitioners to further consider widening their understanding of the scope of student learning and their role in the classroom; and these topics are discussed in Chaps. 4–6.

As well-being is identified as the outcome measure of social support in Chaps. 2 and 3, it further conceptualise the effect of social support and explores the following:

- What does well-being mean and how does well-being relate to social support?
- What are the inner emotional struggles of identified groups of people whom social support could help?
- What are the principles that govern support strategies and other considerations for applying social support?.

In the book, well-being is identified as the outcome of social support. Chapter 2 begins with an exploration of the meaning of well-being. It reports that well-being has become a popular research construct in education literature because of increasing concerns about student learning outcomes in the non-academic aspects of development. This concept, which is generally used to denote the status of happiness, is now widely recommended and applied for evaluating social policies and education (Helliwell, 2006; Michalos, 2012). This implies an important message that the success of human projects is no longer only measured by the cost but has to include human satisfaction as a crucial index of measuring success. The meaning of well-being has revealed diverse approaches. Aristotle's eudaimonic concept of well-being is often adopted in education studies and later discussion in the book will refer to this definition often. The literature generally explains well-being as the status of accepting and living with a person's daimon (demon) or true self (Waterman, 1993), since people would feel alive and authentic when they are allowed to live as 'who they really are'. Another explanation of well-being is significantly applied in education, which is related to social support. According to Ryan and Deci (2001), three principal psychological needs that predict an individual's well-being are suggested based on self-determination theory. These three needs are drawn towards the status of being self-determined, which can generally be described as having a satisfying social network and being closely connected to others (relatedness), making choices and developing volition in one's behavioural regulation (autonomy), and being able to experience the feeling of competence (competence). Other social psychological theories and humanistic theories are drawn into the picture in Chap. 3 to echo the above ideas and to formulate a cluster of concepts that are related to social support and well-being, including self-actualization (Maslow, 1943) and socio-psychological development (Erikson, 1959). The theories altogether highlight the belief that a social relationship helps a person adopt a self-regulated process in the social environment. In such a way, relating to each other and forming social bonds with the others in the social environment represent a crucial process of human growth. Well-being and the other variables discussed in the chapter indicate the theoretical reasons why social support is important for human beings.

To illustrate people's needs for social support, Chap. 3 moves on to describe the psychological adjustment processes of people in need and how social support could help these people, such as in the case of domestic violence victims, ethnic minorities and people living in poverty . Finally, the chapter explores the factors and conditions that facilitate effective social support, and those which inhibit effective social support. Cases are described to illustrate successful and unsuccessful social support stories based on the empirical literature. These case results are further constructed in a framework to illustrate the parameters that guide social support giving, to suggest the conditions support givers should consider in giving social support to ensure that it can be helpful. It shows that social support which means to help people may end up causing great distress to potential support receivers. The resultant framework recommends some common effective support tactics, which can answer the queries such as whether invisible help is more helpful, do people consider relationship closeness in giving support such as in-group members, do people welcome advice from 'similar others' (who had similar experience as the receivers had before), would there be common knowledge in considering the kind of need for support targets such as their evolving needs and who should be the most relevant person to help in particular stages of the situations and circumstances. The chapter also discussed specific cases and situations to highlight the major concerns and effects with reference to gender, culture and personality as these are important variables that determine the effectiveness of social support. Some of these variables are further discussed in Chap. 4, such as gender as a factor that affects social support receiving of school-aged children. As a whole, the tactics discussed in Chap. 3 are useful in helping professionals to develop their expertise in dealing with their clients in different professional contexts that involve social support, and they provide useful knowledge for living for every human individual in society, to support one another to build up a supportive social environment.

An important message is implied in Chap. 3. Given that well-being is the goal of social support and that social support aims to help individuals to become satisfied and healthier in their lifetime, the social aspect of human living has emerged as the consensual principle that supports human development. The building of satisfying social ties and social bonds in the social environment is regarded as key to support human development as the result of discussions in this chapter. From the position of support receivers, gaining help from other human peers may make them feel contented and satisfied, and the feeling of supportiveness is essential as it helps them perceive a supportive environment that facilitates their growth and development. As a whole, the chapter conveys the important message that by living in a social environment with social support as a norm, people will develop 'intrinsic interest' in life and become more 'competent' irrespective of one's living conditions and life circumstances. The analysis of effective social support measures further identifies the subtleties and precautions required in the use of social support, which can be applied for use in general daily life and professional contexts to suit the needs of professionals in various fields. As a whole, the discussion provides insights in creating the educational environment in the classroom and in measuring the outcomes of education to support student development in schools.

Social Support in the Context of Learning and Teaching

Chapter 4 attempts to link social support to the context of learning and teaching, and the social support resources, especially teacher's social support, to draw implications for classroom learning and teaching, after gaining the knowledge, research approaches and realising the benefits of social support in Chaps. 2 and 3. It asks the following:

- What are the theoretical reasons behind the link between social support and education, especially related to teaching and learning in the classroom?
- What are the social support resources documented in the literature, especially teacher social support practices in teaching?
- What impact could social support behaviours and practice from teachers and other support sources have on students in terms of educational outcomes?
- What would be exemplary teaching strategies that utilise social support? and
- What are the implications and further research directions from this approach?

A purposeful review of educational theories is conducted at the beginning of this chapter. The theories being reviewed include attachment theory (Bowlby, 1988), attachment neuroscience (Coan, 2008), broaden-and-build (Fredickson, 2003), social exchange (Blau, 1964), social constructivist learning (Vygotsky, 1978) and affective learning (McCollum, 2014; Reigeluth, 2013). These theories have been used to formulate an overarching theory, which is named a meta-theory to address the importance of social support practice in teaching. Convergence of the social support theories discussed in Chaps. 2 and 3 and the meta-theory derived in Chap. 4 takes into consideration the essential needs of establishing satisfying social relationships, relatedness and supportiveness in the learning and teaching environment; it suggests that the positive relationship experience students gain in learning and teaching in schools is considered crucial as it determines the well-being of students. It conclusively points out that positive social relationships and supportiveness in the learning environment do not only help students overcome difficulties and challenges, they can also nurture the talents and latent abilities of students and engender students' productive learning behaviours and autonomous motivation to learn. Similar to offering social support to needy people, the teachers' role in education is to support learners in developing positive psychological well-being. Disengagement, isolation and deviated behaviours might be the result of a student's previous experience with other people in life which affect their perception of the world and themselves; but positive interaction, such as social support, can help students change their behaviours in healthier ways. The positive influence of social support is therefore potent as it helps create an identity for young people so that they can recognise a clear role to take as their target in social living positively, removed from the statuses of frustration, dissatisfaction and helplessness because of lack of recognition and low self-esteem. In this case, children, adolescents and young adults under the guidance of teachers and parents, would behave more energetically by an enhanced self-esteem and self-identity. As a result, people can live to achieve their life goal and move towards self-actualisation.

The meta-theory also conceptualises the role social support plays in one's cognition. It specifies scaffolding support between human peers stimulates human cognitive development and advances human intellect. Hence, the investigation of social support in Chap. 4 has consolidated a list of important guides to education practitioners, which can be conceived as the direction of school education nowadays. In sum, the meta-theory generated from the cross-disciplinary analysis of educational theories and social support theories suggests that education is to give every individual the opportunities to recognise their own potential, which helps students create self-worth and self-esteem, and supports students to develop and recognise their own strength and overcome adversities. It can be done through building supportive relationships and cultivating positive affect in classrooms and schools. This meta-theory addresses the establishment of satisfying social ties and their primary importance in human development, and the basis of achieving well-being. This theory also implies that paying overwhelming attention to preparing students for examination may not always be appropriate as it will add stressful experiences for students and create isolation and competition early in their life time; instead, establishing a social support culture among students and teachers are the keys for creating successful and meaningful learning experiences for students.

Based on the meta-theory derived in viewing learning and teaching, Chap. 4 further identifies social support sources in schools that support student learning. Teachers' emotional support, relationship with students, and teachers' expectation are identified to be key social support measures in the classroom; these supportive actions are embedded in the classroom environment and form the appropriate teaching strategies and instructional practice. Similarly, the corresponding outcomes of such supportive behaviours of teachers are found to be related to some higher order learning outcomes as addressed in earlier chapters in the social support literature, such as self-esteem, self-efficacy, motivation, socio-emotional competence, prosocial behaviour, adjustment, cognitive learning skills and academic performance. The review exemplifies the important psychological conditions for learning in school which is characterised by teachers' social support behaviours.

The most significant result developed in Chap. 4 is the cognitive aspect of learning that is facilitated by teachers' social support. For example, in giving emotional support, teachers involve students in a crucial learning process that facilitates their mastery of the academic learning content (Meyer & Turner, 2006); teachers' clear expectation and consistent structure communicated to students with autonomy support and respect to learners have an impact on enhancing students' interest in school work and engagement in prosocial behaviour (Hamre & Pianta, 2005; Jang, Reeve, & Deci, 2010; Skinner & Belmont, 1993). The chapter also identifies students as an important source of social support. Students' expectation of positive social behaviour in the classroom may lead to an overall positive attitude towards learning. Student attributes also affect students' attitude and learning behaviours (Wentzel, 2009); for example, students' perception of peers as supportive predicts the learning behaviours and efforts individuals pay to tasks (O'Donnell & O'Kelly, 1994; Ryan, 2000). Social support at the school level is also found to be most crucial in determining student learning outcomes (Russell, 2012); it works in coordination with teachers' support to provide positive effects for student learning.

With reference to effective social support, Chap. 4 identifies that, generally, students from early years to mid-adolescence require social support from teachers. There is a gender differences in the kind of support girls and boys need (Suldo et al., 2009). This feature is consistently reflected in social support studies where, in general, women favour emotional support. The challenges adolescents face in the social environment would also affect their openness to support (Klem & Connell, 2004). Further studies to differentiate the types of social support towards different groups of students are suggested to identify effective support for different learner characteristics.

Chapter 4 also identifies a resourceful list of prototypical pedagogies that characterise a form of pedagogical practice which is oriented to involving learners' exploration and social learning, such as emphasising deliberation, reflection, cooperative learning and feedback, and the feature of caring and concern for individual differences. The pedagogies discussed in Chap. 4 include affective pedagogy (a taxonomy of affective learning) (Anderson et al., 2001), caring practice (Noddings, 2003), cultural responsive teaching (Vavrus, 2008), cooperative learning (Johnson, Johnson, & Smith, 1991; Slavin, 1995), nurture groups (Boxall, 2002), circle time (Mosley, 2005), circle of friends and the restorative justice approach (Morrison, 2002). The last three pedagogical formats are recommended for use with students with special educational needs.

The meta-theory to explain learning and teaching that is derived from the educational literature has been linked to the support literature discussed in Chaps. 2 and 3; this interdisciplinary connection strengthens the social and emotional roles played by teachers in the educational context with substantial support. It has been used as a theoretical linkage across the content of subsequent chapters in discussing social support in education. The discussion in the chapter also makes a strong argument to suggest that the current examination-oriented culture in schools has many defects, one of which is that it forces teachers to engage in short-term planning because of their anxiety in meeting the demands of achieving substantial outcomes. A number of suggestions are made in Chap. 4 to encourage the cultivation of commitment and emotional traits of teachers, and to enhance teachers' professionalism in designing pedagogies based on the characteristics of the cultural context based on the spirit of promoting social support in teaching.

In Chap. 5, an empirical study is reported to discuss expert teachers' social support behaviours and pedagogies that illustrate social support and the related traits of teachers to provide understanding of how social support is executed and implemented through teaching and teachers' interaction with learners in the classroom. This study is explored with reference to the insights drawn from Chap. 4 regarding the benefits of teachers' social support for learners. Since expert teachers' teaching is found to carry 'affective attributes' and that expert teachers make a difference on students' learning outcomes, a study to identify social support behaviours of expert teachers is appropriate to identify social support behaviours in teaching. Chapter 5 seeks to find out the following:

- What are the social support behaviours that the four expert teachers demonstrate in classroom teaching? What are the main features regarding the teaching expertise of teachers?
- Is students' motivation high when studying with the four teachers?
- What are the implications of the study?

The qualitative study reported in Chap. 5 was based on fieldwork mainly through classroom observations and interviews with four teachers regarding their teaching, and a questionnaire survey on students' motivation of four classes of students from junior forms taught by the four teachers in a secondary school in Hong Kong. The results of the study suggested that the four teachers, to varying degrees, turned student learning into a series of moments where the students were prompted to engage in metacognitive learning. Being aware of the factors that influenced students' learning in designing the lesson, they selected the strategies for students to investigate the respective knowledge (knowledge of cognition); they also consciously helped students to adopt 'regulation of cognition' (Ambrose, Bridges, DiPietro, Lovett, & Norman, 2010; Pintrich, 2002), i.e. to ask students to identify learning goals, evaluate outcomes and reflect upon ones' own learning experience. This approach has the benefit that students are thought to reflect upon and reshape their own work, while performing learning tasks through a dialogic discourse.

The dialogic discourse used by the teachers contains teachers' formative feedback, thought provoking questions and stimulation for students to take part in exchanging views, leading students to construct knowledge. This dialogic discourse to a large extent creates a classroom whereby a social environment belongs to each of the members of the class. The four teachers showed their meticulous care for students' need for input and made spontaneous responses to address their needs; students were quite willing to participate even if they were not sure that their answers were correct in their responses to the teachers. All the lessons conducted by the teachers were presented in a productive learning atmosphere. In the students' questionnaire data, students reported a good relationship with teachers, high self-efficacy, high learning goals and low self-handicapping behaviours. These learning outcomes mirror the psychological resources that contribute to students' well-being, a finding that addresses the benefits of social support on well-being.

The practice of the four teachers is conceptualised as demonstrating a 'triad of teaching expertise' which contains teachers' commitment to teaching, communication skills in interacting with learners during the process of teaching, and the meta-cognitive teaching skills of teachers in monitoring students' meta-cognition. The chapter also argues that teachers' genuine care for students enables them to see every individual as a valuable being deserving help; they rendered patience and support to guide students through the learning journey. The social psychology perspective known as 'humanness' (Haslam, 2006) is used to explain the care teachers demonstrate in teaching students in this aspect; the teachers' concerns of establishing a supportive social environment for student learning illustrate how the teachers treat students more with emotional warmth than power. Chapter 5 makes a number of important contributions to the literature. It identifies the 'triad of teaching expertise' and it provides a solid framework for further research regarding the topic of expert teaching, it also identified metacognitive teaching as an important direction to guide teacher training, as an important approach to teacher professional development. The method of study described in the chapter provides a prototypical model of classroom observational study for researchers who are interested in conducting classroom observational research, and a useful instrument for teachers to engage in self-study into one's own teaching.

Social Support Givers and Teacher Development

Chapter 6 investigates teachers' roles as social support givers and the benefits they gain from social support giving to students. This topic is discussed in the context of teaching having become a stressed profession. It makes implications for how teachers can be developed and supported in order to gain a satisfying experience, taking note that teachers' commitment to student learning may be a factor in benefitting teachers' own professional development. The inquiry in this chapter is generated from Chap. 2 regarding support giver's motives and Chaps. 4 and 5 regarding teachers' social support practice in teaching, as a topic that has received relatively scant attention in the literature. The chapter reveals an integrated analysis regarding teacher development. It asks the following:

- How does social support giving relate to teacher satisfaction?
- Does providing social support to students relate positively to teacher development?
- What are the attributes that determine teachers' positive development in the teaching profession?
- Do mental health issues have anything to do with teachers' lack of satisfaction in teaching? If so, why?

The review of literature did not end with answers directly addressing whether social support giving is directly related to teacher development. However, 'love for students' has stood out as a common reason for selecting teaching as a career for teachers, and it is also the reason that has kept teachers in the career despite the heavy workload and challenges teachers encounter in the nature of the job (Hargreaves, 2000; O'Connor, 2008) and the education reform situation in the twenty-first century (Choi & Tang, 2009; Lam 2012; Lam & Yan, 2011). Teachers' love for students is analogous to the motives of social support giving addressed in the social support literature as reported in Chap. 2; it refers to 'empathic concerns' as a motive for altruistic behaviour, such as teachers' strong interest in developing relationships with students and their eagerness to help learners to achieve learning (Hargreaves, 1994, 2000; Lam, 2015). The motives of giving social support to students was described as the 'psychic reward of teaching' (Lortie, 1975) for teachers, which means, teachers' supportive behaviours are driven by their keen interest to see students' growth and take part in supporting students' development path (Hargreaves, 1994); hence, teachers' interest and care become the main sources of satisfaction in teaching for them. The evidences that teachers who show love for students would stay in the career were also explained by the fact that these teachers were more competent in managing teaching in the classroom and that their love giving to students has reduced the distress they felt in the challenging environment of the teaching profession (Choi & Tang, 2009), as 'feeling competence' and 'reducing stress' are beneficial effects as also discussed in the social support literature in Chap. 2. An important strand of inquiry therefore becomes obvious and it is further investigated in this chapter. That is, considering that teachers' social support giving behaviours in teaching are governed by their love for students, and that this intrinsic motivation for teaching helps teachers overcome stress and stay in the career, it is likely to suggest that teachers who are keen on social support giving may also have positive career development.

The chapter has tentatively proved such a link. Since social support giving can give the support givers a sense of competence, the investigation of the link between teachers' social support behaviour and their career development was sought via teachers' self-efficacy and high self-efficacy, i.e. perceived competence. A teacher's self-efficacy is therefore likely to be perceived as having a possible impact on one's motivation to pursue advancement. Assuming that teachers are driven by a strong interest to serve in the profession, they are expected to have a high self-efficacy if the job can give them the opportunity to serve students; and high self-efficacy is found to help a person maintain greater aspirations and anticipate successful achievement. Though investigations of this aspect are not well documented, such a hypothesis was predicted by researchers such as Gecas and Schwalbe (1983), and Ouweneel, Le Blanc, and Schaufeli, (2013). In a study by Lam (2015), it was found that teachers' social support giving to students enhances teachers' self-efficacy in teaching, and that teacher's perceived competence (self-efficacy) enhances their job aspiration.

The positive link between teachers' self-efficacy and career development implies that teacher's perceived competence in teaching may lead to higher positive emotions. This can explain the reason why teachers who are committed to teaching can stay in the profession even though teaching is regarded as a 'high-stressed' profession (Hebson, Earnshaw & Marchington, 2007), as the passion of these teachers may shield them from the challenges and difficulties the teaching profession incurs (e.g. Choi & Tang, 2009; Lam, 2012, Lam & Yan, 2011). The fact that social support has an effect on enhancing support givers' well-being (Piliavin & Siegl, 2007) and health (Schwartz & Sendor, 1999) is proved by different sources as reported in the health psychology section in Chap. 2. The salient psychological processes of how teachers' empathic concerns for helping students can exert a generating effect to drive their creative behaviours in teaching; how this situation associates positively to positive career development of the teachers is explained in Chap. 6, to suggest teachers' love for students is crucial in the personal and professional growth of teachers. A high sense of self-efficacy is the construct used in research on these teachers who show a strong commitment to supporting student development and who have acquired confidence in their career because of the positive engagement in conducting social support practice in teaching.

In Chap. 6, the positive relationships of teachers' social support behaviours and their self-efficacy, and their self-efficacy and career advancement, result in a number of important implications regarding teacher development. For example, schools should develop teachers' self-efficacy by referring to the sources from which teachers can yield satisfaction—i.e. taking the aim of building relationships with students as a major aim of the school. Since self-efficacy could be enhanced by social support giving but diminished by jobs that are not focused on supporting students, increasing the opportunities on events that support student development is appropriate.

The later part of the chapter elucidates the nature of teaching, teacher's personality traits, and the emotional work of teaching, which explain how teachers can proceed with a more satisfying career and advance in the teaching profession. The investigation of these topics has resulted in ideas that are complementary to the earlier part of the discussion in the chapter, conclusively suggesting that commitment to teaching seems to be the prerequisite for a positive teaching career experience. Teaching is regarded as 'emotional work' (Isenbarger & Zembylas, 2006) by teachers who are committed to and enjoy teaching, which implies they utilise the emotional scaffoldings and efforts teachers spend on students. It is different from simply performing 'emotional rules' of teaching by which teachers only discharge their duties and perform standard rules bound by their jobs in teaching (Carson & Templin, 2007). The classroom practices of the former types of teachers, as has been argued through the book, are highly analogous to the practice of social support pedagogies as identified in Chaps. 4 and 5, which stress teacher commitment to learner development as a significant factor that underlines those teachers who have also produced outstanding performance in their teaching. Chapter 6 provides evidence to further elaborate that these teachers possess the character traits that can help them carry out social support giving practice in the classroom, such as emotional competence and being able to be wary of one's own emotions to avoid unconscious emotion that undermines the positive relationship between students and teachers. They tend to solve problems arising in learning and teaching by trying to understand students and reflect on the situations. The discussion further underscores the emotional traits of teachers and their abilities in managing emotions with reference to the nature of the job of teaching within and beyond the classroom.

The main strength of Chap. 6 is that it consolidates the investigation of the book in connecting social support to the field of education in the role of teachers, who are social support givers. It demonstrates, with evidence, that social support can also give the same credits to teachers who care to offer support to learners with genuine interest, as their altruistic giving behaviours in turn make them achieve good teaching, and lead them to develop and advance in their profession. At the end, the chapter discusses with a note of caution, the drawbacks of the predominant performance culture (Ball, 2003; Nicholl & McLellan, 2008) that may undermine the motivation of committed teachers. This form of culture serves standardised performance criteria and examination result (Ball, 2003), which would destroy the motivation of many more committed enthusiastic teachers. Such an education environment would restrict the space for teachers to enjoy the psychic reward of teaching, i.e. the satisfaction teachers would gain from the relationship they develop with students and their emotional support to them. The chapter finally makes recommendations of a holistic plan to support teacher training and development, hopefully to create a social environment that can encourage, sustain and develop teacher's intrinsic interest in teaching.

Overall Conclusion

Chapter 7 of the book includes a brief background introducing social support as a positive virtue that can help human beings make a well-lived life. It continues to discuss the reason for proposing social support as a norm in improving education and the social environment by referring to the decline of the social network system, and the social values that continue to undermine the healthy development of youngsters in the knowledge-based twenty-first century society at this time. It also mentions the rising trend of mental health issues worldwide in society that have prompted the discussion on the topics to promote social support in learning and teaching that both benefit learners and teachers in this book. The chapter further highlights the key concepts and findings explored in Chaps. 2–6 of the book, followed by the key recommendations, contribution of the book, future research directions and limitations.

As a whole, the investigation of social support in the book has created a meta-theory to explain teaching and learning, as a result of an integrated discussion of the social support literature in the health psychology and education disciplines. On the side of learners as support receivers, teachers' social support in teaching is explored. It is found that various types of support given by teachers such as emotional support, teachers' expectation and cognitive scaffoldings serve to support students' well-being, and teachers' support in teaching could also benefit students' psychological and academic outcomes, leading to increased students' intrinsic motivation, positive self-esteem, social development and socio-emotional competence (e.g. Suldo, Shaffer, & Riley, 2008), and fostering pro-social behaviour. An empirical study was reported fully to illustrate the social support behaviours of expert teachers during classroom instruction. The study has demonstrated a triad of teaching expertise factors as the direction for teacher training. The triad includes teacher commitment, communication skills of engaging learners in the classroom and skills of monitoring and guiding students to develop their metacognitive learning which help learners not only become engaged during the lesson but also learn to become self-regulated learners that benefits students' academic functioning. The book has also identified exemplary strategies and pedagogies that illustrate the characteristics of social support in teaching, driven by the meta-theory.

On the other hand, teachers who have a strong motivation to support students' growth and development are found to practice teaching with additional qualities and strengths that are shown in various supportive teaching behaviours. This altruistic teaching motivation is found to give teachers a sense of purpose that motivates them to commit to their work in schools and to develop within themselves a strong identity as teachers; and this psychological condition also serves as an effective buffer against stress and heavy workloads in the teaching profession. Drawing from different sources in the literature, it is possible to suggest that these teachers are also seen to be more likely to be engaged in teaching practices that feature the 'emotional work' of teaching (Hargreaves, 1998); they are keen to support learners by giving scaffoldings and emotional support to achieve affective and cognitive learning outcomes. These teachers are also found to be driven by a feeling of competence, i.e. high self-efficacy, and this competence is derived by the satisfaction gained from social support giving to students in their teaching career, while teachers' high self-efficacy is positively associated with their career progress and advancement (Lam, 2015).

The social support meta-theory derived from the integration of theories and practice across the two fields suggests that reinforcing social bonds in the social environment of teaching and learning can create satisfying experiences for both the students and teachers, where the intended goal is well-being. It suggests a direction of education that can help with growing problems in the twenty-first-century society, such as the social values that continue to undermine the healthy development of youngsters in the globalised economy (Twenge & Kasser, 2013), as well as the growing mental health problems that characterise learners and teachers at this time (World Health Organization, 2017).

This book can help teachers and practitioners examine their own practice and research to accommodate social support in their work. The book has used an evidence-based approach in its investigation of its topics. It has resulted in theorising social support in the professional field of teaching, giving guidelines to practice, and directions for further research. It provides both theoretical and practical implications for learning, teaching and teacher development for improving education and the cultivation of a supportive social environment. It also points out the disadvantages of the prevailing management culture and the examination-oriented education approach that seriously undermine the morale of teachers and create anxiety for learners based on the argument of social support theories. While these issues have been found to be growing in different societies across cultures, this book provides a possible solution to the problems, one that can improve the well-being of young students and teachers, which can benefit the development of our societies.

The book though contains a number of imperfections. Due to the extensive amount of literature on the topics investigated in the book across the fields of health psychology and education, and the inconsistencies in the terms used for locating references for conducting the reviews, the results presented in the book cannot claim to present a full picture but part of the whole of the phenomena under study. As the book involves a huge amount of materials and some of the content is itself a huge area of specialisation, efforts have been made to make the presentation in-depth in order to present as full an understanding as possible to the audience; however, some of the analysis may still emerge as broad strokes to the eyes of expert readers. The study has to a large extent related to the literature published in the English language, however, delineation of the cultural characteristics are not exclusively enabled. Similarly, the empirical study in the book is based in the local country of the author, describing Hong Kong teachers, who, due to the influences of traditional Chinese culture, possibly place more emphasis on relationships with students, and consequently would

Overall Conclusion

demonstrate more the giving of social support to their students than their western counterparts would. It will be necessary to rely on future research to examine the possibility of generalising this finding across cultures.

References

Ahmed, W., Minnaert, A., van der Werf, G., & Kuyper, H. (2010). Perceived social support and early adolescents' achievement: The mediational roles of motivational beliefs and emotions. *Journal of Youth and Adolescence, 39*(1), 36.

Albrecht, T. L., & Adelman, M. B. (1987). *Communicating social support*. Thousand Oaks, CA, US: Sage Publications Inc.

Ambrose, S. A., Bridges, M. W., DiPietro, M., Lovett, M. C., & Norman, M. K. (2010). *How learning works: Seven research-based principles for smart teaching*. USA: Wiley.

Anderson, L. W., Krathwohl, D. R., Airasian, P. W., Cruikshank, K. A., Mayer, R. E., Pintrich, P. R., ... & Wittrock, M. C. (2001). *A taxonomy for learning, teaching, and assessing: A revision of Bloom's taxonomy of educational objectives, abridged edition*. White Plains, NY: Longman.

Arnett, J. J. (2002). The psychology of globalization. *American Psychologist, 57*(10), 774–783.

Arun, P., & Chavan, B. (2009). Stress and suicidal ideas in adolescent students in Chandigarh. *Indian Journal of Medical Sciences, 63*(7), 281–287.

Asad, E. M. M., & Hassan, R. B. (2013). The characteristics of an ideal technical teacher in this modern era. *International Journal of Social Science and Humanities Research, 1*(1), 1–6.

Ball, S. J. (2003). The teacher's soul and the terrors of performativity. *Journal of Education Policy, 18*(2), 215–228.

Bandura, A. (1986). *Social foundations of thought and action: A social cognitive theory*. Englewood Cliffs, NJ, US: Prentice-Hall Inc.

Barrera, M., Jr., & Ainlay, S. L. (1983). The structure of social support: A conceptual and empirical analysis. *Journal of community psychology, 11*(2), 133–143.

Bauer, M. A., Wilkie, J. E., Kim, J. K., & Bodenhausen, G. V. (2012). Cuing consumerism: Situational materialism undermines personal and social well-being. *Psychological Science, 23*(5), 517–523.

Baumeister, R. F., & Leary, M. R. (1995). The need to belong: Desire for interpersonal attachments as a fundamental human motivation. *Psychological Bulletin, 117*(3), 497–529.

Betoret, F. D. (2006). Stressors, self-efficacy, coping resources, and burnout among secondary school teachers in Spain. *Educational Psychology, 26*(4), 519–539.

Blau, P. M. (1964). *Exchange and power in social life*. New Brunswick, NJ: Transaction Publishers.

Blossfeld, H. P., Klijzing, E., Mills, M., & Kurz, K. (2005). *The losers in a globalizing world: Becoming an adult in uncertain times*. London: Routledge.

Borko, H., & Livingston, C. (1989). Cognition and improvisation: Differences in mathematics instruction by expert and novice teachers. *American Educational Research Journal, 26*(4), 473–498.

Bowlby, J. (1988). *A secure base: Parent–child attachment and healthy human development*. New York: Basic Books.

Boxall, M. (2002). *Nurture groups in school: Principles & practice*. USA: Sage.

Bray, M. (2017). Benefits and tensions of shadow education: Comparative perspectives on the roles and impact of private supplementary tutoring in the lives of Hong Kong students. *Journal of International and Comparative Education (JICE), 2,* 18–30.

Caprara, G. V., & Steca, P. (2005). Affective and social self-regulatory efficacy beliefs as determinants of positive thinking and happiness. *European Psychologist, 10*(4), 275–286.

Carson, R. L., & Templin, T. J. (2007, April). Emotional regulation and teacher burnout: Who says that the management of emotional expression doesn't matter. In *American Education research association annual convention*, Chicago.

Centers for Disease Control. (2013). Make a difference at your school. *Chronic Disease*. Paper 31. Retrieved from http://digitalcommons.hsc.unt.edu/disease/31.

Chan, K. B., Lai, G., Ko, Y. C., & Boey, K. W. (2000). Work stress among six professional groups: The Singapore experience. *Social Science and Medicine, 50*(10), 1415–1432.

Cheng, Y. C. (1999). Recent education developments in South East Asia: An introduction. *School Effectiveness and School Improvement, 10*(1), 3–9.

Cheung, E. & Chiu, P. (2016, March 12). Students at breaking point: Hong Kong announces emergency measures after 22 suicides since the start of the academic year. *The South China Morning Post*. Retrieved from http://www.scmp.com/news/hong-kong/health-environment/article/1923465/students-breaking-point-hong-kong-announces.

Cheung, A. C., & Wong, P. M. (2012). Factors affecting the implementation of curriculum reform in Hong Kong: Key findings from a large-scale survey study. *International Journal of Educational Management, 26*(1), 39–54.

Chiu, P. (2017, March 21). Testing times for Hong Kong's controversial exam, despite government awarding itself a pass: Parents fear repetitive drilling exercises will continue and are calling for assessment to be scrapped while planning a citywide boycott. *The South China Morning Post*. Retrieved from http://www.scmp.com.

Choi, P. L., & Tang, S. Y. F. (2009). Teacher commitment trends: Cases of Hong Kong teachers from 1997 to 2007. *Teaching and Teacher Education, 25*(5), 767–777.

Coan, J. A. (2008). Toward a neuroscience of attachment. In J. Cassidy & P. R. Shaver (Eds.), *Handbook of attachment: Theory, research, and clinical applications* (2nd ed., pp. 241–265). New York: The Guilford Press.

Cohen, S. (2004). Social relationships and health. *American Psychologist, 59*(8), 676–684.

Cohen, S., & McKay, G. (1984). Social support, stress and the buffering hypothesis: A theoretical analysis. *Handbook of Psychology and Health, 4*, 253–267.

Coleman, J. S. (1990). *Foundations of social theory*. Cambridge: Harvard University Press.

Durkheim, E. (2013). *Durkheim: The rules of sociological method: And selected texts on sociology and its method*. Palgrave Macmillan.

Education Support Partnership. (2015). *2015 education sector health survey*. Retrieved from https://www.educationsupportpartnership.org.uk/resources/research-reports/2015-health-survey.

Emmer, E. T., & Stough, L. M. (2001). Classroom management: A critical part of educational psychology, with implications for teacher education. *Educational Psychologist, 36*(2), 103–112.

Erikson, E. H. (1959). *Identity and the life cycle: Selected papers*. Oxford, England: International Universities Press.

Feeney, B. C., & Collins, N. L. (2015). A new look at social support: A theoretical perspective on thriving through relationships. *Personality and Social Psychology Review, 19*(2), 113–147.

Feld, L. D., & Shusterman, A. (2015). Into the pressure cooker: Student stress in college preparatory high schools. *Journal of Adolescence, 41*, 31–42.

Fredrickson, B. L. (2003). The value of positive emotions: The emerging science of positive psychology is coming to understand why it's good to feel good. *American Scientist, 91*(4), 330–335.

Fredricks, J., Blumenfeld, P., Friedel, J., & Paris, A. (2005). School engagement. In K. A. Moore & L. H. Lippman (Eds.), *What do children need to flourish?* (pp. 305–321). New York: Springer.

Gecas, V., & Schwalbe, M. L. (1983). Beyond the looking-glass self: Social structure and efficacy-based self-esteem. *Social Psychology Quarterly, 46*(2), 77–88.

Goldsmith, D. J. (2004). *Communicating social support*. Cambridge: Cambridge University Press.

Guay, S., Billette, V., & Marchand, A. (2006). Exploring the links between posttraumatic stress disorder and social support: Processes and potential research avenues. *Journal of Traumatic Stress, 19*(3), 327–338.

References

Hamre, B. K., & Pianta, R. C. (2005). Can instructional and emotional support in the first-grade classroom make a difference for children at risk of school failure? *Child Development, 76*(5), 949–967.

Hargreaves, A. (1994). *Changing teachers, changing times: Teachers' work and culture in the postmodern age.* New York: Teachers College Press.

Hargreaves, A. (1998). The emotional practice of teaching. *Teaching and Teacher Education, 14*(8), 835–854.

Hargreaves, A. (1999). The psychic rewards (and annoyances) of teaching. In M. Hammersley (Ed.), *Researching school experience: Ethnographic studies of teaching and learning* (pp. 85–104). London & New York: Falmer Press.

Hargreaves, A. (2000). Mixed emotions: Teachers' perceptions of their interactions with students. *Teaching and Teacher Education, 16*(8), 811–826.

Haslam, N. (2006). Dehumanization: An integrative review. *Personality and Social Psychology Review, 10*(3), 252–264.

Hattie, J. (2003, October). Teachers make a difference: What is the research evidence? In *Paper presented at the Australian Council for Educational Research Annual Conference on Building Teacher Quality*, Melbourne.

Hebson, G., Earnshaw, J., & Marchington, L. (2007). Too emotional to be capable? The changing nature of emotion work in definitions of 'capable teaching'. *Journal of Education Policy, 22*(6), 675–694.

Helliwell, J. F. (2006). Well-Being, social capital and public policy: What's new? *The Economic Journal, 116,* C34–C45.

Hong Kong Federation of Education Workers. (2015). Teacher well-being survey. Retrieved May 17, 2018, from https://hkfew.org.hk/UPFILE/ArticleFile/201552117534113.pdf.

Hong Kong Institute of Asia-Pacific Studies. (2016). *Survey findings on views on "winning at the starting line" in Hong Kong.* Retrieved from http://www.cuhk.edu.hk/hkiaps/tellab/pdf/telepress/16/SP_Press_Release_20160808.pdf.

Hong Kong Primary Education Research Association, & Education Convergence. (2006). *Education research study on Hong Kong teachers' stress: Preliminary analysis.* Hong Kong: Hong Kong Primary Education Research Association and Education Convergence. (in Chinese).

Isenbarger, L., & Zembylas, M. (2006). The emotional labour of caring in teaching. *Teaching and Teacher Education, 22*(1), 120–134.

Jang, H., Reeve, J., & Deci, E. L. (2010). Engaging students in learning activities: It is not autonomy support or structure but autonomy support and structure. *Journal of Educational Psychology, 102*(3), 588–600.

Jeffrey, B., & Woods, P. (1996). Feeling deprofessionalised: The social construction of emotions during an OFSTED inspection. *Cambridge Journal of Education, 26*(3), 325–343.

Johnson, D. W., Johnson, R. T., & Smith, K. A. (1991). Cooperative learning: Increasing college faculty instructional productivity. *ASHE-ERIC Higher Education Report* No.4. Washington, DC: School of Education and Human Development, The George Washington University.

King, R. B., Caleon, I. S., Tan, J. P. L., & Ye, S. (2016). Positive Education in Asia. *Asia-Pacific Educational Research, 25*(3), 361–365.

Klem, A. M., & Connell, J. P. (2004). Relationships matter: Linking teacher support to student engagement and achievement. *Journal of School Health, 74*(7), 262–273.

Kushner, H. I., & Sterk, C. E. (2005). The limits of social capital: Durkheim, suicide, and social cohesion. *American Journal of Public Health, 95*(7), 1139–1143.

Lai, K. C., Chan, K. W., Ko, K. W., & So, K. S. (2005). Teaching as a career: A perspective from Hong Kong senior secondary students. *Journal of Education for Teaching, 31*(3), 153–168.

Lakey, B., & Cohen, S. (2000a). Social support and theory. In S. Cohen, L. G., Unerwood, & B. H. Gottlieb (Eds.), *Social support measurement and intervention: A guide for health and social scientists* (pp. 29–52). Oxford: Oxford University Press.

Lakey, B., & Cohen, S. (2000b). Social support theory and measurement. In S. Cohen, L. Underwood, & B. Gottlieb (Eds.), *Measuring and intervening in social support*. New York: Oxford University Press.

Lam, B. H. (2011a). A reflective account of a pre-service teacher's effort to implement progressive curriculum in field practice. *Schools: Studies Education, 8*(1), 22–39.

Lam, B. H. (2011b). The contexts of teaching in the 21st century. In S. N. Phillipson & B. H. Lam (Eds.), *Learning and teaching in the Chinese classroom* (pp. 1–30). Hong Kong: Hong Kong University Press.

Lam, B. H. (2012). Why do they want to become teachers? A study on prospective teachers' motivation to teach in Hong Kong. *The Asian Pacific Education Researcher, 21*(2), 307–314.

Lam, B. H. (2014). Challenges beginning teachers face. *Schools: Studies Education, 11*(1), 156–169.

Lam, B. H. (2015). There is no fear in love—The giving of social support to students enhances teachers' career development. In R. Osbourne (Ed.), *Job satisfaction: Determinants, workplace implications and impacts on psychological well-being* (pp. 73–96). Hauppauge, NY: Nova Science Publishers.

Lam, B. H. (2015, June). There is no fear in love: The giving of social support to students enhances teachers' career development. In *Paper presented at the Education and Cognitive Development Lab research seminar series of the National Institute of Education*, Singapore.

Lam, B. H. (2017). Positive education and education of Hong Kong. *Hong Kong Economic Journal*. Retrieved 07-08-2017 http://www1.hkej.com/dailynews/culture/article/1624623/%E6%AD%A3%E9%9D%A2%E6%95%99%E8%82%B2%E8%88%87%E9%A6%99%E6%B8%AF%E6%95%99%E8%82%B2.

Lam, B. H., & Yan, H. F. (2011). Beginning teachers' job satisfaction: The impact of school-based factors. *Teacher Development, 15*(3), 333–348.

Larson, R. W., Wilson, S., Brown, B. B., Furstenberg, F. F., Jr., & Verma, S. (2002). Changes in Adolescents' Interpersonal Experiences: Are they being prepared for adult relationships in the twenty-first century? *Journal of Research on Adolescence, 12*(1), 31–68.

Lazarus, R. S., & Folkman, S. (1984). Coping and adaptation. *The handbook of behavioral medicine*, 282325.

Li, H. C. W., Chan, S. L. P., Chung, O. K. J., & Chui, M. L. M. (2010). Relationships among mental health, self-esteem and physical health in Chinese adolescents: An exploratory study. *Journal of Health Psychology, 15*(1), 96–106.

Lin, N. (1999). Social networks and status attainment. *Annual review of sociology, 25*(1), 467–487.

Lin, N. (2017). Building a network theory of social capital. In *Social capital* (pp. 3–28). UK: Routledge.

Lin, N., Ensel, W. M., Simeone, R. S., & Kuo, W. (1979). Social support, stressful life events, and illness: A model and an empirical test. *Journal of Health and Social Behavior, 20*(2), 108–119.

Liu, X., & Tein, J. Y. (2005). Life events, psychopathology, and suicidal behavior in Chinese adolescents. *Journal of Affective Disorders, 86*, 195–203.

López, M. L., & Cooper, L. (2011). *Social support measures review*. National Center for Latino Child & Family Research. Retrieved from http://www.first5la.org/files/SSMS_LopezCooper_LiteratureReviewandTable_02212011.pdf.

Lortie, D. (1975). *Schoolteacher: A sociological analysis*. Chicago: University of Chicago.

Martin, A. J., Collie, R. J., & Frydenberg, E. (2017a). Social and emotional learning: Lessons learned and opportunities going forward. In E. Frydenberg, A. J. Martin, & R. J. Collie (Eds.), *Social and emotional learning in Australia and the Asia-Pacific: Perspectives, programs and approaches* (pp. 459–471). Singapore: Springer.

Martin, A. J., Collie, R. J., & Frydenberg, E. (2017b). Social and emotional learning: Lessons learned and opportunities going forward. In E. Frydenberg, A. J. Martin, & R. J. Collie (Eds.), *Social and emotional learning in Australia and the Asia-Pacific: Perspectives, programs and approaches* (pp. 459–471). Singapore: Springer Singapore.

Maslow, A. H. (1943). A theory of human motivation. *Psychological Review, 50*(4), 370.

References

McCollum, B. D. (2014). The caring beliefs and practices of effective teachers. *Electronic Theses & Dissertations, 1186*. Retrieved from https://digitalcommons.georgiasouthern.edu/etd/1186/.

McNeil, L. (2002). *Contradictions of school reform: Educational costs of standardized testing*. UK: Routledge.

Meyer, D. K., & Turner, J. C. (2006). Re-conceptualizing emotion and motivation to learn in classroom contexts. *Educational Psychology Review, 18*(4), 377–390.

Michalos, A. C. (2012). *Global report on student well-being: Volume IV: Religion, education, recreation, and health*. Berlin: Springer Science & Business Media.

Mills, M., Blossfeld, H. P., & Klijzing, E. (2005). Becoming an adult in uncertain times: A 14-country comparison of the losers of globalization. In H. -P., Blossfeld, E. Kligzing, M. Mills, & K. Kurz (Eds.), *Globalization, uncertainty and youth in society* (pp. 438–459). London: Routledge.

Morrison, B. (2002). *Bullying and victimisation in schools: A restorative justice approach. Australian Institute of Criminology: Trends & issues in crime and criminal justice* (p. 219). Retrieved from http://www.aic.gov.au.

Mosley, J. (2005). *Circle time for young children*. USA: Routledge.

Nicholl, B., & McLellan, R. (2008). 'We're all in this game whether we like it or not to get a number of As to Cs'. Design and technology teachers' struggles to implement creativity and performativity policies. *British Educational Research Journal, 34*(5), 585–600.

Nickerson, R. S., Butler, S. F., & Carlin, M. (2009). Empathy and knowledge projection. In J. Decety & W. Ickes (Eds.), *The social neuroscience of empathy* (pp. 44–56). Cambridge, Massachusetts: The MIT Press.

Niemiec, C. P., & Ryan, R. M. (2009). Autonomy, competence, and relatedness in the classroom: Applying self-determination theory to educational practice. *School Field, 7*(2), 133–144.

Noddings, N. (2003). *Happiness and education*. Cambridge, UK: Cambridge University Press.

O'Connor, K. E. (2008). "You choose to care": Teachers, emotions and professional identity. *Teaching and Teacher Education, 24*(1), 117–126.

O'Donnell, A. M., & O'Kelly, J. (1994). Learning from peers: Beyond the rhetoric of positive results. *Educational Psychology Review, 6*(4), 321–349.

Ouweneel, E., Le Blanc, P. M., & Schaufeli, W. B. (2013). Do-it-yourself: An online positive psychology intervention to promote positive emotions, self-efficacy, and engagement at work. *Career Development International, 18*(2), 173–195.

Piliavin, J. A., & Siegl, E. (2007). Health benefits of volunteering in the Wisconsin longitudinal study. *Journal of Health and Social Behavior, 48*(4), 450–464.

Pintrich, P. R. (2002). The role of metacognitive knowledge in learning, teaching, and assessing. *Theory into Practice, 41*(4), 219–225.

Polanczyk, G. V., Salum, G. A., Sugaya, L. S., Caye, A., & Rohde, L. A. (2015). Annual Research Review: A meta-analysis of the worldwide prevalence of mental disorders in children and adolescents. *Journal of Child Psychology and Psychiatry, 56*(3), 345–365.

Reeve, J., Deci, E. L., & Ryan, R. M. (2004). Self-determination theory: A dialectical framework for understanding socio-cultural influences on student motivation. In D. McInerney & S. Van Etten (Eds.), *Big theories revisited: Volume 4 in Research on sociocultural influences on motivation and learning* (pp. 31–60). Greenwich, CT: Information Age Publishing.

Reigeluth, C. M. (2013). *Instructional-design theories and models: A new paradigm of instructional theory* (Vol. II). UK: Routledge.

Reis, H. T., Sheldon, K. M., Gable, S. L., Roscoe, J., & Ryan, R. M. (2000). Daily well-being: The role of autonomy, competence, and relatedness. *Personality and Social Psychology Bulletin, 26*(4), 419–435.

Richardson, V., & Fallona, C. (2001). Classroom management as method and manner. *Journal of Curriculum Studies, 33*(6), 705–728.

Russell, S. L. (2012). *Individual-and classroom-level social support and classroom behavior in middle school*. Ph.D. dissertation. University of Maryland, College Park, ProQuest Dissertations Publishing.

Ryan, A. M. (2000). Peer groups as a context for the socialization of adolescents' motivation, engagement, and achievement in school. *Educational Psychologist, 35*(2), 101–111.

Ryan, R. M., & Deci, E. L. (2001). On happiness and human potentials: A review of research on hedonic and eudaimonic well-being. *Annual Review of Psychology, 52*(1), 141–166.

Ryan, R. M., & Deci, E. L. (2017). *Self-determination theory: Basic psychological needs in motivation, development, and wellness.* New York: Guilford Publications.

Sarason, B. R., Sarason, I. G., & Pierce, G. R. (1990a). Traditional views of social support and their impact on assessment. In B. R. Sarason, I. G. Sarason, & G. R. Pierce (Eds.), *Wiley series on personality processes. Social support: An interactional view* (pp. 9–25). Oxford, England: Wiley.

Sarason, B. R., Sarason, I. G., & Pierce, G. R. (1990b). *Social support: An interactional view.* New York: John Wiley.

Sarason, I. G., Sarason, B. R., Shearin, E. N., & Pierce, G. R. (1987). A brief measure of social support: Practical and theoretical implications. *Journal of Social and Personal Relationships, 4*(4), 497–510.

Schwartz, C. E., & Sendor, R. M. (1999). Helping others helps oneself: response shift effects in peer support. *Social Science and Medicine, 48*(11), 1563–1575.

Seligman, M. (2011). *Flourish: A visionary new understanding of happiness and well-being.* New York: Free Press.

Sharma, S., & Sharma, M. (2010). Globalization, threatened identities, coping and well-being. *Psychological Studies, 55*(4), 313–322.

Sherbourne, C. D., & Stewart, A. L. (1991). The MOS social support survey. *Social Science & Medicine, 32*(6), 705–714.

Skinner, E. A., & Belmont, M. J. (1993). Motivation in the classroom: Reciprocal effects of teacher behavior and student engagement across the school year. *Journal of Educational Psychology, 85*(4), 571–581.

Slavin, R. E. (1995). Best evidence synthesis: An intelligent alternative to meta-analysis. *Journal of Clinical Epidemiology, 48*(1), 9–18.

Steinhardt, M. A., Smith Jaggars, S. E., Faulk, K. E., & Gloria, C. T. (2011). Chronic work stress and depressive symptoms: Assessing the mediating role of teacher burnout. *Stress and Health, 27*(5), 420–429.

Storrie, K., Ahern, K., & Tuckett, A. (2010). A systematic review: students with mental health problems—A growing problem. *International Journal of Nursing Practice, 16*(1), 1–6.

Suldo, S. M., Friedrich, A. A., White, T., Farmer, J., Minch, D., & Michalowski, J. (2009). Teacher support and adolescents' subjective well-being: A mixed-methods investigation. *School Psychology Review, 38*(1), 67–85.

Suldo, S. M., Shaffer, E. J., & Riley, K. N. (2008). A social-cognitive-behavioral model of academic predictors of adolescents' life satisfaction. *School Psychology Quarterly, 23*(1), 56–69.

Sun, R. C., & Shek, D. T. (2010). Life satisfaction, positive youth development, and problem behaviour among Chinese adolescents in Hong Kong. *Social Indicators Research, 95*(3), 455–474.

Taylor, S. E. (2007). Social support. In H. S. Friedman & R. C. Silver (Eds.), *Foundations of health psychology* (pp. 145–171). Oxford: Oxford University Press.

Teven, J. J., & Hanson, T. L. (2004). The impact of teacher immediacy and perceived caring on teacher competence and trustworthiness. *Communication Quarterly, 52*(1), 39–53.

The Hong Kong institute of Family Education (2013). 虎爸虎媽影響學童發展 [*Tiger dad and mom affects student's development*]. Retrieved from http://www.ife.org.hk/media_detail.php?id=122.

Thoits, P. A. (2011). Mechanisms linking social ties and support to physical and mental health. *Journal of Health and Social Behavior, 52*(2), 145–161.

Twenge, J. M., & Kasser, T. (2013). Generational changes in materialism and work centrality, 1976–2007: Associations with temporal changes in societal insecurity and materialistic role modeling. *Personality and Social Psychology Bulletin, 39*(7), 883–897.

Uchino, B. N. (2009). What a lifespan approach might tell us about why distinct measures of social support have differential links to physical health. *Journal of Social and Personal Relationships, 26*(1), 53–62.

References

Uchino, B. N., Bowen, K., Carlisle, M., & Birmingham, W. (2012). Psychological pathways linking social support to health outcomes: A visit with the "ghosts" of research past, present, and future. *Social Science and Medicine, 74*(7), 949–957.

Vavrus, M. (2008). Culturally responsive teaching. *21st century education: A reference handbook, 2*, 49–57. Retrieved from https://static1.squarespace.com/static/55a68b71e4b075daf6b2aa0b/t/55a7322ae4b0a573ba71de46/1437020714535/CulturallyResponsiveTeaching.pdf.

Vohs, K. D., Mead, N. L., & Goode, M. R. (2006). The psychological consequences of money. *Science, 314*(5802), 1154–1156.

Vygotsky, L. S. (1978). *Mind in society: The development of higher psychological processes*. Cambridge, MA: Harvard University Press.

Waterman, A. S. (1993). Two conceptions of happiness: Contrasts of personal expressiveness (eudaimonia) and hedonic enjoyment. *Journal of Personality and Social Psychology, 64*(4), 678–691.

Wentzel, K. R. (1994). Relations of social goal pursuit to social acceptance, classroom behavior, and perceived social support. *Journal of Educational Psychology, 86*(2), 173.

Wentzel, K. R. (2009). Peers and academic functioning at school. In K. H. Rubin, W. M. Bukowski, & B. Laursen (Eds.), *Social, emotional, and personality development in context. Handbook of peer interactions, relationships, and groups* (pp. 531–547). New York, NY, US: Guilford Press.

Wilcox, P., Winn, S., & Fyvie-Gauld, M. (2005). 'It was nothing to do with the university, it was just the people': the role of social support in the first-year experience of higher education. *Studies in Higher Education, 30*(6), 707–722.

World Health Organization (2014). *Preventing suicide: A global imperative*. Retrieved from http://apps.who.int/iris/bitstream/10665/131056/1/9789241564779_eng.pdf?ua=1&ua=1.

World Health Organization (2017 April). *Mental disorders fact sheet*. Retrieved from http://www.who.int/mediacentre/factsheets/fs396/en/.

Chapter 2
Understanding Social Support

Abstract The chapter gives readers a comprehensive understanding of the research on social support in the field of health psychology. It acts as the foundation of this book to provide readers with a fundamental knowledge of social support; and the ideas in this chapter are linked to the other chapters of the book. The first two parts of the content cover the discussion of the meaning of social support and the research approaches of this topic in the literature. The third part discusses the implications of social support for education. It seeks to accomplish the following purposes:

(1) To describe the key perspectives of conceptualising social support research, and relevant concepts which explain each of the study approaches with reference to theoretical and empirical literature;
(2) To discuss some pertinent issues that relate to research in social support and suggest instruments to be used for the topics of study;
(3) To draw implications for education and discuss potential topics for further study in subsequent chapters of the book.

The preliminary ideas suggested in the chapter will be the guide to the direction of this book, which will be followed-up and investigated in subsequent chapters of the book, to draw connections between social support and the practice of education. The chapter suggests the potential of connecting social support to education in order to generate theory and practice that benefits students as support receivers. The chapter also hints at the potential area of studying the benefits of social support for support givers. The potential topics related to learners and teachers as recipients and providers of social support in the context of education will be further explored in subsequent chapters of the book.

Why Study Social Support?

The description in Chap. 1 about the societal background in the twenty-first century suggests a catalyst for promoting social support in society. In schools, the lack of motivation for academic activities is a prominent problem of school-aged students (Legault, Green-Demers, & Pelletier, 2006). Students' feeling of disconnection from

© Springer Nature Singapore Pte Ltd. 2019
B. LAM, *Social Support, Well-being, and Teacher Development*,
https://doi.org/10.1007/978-981-13-3577-8_2

school has created a serious problem of disengagement, and the problems increase as students grow (Fredricks, Blumenfeld, Friedel, & Paris, 2005). Propelled by this, much effort has been put forward to reinvent education to fit the needs of a changing society. Researchers have started to re-conceptualise education as helping students to attain a fulfilling and actualizing self (Jang, Reeve, Ryan, & Kim, 2009). Teaching to promote learners' interest, motivation, social and emotional development has been given a more prominent place in schools, and the affective attributes and emotional support to learners are fully recognised as exemplary traits of teaching (Hattie & Jaeger, 2003). Stakeholders bestow a higher expectation on teachers from whom students could expect nurturance, and more is expected from teachers to play the role of a warm and supportive teacher as these characteristics are found to produce better learning outcomes (Reddy, Rhodes, & Mulhall, 2003; Rosenfeld, Richman, & Bowen, 2000). At the classroom level, however, the practice of an emotional role in teaching remains a myth for teachers, partly because the practice of supportive behaviours in the classroom is open-ended, is subject to contextual factors (such as teacher's personal style) and has a boundless scope to deal with; and partly because of the interference of the measurement culture in schools that discourages teachers from pursuing this topic further (Sachs, 2003). All in all, there is a perceived need for teachers to reflect on their expanding role in teaching at this time. The present educational environment reveals a particular need for research to theorise teachers' supportive behaviour in teaching that highlight teachers' commitments to student psychological well-being in learning. Such investigations can provide evidence to recommend to policymakers the directions of education that can improve education; the results can also have implications for the professional knowledge of teaching and strengthen the scholarship of teaching.

Supportive teachers and supportive teaching behaviours are explored in this book by referring to social support as a construct. Social support first appeared as a topic of intuitive interest to me when I began to realise that 'enthusiasm', 'feedback' and 'concern for learner diversity' are areas that my students valued, even when they were university teachers. It did not take me long to realise that enthusiasm, caring and empathy are recognisable traits of expert teachers in the educational literature. However, these traits in teaching have not been addressed formally in practice, either in the selection of teachers, curriculum of teacher education (Casey & Childs, 2017), or in the formal assessment of teaching in different educational settings. Social support was originally developed in the health care disciplines; however education has produced similar contexts that bring connection to this term. First of all, education involves interaction between the teacher as giver and students as receivers, and the communication between supportive teachers and their learners should resemble the features of support giver and taker. It is expected that practitioners in education could learn from the concerns of such interaction and communication to guide practice in teaching. Second, support for students can happen by different means, of a different nature. What the field of education could borrow from the practice of social support in health psychology is its strong tradition of research, such as assumptions, approaches and skills. Third, social support is known to affect the well-being and supports people in distress (Taylor, 2007), since the background of students even in mainstream schools has become very diverse nowadays, and mental health problems have become common among school-aged children (Cheung & Chiu, 2016; Centers for Disease Control, 2003). The strategies and outcomes to be expected for teaching in schools can be considered along with the knowledge as found in social support research. Finally, studying social support can broaden the horizon of knowledge in education. Education has an applied knowledge nature. It is often used to solve problems (Biglan, 1973) and is subject to specific values and social purposes of a particular context (Labaree, 1998). The exploration on social support in the healthcare disciplines and the insights it draws from education as an interdisciplinary investigation is, therefore, appropriate, especially due to the societal background that makes this topic of high relevance to education nowadays.

This chapter attempts to take one stride forward to understand the intriguing nature of social support which is often used as a general term; and explore its connections to learning and teaching, and teacher development. While it provides a theoretical framework to study the theory and practice of social support in education in the forthcoming chapters, it is a chapter unique for understanding the research and practice of social support.

What Is Social Support?

Psychologists, medical practitioners and other health specialists have started to investigate the impact of transaction between people and the effect of support from others to one's own health situation, which creates the terrain of social support research in health psychology (Cobb, 1976; Sarason & Sarason, 1985; Taylor, 2007). Being a relatively new discipline, originating in the 1970s, health psychology focuses on the scientific study of psychological processes related to health and health care (Adler & Kwon, 2002; Taylor, 2007), by combining 'psycho' and 'soma' (body and mind) in looking at human's health condition. Social support is regarded as a major component of health psychology to help with health issues including depressive symptomatology and physical and mental illness (Taylor, Welch, Kim, & Sherman, 2007; Thoits, 2011), by involving different categories of help from professionals in specialised fields and members of the social environment. It has developed as a field of interest in the medical, psychology and social science literature (Callaghan & Morrissey, 1993; Turner & Marino, 1994).

Social support has a complex meaning as it is subject to a series of interactions and processes, which covers the conditions (such as different situations that involve social support and in which social support takes effect), types of support and effects (outcomes based on different situations). Lin, Ensel, Simeone, and Kuo (1979, p. 109) defined social support as the 'support accessible to an individual through social ties to other individuals, groups, and the larger community'. To emphasise the effect of social support on human healthy functioning, Farmer and Farmer (1996, p. 483) defined social support as the 'processes of social exchange that contribute to the development of individuals' behavioural patterns, social cognition and values'. Conclusively, social support is found to positively affect both physical and psychological health (Thoits, 2011). The beneficial effects of social support can be explained by two different models:

(1) stress buffering effect, in which social support buffers the adverse impacts of a stressor, either by enhancing an individual's coping strategy or leading him/her to reinterpret the situation to be less adverse due to the available support; and

(2) main effect, through which social bonds have a direct positive effect on a person's well-being regardless of stress.

Apparently, buffering stress is commonly recognised as a key function of social support in helping one feel less distress and resolving the problems that may cause stress, yet, the importance of social support regarding a person's interpersonal relationship with the other is considered to be crucial to living which can benefit health and well-being (Lakey & Cronin, 2008; Uchino, 2004, 2009). In the discussion below, health and well-being will generally be posited as valid outcomes of social support.

Major Conceptions of Social Support

Researchers have used a variety of approaches and terminologies to define social support, resulting in a bewildering range of measures in studying it (Heaney & Israel, 2008; House, 1987; Lakey & Cohen, 2000; López & Cooper, 2011; Reblin & Uchino, 2008), accompanied by findings which are not always comparable (Barrera, 1986; Cohen & McKay, 1984; Heller, 1979; Nurullah, 2012; Taylor, 2007; Uchino, Cacioppo, & Kiecolt-Glaser, 1996). Regarding the approaches of such study, researchers in health psychology have used several approaches which can be referred to in initiating a discussion of social support. For example, Sarason, Sarason and Pierce (1990a, 1990b) suggested that social support can be viewed from the perspective of three models, namely, the network model, received model and perceived model. Barrera & Ainlay (1983) as well as Sherbourne and Stewart (1991a, 1991b) examined social support functions, while both of their analyses focus on tangible types of support; their analyses commonly address the perceived availability of support, social structure (e.g. quantity and connectedness) and quality of social support (e.g. intimacy) in a person's social network. With a specific focus, House (1987) studied social support in relation to stress and health, focusing on the study of social structure. More comprehensively, Lakey and Cohen (2000) classified social support research into three theoretical perspectives to explain how social support influence people's health, namely, the stress buffering and coping perspective, social constructionist perspective and relationship perspective. These three perspectives are interrelated while each of them has a distinct association with health (Heller & Swindle, 1983; Lakey & Cohen, 2000). Reviews of social support research conducted after 2000 (e.g. Goodman, Potts, & Pasztor, 2007; López &

Major Conceptions of Social Support 33

Cooper, 2011; Matin et al., 2014; Rees, Mitchell, Evans, & Hardy, 2010) continued to explore social support focusing on stress buffers and functions of social support, perceived support and human interpersonal relationship.

To come up with a more comprehensive review, both review documents and original published articles were located as the sources for compiling this review. The process of searching was managed through the library I-Search database and the Google Scholar browsing engine based on the theme 'social support', from the year 1970 onwards, which was the time when social support research had begun to take shape. English language materials are used to yield a wide coverage of academic literature sources to support the investigation. In the following, five major approaches to studying social support are discussed. The compilation of the results is based on the literature drawn from the academic resource database described above. They are largely based on the investigations suggested by Barrera and Ainlay (1983), Cohen (2004a, 2004b), Coleman (1990), Goldsmith (2004), Guay et al. (2006), López and Cooper (2011), Lazarus and Folkman (1984), Lin (1999, 2017), Sarason, Sarason, Shearin, and Pierce (1987); Sarason, Sarason, and Pierce (1990a, 1990b), Uchino (2009), House (1987), Barrera and Ainlay (1983), Sherbourne and Stewart (1991a, 1991b) and Nurullah (2012). The meta-level analysis of social support research produced by Feeney and Collins (2015), Taylor (2007), Lakey and Cohen (2000), and Uchino, Bowen, Carlisle, and Birmingham (2012) are also referenced in formulating the analysis. In explaining different approaches, examples and research findings located from both theoretical and empirical literature are included to elaborate the meaning.

Stress Buffering, Coping and Adjustment

The stress and coping approach of conceptualising social support (Lakey & Cohen, 2000; Lakey & Orehek, 2011; Goldsmith, 2004) has been the most popular approach of research in health psychology (e.g. Cohen & Wills, 1985; Cutrona & Russell, 1990; Simoni, Frick, & Huang, 2006). It hypothesises that social support protects individuals from the negative health outcomes of stressful events (i.e. acting as a buffer of stress), via the functions of 'stress buffering' (Cassel, 1976; Cobb, 1976). Stress buffering means either (1) received support, 'supportive actions' the person actually received in reality or (2) perceived support, the perception of available support in the absence of actual assistance. The former can improve the coping performance of the stressed individual while the latter soothes the individual's evaluation of the event to make it less stressful (López and Cooper, 2011). Coping is the behaviour and action that mainly serves to regulate emotions and distress, and it is used to manage the problem that has caused the distress (Lakey & Cohen, 2000; Cutrona & Russell, 1990). The two conceptualizations of stress buffering effect of social support that is discussed below are illustrated in Fig. 2.1.

Received Support Buffers Stress. Received support promotes one's coping strategy in a negative event and thus buffers the adverse effect of stress on health. Shut-

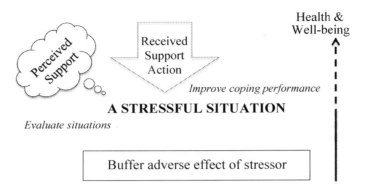

Fig. 2.1 Social support buffers stress by 'support action' received and 'perceived support'; it improves a person's coping performance and enables the person to perceive the situation as less stressful. Representative works that explain this approach include Goldsmith (2004), Guay, Billette, and Marchand (2006), Lazarus and Folkman (1984), and Lakey and Cohen (2000)

terstock (2011) explained the situation by referring to the situation of a patient taking a blood test. A patient feels worried as she is not sure what will be done for a blood test. The nurse thus explains to her the exact procedure of the blood test, its duration, the steps to be taken and the level of pain to be involved. The nurse also explains how the test results will be determined and what the possible follow-up steps are after the test. The information provided by the nurse helps the patient clarify the uncertain situation and ease the patient's anxiety because the patient is then clear about what one should do when preparing for the test. The patient may also expect to receive other types of support, such as encouragement and reassurance that the test is just not difficult to do (emotional support), or the advice to the patient about preparing well for the examination and the trust of the patient that she/he can manage to follow the instructions well and comply with the test follow-up procedures (self-esteem support). The types of social support may vary according to situations and the receiver's needs. The following discussion will elaborate further the different angles and perspectives of studying social support.

Apart from tangible support which provides physical assistance such as information support, the actual received support can come in many forms. For example, emotional support encourages an individual to evaluate the coping methods and enhance stress management (Folkman, Schaefer, & Lazarus, 1979; Gore, 1978; Helgeson & Cohen, 1996; Cohen, 2011); informational support may affect the coping strategy of the recipient by suggesting alternative solutions to a problem, whereas esteem support may encourage the individual to take a certain action to tackle the problem as higher self-esteem will lead to more proactive coping behaviours (Lo, 2002).

Effective stress coping can be promoted by optimal matching (Cohen & McKay, 1984; Cutrona & Russell, 1990; Cutrona, Shaffer, Wesner, & Gardner, 2007; Dunkel-Schetter, Blasband, Feinstein, & Herbert, 1992; Lakey & Cohen, 2000). It is a model of social support study to identify the type of social support that is most beneficial to a particular stressor, to help an individual in coping with and reducing the negative impact of stress effectively in a stressful situation. A simple example to explain optimal matching is that imagine if you are hungry; comforting words from a friend may make you feel a little bit better, but the best kind of support must be offering you food directly because in such case the support your friend offer (food) you can replace the nature of your loss or need (hungry) on that point (Goldsmith, 2004).

Cutrona & Russell's (1990) framework attempted to identify a sophisticated, multiple-dimensional model of considering social support based on the optimal matching model of social support study. The framework specifies that the situations of strains, challenges and needs that people encounter in life are defined by several dimensions of life events, namely, desirability, controllability, duration of consequence and life domain. Different situations and conditions are then created to determine the types of social support behaviours that will be needed by people in the situation, which may lead to positive health outcomes (Barrera, 1986; Cohen & Mckay, 1984; Cutrona & Russell, 1990; Hobfoll & Vaux, 1993). According to Cutrona and Russell (1990), the four determinant of psychological consequences can be explained as: (a) *desirability* determines the intensity and the nature of the stress people experience; stress that is caused by desirable events create anxiety, such as promotion, and stress that is caused by undesirable events create depression; (b) *controllability* means whether one can take control of the situation to create a desirable situation, or can prevent an undesired goal that causes the stress. (c) Duration of consequence refers to the period the event causes stress may last; (d) *life domain* comprises aspects of life circumstances including assets (e.g. material goods and health), relationships (e.g. interpersonal challenges or losses of family and friends) and achievement (e.g. status and competition). Some salient results were generated from the optimal matching model of study. These results provide hints regarding effective support measures, which are useful to researchers and practitioners in the field of health psychology. For example, people who are under uncontrollable situations for a long period of time are in need of both emotional support and instrumental support, they also require emotional-focused coping strategies to manage the situation, such as in the situation of financial strain, losing job and the loss of a long-term partner or spouse (Cobb, 1976; Cutrona & Russell, 1990; Cutrona, Shaffer, Wesner, & Gardner, 2007). For the situation of work stress that are commonly encountered by people in the modern society, esteem support for reassuring self-worth and tangible support such as supervisor's help to review their work situation were found to be crucial factors that can eliminate the situation of burnout (Hämmig, 2017; Mäkikangas & Kinnunen, 2003). As for people who are experiencing role changes (expecting to be parents of a child or retirement), esteem support is most critical (Cobb, 1976; Cohen, 1992; Cutrona & Russell, 1990) for them to adjust to their new roles more confidently with a positive perception of themselves.

The matching model also received criticisms (Mattson & Hall, 2011). Heaney and Irsael (2008) suggesting that a helping act may provide one or more types of support at the same time and it is hard to empirically study the types of support separately. Another criticism is that a single support action can fulfill multiple needs at a time. For example, giving a piece of relevant information to a friend who is going to attend an interview for an important position in an organisation which

Table 2.1 Summary of types of support

Types of support	Description
Emotional support	Giving someone the feeling of being loved and cared for
Esteem support	Boosting someone's self-esteem and self-efficacy (e.g. giving praise)
Network support	Recognising someone as a member of a group, which creates a sense of belongingness and companionship for the person in the group
Information support	Providing useful information concerning the situation
Tangible support	Providing actual physical assistance (e.g. money, food)

you are familiar with not only would provide the person useful tips (information support) for preparing the job interview, it would also give the person the feeling of being cared for (emotional support) and enhance the person's self-confidence (esteem support). Therefore, it is hard to single out an action that helps with a situation of a life domain. Nonetheless, the stress support matching model nowadays still serves as an important basis to demonstrate how social support is provided and received (e.g. Torsheim & Wold, 2001) and is proven as a prominent approach of study in social support research (Cohen, 2004a, 2004b; Lakey & Cohen, 2000). Social support research based on optimal matching has resulted to a list of useful recommendations of certain types of support that can help achieve optimal adjustment for people in different circumstances, to improve their coping strategies and opportunities of recovery that lead to better health and well-being. The following list provides the common types of support functions that have explained the general function of each type of support based on the constructs commonly used by researchers (Cobb, 1976; Coyne, Aldwin & Lazarus, 1981; Folkman, Schaefer, & Lazarus, 1979; Gore, 1978) (Table 2.1).

Evaluation of Stressful Situations to Make People Feeling Less Stressed. Social support can also protect a person from the negative impacts of a stressful event by leading him/her to interpret the stressful situation so it becomes less aversive. Lazarus and Folkman (Lazarus & Folkman, 1984; Folkman, Lazarus, Gruen, & DeLongis, 1986) were early researchers who proposed the subjective perspectives of stress. They defined cognitive appraisal as an evaluation that reflects an individual's subjective interpretation of the event. Many researchers began to contribute to this point of view (e.g. Haley, Levine, Brown, & Bartolucci, 1987; Jackson & Warren, 2000; Pakenham, Chiu, Bursnall, & Cannon, 2007). According to appraisal theory (Lazarus, 1966), people's appraisal of a situation is very crucial in determining how stressful an event is (Lazarus, 1966; Lazarus & Folkman, 1984), and how it creates emotional responses such as stress in a person, since emotional responses can be changed (Lazarus, 1966, cited in Ellsworth & Scherer, 2003). 'Perceived support' may influence a person's initial response to the stressful situation and therefore elicit more positive emotions that benefit one's health. For instance, esteem support may offset threats to self-esteem that usually occur as a response to stress appraisal when the individual is believed to have the ability to solve the problem. Informational support helps one reappraise a stressor as less harmful when the individual understands more about the situation and possible resources. Emotional support may reduce the stress by distracting the person from worrying about stressful situations or directly uplifting positive affection. Tangible support may provide the recipient with increased time as if someone takes care of your children when you are busy with work, you are able to pay full attention to the challenges at work for the time being. The perception of these available supports from others may lead to reexamining the potential threat of a situation and thus alleviate stress (Thoits, 2013).

According to Folkman, Lazarus, Gruen, and DeLongis (1986), there are two stages of appraisal of an event: *primary appraisals* are judgments of the event, deciding whether it is stressful or threatening. The person may question 'What is going on?' Then during the process of *secondary appraisal*, the person evaluates available resources that are useful for coping with the situation and ask the question 'What can I do with it?' For example in the situation that a suspected health problem is diagnosed after taking the blood test, some patients will feel overwhelmed and think of the worst situation, therefore creating huge emotional turbulence for oneself. The more negative the appraisals are, the greater emotional stress results (Compas, Worsham, Ey, & Howell, 1996; Lazarus & Folkman, 1984; Pakenham, 2002) and leads to destructive outcomes. In another example, imagine when you realise the deadline for an assignment is approaching but you still haven't started doing it. First, you might ask yourself questions like 'why didn't I know about the assignment? Was I absent from that class?' Then you would try to look for resources that could help with the assignment, such as friends who have finished it or reference books and lecture notes. If you think there would be no chance of meeting the deadline, you might give up finishing the assignment and receive a bad grade, and feel disturbed and discouraged by it. Or you may estimate you have enough resources to help you finish the task and try your best to finish it and hand it in.

Appraisals essentially affect the outcomes of an event eventually, and determine successful and positive outcomes so that even within the same situation, people can be successful, while some do not. The belief of available social support reduces the impact of stress by appraising the stressful situation to be less negative or by reducing the significance of the negative meaning of the stressful events (Ehlers & Clark, 2000; Guay, Billette, & Marchand, 2006).

In Hitchock, Ellis, Williamson, and Nixon's (2015) study of children's post-traumatic stress, 91 hospitalised children aged from 7 to 17, who had experienced a single incident trauma (e.g. car accident, severe injury) were interviewed about their perceived support from family, an important person and friends, as well as their appraisals of the traumatic events. Their parents were also examined in terms of their perceptions of their support for their child.

Some parents avoided discussing the trauma with their child in order not to upset him/her. Surprisingly, when people were less willing to mention the traumatic incidents with their children, it is possible that the children might assume that they were blamed for the trauma and feel unsupported, thus perceiving the events as more negative than others might. In contrast, when the children felt they could discuss it with some significant others, they perceived more social support. Another finding of the study suggests that the benefits of children's perception of social support in post-traumatic symptom development are greater than their parent's report of support. These indicate that the interpretation of support rather than the actual support provided by others alter the appreciation of an event, which can help people view the same event more positively.

Appraisals of traumatic events are crucial for post-traumatic responses (Ehlers & Clark, 2000). Hitchock and colleagues also found that negative appraisal mediated the relationship between social support and post-traumatic stress. That is, social support helped reduce the post-traumatic stress of these children when they had less negative appraisal toward the trauma. In other words, perceived social support buffers the adverse effect of the traumatic event by inducing the sufferers to evaluate the event as less negative, and protecting them from stress. Persons need support if they always interpret circumstances as negative, as an interpretation of events is also predicted by one's emotions (Ellsworth & Scherer, 2003).

The Social Constructionist and Interactionalist Approaches

In contrast with the stress and coping approach where people are active agents acting in situations and changed living circumstances, social constructionist and interactionalist approaches of conceptualising social support suggest that an individual's perceived support affects his/her self-esteem and identity and thus indirectly leads to better health and well-being (e.g., Kaul & Lakey, 2003). Inspired by Kelly's (1963) *Personal Constructs Theory* and Mead's (1934) *Symbolic Interactionist* theory, the social constructionist assumes that there is no 'real' reality since everyone perceives the same world differently. The symbolic interactionalist also agrees this position, researchers who think the same way suppose that everyone creates the world by acting in relation to others. As the world is 'constructed' by individual selves, it means the concepts we use to interpret the world depend on our personalities, personal beliefs and values in a cultural context. Based on this understanding, human beings construct assumptions and theories about the 'world' that reflect their social context (Dewey, 1917; Young and Collin, 2004), therefore the 'self' and the social world are inseparable (Mahoney, 2002; Mead, 1934). Therefore, it is the individual's own judgement of support, instead of the actual received support, that leads directly to outcomes. Previous research points out that received support and perceived support are only weakly associated (Lakey, Orehek, Hain, & VanVleet, 2010). As suggested by Hobfoll (2009), received support usually refers to the actual support we get during a particular stressful situation or period of time, whereas perceived support is the overall generalisation of various assistance provided by our network members in our past experiences. Some studies have proved perceived support has a much stronger

Major Conceptions of Social Support   39

effect on both physical and psychological health than received support (e.g. Lakey & Cronin, 2008; Uchino, 2004, 2009). Since health is a long-term issue, a generalised perception of support should predict health outcomes more accurately than a specific support action in a limited time frame.

Social Cognition Monitors Perceived Support. To simply define this concept, social cognition asserts that a person's understanding develops through social inter-action and social learning (Barone, Maddux, & Snyder, 1997). From this point of view, social support is one's perception of available support and this perception influ-ences the perception of self (i.e. self-esteem) (Lakey & Cohen, 2000; Uchino, 2009). Once an individual has formed a stable belief regarding the supportiveness of oth-ers, his/her usual judgements about social support will fit their existing beliefs. It, therefore, becomes likely that those who have a high level of perceived support will expect support to be given and thus have greater confidence in living, compared to those with a low level of perceived support who may experience anxiety because of anticipated rejection (Beck, Rush, Shaw, & Emery, 1979; Dozois & Beck, 2008). Therefore, the perception of support depends largely on an individual's impression of the support provider than the nature of the actual support (Kaul & Lakey, 2003; Mak, Bond, Simpson & Rholes, 2010). As a whole, the perception of available support in the social environment affects one's self-esteem and self-efficacy, which causes a mediating effect on health and well-being (Lakey & Cohen, 2000; Uchino, 2009).

This perspective is important as it suggests the powerful influence of human perception, and a person's perception once formed, may affect one's behaviour and create results which are long in affecting one's self-concept and directing one's life experience. As explained by the notion of a 'self-fulfilling prophecy' (Watzlawick, 1984), a strongly held belief, once formed, may influence a person's behaviour, and would ultimately lead to the fulfillment of the once false prediction of the person. While a person's belief of supportiveness of the environment may be formed upon a false impression or a particular event, this belief could still be influential in governing the behaviour of the person in their interaction with others in the social environment.

An example from daily life may illustrate how social cognition affects one's self-esteem and satisfaction. Supposed that you are having a tight schedule in submitting an application to a prestigious university for your higher education degree, you have to fill in the forms and prepare your CV, but have found that you may not have time to arrange the delivery because you are not familiar with the procedure of requesting a courier to send the parcel to a foreign country overseas. As you have this problem, your reaction is that since you cannot manage the whole task in this urgent timeframe, you must seek help from your brother and your friends as they might have experienced finding the sources for delivery and the experience of writing up a presentable CV; because of this, you are sure that you can cope with the situation and handle the application even within a tight timeframe. However, if you do not think anyone can help you even if you have friends and relatives who may have gone through the same procedure before, your past experience of seeking help inhibits you. You will just think that you have to rely on your own resources and will not ask anyone around you to help. You might also feel very anxious about their failure to help you. Eventually, you may give up the application because you are unable to handle it and no support can be accessed. Vice versa, if you often receive help and you believe that support is always around you, you remember clearly the supportiveness of others; that memory then assures you that support is out there when you need it;, you are at ease and calm when encountering the same situation; you will be expecting help and would ask for help if you need to.

The empirical literature also provides examples to explain how social cognition determines social support perception, which leads to life satisfaction. In a study of academic and career self-efficacy with 486 American undergraduate psychology students (Wright, Perrone-McGovern, Boo, & White, 2014), their attachment, perception of support, career barrier, career decision self-efficacy (i.e. confidence in one's ability to make decision to pursue a career path) and academic self-efficacy (i.e. self-efficacy in performing academic-related tasks) were measured. Attachment security (see also Chap. 2) is positively related to social support experience (Davila & Kashy, 2009); this means that individuals who develop a close relationship with family and friends are more approaching and confident. Consequently, they are more proactive in reaching out for social support (Feeney, Cassidy, & Ramos-Marcuse, 2008). Therefore, they are likely to perceive more support than 'avoidant individuals', who tended to refuse support from the others (Vogel & Wei, 2005). It has been found that attachment could positively predict perceived support and students who perceived more support also reported greater academic and career decision-making self-efficacy. In sum, past experiences of an individual influence his/her perception of social support and hence affect his/her well-being.

There are two possible explanations for this model to link up social support and health outcomes. (1) Positive appraisals of social relationships enhance positive cognition about oneself and thus lead to positive affect (Pierce, Baldwin, & Lydon, 1997). This will be discussed more in the part on the relationship perspective. (2) In Maslow's hierarchy of needs (1943), belongingness and love are basic psychological human needs. Failure to fulfill this need will directly lead to distress (Baumeister & Leary, 1995). Therefore, when a person perceives lack of support within their social environment because of past experiences, his/her psychological needs are unfulfilled. This will then lead to a negative impact on his/her psychological well-being.

Symbolic Interactionism Enhances Engagement. Symbolic Interactionalism holds that the regularisation of social interaction is responsible for an effect on well-being (Thoits, 1985, cited in Lakey & Cohen, 2000; Thoits, 2011). In this sense, acting in relation to others in the social environment suggests to us what roles to play and the support we may receive. These interactionalist activities give us a sense of self (i.e. who you are in this world) and create a meaning of life for ourselves, enabling us to develop an understanding of ourselves and this understanding monitors the way we act in the social environment, governed by a clear identity. By such identity formation interactively reinforced in the social environment, our health and well-being can be promoted (e.g. Berkman, Glass, Brissette, & Seeman, 2000; Cohen, 2004a, 2004b) (see Fig. 2.2). 'Self' is an essential concept in symbolic interactionism. Cooley's (1902) 'looking-glass self' suggested that sometimes people see themselves as they think others see them. These kinds of perception of self-image lead to self-concepts and emotional affects. As people make use of social interaction to evaluate

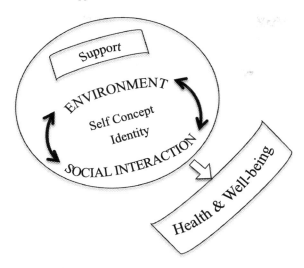

Fig. 2.2 Social interaction in the social environment helps develop one's self-identity; it leads to health and well-being outcomes. Representative works that explain this approach include Berkman, Glass, Brissette, and Seeman (2000); Cohen (2004a, 2004b), and Lakey and Cohen (2000)

and form a self-concept, roles become a point of reference to view themselves. People's roles in social contexts guide their behaviour (how to act) as a member of the group and give people a sense of identity of self (Lakey & Cohen, 2000; Stryker, 1994). According to Stryker's (1994), when a person is committed to a particular role identity, he/she is motivated to act according to the conception of such identity; in enacting role performance, the person's self-esteem is realised and ascertained. For example, imagine you are a student at school, who is expected to study hard to achieve good grades. If you work hard and perform well in the examinations, you will have higher self-esteem.

The Social Cognitive Theory (Lent, Brown, & Hackett, 2000) further explains how the interactionalist self that develops in the environment gears people with a sense of direction in their life. External factors such as social support, gender and role may have a greater influence on decision-making than personal or other internal factors. Gender role is a good example to illustrate the idea. Through gender socialisation, we learn about social expectation associated with our gender from the moment we are born. For instance, clothes for baby boys are usually blue in colour while those for girls are pink, not vice versa. And gradually males and females behave differently as they learn about social roles. When pursuing a career, people tend to rely on traditional gender stereotype, for example engineers are men and nurses are women, rather than personal interests (Holland, 1997; Wright et al., 2014, Duncan, Peterson, & Ax, 2003). The commitments to and responsibility of a role can exert invisible pressure on an individual to regulate his/her behaviours (Thoits, 2011). This mechanism predisposes human beings in how they act in a social environment.

Social network ties people together closely through social influence, attitudes and behaviour regulation (Laumann, 1973; Krohn, 1986). People regulate themselves by applying the social norms to their own behaviours (Mead, 1934), by comparing themselves with similar others in the reference group (Festinger, 1954), which is a collection of people we regard as a standard for comparison. For example, when choosing what clothes to buy, we usually refer to our peers or celebrities of similar age instead of our parents, because their style is more suitable for us. Similarly, we would find it awkward if our parents dressed like us. This is because of social influence, under which people assess the appropriateness of their behaviour and belief by comparing themselves with the norms. This explains the reason why it is not surprising to see that teenagers have almost the same outfit everywhere in the street when there is a 'fashion trend' to follow.

Similarly, social influence can promote an individual's well-being in the same way. Norms about health habits are acquired through social interactions, such that undesired behaviours will be inhibited among a social network. In a study of alcohol consumption behaviour (Green, Freeborn, & Polen, 2001), 7019 participants were asked about their alcohol drinking habits and social integration, for example how often they had contact with friends and how frequently they participated in religious and non-religious activities. It was found that gathering with friends more often and frequent participation in clubs was associated with greater alcohol consumption. By contrast, married people and those who attended more religious services significantly drank less, regardless of gender. This study shows that social context can effectively regulate people's behaviours and therefore affect their health outcomes. Of course, some reference groups may encourage undesirable or dangerous behaviours, such as gangs and gangster groups that involve behaviours such as fighting and drug abuse. Therefore, the direction of social interaction's effect on health consequence depends mainly on the reference groups researchers choose.

In this approach, the functions of social support are to help create and uphold self-esteem and one's identity development. The size and tightness of an individual's social network impact the receipt of support (Barrera, 1986). In Benson's (2012) study of support networks of mothers of children with Autism Spectrum Disorder (ASD), network size and composition of the support network of 106 mothers were examined. Their perceived levels of social support, levels of depressed mood, as well as subjective well-being were also measured. Larger network size and network emotional support were found to be directly related to increased perceived social support (Turner & Brown, 2010). Mothers who identified more people in their support networks perceived more social support in which support was mainly provided by close individuals in their inner circle. This is consistent with the previous finding that the benefits of social networks may be the greatest when the network members are perceived as significant or intimate to the support recipient (e.g. McLaughlin, Horwitz, & White, 2002, Thoits, 1995). So, how is a social network related to health outcomes? Mothers who have a larger and closer support network perceive more social support and they have lower levels of depression and a better feeling of well-being. Therefore, Benson (2012) concluded in his study that the size and functions of the network indirectly influence depressed mood and well-being through its effect on perceived social support.

Social Capital Strengthens Social Resources

Social capital is a specific term used in the sociological tradition which originally referred to the creation of capital that can facilitate one's instrumental action for production (Coleman, 1990). Unlike the symbolic interactionalist assumption which examines social support by the social influence a reference group has on the actor, social capital focuses on the accumulated resources one receives from his/her social relationships (Lin, 1999). In this approach, a focal person (known as ego) is the object who is tied to other people in his or her social network (known as alters) (DeJordy & Halgin, 2008). Social capital is studied by identifying the accumulated resources created for the ego or in the ego's social networks through the 'close ties', with whom the ego maintains a close social bond, such as friends and family, as well as the 'weak ties' who are alters outside the reach of one's social clique (Lin, 1999, 2017). The pattern of alters may create capital to benefit the focal person in different events (Putnam, 2000) such as in a career hunting situation where the ego may receive information from his or her alters who gain information from their own network. If the ego is connected to many alters who are not connected to the ego's network, the ego may have the benefit of access to timely information and have greater control of information (Burt, 1997, cited in Seibert, Kraimer, & Liden, 2001). Bonding social capital (close ties) benefits people in psychological well-being, such as self-esteem and emotional support (Ellison, Steinfield, & Lampe, 2007). The concept of social capital generated from network support, as a perspective of viewing social support, is illustrated in Fig. 2.3. A study of bridging capital via a social media network site is discussed below.

In Steinfield, Ellison, and Lampe's (2008) longitudinal study on 286 students in a university context, the authors investigated the relationship between participants' intensity of using Facebook as a social network site, self-esteem and loose connections between individuals (i.e. bridging social capital). Students were asked to record

Fig. 2.3 Social capital defines one's support in their social network via close ties and loose ties; it benefits psychological health and physical health. Representative works that explain this approach include Lin (2017), and Ellison, Steinfield, and Lampe (2007)

data on the time of using Facebook on average per day and the people they interacted with. They also filled in surveys to indicate how they felt about the use of Facebook on a 5-point Likert scale on items such as 'Facebook is part of my everyday activity', at some points of time in a school year. The authors used the Rosenberg Self-Esteem Scale (Rosenberg, 1989) for measuring students' self-esteem. Bridging social capital was measured by a survey, constructed by the authors, to examine if participants' Facebook use engaged them in a large and heterogeneous network of friends and their perceptions about the event. Sample items included such as 'I come into contact with new people all the time' and 'interacting with people in the site makes me want to try new things'. The study reported that participants spent significantly more time per day actively using Facebook and as a social media site Facebook has been shown to have growing importance in the lives of students according to the study results. The study reported the potential use of Facebook in gaining social capital for students with low self-esteem by the evidence of high scores on bridging social capital.

Social capital is used to examine career success (Seibert, Kraimer, & Liden, 2001), organisational success (Taylor, 2000) and academic success (Goddard, 2003), and it benefits both psychological health and physical health (Kim, Subramanian, & Kawachi, 2008). The effect of social capital is often measured by variables such as self-esteem, motivation and well-being. Many different operationalisations of social capital research are found due to the diverse conceptualization of this construct. It remains as a unique way of measuring the importance of people and networks in different domains of people's life.

Supportive Relationships and Social Integration

Another perspective of viewing social support identifies that people who maintain good quality relationships with other people in the social network and who are socially integrated have better health and well-being (Cohen, 2004a, 2004b; Cohen and Wills, 1985; Feeney & Collins, 2015; Lakey & Cohen, 2000; Sarason, 1974; Sarason, Sarason, Shearin, & Pierce, 1987; Thompson, Flood, & Goodvin, 2006). This assumption means we should look at the relationship qualities of a person in his/her own network, and whether these qualities affect one's perceived and/or received support (Lakey & Cohen, 2000; Kawachi & Berkman, 2001). According to Lakey and Cohen (2000), good relationship qualities include low conflict, companionship and intimacy. The supportive relationship and social integration perspective assumes that the relationship qualities a person maintains in his/her social network, including spouse, classmates, teachers, the friendship network, relative network and other affiliated association network of professional and personal types (such as professional association, church and interest groups) would simultaneously affect both perceived and/or received social support and the actual health outcomes of the person (Cohen, 2004a, 2004b; Cohen & Wills, 1985). People who maintain supportive relationship qualities are also found to be socially integrated as good relationship

Major Conceptions of Social Support

qualities enable them to perceive social support positively and also receive actual support to help with their aversive life situations.

Rini, Dunkel-Schetter, Glynn, Hobel, and Sandman (2006) showed that by having a quality relationship with a partner, a woman would perceive the support provided by her partner to be more effective. 176 pregnant women rated their relationship with their partner and their appraisal of the effectiveness of support by their partner. It was found that the higher the quality of the relationship with the partner, with more intimacy and emotional closeness and greater perceived equity in the relationship, the more effective the support provided by her partner was perceived. It is commonly suggested that marital satisfaction highly influences the appraisals of spouses (Waldinger & Schulz, 2006). It is expected that a woman who has an optimistic relationship with her partner will have more positive expectations of her partner during pregnancy, as a result perceiving her partner and his support more favourably (Beach, Fincham, Katz, & Bradburyet, 1996; Rini et al., 2006). Besides, as the perceived support effectiveness increases, the support is found to address stress more efficiently. Pregnant women who have a better relationship with their partner are less likely to suffer from prenatal anxiety (Rini et al., 2006; Stapleton et al., 2012). This confirms that better quality relationships directly lead to positive well-being.

Perceived support from close relationships such as family and friends during times of stress also have been found to be related to positive health outcomes (e.g. Hazel, Oppenheimer, Technow, Young, & Hankin, 2014; Lakey & Cronin, 2008; Rothon, Head, Klineberg, & Stansfeld, 2011). More recently, van Harmelen et al., (2016) conducted a longitudinal study on 711 British secondaries on their early life stress at the age of 14 or/and 17. The participants were examined based on their recalled negative experiences within the family environment (e.g. negative parenting style, family discard, child abuse, etc.) in the past, primary school peer bullying experiences, quality of friendship, perceived family support and depression symptoms. It was shown that friendships and family support buffered the effect of childhood family adversity (CFA) and/or peer bullying on depressive symptoms at age 17. That is, teenagers who suffered from CFA and/or peer bullying during primary studies were more likely to show symptoms of depression when they were 17. However, friendships and supporting family acted as a buffer to help prevent depression. Besides, by reducing depressive symptoms at age 14 and enhancing friendships and/or family support at age 17, adolescent's friendships and family support can indirectly affect depression symptoms at age 17, Fig. 2.4 illustrates this idea graphically. In sum, research has reported that positive relationships with family and friends in adolescence lower the risk of depressive symptoms later in life (Sheeber, Hops, Alpert, Davis, & Andrews, 1997; van Harmelen et al., 2016).

There is still no consensus on how relationship qualities influence physical and emotional health (Uchino, et al., 2012). Nevertheless, there are some directions to the question. Some suggest that quality relationship enhances self-esteem (Sapouna & Wolke, 2013), and others say it leads to positive appraisals or active coping strategies (Lakey & Cohen, 2000; Sarason, Sarason, & Pierce, 1990a, 1990b), or it polishes resilience and interpersonal skills (Fitzpatrick & Bussey, 2014; Hazel et al., 2014).

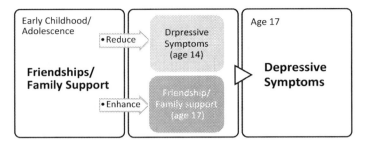

Fig. 2.4 Illustration of quality of relationship that affects well-being. Friendships and/or family support in early childhood/adolescence indirectly predict depressive symptoms at the age of 17 based on the work of van Harmelen et al. (2016)

Support Giving and Support Givers

Unlike the above conceptualisations which explain social support from the support receiver's position, giving social support has emerged as a potential topic in the social support literature which studies the motives and benefits of social support givers.

Batson and Shaw (1991) proposed three motives for people to carry out altruistic helping behaviours, namely, (1) *social reward*, which motivates helping acts in order to impress others; (2) *experienced distress*, which motivates people to help others in order to reduce their own distress; and (3) *empathic concern*, an unselfish motive people have when they identify someone in need and intend to benefit the well-being of the needy, which is considered a primary determinant of prosocial bahviours (Omoto, Malsch, & Barraza, 2009). Several studies have reported the benefits of giving helping behaviours on physical health and well-being, for instance individuals who offer support to others experience lower risk of mortality (Brown, Nesse, Vinokur, & Smith, 2003; Kahana, Bhatta, Lovegreen, Kahana, & Midlarsky, 2013) and have better health (Schwartz & Sendor, 2000); these people experience greater positive affect and life satisfaction (Kahana, Bhatta, Lovegreen, Kahana, & Midlarsky, 2013), and reduced distress (Midlarsky, 1991). In the case of volunteers engaging in service to help people in need, it is reported that they are at lower risk of depression, are generally happier and have higher self-esteem.

There are a few possible hypotheses raised, trying to explain the relationships between providing social support/informal help to others and well-being. First, kin-selection theory (Hamilton, 1964) and reciprocal-altruism theory (Trivers, 1971) hypothesise that an individual's sense of success depends on his/her ability to provide resources to relationship partners. Engaging in helping behaviours promotes one's feeling of competence, involvement and usefulness (Caprara & Steca, 2005) and satisfies one's psychological needs for competence. According to kin-selection theory, people tend to offer help to close kin in order to increase their family's chance of survival, while the reciprocal-altruism theory suggests that people help others with the expectation that they will be helped in return later on. In other words, offering help to others enlarges an individual's social capital so that he/she will be more likely to receive support whenever needed and enhance his/her chances of survival. Secondly, human beings are evolutionarily bonded to relatedness via offering help to others (Caprara & Steca, 2005). Helping behaviours enhance interpersonal relationships and intimacy by receiving a positive response from the recipient. The subjective feeling of being recognised, feeling important and relied upon arising from helping behaviours mediate the positive effects of supporting others on well-being (Piliavin and Siegl, 2007). However, it should be noted that not all helping behaviours generate well-being.

The Self-Determination Theory (SDT) derived by Deci and Ryan (1985), proposes that autonomy is one of the core elements of psychological need (please see Chap. 3 for an explanation of SDT). When a helping behaviour is controlled (i.e. not doing it willingly), the basic psychological need of autonomy is unsatisfied, then the helper would not feel the achievement of such helping act as the helper feels he/she does not own the behaviour (deCharms, 1968; Deci & Ryan, 1985). The relatedness caused by such controlled helping behaviours is also diminished because connection and caring may be lacking in the helping behaviour (Weinstein & Ryan, 2010). Evidence of this is shown in one of Weinstein and Ryan's (2010) studies with 124 university students. The participants attended in pairs, first filling out questionnaires examining baseline well-being and then completing a remote-association test (Mednick, 1962) that required them to find the associations for sets of given terms. Participants were divided into a *help* or *no-help* condition by random order. In the help condition, participants were randomly assigned to be the helper or the help recipient. The helper was told that he/she would not be eligible for a raffle, but he/she could still help another participant (the recipient) in the task to win the prize. Participants in the no-help conditions were told that each of them could work toward an individual opportunity to be entered in the raffle.

While in the no-help condition, participants received the same set of instructions but they were told that each of them could work toward an individual opportunity to be entered in the raffle. Upon completion of the task, the participants filled out another set of questionnaires assessing well-being, task enjoyment and engagement, relatedness to another participant, their motivation to help another participant and other demographic data. It was found that autonomous helpers experienced more positive emotion, vitality and self-esteem than did non-helpers or controlled helpers upon completing the task. They also offered more and effective help during the task. Autonomous helpers and recipients both experienced a higher level of relatedness to one another. The literature on social support giving as a whole concludes that social support giving shares the same benefits as social support receiving, on physical health and well-being. It also indicates that autonomous helping behaviours will lead to engagement into the helping acts, therefore, promoting the intrinsic drive to help may be useful to establish a culture of support in the environment.

The review of the literature on social support explains different conceptualizations of social support research. A summary of the two models and the assumptions of studying social support are provided in Tables 2.2 and 2.3.

Table 2.2 Two models of conceiving social support

Model	Description
Stress buffering effect	Social support buffers the aversive effects of a stressor, relieving pressure on the person or helping them reinterpret the stressful situation
Main effect	Social relationships directly enhance well-being regardless of stress, and have a number of positive effects such as leading to higher self-esteem, increased sense of belonging and positive affect

Table 2.3 Summary of social support processes and effects

Social support conceptions		
Types	Assumptions	Psychological mechanism
Stress buffering, coping and adjustment	Received support buffers stress: Other people's supportive actions can enhance an individual's coping strategy against a stressor	The specific support helps the person adjust coping strategy and deal with the stressor better, thus suffer from less distress
	Evaluation of stressful situations: A person who believes social support is available may perceive the stressful situation less negatively	The person can evaluate the same stressor less aversive. This leads to psychological regulation and less negative emotions
The social constructionism and symbolic interactionalism	Social cognition monitors perception of support and affects people's behaviour: Once a person establishes stable beliefs about the supportiveness of his/her social network, his/her perceived social support will be fixed according to the existing beliefs	People who have a high level of perceived support are more attentive to supportive actions. They are more confident and willing to reach out for support and benefit from a supportive network
	Symbolic interactionism enhances engagement: The social norms within a social network govern network members' behaviour, it regulates the behaviours of members, this promotes a member's self-identity and may enhance one's self-esteem which positively influences well-being	The interaction in a social group is a process of regularisation for oneself to develop self-concept and form identity. This process helps people adopt desirable behaviours and lead to well-being of members. The impact serves the psychological and social well-being
Social capital strengthens resources	Individuals gain accumulated resources from people who are tied to their social network, via close ties or weak ties, giving support and benefits of various types such as emotional and cognitive	Resources accumulated through the social network helps the focal person to access useful information, leading to greater control of situations and beneficial outcomes in different types of events

(continued)

Social Support Research—Methods and Studies   49

Table 2.3 (continued)

Social support conceptions

Types	Assumptions	Psychological mechanism
Quality of relationships creates a positive experience	The quality of good relationships, such as low conflict and intimacy, affect a person's perceived and received social support and affect their life experience more positively	People who have good quality social relationships may anticipate support and the support they receive will be more effective. They are more resilient
Support giving is beneficial to support givers	The benefits of support giving shared the same benefits of support receiving, on physical health and well-being	Giving support is generated from empathic concerns of the others' well-being, helping can reduce the giver's own distress and show one's competence

Social Support Research—Methods and Studies

This section discusses the issues researchers have to consider when designing social support studies. This has implications for the approach researchers may take and the relevant instruments they may choose in order to ensure a well-framed study with consideration of the issues identified in this area of research.

Considering the Research Approaches to Be Taken and the Instruments to Be Used

In approaching social support research, researchers have to consider if perceived support or received support should be measured when developing their research design. Some researchers have challenged the effectiveness of received support and suggested that perceived support is more useful in predicting adjustment to stressful events (e.g. Lakey & Cronin, 2008; Uchino, 2004, 2009), though, as discussed earlier, received support is found to be related to stress coping and health. The following highlights some parameters for considering the choice of measures in social support research regarding different assumptions discussed earlier.

When studying support actions that enhance people's well-being in stressful situations by improving their coping strategy, measures of stress must be included. In many studies, a particular group of people facing the same stressor is recruited (e.g. cancer patients; Schulz & Schwarzer, 2004). In this case, some measures of stress severity brought about by a particular stress may be used, such as the Coping with Surgical Stress Scale developed by COSS; Krohne, de Bruin, El Giamal, and Schmukle (2000), which measures stress induced by surgery. It is also important to measure the effect of received social support on coping strategy and/or performance. Many previous studies used a mediation model to explain such relationship (e.g. Luszczynska, Mohamed, & Schwarzer, 2005). For example, in Iwasaki's (2001) study of college students' coping methods, coping was measured with the Leisure Coping Scale, which was specified for measuring leisure coping. Received social support was examined by a self-developed modified version of the Social Support Resource Scale (Vaux & Harrison, 1985), which was tailor made to match the study objective. It is noteworthy that stress was not measured with any already-made scales in the study, instead a diary-keeping method to record regular stressful events method was employed. Researchers may consider designing qualitative instruments to supplement other measures.

Research on the evaluation of stressful situations proposes that a belief in the availability of social support reduces the level of stress encountered by a person through influencing his/her evaluation of the situation. Therefore, measures of perceived support, stressors and evaluation should be included in such a research approach. However, only a few measurement tools manage to assess both primary and secondary appraisal (e.g. Stress Appraisal Measure; Peacock & Wong, 1990). Hitchcock et al.'s (2015) research may illustrate the use of such an approach. The researchers studied children's post-traumatic stress; children's perceived social support was measured with the Multidimensional Scale of Perceived Social Support (MSPSS) developed by Zimet, Dahlem, Zimet, and Farley (1988) and their appraisals of the traumatic event were examined using the Child Posttraumatic Cognitions Inventory (CPTCI) developed by Meiser-Stedman et al., (2009), which was specified for post-traumatic use. As stress is one of the key components in studies of appraisal approach, stress was assessed here with the Posttraumatic Stress Scale (CPSS) developed by Foa, Johnson, Feeny, and Treadwell (2001), which was a partly self-report and partly interview measure assessing the level of post-traumatic stress. It included items like 'acting or feeling as if the event was happening again' and 'having trouble falling or staying asleep', in which the child had to indicate the frequency with which the statement described had bothered them. In this study, the researchers used Posttraumatic Stress Disorder (PTSD) and depression as references of well-being; they were measured with the Clinician-Administered PTSD Scale for Children (CAPS) (Nader, Kriegler, Blake, & Pynoos, 1994) and the Child Depression Inventory (CDI) (Kovacs, 1992), respectively. The former being a standard diagnostic tool for PTSD in children and the latter an instrument to assess the severity of depressive symptoms in children.

In researching people's social cognition, the measurement of stress does not need to be included as this perspective emphasises the effect of perceived support on health outcomes. This approach also suggests that the perception of available support affects self-concept. The measure of self is key and it should be included in the mediational analyses (Lakey & Cohen, 2000). In Wright et al.'s (2014) study, for example, career and academic decision self-efficacy was used as the measures of self-concept. They were measured with the Career Decision Self-Efficacy Scale-Short Form (CDSE-SF; Betz & Taylor, 2001), as well as the Academic Self-Efficacy Scale (ASES; Schmitt, 2008) and the College Self-Efficacy Instrument (CESI; Solberg, O'Brien, Villarreal, Kennell and Davis, 1993), respectively. The former assessed students' self-efficacy related to academic performance and the latter reflected college self-efficacy in three areas, namely Social, Class and Roommate. Participants' perception of support was assessed by the Social Support Questionnaire (SSQ; Sarason, Sarason, Shearin, &

Pierce, 1987) and the UCLA Loneliness Scale-Version 3 (UCLA-3; Russell, 1996), which examined respondent's subjective feeling of loneliness and social isolation. Of particular interest in the aforementioned study is that the UCLA scale is designed to assess loneliness. As the total score of UCLA-3 was reverse coded, the authors assumed less loneliness would suggest more perceived support.

Nevertheless, the focus of the interactionalist approach of social support study is on how people act in relation to others in the social environment, the responsive and reactive roles they play and the support they receive in interacting with others. It is through the social roles people negotiate in a social interaction with others that build up their self-identity and self-esteem. The formulation of the sense of 'self' in people functions to achieve the fulfillment of goals of different parties in the social environment, that can promote well-being (McNulty & Swann, 1994). To delimit the focus, researchers may choose a certain network feature to focus on when researching with the interactionalist approach, such as network size or density. There are measures that are designed to examine these characteristics of a social network. Furthermore, the measures of stress in a symbolic interactionalist approach are optional since this approach examines the social roles that influence a person's well-being in the absence of a stressor. An example by Avanzi, Schuh, Fraccaroli, and van Dick (2015) may illustrate the creation of an interactionalist design approach. The researchers used the Italian version (Bergami & Bagozzi, 2000) of the Mael and Ashforth scale (1992) to measure organisational identification, and the UK Health and Safety Executive's four-item scale (Edwards, Webster, Van Laar, & Easton, 2008) to examine participants' perceived social support within the organisation with items such as 'I get the help and support I need from colleagues'. Burnout was used as a measure of well-being in this study. They measured three dimensions of burnout (Maslach, Jackson, and Schwab, 1996): *emotional exhaustion* with the Maslach Burnout Inventory—Educators Survey (MBI-ES) (Maslach et al., 1996), *cynicism* with the Maslach Burnout Inventory—General Survey (Schaufeli, Leiter, Maslach, & Jackson, 1996), and *reduced personal accomplishment* with the reversely coded efficacy scale from the MBI-ES. Benson's (2012) study, as discussed earlier, shows that it is possible to study only the properties of the participants' social networks, which were found to be related to the participants' perceived social support and well-being.

The study of social capital should be defined according to the types of capital one may wish to research. Given its diverse conceptualizations, the scope of social capital research is very large. Recent studies focus on media network sites for knowledge development with specific interests on collective action, community involvement and differential social achievement (Wasko & Faraj, 2005). Specific survey has been developed to identify the sophistication and complexities regarding interaction and time of engagement (Ellison et al., 2007). Computer technologies may be deployed to identify social capital as the site data can be multiple. The measurement used may include self-esteem and satisfaction apart from the communication data in the network.

Lastly, a study of the qualities of relationships can conclude relationship quality directly affects both social support and well-being. It can be generic quality between romantic partners, among family and friends or some characteristics of a good rela-

52   2   Understanding Social Support

Table 2.4 Key variables in social support research perspectives and sample measurements

Approach	Variables	Example of measures
Supportive actions	Received support Types of support Coping Strategy Stress	Inventory of Socially Supportive Behaviors (ISSB) UCLA Social Support Inventory (UCLA-SSI) COPE Inventory
Evaluation of stressful situations	Perceived support Appraisal of the event Stress	Social Support Questionnaire (SSQ) Stress Appraisal Measure (SAM)
Social cognition	Perceived support	Social Provisions Scales (SPS)
	Self-concept	Rosenberg Self-esteem Scale
	Well-being	
	*Remark: stress need not be involved	
Symbolic interactionalist	Social Network Role (identity) Well-being	Lubben Social Network Scale-6 (LSNS-6) Sense of Community Index (SCI)
Social capital	Bridging social capital Self-Esteem Well-being	Rosenberg Self-Esteem Scale The Scales of Psychological Well-being
Quality of relationships	Quality of relationships Well-being	Quality of Relationships Inventory (QRI)

tionship such as low conflict, intimacy and companionship. Therefore, measures of the quality of one or more relationships would also be suitable in a study. In Rini et al.'s (2006) study of partner's support during pregnancy, they measured three characteristics of marital relationship: relationship quality, relationship intimacy and relationship equity. All of the three aspects were found to be positively related to the effectiveness of perceived social support.

To sum up, Table 2.4 summarises the variables according to different social support assumptions, with suggestions of sample measurements, to provide an overall view of the variables of social support research and the measures that enable the study of them. The examples above illustrate how the different dependent variables are considered with reference to the approach(es) the study adopts.

Complications When Measuring Social Networks

When we plan to investigate a social network, there should be target group(s) or features of a network since the range of a social network can be very broad: romantic partner, family, friends, neighbours and co-workers and they can all be considered as one's network members. So, some researchers have tried to classify these network members into groups. For example, Sullivan (1953) differentiated people in primary

Social Support Research—Methods and Studies 53

and secondary groups. The term primary group members refers to our significant others, who are important to and emotionally tied to the individual (such as spouse); while secondary groups are more likely to be larger in group size and the in-group interactions are more formal (such as colleagues). Similarly, Granovetter (1973) grouped network members by strong or weak ties, the tie is considered by the time spent together, intensity of emotional exchange, intimacy, etc. The variations in bonding and some other characteristics of social structure are found to be relevant to favourable health outcomes (e.g. Haines, Beggs, & Hurlbert, 2008; Hall & Wellman, 1985; Suitor & Pillemer, 2002). Some scales measure the size of social network in a wide range, such as the Lubben Social Network Scale (LSNS) (Lubben, 1988), which is designed to assess the level of social isolation in elderly populations. Its abbreviated version (LSNS-6) measures the level of perceived social support provided by family, friends and neighbours in a wide range of settings, from community to hospitals (Lubben et al., 2006).

Similarly, in the relationship approach, various kinds of relationship can be taken account of. Some previous studies have focused on marital relationships (e.g. Rini et al., 2006), while the others put the emphasis on family and friendships or even relationships among colleagues in workplaces (e.g. Avanzi et al., 2015). Therefore, there is a wide range of literature regarding the relationship perspective of social support. The majority of the research focuses on the overall quality of a relationship, but it is also feasible to break down the features of the relationship (e.g. intimacy, equity) to look at their relative importance for a person's well-being.

The Quality of Relationships Inventory (QRI) (Pierce, Sarason, & Sarason, 1991) suggests an example of measuring the quality of a particular relationship with respect to its salient features, on three areas: support, conflict and depth stemming relationship. As Pierce and his team developed the inventory, they found that these characteristics were distinct aspects of a specific relationship as they correlated with personal effects and perceived support differently. Therefore, it was preferable to measure more than one dimension of the relationship so as to investigate the connections between relationships and well-being and the rationale behind them. Table 2.5 lists some concrete characteristics of variables in social support studies to give more explanation to the variables.

A collection of measures that are commonly used in studies of social support is provided in Table 2.6. The instruments are categorised and introduced according to their aims of assessment, including social support, stress, coping, appraisals and well-being, with the subscales, number of items and psychometric property of each scale listed. Remarks are given if the scales target a specific group. Most of the scales under the same category (such as perceived support) serve similar purposes, therefore, investigators may use the instrument for study according to the set purpose of the study, length of the questionnaire and target participants. For example, in Wright et al. (2014) study mentioned in the previous section, they used Sarason et al.'s (1987) Social Support Questionnaire (SSQ) () to measure participants' perception of support and the UCLA Loneliness Scale-Version 3 (UCLA-3) (Russell, 1996) to measure

Table 2.5 Variable characteristics in social support studies

Variable	Characteristics	What are usually measured
Social network	Size	• No. of network members
	Density	• The proportion of network member considered as primary group/strong tie
	Composition Role	• Who is included (e.g. kin, friends, similar others) • Participation in different types of social roles
Relationship	Low conflicts	• Frequency of conflicts, conflicts management
	Intimacy Equity	• The degree of emotional closeness • The extent the relationship is reciprocal
	Quality of relationship	• In general the quality of relationship with a specific person/group
Well-being	Physical health	• Rate of recovery
	Mental health	• Depressive symptoms, anxiety, distress
	Self-concept	• Self-esteem, Self-efficacy

their loneliness. Actually, these measures can be replaced by other interchangeable scales under the same column of the table, such as Lubben's Social Network Scale-6 (LSNS-6) (Lubben et al., 2006) for the UCLA-3, as long as they are measuring the same construct.

Relating Social Support to Well-being Measures

Social support is related to humans' well-being in many ways. It is positively related to mental (Lakey & Cronin, 2008) and physical health (Uchino, 2004, 2009). The stress and buffering perspectives as described propose a clear theoretical pathway of how social support helps reduce stress and leads to positive health outcomes. However, many researchers have pointed out that the mechanism of social ties' main/direct effect on health is still ambiguous (Cohen & Janicki-Deverts, 2009; Thoits, 2011; Uchino, 2004). Many of the recent studies have sought to investigate the main effect of social support with reference to other higher order concepts. Well-being is commonly referred to, and other related variables include sense of mattering, self-esteem, mastery, belonging, social influence and so on (Thiots, 2011), in addition to mental and physical health. Self-esteem and self-efficacy are two common measures as they are the key components of Bandura's (1986) social cognitive theory that comprises a person's perceptions of his/her own ability and self-worth. A range of studies have proved that supportive networks or relationships have positive correlations with both self-esteem and self-efficacy (e.g. Waters & Moore, 2002; Wright et al., 2014).

Social Support Research—Methods and Studies 55

For instance, in a study of social support and unemployment (Maddy, Cannon, & Lichtenberger, 2015), the investigators examined the effect of social support on both self-esteem and self-efficacy of unemployed individuals. The Rosenberg Self-Esteem Scale (Rosenberg, 1965) and the New General Self-Efficacy Scale (NGSES; Chen, Gully, & Eden, 2001) were used as measurement tools for the two dependent variables, respectively. Therefore, studying the effect of social support on one's well-being can go beyond physical and mental health outside of the clinical settings.

Quantitative or Qualitative Approach to Studying Social Support

In social support research, most designed measures are in a quantitative self-report questionnaire format, as it is easier to analyze the data and more time-and-cost-effective when collecting the data. However, self-reported data sometimes may have common-method bias, which means that the correlation found between the two variables is due to the shared method used for data collection instead of the variables per se. Method biases are considered one of the main sources of measurement error (Podsakoff, MacKenzie, Lee, & Podsakoff, 2003). A great deal of research shows that mood states affect recall of memory (e.g. Isen & Baron, 1991; Podsakoff et al., 2003). Therefore, for example when measuring received support, if we depend only on the participants' report of support received, (1) it is difficult for the participants to recall all support received, especially over a long period of time; and (2) some invisible support they received may not be recognised by the participants. Thus, it is preferable to utilise multiple measurements when conducting a study. For instance, researchers can support their findings on social support and networks with both self-report questionnaires and observed interpersonal interactions or gather more data from support providers or network members than from the support recipients alone, in order to draw a valid and strong conclusion.

Potential Confound

Direction of effect. Directionality is often a limitation in social support literature. Researchers have proposed that social support and a social network lead to decreasing distress and better health outcomes. However, viewing it the other way round, depressive symptoms also can influence an individual's social network and his/her perception of availability of social support (Rini et al., 2006), therefore, the causal relationship between social support and health is considered doubtful by some researchers (e.g. Berkman et al., 2000; House, 2001; Uchino, 2009). It is also not clear whether better-adjusted people are more eager to engage in prosocial behaviours or that prosocial actions help people to adjust better (Piliavin, 2009; Bokszczanin,

2012). Therefore, it is suggested that a longitudinal study can establish better causal relationships between the nature of social context and health outcomes (Rini et al., 2006), as well as to reduce common-method variance (Avanzi et al., 2015), compared with a cross-sectional study.

Gender and cultural difference. This is always one of the major confounds in most scientific studies. In the field of social support, for example social networks of men and women have proven to be significantly different from one another and this differentiation also creates different influences on social support and health outcomes (Ajrouch, Blandon, & Antonucci, 2005; Haines et al., 2008). Therefore, it is hard to generalise the research findings if we include only participants of single ethnicity or if we do not investigate the effect of gender difference in the study.

Limitations of the Current Scales for Studying Social Support

Research on social support started a few decades ago, and many fundamental theories and studies were published in the 1980s. These classics are still influential nowadays. A number of measuring tools were also developed at that time. Therefore, some popular measures may not be up-to-date to some extent. They are still widely used due to their convenience and familiarity (López & Cooper, 2011). Another problem concerns translation. Most scales were developed in English and used with Western-based samples. The direct translation of a measure into other language(s) may affect its psychometric properties and over-generalise a phenomenon of one population group to another ethnic group.

Besides, scales from old days may not be able to reflect today's norms. For example, some measures of social networks ask participants how often they visit their friends at their homes or how often they chat on the phone with their friends, in which a higher frequency indicates a closer relationship with their network members. However, nowadays in general, people live in the city and seldom visit one another very often due to their busy schedules or their flats being too small for gatherings. And due to technology advancement, we can utilise all kinds of online social networks to interact instead of calling or meeting each other in person. Therefore, when choosing suitable measures we have to consider whether the items or the scoring criteria are relevant to the social context.

Implications to Study Social Support in Education

The following section discusses a few ideas taken from the social support literature review, and ideas about the connections between social support and the practice of education to suggest the content to be discussed in subsequent chapters of the book.

Satisfying Social Ties Enhance Human Development

Developing Social Bonds as Core Value. As mentioned earlier, social support refers to an interaction of receivers and givers, and the interaction can closely resemble the roles of learners and teachers in education. Nowadays, the student population in mainstream schools has become very diverse. Students who are less capable and less motivated in learning study together with everyone else in a class. Therefore, the theoretical assumptions discussed in the social support literature which values the social and emotional development of human beings can be applied to education, and the knowledge of social support is useful to teachers who are involved in day-to-day interaction with children and young people in the classroom social environment. Education comprises a crucial part of a person's social environment. According to Bronfenbrenner (2005), each individual is involved in a process of reciprocal interaction in the ecological social environment. A substantial part of a person's growth is their interaction with the immediate environment. Family and schools are the sources of immediate influence on a child's development, known as a microsystem. The review of social support echoes the ecological systems proposed in Bronfenbrenner's model, and the social construction and interactionalist assumptions of the social support literature provide insights to suggest that support given to students, such as emotional support, esteem support and respect to individuals as a kind of support, can form a protective measure for students that facilitates their development significantly. Adopting social relationships and social bonds as core values in the school and classroom environment do not only help students overcome personal problems they come across in their personal lives, it also helps students to perceive supportiveness about the environment. According to social support literature, the perception of supportiveness is an important psychological mechanism for human beings which has important implications for a person's 'self-development', such as shielding students from stressful environments and low self-esteem (how students value or feel about themselves) and cultivating a positive self-concept in the process of socialisation.

Schools can also act as a more proactive agent in the twenty-first century, as the effect of traditional social support systems is diminishing in the social environment (Sharma & Sharma, 2010). By forging positive social relationships as a common norm, schools and teachers could coordinate with parents and other social welfare organisations in society to make these different sources of influences beneficial for students to reinforce the effect of social support in order to support students' growth and development. Adopting a social support perspective to view the education environment can also help teachers and school managers think broadly about their professional role in schools, since each player in the educational setting would be a part of the social environment perceived by students and the alignment of aims and coordinating efforts will definitely help. The perception of support does not only come from teachers' supportive actions but also from student peers in the classroom;

therefore, social support is a factor that can make a number of potential contributions to the environment, including learning, teaching and the planning of the educational environment.

Strengthening Moral Education and Teachers' Moral Role. At the micro-level, teaching in the classroom involves intensive interaction with students who come from different classes, genders and ethnicities. The social support literature inspires teachers to think about the importance of their moral role in the classroom, and the need to build up a trustful environment to support student learning. Since teachers' own actions directly and indirectly have a strong influence on students, they should be aware of their manner and communication with students in the classroom, and the decision they make in the school environment. The suggestion of giving more attention to the moral role of teaching is therefore implied from the discussion of social support. In fact, the concerns of moral education are also shared by other researchers, suggesting a decline of a common moral standard in the globalised society (e.g. Campbell, 2008; Murrell, Diez, Feiman-Nemser, & Schussler, 2010). Moreover, the cultivation of morally valued principles in youngsters is deemed necessary in the twenty-first century as people in society are now being influenced by the predominantly materialistic and consumeristic culture (Twenge & Kasser, 2013), which have brought about a lower sense of personal responsibility and a declining willingness to offer help as a general phenomenon (Kasser & Ryan, 2001; Bauer, Wilkie, Kim, & Bodenhausen, 2012). As discussed earlier, the assumptions behind social support indicate that values such as responsibility, respect, caring and civic virtues can be emphasised in the school and classroom environment for cultivating the value of social support among students and the classroom environment.

Examination-Oriented Culture is Detrimental. The review of social support literature highlights the powerful influence of social relationships in the social environment. Social support has a crucial role to play in contributing to the psychological well-being of the self in the process of socialisation (e.g. via self-esteem and self-concept formation). It implies that the current examination-oriented culture existing in the schools and the societal environment must be changed. An examination-oriented environment would certainly create learning anxiety and tension for students (Cheung & Chiu, 2016). It will also create tension for teachers who have to fulfill their accountability for the demands of achievement outcomes (Ball, 2003). It creates a vicious circle for education in society as teachers have less time to build relationships with and offer emotional support to students and where students are situated in a highly competitive environment in which individual learning for the competition is encouraged. Teachers may also feel helpless and unsupported in an environment with a heavy accountability system. The result of declining health and psychological well-being of young people and teachers over the world has already given warning signals (Hong Kong Primary Education Research Association and Education Convergence, 2006; World Health Organization, 2017). Investigation of the potential of social support in educational practice would definitely provide insights in the field of education.

Insights on Learner-Centred Education and Teacher Development. The theoretical assumptions of social support to a large extent echoes many of the other streams of thoughts in education, such as learner-centred education, which is a prevalent approach in the field of education. The theories of both social support and learner-centred education similarly argue for the importance of self-esteem, social relationships and positive emotions in a person's growth and development. Further investigation of the ideas of social support in education may help to elaborate learner-centred education, which is an area in need of more research and discussion to guide practice in the classroom (O'Neill & McMahon, 2005). Subsequent chapters will explore how social support is practiced in the classroom in order to follow-up with this idea.

A topic of interest arising from this review which has the potential to contribute to both the field of health care and education is the study of social support givers. Evidence indicates that social support giving can enhance social support givers' self-worth, relieve anxiety and develop satisfaction in their lives. Research into the link between teachers' social support giving to students and teacher development is considered a topic that has significant implications for the field of education. Since support of students is argued as a key trait of good teachers (Hattie & Jaeger, 2003), the link of teachers' supportive action in their professional practice to their own professional development has significant potential for the direction of teacher development. This is a topic of popular interest especially at the current time when the teaching profession is undergoing a difficult period, with a large number of teachers experiencing mental health problems (O' Brennan, Pas, & Bradshaw, 2017; Yeung & Liu, 2007). This topic will be further investigated in the later part of the book.

Conclusion and Limitations of the Chapter

The goal of this chapter is to provide readers with fundamental concepts of social support research and the knowledge of social support in the theoretical and empirical literature. In addition, the chapter aims to provide a guide to researchers and practitioners who are interested in social support studies, and draw their interest to this topic which may have the potential to be explored in different fields and settings.

The review shows that efforts in social support research date back to the 1970s and is nowadays speeding up quickly in multiple disciplines. It is an emerging area in psychology and is still very new, so has much potential to contribute to different fields. The key approaches to understanding social support are discussed, which can be summarised as: (1) support reduces the negative effect of stressful events through support received or through the perception of available support; (2) people construct understanding through interaction with other people in their social network, and they construct understanding, form beliefs and develop self-identity about themselves that affect both their behaviour and perception of supportiveness of other people; (3) social capital can be found in every individual's network which can provide resources and support of different kinds, and one can benefit from these resources to accomplish life events more satisfactorily; (4) the good qualities in different relationships are positively related to their life experience; and (5) social support giving is beneficial to support providers. These assumptions have their distinct associations with a person's physical health and well-being. It is suggested from the review that the outcome measures of social support are found in the psychological processes of human development. It informs a cluster of theoretical assumptions of social support research explained by psychological measures including self-esteem, self-efficacy, belongingness and social integration, as well as mental and physical health. Since social support happens between people, the theoretical assumptions can also be applied in other professional contexts that serve people. Education appears to be one context that can benefit from this topic.

In order to facilitate research on this topic, the second part of the chapter has discussed some methodological issues of social support research. It discusses some important ideas about measurement, operationalisation and precautions for the research design of different approaches, and potential confounds of general interest to researchers. Moreover, an inventory has been compiled illustrating the instruments that are commonly used in social support studies, specifying their properties and their different research approaches. The recommendations can provide some direction for future research.

The final part of the chapter attempts to imply the ideas of social support research for education. It highlights social bonds, social interaction and the outcome measures of social support that are the common content shared in the field of education. Some suggestions and comments are made about the general situation of education of the twenty-first century based on the core values identified from the social support literature. Preliminary ideas about inquiry in education are discussed and they will be further explored in subsequent parts of the book.

In writing this chapter, updated research literature was used to explain key assumptions and research approaches in this topic, and examples were carefully selected to balance the interest of the audience and the content relevancy. When handling the review, it has been found that social support is also studied in many other fields, such as management and organisational studies. The current review is largely based on health psychology and psychology in different areas, therefore, this review cannot be claimed to be an exhaustive one, and thus, the findings cannot be regarded as conclusive. There are some areas, particularly social support in medical literature, that have not been largely included, in that the nature of medical knowledge cannot be translated accurately by the author who is from the field of education. It is hoped that this will be addressed by other researchers in the field based on this preliminary work. Also, due to the extensive literature on this topic, while efforts have been devoted to make the writing highly structured and user-friendly, the balance of the author's intention to give a broader view on this topic to benefit a larger audience and for further development in the book may make the chapter a lengthy one.

The next chapter will explore the context and practice of social support. It will introduce the meaning of well-being, which is a construct used to conceptualise the outcomes of social support. It will also discuss the psychological processes of selected groups of people who need social support in real contexts, and the factors and conditions for effective support.

Table 2.6 Measures used in social support studies

Social support measures					
Measure (abbreviated name; authors)		Description	Subscales	No. of items (short ver.)	Psych. properties
Received	**Inventory of Socially Supportive Behaviors** (ISSB; Barrera, Sandler, & Ramsay, 1981)	It assesses the frequency of an individual receiving different forms of assistance in the previous month. Frequency of each item on 5-point Likert scales, from 1 (not at all) to 5 (about every day) is rated	1. Guidance 2. Emotional Support 3. Tangible Support	40 (19)	$\alpha = .93–.94$ Test–retest $= .88$
	UCLA Social Support Inventory (UCLA-SSI; Dunkel-Schetter, Feinstein, & Call 1986)	It examines the respondent's need for social support, how support is sought and received, and satisfaction with support. Relationships with the support providers are also measured	Types of support: 1. Information or advice 2. Tangible Assistance/aid 3. Emotional support Social network member: 1. Parent 2. Friend 3. Romantic partner	70	N/A
Perceived	**Interpersonal support evaluation list** (Cohen & Hoberman, 1983; Cohen, Mermelstein, Kamarck, &, Hoberman, 1985)	It measures three/four dimensions of perceived social support. A 4-point scale is used to rate the items in each dimension The higher the score in a subscale, the more social support the participant perceives	1. Appraisal 2. Belonging 3. Tangible 4. (Self-esteem)	40 (12)	$\alpha = .88–.90$ Test–retest $= .63–.70$

(continued)

Table 2.6 (continued)

Social support measures

Measure (abbreviated name; authors)		Description	Subscales	No. of items (short ver.)	Psych. properties
	Social Support Questionnaire (SSQ; Sarason, Sarason, Shearin, & Pierce, 1987)	It measures the participant's perceptions of social support and satisfaction with that type of support. In Part 1, the participants had to list all the people who match the description of the question; while in Part 2, participants rated the satisfaction with the listed people	N/A	45	
	Social Provisions Scales (SPS; Cutrona & Russell, 1987)	It accesses the degree to which respondent's social relationships provide different dimensions of social support. Responses range from 1 (strongly disagree) to 4 (strongly agree). Half of the items among the six subscales describe the availability of a type of support and the remaining describe the absence of a type of support.	1. Attachment 2. Social integration 3. Reassurance of worth 4. Reliable alliance 5. Guidance 6. Opportunity for nurturance	24	$\alpha = <.70$ Test–retest $= .37–.66$
	Arizona social support interview schedule (Barrera, 1980)	It examines respondent's psychosocial functioning and perceived social support by assessing the respondent's social network in the past 6 months. The interview has to be conducted by a trained interviewer and responses should be coded accordingly. Trained interviewer needed	1. Assistance received 2. Material aid 3. Advice 4. Positive feedback 5. People to confide in	27	$\alpha = .78$

(continued)

Table 2.6 (continued)

Social support measures

Measure (abbreviated name; authors)	Description	Subscales	No. of items (short ver.)	Psych. properties
Social Support Appraisals scale (SSA; Vaux et al., 1986)	It measures subjective appraisal of social support. Respondents have to rate whether he/she is loved by, esteemed by, and involved with family, friends on a 4-point scale	1. Attachment 2. Social Integration 3. Reassurance of Worth 4. Reliable Alliance, Guidance 5. Opportunity for Nurturance	23	$\alpha > .70$
Medical Outcomes Study: Social Support Survey (MOS-SSS; Sherbourne & Stewart, 1991a, 1991b)	It examines the respondent's perceived availability of support. Each item is rated on a 5-point scale ranging from 'none of the time' to 'all of the time', with a high subscale and/or overall score representing a high level of social support	1. Emotional/Informational support 2. Affectionate support 3. Tangible support scale 4. Positive interaction scale	19	$.91 - .97$
McMaster Family Assessment Device-General Functioning scale (FAD-GF; Epstein, Baldwin, & Bishop 1983)	It is a subscale of the McMaster Family Assessment Device, which examines the overall health/pathology of the family. Participants have to rate the extent they agree or disagree with the statements describing their families on a 4-point scale. For use on adolescent and family	N/A	12	$\alpha = .92$

(continued)

Table 2.6 (continued)

Social support measures

Measure (abbreviated name; authors)		Description	Subscales	No. of items (short ver.)	Psych. properties
Received & Perceived	**Berlin Social Support Scales** (BSSS; Schwarzer & Schulz, 2003)	It accesses both the cognitive and behavioural aspects of social support. Respondents rate their agreement with the items on a 4-point Likert scale. Scale scores are obtained by summing up the corresponding item responses or by generating a mean score	1. Perceived 2. Actual provided 3. Received social support 4. Need for support 5. Support seeking 6. Proactive buffering	45	$\alpha = .63–.83$
	Perceived Stress Scale (PSS; Cohen Kamarck, Mermelstein, 1983)	It assesses the degree to which people perceive their lives as stressful. Participants need to indicate how often they have found their lives unpredictable, uncontrollable and overloaded in the past month. Total score over 20 will be considered as highly stressed	N/A	10	
	The Holmes and Rahe stress scale (Holmes & Rahe, 1967)	It includes 43 major stressful life events. Each event was assigned a Life Change Unit according to how traumatic it was felt to be by a large sample of the population. The total score is calculated by summing up the unit score for each event experienced in the past 12-month period	N/A	43	

(continued)

Table 2.6 (continued)

Social support measures

Measure (abbreviated name; authors)	Description	Subscales	No. of items (short ver.)	Psych. properties
Life Experiences Survey (LES; Sarason, John, & Siegel, 1978)	Respondents have to rate the occurrence of discrete life events in two stages including 'the past 0 to 6 months' and the past '7 months to a year'. Respondent has to rate the events for which they have actually experienced and its impact. Section I of the LES consists of 47 particular events is designed for all respondents. Section II consists of 10 events related to changes experienced in the academic environment which is used by students only which	1. Positive events 2. Negative events 3. Total events	57 (44)	
Coping with Surgical Stress Scale (COSS; Krohne et al., 2000)	It assesses the coping strategies respondents employ for dealing with the stress of surgery. Respondents have to indicate whether they agree with the coping-related thought statements in a yes–no response format. For use on patients who are undergoing or waiting for surgery	1. Rumination 2. Optimism and trust 3. Turning to social and religious resources 4. Threat avoidance 5. Information seeking	27	$\alpha = .55–.79$

Health/well-being measures

Physical	**Cohen-Hoberman Inventory of Physical Symptoms** (CHIPS; Cohen & Hoberman, 1983)	It consists of a list of 33 common physical symptoms. Items were selected so as to exclude items of an obvious psychological nature (feel nervous). Each item is rated on a 5-point Likert scale for how much that item troubled the respondent during the past 2 weeks	N/A	33

(continued)

Table 2.6 (continued)

Social support measures

	Measure (abbreviated name; authors)	Description	Subscales	No. of items (short ver.)	Psych. properties
	Pennebaker Inventory of Limbic Languidness (PILL; Pennebaker, 1982)	It consists of a list of physical symptoms. Participants are required to rate the frequency of each symptom experienced. A high score means worse health condition than the general population	N/A	54	α = .93–.95
Psychological	**Center for Epidemiologic Studies Depression scale** (CES-D; Radloff, 1977)	It is rated how often over the past week the respondent experienced depressive symptoms, such as restless sleep, poor appetite and feeling of loneliness. Response options range from 0 to 3 for each item, from 0 (rarely or none of the time) to 3 (most or almost all the time). Scores range from 0 to 60, with high scores indicating greater depressive symptoms	N/A	20	
	Beck Depression Inventory (BDI; Beck, Steer, & Brown, 1996)	It is a self-report rating inventory that measures characteristic attitudes and symptoms of depression (Beck et al. 1961). The total score reflects the level of depression of the respondent	N/A	21	α = .91 Test–retest = .93

(continued)

Table 2.6 (continued)

Social support measures

Measure (abbreviated name; authors)		Description	Subscales	No. of items (short ver.)	Psych. properties
	The Positive and Negative Affect Schedule (PANAS; Watson Clark, & Tellegen., 1988)	It comprises two mood scales, one measures positive affect and another measures negative affect. The 20-item test is scored by a 5-point Likert scale	1. Positive affect 2. Negative affect	20	
	Mental Health Inventory (MHI; Veit & Ware, 1983)	It provides an assessment of multiple domains of mental health including anxiety, depression, behavioural control, positive affect, and general distress	1. Anxiety 2. Depression 3. Behavioural control 4. Positive affect 5. Emotional ties	38 (18)	$\alpha = .93$ (.82)
	The Scales of Psychological Well-being (SPWB; Ryff, 1989)	Both the long and medium forms consist of a series of statements reflecting the six areas of psychological. Respondents rate statements on a 6-point Likert scale, from 1 (strong disagreement) to 6 (strong agreement). Scores are summed up for each of the six categories. For each category, a high score indicates that the respondent has a satisfaction of that aspect in his/her life; while a low score shows that the respondent struggles to feel comfortable with that particular area	1. Autonomy 2. Environmental mastery 3. Personal growth 4. Positive relations with others 5. Purpose in life 6. Self-acceptance	84 (54)	

(continued)

Table 2.6 (continued)

Social support measures

Measure (abbreviated name; authors)	Description	Subscales	No. of items (short ver.)	Psych. properties
Profile Of Mood States (POMS; McNair, Lorr, & Droppleman, 1981)	It contains a list of adjectives that describe feelings. Respondents are required to indicate for each adjective how they have been feeling in the past week (today inclusive) on a 5-point scale	1. Anxiety 2. Depression 3. Hostility 4. Vigor 5. Fatigue 6. Confusion	65	$\alpha = .63-.96$
Self-esteem **Rosenberg self-esteem scale** (Rosenberg, 1965)	It examines global self-worth by measuring both positive and negative feelings about oneself. Respondent answers to the extent he/she agrees with the statements using a 4-point Likert scale. A higher total score indicates higher self-esteem	N/A	10	
Coping				
Ways of ping (Folkman & Lazarus, 1988)	It measures the coping processes used by the respondent in a particular stressful encounter instead of copying style or traits. Each item in the questionnaire is rated on a 4-point Likert scale and Each subscale is the sum of the scores of its corresponding items	1. Confrontive coping 2. Distancing 3. Self-controlling 4. Seeking social support 5. Accepting responsibility 6. Escape-avoidance 7. Planful Problem-solving 8. Positive reappraisal	66	$\alpha = .53-.82$

(continued)

Table 2.6 (continued)

Social support measures

Measure (abbreviated name; authors)	Description	Subscales	No. of items (short ver.)	Psych. properties
COPE inventory (Carver, Scheier, & Weintraub, 1989)	It measures in general how the participant responds to difficult or stressful events in life. The score of each subscale is summed by the total scores of the corresponding items. The higher one scores in a particular subscale, the higher the tendency he/she respond to stress in such manner	1. Positive reinterpretation and growth 2. Mental disengagement 3. Focus on and venting of emotions 4. Use of instrumental social support 5. Active coping 6. Denial 7. Religious coping 8. Humour 9. Behavioural disengagement 10. Restraint 11. Use of emotional social support 12. Substance use 13. Acceptance 14. Suppression of competing activities 15. Planning	60	Avg. $\alpha = .79$

Appraisal

Measure (abbreviated name; authors)	Description	Subscales	No. of items (short ver.)	Psych. properties
Stress Appraisal Measure (SAM; Peacock, & Wong, 1990)	It measures an individual's appraisal of a particular stressful event. The SAM includes measures of primary stress appraisal, secondary stress appraisal and overall perceived stressfulness (Peacock, 1990). The subscales are scored by averaging the total of the corresponding items	1. Threat 2. Challenge 3. Centrality 4. Controllable-by-self 5. Controllable-by-others 6. Uncontrollable-by-anyone 7. Stressfulness	28	$\alpha = .65-.90$

(continued)

Table 2.6 (continued)

Social support measures

Measure (abbreviated name; authors)	Description	Subscales	No. of items (short ver.)	Psych. properties
Background to the Appraisal of Life Events Scale (ALE; Ferguson, Matthews, & Cox, 1999)	It is a checklist of adjectives for assessing appraisals of a particular stressful event. Respondents have to rate the extent of the feeling of each adjective on a 6-point Likert scale	1. Threat 2. Challenge 3. Loss	16	
Social Network				
Lubben Social Network Scale-6 (LSNS-6; Lubben et al., 2006)	It accesses social isolation of an individual by measuring perceived social support by friends and family. The total score is the sum of all questions, which are on a 5-point Likert scale. Applicable to age 65 or above	1. Family 2. Friendships	6	$\alpha = .83$
Berkman's Social Network Index (SNI; Berkman & Syme, 1979)	It considers both the number and relative importance of social ties across the four subscales. Each of the subscales is weighted differently to sum up a total	1. Marital status 2. Sociability 3. Church group membership 4. Membership in other community organisations	11	

(continued)

Table 2.6 (continued)

Social support measures

Measure (abbreviated name; authors	Description	Subscales	No. of items (short ver.)	Psych. properties
Sense of Community Index (SCI; McMillan & Chavis, 1986)	It measures the sense of belonging and commitment of the respondent as a member of his/her community	1. Membership 2. Influence 3. Fulfillment of needs 4. Emotional connection	12	
UCLA loneliness scale-version 3 (UCLA-3; Russell, 1996)	It measures the respondent's subjective feeling of loneliness and social isolation. Respondents have to rate how accurate each item is descriptive to him/her	N/A	20	$\alpha = .89-.94$ Test–retest $= .73$
Work Relationship Index (WRI; Moos, 1981; Moos & Insel, 1974)	It is based on three subscales of the relationship domain of the Work Environment Scale, which measures work-based support, and predictably related to respondents' level of depressive and psychosomatic symptoms. Items are scored on a true/false format. Use in workplace settings	1. Involvement-concern with and commitment to job 2. Peer cohesion-support from co-workers 3. Support to and from supervisors		$\alpha = .88$
Scale of Perceived Organizational Support (POS; Eisenberger, Cummings, Armeli, & Lynch, 1997)	It examines the extent an employee believes the organisation values his/her contribution, and care about the employee's well-being. Respondents need to indicate the degree to which they agree with questions on a 7-point Likert scale. Use in workplace settings	N/A	36(8)	$\alpha = .90$

(continued)

Table 2.6 (continued)

Social support measures

Measure (abbreviated name; authors)	Description	Subscales	No. of items (short ver.)	Psych. properties
Relationships				
Quality of Relationships Inventory (QRI; Pierce, Sarason, & Sarason, 1991)	It measures the quality of an individual's relationship with a specific person. Participant has to judge the degree or frequency of the situations described on a 4-point scale. The subscales are to be calculated separately by averaging the relevant items scores.	1. Support Scale 2. Conflict Scale 3. Depth Scale	25	$\alpha = .83, .88, .83$
Relationship assessment scale (Hendrick, 1988)	It measures general relationship satisfaction. Respondent answers each item using a 5-point scale ranging from 1 (low satisfaction) to 5 (high satisfaction). The higher the total score, the more satisfied the respondent is with his/her relationship	N/A	7	
Relationship closeness Inventory (Berscheid, Snyder, & Omoto, 1989)	It measures the subject's relationship with a particular person. One part of the questionnaire comprises of Yes/No responses and the other part consists of questions using 7-point scales	1. Frequency 2. Diversity 3. Strength		Test–retest =.61–.82
Cambridge Friendships Questionnaire (CFQ: Goodyer, Wright, Alrham, 1989)	It assesses the number, availability and quality of friendships. The total score is computed by summing up the item scores. A higher score indicates the better perceived overall quality of friendships. For studying friendship	N/A	8	Test–retest = .80

References

Adler, P. S., & Kwon, S. W. (2002). Social capital: Prospects for a new concept. *Academy of Management Review, 27*(1), 17–40.

Ajrouch, K. J., Blandon, A. Y., & Antonucci, T. C. (2005). Social networks among men and women: The effects of age and socioeconomic status. *The Journals of Gerontology Series B: Psychological Sciences and Social Sciences, 60*(6), S311–S317.

Avanzi, L., Schuh, S. C., Fraccaroli, F., & van Dick, R. (2015). Why does organizational identification relate to reduced employee burnout? The mediating influence of social support and collective efficacy. *Work & Stress, 29*(1), 1–10.

Ball, S. J. (2003). The teacher's soul and the terrors of performativity. *Journal of education policy, 18*(2), 215–228.

Bandura, A. (1986). *Social foundations of thought and action: A social cognitive theory.* Upper Saddle River, NJ: Prentice-Hall.

Barone, D. F., Maddux, J. E., & Snyder, C. R. (1997). *Social cognitive psychology: History and current domains.* New York, NY, US: Plenum Press.

Barrera, M., Jr., & Ainlay, S. L. (1983). The structure of social support: A conceptual and empirical analysis. *Journal of community psychology, 11*(2), 133–143.

Barrera, M. (1980). A method for the assessment of social support networks in community survey research. *Connection, 3,* 8–13.

Barrera, M. (1986). Distinctions between social support concepts, measures, and models. *American Journal of Community Psychology, 14*(4), 413–445.

Barrera, M., Sandler, I. N., & Ramsay, T. B. (1981). Preliminary development of a scale of social support: Studies on college students. *American Journal of Community Psychology, 9*(4), 435–447.

Batson, C. D., & Shaw, L. L. (1991). Evidence for altruism: Toward a pluralism of prosocial motives. *Psychological Inquiry, 2*(2), 107–122.

Bauer, M. A., Wilkie, J. E., Kim, J. K., & Bodenhausen, G. V. (2012). Cuing consumerism: Situational materialism undermines personal and social well-being. *Psychological Science, 23*(5), 517–523.

Baumeister, R. F., & Leary, M. R. (1995). The need to belong: Desire for interpersonal attachments as a fundamental human motivation. *Psychological Bulletin, 117*(3), 497–529.

Beach, S. R. H., Fincham, F. D., Katz, J., & Bradbury, T. N. (1996). Social support in marriage. In G. R. Pierce, B. R. Sarason, & I. G. Sarason (Eds.), *Handbook of social support and the family* (pp. 43–65). New York: Plenum Press.

Beck, A. T., Rush, A. J., Shaw, B. F., & Emery, G. (1979). *Cognitive therapy of depression.* New York: Guilford.

Beck, A. T., Steer, R. A., & Brown, G. K. (1996). *Beck depression inventory-II.* San Antonio, TX: Psychological Corporation.

Beck, A. T., Ward, C. H., Mendelson, M., Mock, J., & Erbaugh, J. (1961). An inventory for measuring depression. *Archives of General Psychiatry, 4*(6), 561–571.

Benson, P. R. (2012). Network characteristics, perceived social support, and psychological adjustment in mothers of children with autism spectrum disorder. *Journal of Autism and Developmental Disorders, 42*(12), 2597–2610.

Bergami, M., & Bagozzi, R. P. (2000). Self-categorization, affective commitment and group self-esteem as distinct aspects of social identity in the organization. *British Journal of Social Psychology, 39*(4), 555–577.

Berkman, L. F., & Syme, S. L. (1979). Social networks, host resistance, and mortality: A nine-year follow-up study of Alameda County residents. *American Journal of Epidemiology, 109*(2), 186–204.

Berkman, L. F., Glass, T., Brissette, I., & Seeman, T. E. (2000). From social integration to health: Durkheim in the new millennium. *Social Science and Medicine, 51*(6), 843–857.

Berscheid, E., Snyder, M., & Omoto, A. M. (1989). The relationship closeness inventory: Assessing the closeness of interpersonal relationships. *Journal of Personality and Social Psychology, 57*(5), 792–807.

Betz, N. E., & Taylor, K. M. (2001). *Manual for the career decision self-efficacy scale and CDMSE-Short Form*. Unpublished manuscript, Ohio State University, Columbus, OH.

Biglan, A. (1973). The characteristics of subject matter in different academic areas. *Journal of Applied Psychology, 57*(3), 195–203.

Bokszczanin, A. (2012). Social support provided by adolescents following a disaster and perceived social support, sense of community at school, and proactive coping. *Anxiety Stress and Coping, 25*(5), 575–592.

Bronfenbrenner, U. (2005). *Making human beings human: Bioecological perspectives on human development*. USA: Sage.

Brown, S. L., Nesse, R. M., Vinokur, A. D., & Smith, D. M. (2003). Providing social support may be more beneficial than receiving it results from a prospective study of mortality. *Psychological Science, 14*(4), 320–327.

Burt, R. S. (1997). A note on social capital and network content. *Social Networks, 19*(4), 355–373.

Callaghan, P., & Morrissey, J. (1993). Social support and health: A review. *Journal of Advanced Nursing, 18*(2), 203–210.

Campbell, E. (2008). The ethics of teaching as a moral profession. *Curriculum Inquiry, 38*(4), 357–385.

Caprara, G. V., & Steca, P. (2005). Self-efficacy beliefs as determinants of prosocial behavior conducive to life satisfaction across ages. *Journal of Social and Clinical Psychology, 24*(2), 191–217.

Carver, C. S., Scheier, M. F., & Weintraub, J. K. (1989). Assessing coping strategies: A theoretically based approach. *Journal of Personality and Social Psychology, 56,* 267–283.

Casey, C., & Childs, R. (2017). Teacher education program admission criteria and what beginning teachers need to know to be successful teachers. *Canadian Journal of Educational Administration and Policy,* (67).

Cassel, J. (1976). The contribution of the social environment to host resistance. *American Journal of Epidemiology, 104,* 107–123.

Centers for Disease Control. (2003). *Suicide in the United States*. Retrieved from www.cdc.gov. ncipc/factsheets/suitfacts.htm.

Chen, G., Gully, S. M., & Eden, D. (2001). Validation of a new general self-efficacy scale. *Organizational Research Methods, 4*(1), 62–83.

Cheung, E., & Chiu, P. (2016, March 12). Students at breaking point: Hong Kong announces emergency measures after 22 suicides since the start of the academic year. *The South China Morning Post*. Retrieved from http://www.scmp.com/news/hong-kong/health-environment/article/1923465/students-breaking-point-hong-kong-announces.

Cobb, S. (1976). Social support as a moderator of life stress. *Psychosomatic Medicine, 38*(5), 300–314.

Cohen, S. (1992). *Stress, social support, and disorder. The meaning and measurement of social support* (pp. 109–124).

Cohen, J. (2011). *Social support received online and offline by individuals diagnosed with cancer* (Doctoral dissertation). Virginia Commonwealth University, Richmond, Virginia. Retrieved from http://scholarscompass.vcu.edu/cgi/viewcontent.cgi?article=3508&context=etd.

Cohen, S. (2004a). Social relationships and health. *American psychologist, 59*(8), 676.

Cohen, S. (2004b). Social relationships and health. *American Psychologist, 59*(8), 676–684.

Cohen, S., & Hoberman, H. M. (1983). Positive events and social supports as buffers of life change stress. *Journal of Applied Social Psychology, 13*(2), 99–125.

Cohen, S., & Janicki-Deverts, D. (2009). Can we improve our physical health by altering our social networks? *Perspectives on Psychological Science, 4*(4), 375–378.

Cohen, S., & McKay, G. (1984). Social support, stress and the buffering hypothesis: A theoretical analysis. *Handbook of Psychology and Health, 4,* 253–267.

References

75

Cohen, S., & Wills, T. A. (1985). Stress, social support, and the buffering hypothesis. *Psychological Bulletin, 98*(2), 310–357.

Cohen, S., Kamarck, T., & Mermelstein, R. (1983). A global measure of perceived stress. *Journal of Health and Social Behavior, 24*, 385–396.

Cohen, S., Mermelstein, R., Kamarck, T., & Hoberman, H. M. (1985). Measuring the functional components of social support. In I. G. Sarason & B. R. Sarason (Eds.), *Social support: Theory, research and applications* (pp. 73–94). Netherlands: Springer.

Coleman, J. S. (1990). *Foundations of social theory*. Cambridge: Harvard University Press.

Compas, B. E., Worsham, N. L., Ey, S., & Howell, D. C. (1996). When mom or dad has cancer: II. Coping, cognitive appraisals, and psychological distress in children of cancer patients. *Health Psychology, 15*(3), 167–175.

Cooley, C. H. (1902). The looking-glass self. *O'brien*, 126–128.

Coyne, J. C., Aldwin, C., & Lazarus, R. S. (1981). Depression and coping in stressful episodes. *Journal of Abnormal Psychology, 90*(5), 439.

Cutrona, C. E., & Russell, D. W. (1987). The provisions of social relationships and adaptation to stress. *Advances in Personal Relationships, 1*(1), 37–67.

Cutrona, C. E., & Russell, D. W. (1990). Type of social support and specific stress: Toward a theory of optimal matching. In B. R. Sarason, I. G. Sarason, & G. R. Pierce (Eds.), *Social support: An interactional view* (pp. 319–366). New York: Wiley.

Cutrona, C. E., Shaffer, P. A., Wesner, K. A., & Gardner, K. A. (2007). Optimally matching support and perceived spousal sensitivity. *Journal of Family Psychology, 21*(4), 754.

Davila, J., & Kashy, D. A. (2009). Secure base processes in couples: Daily associations between support experiences and attachment security. *Journal of Family Psychology, 23*(1), 76–88.

deCharms, R. (1968). *Personal causation*. New York: Academic Press.

Deci, E. L., & Ryan, R. M. (1985). *Intrinsic motivation and self-determination in human behavior*. New York: Plenum Press.

DeJordy, R., & Halgin, D. (2008). *Introduction to ego network analysis*. Boston, MA: Boston College and the Winston Center for Leadership & Ethics.

Dewey, J. (1917). The need for a recovery of philosophy. In J. Dewey (Ed.), *Creative intelligence: Essays in the pragmatic attitude* (pp. 3–69). New York: Holt.

Dozois, D. J., & Beck, A. T. (2008). Cognitive schemas, beliefs and assumptions. *Risk Factors in Depression, 1*, 121–143.

Duncan, L. E., Peterson, B. E., & Ax, E. E. (2003). Authoritarianism as an agent of status quo maintenance: Implications for women's careers and family lives. *Sex Roles, 49*(11–12), 619–630.

Dunkel-Schetter, C., Blasband, D. E., Feinstein, L. G., & Herbert, T. B. (1992). Elements of supportive interactions: When are attempts to help effective? In S. Spacapan & S. Oskamp (Eds.), *Helping and being helped: Naturalistic studies* (pp. 83–114). Thousand Oaks, CA, USA: Sage Publications.

Dunkel-Schetter, C., Feinstein, L., & Call, J. (1986). *UCLA social support inventory*. Unpublished manuscript, University of California, Los Angeles.

Edwards, J. A., Webster, S., Van Laar, D., & Easton, S. (2008). Psychometric analysis of the UK health and safety executive's management standards work-related stress indicator tool. *Work & Stress, 22*(2), 96–107.

Ehlers, A., & Clark, D. M. (2000). A cognitive model of posttraumatic stress disorder. *Behaviour Research and Therapy, 38*, 319–345.

Eisenberger, R., Cummings, J., Armeli, S., & Lynch, P. (1997). Perceived organizational support, discretionary treatment, and job satisfaction. *Journal of Applied Psychology, 82*(5), 812–820.

Ellison, N. B., Steinfield, C., & Lampe, C. (2007). The benefits of Facebook "friends:" Social capital and college students' use of online social network sites. *Journal of Computer-Mediated Communication, 12*(4), 1143–1168.

Ellsworth, P. C., & Scherer, K. R. (2003). Appraisal processes in emotion. *Handbook of Affective Sciences, 572*, V595.

Epstein, N. B., Baldwin, L. M., & Bishop, D. S. (1983). The McMaster family assessment device. *Journal of Marital and Family Therapy, 9*, 171–180.

Farmer, T. W., & Farmer, E. M. Z. (1996). Social relationships of students with exceptionalities in mainstream classrooms: Social networks and homophily. *Exceptional Children, 62*, 431–450.

Feeney, B. C., & Collins, N. L. (2015). A new look at social support: A theoretical perspective on thriving through relationships. *Personality and Social Psychology Review, 19*(2), 113–147.

Feeney, B. C., Cassidy, J., & Ramos-Marcuse, F. (2008). The generalization of attachment representations to new social situations: predicting behavior during initial interactions with strangers. *Journal of Personality and Social Psychology, 95*(6), 1481–1498.

Ferguson, E., Matthews, G., & Cox, T. (1999). The appraisal of life events (ALE) scale: reliability, and validity. *British Journal of Health Psychology, i*, 97–116.

Festinger, L. (1954). A theory of social comparison processes. *Human Relations. 7*(2), 117–140.

Fitzpatrick, S., & Bussey, K. (2014). The role of perceived friendship self-efficacy as a protective factor against the negative effects of social victimization. *Social Development, 23*(1), 41–60.

Foa, E. B., Johnson, K., Feeny, N. C., & Treadwell, K. R. T. (2001). The Child PTSD Symptom Scale (CPSS): Preliminary psychometrics of a measure for children with PTSD. *Journal of Clinical Child Psychology, 30*(3), 376–384.

Folkman, S., & Lazarus, R. S. (1988). The relationship between coping and emotion: Implications for theory and research. *Social Science and Medicine, 26*(3), 309–317.

Folkman, S., Lazarus, R. S., Gruen, R. J., & DeLongis, A. (1986). Appraisal, coping, health status, and psychological symptoms. *Journal of Personality and Social Psychology, 50*(3), 571.

Folkman, S., Schaefer, C., & Lazarus, R. S. (1979). Cognitive processes as mediators of stress and coping. In V. Hamilton & D. M. Warburton (Eds.), *Human stress and cognition: An information-processing approach*. London: Wiley.

Fredricks, J. A., Blumenfeld, P., Friedel, J., & Paris, A. (2005). School engagement. In K, A. Moore, & L. H. Lippman (Eds.), *What do children need to flourish? Conceptualizing and measuring indicators of positive development* (pp. 305–321). Boston, MA: Springer.

Goddard, R. D. (2003). Relational networks, social trust, and norms: A social capital perspective on students' chances of academic success. *Educational Evaluation and Policy Analysis, 25*(1), 59–74.

Goldsmith, D. J. (2004). *Communicating social support*. Cambridge: Cambridge University Press.

Goodman, C. C., Potts, M. K., & Pasztor, E. M. (2007). Caregiving grandmothers with vs. without child welfare system involvement: Effects of expressed need, formal services, and informal social support on caregiver burden. *Children and Youth Services Review, 29*(4), 428–441.

Goodyer, I. M., Wright, C., & Alrham, P. M. E. (1989). Recent friendships in anxious and depressed school age children. *Psychological Medicine, 19*(1), 165–174.

Gore, S. (1978). The effect of social support in moderating the health consequences of unemployment. *Journal of Health and Social Behavior, 19*(2), 157–165.

Granovetter, M. S. (1973). The strength of weak ties. *American Journal of Sociology, 78*, 1360–1380.

Green, C. A., Freeborn, D. K., & Polen, M. R. (2001). Gender and alcohol use: The roles of social support, chronic illness, and psychological well-being. *Journal of Behavioral Medicine, 24*(4), 383–399.

Guay, S., Billette, V., & Marchand, A. (2006). Exploring the links between posttraumatic stress disorder and social support: Processes and potential research avenues. *Journal of Traumatic Stress, 19*(3), 327–338.

Haines, V. A., Beggs, J. J., & Hurlbert, J. S. (2008). Contextualizing Health outcomes: Do effects of network structure differ for women and men? *Sex Roles, 59*(3–4), 164–175.

Haley, W. E., Levine, E. G., Brown, S. L., & Bartolucci, A. A. (1987). Stress, appraisal, coping, and social support as predictors of adaptational outcome among dementia caregivers. *Psychology and Aging, 2*(4), 323–330.

Hall, A., & Wellman, B. (1985). Social networks and social support. In S. Cohen, & S. S. Leonard (Eds.), *Social support and health* (pp. 23–41). San Diego, CA, US: Academic Press.

References

Hamilton, W. D. (1964). The genetical evolution of social behaviour. I & II. *Journal of Theoretical Biology, 7*(1), 1–52.

Hämmig, O. (2017). Health and well-being at work: The key role of supervisor support. *SSM-Population Health, 3*, 393–402.

Hattie, J. A., & Jaeger, R. J. (2003). *Distinguishing expert teachers from experienced and novice teachers.* Australian: University of Auckland.

Hazel, N. A., Oppenheimer, C. W., Technow, J. R., Young, J. F., & Hankin, B. L. (2014). Parent relationship quality buffers against the effect of peer stressors on depressive symptoms from middle childhood to adolescence. *Developmental Psychology, 50*, 2115–2123.

Heaney, C. A., & Israel, B. A. (2008). Social networks and social support. *Health Behavior and Health Education: Theory, Research, and Practice, 4*, 189–210.

Helgeson, V. S., & Cohen, S. (1996). Social support and adjustment to cancer: Reconciling descriptive, correlational, and intervention research. *Health Psychology, 15*(2), 135.

Heller, K. (1979). The effects of social support: Prevention and treatment implications. In A. P. Goldstein & F. H. Kanfer (Eds.), *Maximizing treatment gains: Transfer enhancement in psychotherapy* (pp. 253–382). New York: Academic Press.

Heller, K., & Swindle, R. W. (1983). Social networks, perceived social support and coping with stress. In R. D. Felner, L. A. Jason, J. Moritsugu, & S. S. Farber (Eds.), *Preventive psychology, research and practice in community intervention* (pp. 87–103). New York: Pergamon.

Hendrick, S. S. (1988). A generic measure of relationship satisfaction. *Journal of Marriage and the Family, 50*(1), 93–98.

Hitchcock, C., Ellis, A. A., Williamson, P., & Nixon, R. D. (2015). The prospective role of cognitive appraisals and social support in predicting children's posttraumatic stress. *Journal of Abnormal Child Psychology, 43*(8), 1485–1492.

Hobfoll, S. E. (2009). Social support: The movie. *Journal of Social and Personal Relationships, 26*(1), 93–101.

Hobfoll, S. E., & Vaux, A. (1993). Social support: Social resources and social context. In Shlomo Breznitz (Ed.), *Handbook of stress: Theoretical and clinical aspects* (2nd ed., pp. 685–705). New York: Free Press.

Holland, J. L. (1997). *Making vocational choices: A theory of vocational personalities and work environments.* Odessa: Psychological Assessment Resources.

Holmes, T. H., & Rahe, R. H. (1967). The social readjustment rating scale. *Journal of Psychosomatic Research, 11*, 213–218.

Hong Kong Primary Education Research Association, & Education Convergence. (2006). *Education research study on Hong Kong teachers' stress: Preliminary analysis.* Hong Kong: Hong Kong Primary Education Research Association and Education Convergence. (in Chinese).

House, J. S. (1987, December). Social support and social structure. In *Sociological forum* (Vol. 2, No. 1, pp. 135–146). Kluwer Academic Publishers.

House, J. S. (2001). Social isolation kills, but how and why? *Psychosomatic Medicine, 63*(2), 273–274.

Isen, A. M., & Baron, R. A. (1991). Positive affect as a factor in organizational-behavior. *Research in Organizational Behavior, 13*, 1–53.

Iwasaki, Y. (2001). Testing an optimal matching hypothesis of stress, coping and health: Leisure and general coping. *Loisir et Société/Society and Leisure, 24*(1), 163–203.

Jackson, Y., & Warren, J. S. (2000). Appraisal, social support, and life events: Predicting outcome behavior in school-age children. *Child Development, 71*(5), 1441–1457.

Jang, H., Reeve, J., Ryan, R. M., & Kim, A. (2009). Can self-determination theory explain what underlies the productive, satisfying learning experiences of collectivistically oriented Korean students? *Journal of Educational Psychology, 101*(3), 644–661.

Kahana, E., Bhatta, T., Lovegreen, L. D., Kahana, B., & Midlarsky, E. (2013). Altruism, helping, and volunteering: pathways to well-being in late life. *Journal of Aging and Health, 25*(1), 159–187.

Kasser, T., & Ryan, R. M. (2001). Be careful what you wish for: Optimal functioning and the relative attainment of intrinsic and extrinsic goals. In P. Schmuck, Peter & K. M. Sheldon (Eds.), Life goals and well-being: Towards a positive psychology of human striving (pp. 116–131). Ashland, OH, US: Hogrefe & Huber Publishers.

Kaul, M., & Lakey, B. (2003). Where is the support in perceived support? The role of generic relationship satisfaction and enacted support in perceived support's relation to low distress. *Journal of Social and Clinical Psychology, 22*(1), 59–78.

Kawachi, I., & Berkman, L. F. (2001). Social ties and mental health. *Journal of Urban health, 78*(3), 458–467.

Kelly, G. A. (1963). *A theory of personality: The psychology of personal constructs.* New York: W.W. Norton & Company.

Kim, D., Subramanian, S. V., & Kawachi, I. (2008). *Social capital and physical health. In Social capital and health* (pp. 139–190). New York, NY: Springer.

Kovacs, M. (1992). *Children depression inventory (CDI) manual.* New York: Multi-Health Systems.

Krohn, M. D. (1986). The web of conformity: A network approach to explanation of delinquent behavior. *Social Problems, 33*(6), S81–S93.

Krohne, H. W., de Bruin, J. T., El Giamal, M., & Schmukle, S. C. (2000). The assessment of surgery-related coping: The Coping with Surgical Stress Scale (COSS). *Psychology and Health, 15*, 135–149.

Labaree, D. F. (1998). Educational researchers: Living with a lesser form of knowledge. *Educational Researcher, 27*(8), 4–12.

Lakey, B., & Cohen, S. (2000). Social support theory and measurement. In S. Cohen, L. Underwood, & B. Gottlieb (Eds.), *Measuring and intervening in social support.* New York: Oxford University Press.

Lakey, B., & Cronin, A. (2008). Low social support and major depression: Research, theory and methodological issues. In K. S. Dobson & D. J. A. Dozois (Eds.), *Risk factors for depression* (pp. 385–408). Oxford: Academic Press.

Lakey, B., & Orehek, E. (2011). Relational regulation theory: A new approach to explain the link between perceived social support and mental health. *Psychological Review, 118*(3), 482–495.

Lakey, B., Orehek, E., Hain, K. L., & VanVleet, M. (2010). Enacted support's links to negative affect and perceived support are more consistent with theory when social influences are isolated from trait influences. *Personality and Social Psychology Bulletin, 36*(1), 132–142.

Laumann, E. O. (1973). *Bonds of Pluralism: The Form and Substance of Urban Social Networks.* New York, NY: John Wiley and Sons.

Lazarus, R. S. (1966). *Psychological stress and the coping process.* New York: McGraw-Hill.

Lazarus, R. S., & Folkman, S. (1984). *Stress, appraisal, and coping.* New York: Springer Publishing Company.

Legault, L., Green-Demers, I., & Pelletier, L. (2006). Why do high school students lack motivation in the classroom? Toward an understanding of academic amotivation and the role of social support. *Journal of Educational Psychology, 98*(3), 567–582.

Lent, R. W., Brown, S. D., & Hackett, G. (2000). Contextual supports and barriers to career choice: A social cognitive analysis. *Journal of Counseling Psychology, 47*(1), 36–49.

Lin, N. (1999). Social networks and status attainment. *Annual Review of Sociology, 25*(1), 467–487.

Lin, N. (2017). *Building a network theory of social capital. In Social capital* (pp. 3–28). UK: Routledge.

Lin, N., Ensel, W. M., Simeone, R. S., & Kuo, W. (1979). Social support, stressful life events, and illness: A model and an empirical test. *Journal of Health and Social Behavior, 20*(2), 108–119.

Lo, R. (2002). A longitudinal study of perceived level of stress, coping and self-esteem of undergraduate nursing students: an Australian case study. *Journal of Advanced Nursing, 39*(2), 119–126.

López, M. L., & Cooper, L. (2011). *Social support measures review.* National Center for Latino Child & Family Research.

Lubben, J. E. (1988). Assessing social networks among elderly populations. *Family & Community Health, 11*(3), 42–52.

References 79

Lubben, J., Blozik, E., Gillmann, G., Iliffe, S., von Renteln Kruse, W., Beck, J. C., et al. (2006). Performance of an abbreviated version of the Lubben Social Network Scale among three European community-dwelling older adult populations. *The Gerontologist, 46*(4), 503–513.

Luszczynska, A., Mohamed, N. E., & Schwarzer, R. (2005). Self-efficacy and social support predict benefit finding 12 months after cancer surgery: The mediating role of coping strategies. *Psychology, Health & Medicine, 10*(4), 365–375.

Mäkikangas, A., & Kinnunen, U. (2003). Psychosocial work stressors and well-being: Self-esteem and optimism as moderators in a one-year longitudinal sample. *Personality and Individual Differences, 35*(3), 537–557.

Maddy, L. M., Cannon, J. G., & Lichtenberger, E. J. (2015). The effects of social support on self-esteem, self-efficacy, and job search efficacy in the unemployed. *Journal of Employment Counseling, 52*(2), 87–95.

Mael, F., & Ashforth, B. E. (1992). Alumni and their alma mater: A partial test of the reformulated model of organizational identification. *Journal of Organizational Behavior, 13*(2), 103–123.

Mahoney, M. J. (2002). Constructivism and positive psychology. In C. R. Snyder & S. J. Lopez (Eds.), *Handbook of positive psychology* (pp. 745–750). Oxford: Oxford University Press.

Mak, M. C. K., Bond, M. H., Simpson, J. A., & Rholes, W. S. (2010). Adult attachment, perceived support, and depressive symptoms in Chinese and American cultures. *Journal of Social and Clinical Psychology, 29*(2), 144–165.

Maslach, C., Jackson, S. E., & Schwab, R. L. (1996). Maslach burnout inventory-educators survey (MBIES). In C. Maslach, S. E. Jackson, & M. P. Leiter (Eds.), *Maslach burnout inventory (MBI) manual* (3rd ed.). Palo Alto: Consulting Psychologists Press.

Maslow, A. H. (1943). A theory of human motivation. *Psychological Review, 50*(4), 370–396.

Matin, B. K., Jalilian, F., Alavijeh, M. M., Ashtarian, H., Mahboubi, M., & Afsar, A. (2014). Using the PRECEDE model in understanding determinants of quality of life among Iranian male addicts. *Global Journal of Health Science, 6*(6), 19–27.

Mattson, M., & Hall, J. G. (2011). Linking Health Communication with social support. *Junker Shutter Stock, 23*(4), 22–45.

McLaughlin, J., Horwitz, A. V., & White, H. R. (2002). The differential importance of friend, relative, and partner relationships for the mental health of young adults. In J. A. Levy & B. A. Pescosolido (Eds.), *Social networks and health* (pp. 223–246). New York: Elsevier.

McMillan, D. W., & Chavis, D. M. (1986). Sense of community: A definition and theory. *Journal of Community Psychology, 14*(1), 6–23.

McNair, D. M., Lorr, M., & Droppleman, L. F. (1981). *Profile of mood states*. San Diego, CA: Educational and Industrial Testing Service.

McNulty, S. E., & Swann, W. B., Jr. (1994). Identity negotiation in roommate relationships: The self as architect and consequence of social reality. *Journal of Personality and Social Psychology, 67*(6), 1012.

Mead, G. H. (1934). *Mind, self and society*. Chicago: University of Chicago Press.

Mednick, S. (1962). The associative basis of the creative process. *Psychological Review, 69*(3), 220–232.

Meiser-Stedman, R., Smith, P., Bryant, R., Salmon, K., Yule, W., Dalgleish, T., et al. (2009). Development and validation of the child post-traumatic cognitions inventory (CPTCI). *Journal of Child Psychology and Psychiatry, 50*(4), 432–440.

Midlarsky, E. (1991). Helping as coping. In Margaret S. Clark (Ed.), *Prosocial behavior* (pp. 238–264). Thousand Oaks, CA, US: Sage Publications.

Moos, R. H. (1981). *Work environment scale manual*. Palo Alto, CA: Consulting Psychologists Press.

Moos, R. H., & Insel, P. (1974). *Work Environment Scale Preliminary Manual*. Palo Alto, CA: Consulting Psychologists Press.

Murrell Jr, P. C., Diez, M. E., Feiman-Nemser, S., & Schussler, D. L. (2010). *Teaching as a moral practice: Defining, developing, and assessing professional dispositions in teacher education*. Harvard Education Press. 8 Story Street First Floor, Cambridge, MA 02138.

Nader, K. O., Kriegler, J. A., Blake, D. D., & Pynoos, R. S. (1994). *Clinician administered PTSD scale for children (CAPS-C)*. Los Angeles: Western Psychological Services.

Nurullah, A. S. (2012). Received and provided social support: A review of current evidence and future directions. *American Journal of Health Studies, 27*(3), 173–188.

O' Brennan, L., Pas, E., & Bradshaw, C. (2017). Multilevel examination of burnout among high school staff: Importance of staff and school factors. *School Psychology Review, 46*(2), 165–176.

O'Neill, G., & McMahon, T. (2005). *Student-centred learning: What does it mean for students and lecturers*.

Omoto, A. M., Malsch, A. M., & Barraza, J. A. (2009). Compassionate acts: Motivations for and correlates of volunteerism among old adults. In B. Fehr, S. Sprecher, & L. G. Underwood (Eds.), *The science of compassionate love: Theory, research, and applications* (pp. 257–282). Malden, MA: Wiley-Blackwell.

Pakenham, K. (2002). Development of a measure of coping with multiple sclerosis caregiving. *Psychology and Health, 17*(1), 97–118.

Pakenham, K. I., Chiu, J., Bursnall, S., & Cannon, T. (2007). Relations between social support, appraisal and coping and both positive and negative outcomes in young carers. *Journal of Health Psychology, 12*(1), 89–102.

Peacock, E. J., & Wong, P. T. (1990). The stress appraisal measure (SAM): A multidimensional approach to cognitive appraisal. *Stress Medicine, 6*(3), 227–236.

Pennebaker, J. W. (1982). *The psychology of physical symptoms*. New York: Springer.

Pierce, G. R., Sarason, I. G., & Sarason, B. R. (1991). General and relationship-based perceptions of social support: are two constructs better than one? *Journal of Personality and Social Psychology, 61*(6), 1028–1039.

Pierce, T., Baldwin, M. W., & Lydon, J. E. (1997). A relational schema approach to social support. *Sourcebook of social support and personality* (pp. 19–47). New York: Springer.

Piliavin, J. A. (2009). Altruism and helping: The evolution of a field: The 2008 Cooley-Mead presentation. *Social Psychology Quarterly, 72*(3), 209–225.

Piliavin, J. A., & Siegl, E. (2007). Health benefits of volunteering in the Wisconsin longitudinal study. *Journal of Health and Social Behavior, 48*(4), 450–464.

Podsakoff, P. M., MacKenzie, S. B., Lee, J. Y., & Podsakoff, N. P. (2003). Common method biases in behavioral research: A critical review of the literature and recommended remedies. *Journal of Applied Psychology, 88*(5), 879–903.

Putnam, R. D. (2000). *Bowling alone: America's declining social capital. In culture and politics* (pp. 223–234). New York: Palgrave Macmillan.

Radloff, L. S. (1977). Center for epidemiological studies depression scale. *Applied Psychological Measurement, 1*, 385–401.

Reblin, M., & Uchino, B. N. (2008). Social and emotional support and its implication for health. *Current Opinion in Psychiatry, 21*(2), 201.

Reddy, R., Rhodes, J. E., & Mulhall, P. (2003). The influence of teacher support on student adjustment in the middle school years: A latent growth curve study. *Development and Psychopathology, 15*(1), 119–138.

Rees, T., Mitchell, I., Evans, L., & Hardy, L. (2010). Stressors, social support and psychological responses to sport injury in high-and low-performance standard participants. *Psychology of Sport and Exercise, 11*(6), 505–512.

Rini, C., Dunkel Schetter, C., Glynn, L. M., Hobel, C., & Sandman, C. A. (2006). Effective social support: Antecedents and consequences of partner support during pregnancy. *Personal Relationships, 13*(2), 207–229.

Rosenberg, M. (1965). *Society and the adolescent self-image*. Princeton, NJ: Princeton University Press.

Rosenberg, I. H. (1989). Summary comments. *The American Journal of Clinical Nutrition, 50*(5), 1231–1233.

Rosenfeld, L. B., Richman, J. M., & Bowen, G. L. (2000). Social support networks and school outcomes: The centrality of the teacher. *Child and Adolescent Social Work Journal, 17*(3), 205–226.

References 81

Rothon, C., Head, J., Klineberg, E., & Stansfeld, S. (2011). Can social support protect bullied adolescents from adverse outcomes? A prospective study on the effects of bullying on the educational achievement and mental health of adolescents at secondary schools in East London. *Journal of Adolescence, 34*(3), 579–588.

Russell, D. (1996). UCLA loneliness scale (Version 3): Reliability, validity, and factor structure. *Journal of Personality Assessment, 66,* 20–40.

Ryff, C. (1989). Happiness is everything, or is it? Explorations on the meaning of psychological well-being. *Journal of Personality and Social Psychology, 57,* 1069–1081.

Sachs, J. (2003). *The activist teaching profession.* Buckingham: Open University Press.

Sapouna, M., & Wolke, D. (2013). Resilience to bullying victimization: The role of individual, family and peer characteristics. *Child Abuse and Neglect, 37*(11), 997–1006.

Sarason, B. R., Sarason, I. G., & Pierce, G. R. (1990a). Traditional views of social support and their impact on assessment. In B. R. Sarason, I. G. Sarason, & G. R. Pierce (Eds.), *Wiley series on personality processes. Social support: An interactional view* (pp. 9–25). Oxford, England: Wiley.

Sarason, B. R., Sarason, I. G., & Pierce, G. R. (1990b). *Social support: An interactional view.* New York: Wiley.

Sarason, I. G., & Sarason, B. R. (1985). Social support-Insights from assessment and experimentation. In I. G. Sarason & B. R. Sarason (Eds.), *Social support: Theory, research and applications* (pp. 39–50). Netherlands: Springer.

Sarason, I. G., Johnson, J. H., & Siegel, J. M. (1978). Assessing the impact of life changes: Development of the Life Experiences Survey. *Journal of Consulting and Clinical Psychology, 46*(5), 932–946.

Sarason, I. G., Sarason, B. R., Shearin, E. N., & Pierce, G. R. (1987). A brief measure of social support: Practical and theoretical implications. *Journal of Social and Personal Relationships, 4*(4), 497–510.

Sarason, S. B. (1974). *The psychological sense of community: Prospects for a community psychology.* San Francisco, CA: Jossey-Bass.

Schaefer, C., Coyne, J. C., & Lazarus, R. S. (1981). The health-related functions of social support. *Journal of Behavioral Medicine, 4*(4), 381–406.

Schaufeli, W. B., Leiter, M. P., Maslach, C., & Jackson, S. E. (1996). The MBI-general survey. In C. Maslach, S. E. Jackson, & M. P Leiter (Eds.), *Maslach burnout inventory manual* (3rd ed., pp. 19–26). Palo Alto, CA: Consulting Psychologists Press.

Schmitt, N. (2008). The interaction of neuroticism and gender and its impact on self-efficacy and performance. *Human Performance, 21,* 49–61.

Schulz, U., & Schwarzer, R. (2004). Long-term effects of spousal support on coping with cancer after surgery. *Journal of Social and Clinical Psychology, 23*(5), 716–732.

Schwartz, C., & Sendor, M. (2000). Helping others helps oneself: Response shift effects in peer support. In K. Schmaling (Ed.), *Adaptation to changing health: Response shift in quality-of-life research* (pp. 43–70). Washington, DC: American Psychological Association.

Schwarzer, R., & Schulz, U. (2003). Social support in coping with illness: The Berlin Social Support Scales (BSSS). *Diagnostica, 49*(2), 73–82.

Seibert, S. E., Kraimer, M. L., & Liden, R. C. (2001). A social capital theory of career success. *Academy of Management Journal, 44*(2), 219–237.

Sharma, S., & Sharma, M. (2010). Globalization, threatened identities, coping and well-being. *Psychological Studies, 55*(4), 313–322.

Sheeber, L., Hops, H., Alpert, A., Davis, B., & Andrews, J. (1997). Family support and conflict: Prospective relations to adolescent depression. *Journal of Abnormal Child Psychology, 25*(4), 333–344.

Sherbourne, C. D., & Stewart, A. L. (1991a). The MOS social support survey. *Social Science and Medicine, 32*(6), 705–714.

Sherbourne, C. D., & Stewart, A. L. (1991b). The MOS social support survey. *Social Science and Medicine, 32*(6), 705–714.

Shutterstock, J. (2011). *Linking health communication with social support. Mattson's Health as communication nexus.* Dubuque, IA: Kendall Hunt Publishing.

Simoni, J. M., Frick, P. A., & Huang, B. (2006). A longitudinal evaluation of a social support model of medication adherence among HIV-positive men and women on antiretroviral therapy. *Health Psychology, 25*(1), 74–81.

Solberg, V. S., O'Brien, K., Villareal, P., Kennel, R., & Davis, B. (1993). Self-efficacy and Hispanic college students: Validation of the college self-efficacy instrument. *Hispanic Journal of Behavioral Sciences, 15*(1), 80–95.

Stapleton, L. R. T., Schetter, C. D., Westling, E., Rini, C., Glynn, L. M., Hobel, C. J., et al. (2012). Perceived partner support in pregnancy predicts lower maternal and infant distress. *Journal of Family Psychology, 26*(3), 453–463.

Steinfield, C., Ellison, N. B., & Lampe, C. (2008). Social capital, self-esteem, and use of online social network sites: A longitudinal analysis. *Journal of Applied Developmental Psychology, 29*(6), 434–445.

Stryker, Sheldon. (1994). Identity theory: Its development, research base, and prospects. *Studies in Symbolic Interaction, 16,* 9–20.

Suitor, J. J., & Pillemer, K. (2002). Gender, social support, and experiential similarity during chronic stress. *Advances in Medical Sociology, 8,* 247–266.

Sullivan, H. S. (1953). *The interpersonal theory of psychiatry.* Washington, DC: William Alanson White Psychiatric Foundation.

Taylor, M. (2000). Communities in the lead: Power, organisational capacity and social capital. *Urban Studies, 37*(5–6), 1019–1035.

Taylor, S. E. (2007). Social support. In H. S. Friedman & R. C. Silver (Eds.), *Foundations of health psychology* (pp. 145–171). Oxford: Oxford University Press.

Taylor, S. E., Welch, W. T., Kim, H. S., & Sherman, D. K. (2007). Cultural differences in the impact of social support on psychological and biological stress responses. *Psychological Science, 18*(9), 831–837.

Thoits, P. A. (1985). Social support and psychological well-being: Theoretical possibilities. In I. G. Sarason & B. R. Sarason (Eds.), *Social support: Theory, research and applications* (pp. 51–72). Netherlands: Springer.

Thoits, P. A. (1995). Stress, coping, and social support processes: Where are we? What next? *Journal of Health and Social Behavior, Forty Years of Medical Sociology: The State of the Art and Directions for the Future,* 53–79.

Thoits, P. A. (2011). Mechanisms linking social ties and support to physical and mental health. *Journal of Health and Social Behavior, 52*(2), 145–161.

Thoits, P. A. (2013). Self, identity, stress, and mental health. In C. S. Aneshensel, J. C. Phelan, & A. Bierman (Eds.), *Handbook of the sociology of mental health* (pp. 357–377). Netherlands: Springer.

Thompson, R. A., Flood, M. F., & Goodvin, R. (2006). Social support and developmental psychopathology. *Developmental Psychopathology, 3,* 1–37.

Torsheim, T., & Wold, B. (2001). School-Related Stress, School Support, and Somatic Complaints A General Population Study. *Journal of Adolescent Research, 16*(3), 293–303.

Trivers, R. L. (1971). The evolution of reciprocal altruism. *The Quarterly Review of Biology, 46*(1), 35–57.

Turner, R. J., & Brown, R. L. (2010). Social support and mental health. In T. L. Scheid & T. N. Brown (Eds.), *A handbook for the study of mental health: Social contexts, theories, and systems* (pp. 200–212). Cambridge: Cambridge University Press.

Turner, R. J., & Marino, F. (1994). Social support and social structure: A descriptive epidemiology. *Journal of Health and Social Behavior, 35*(3), 193–212.

Twenge, J. M., & Kasser, T. (2013). Generational changes in materialism and work centrality, 1976–2007: Associations with temporal changes in societal insecurity and materialistic role modeling. *Personality and Social Psychology Bulletin, 39*(7), 883–897.

References

Uchino, B. N. (2004). *Social support and physical health: Understanding the health consequences of relationships*. New Haven: Yale University Press.

Uchino, B. N. (2009). Understanding the links between social support and physical health: A lifespan perspective with emphasis on the separability of perceived and received support. *Perspectives on Psychological Science, 4*, 236–255.

Uchino, B. N., Bowen, K., Carlisle, M., & Birmingham, W. (2012). Psychological pathways linking social support to health outcomes: A visit with the "ghosts" of research past, present, and future. *Social Science and Medicine, 74*(7), 949–957.

Uchino, B. N., Cacioppo, J. T., & Kiecolt-Glaser, J. K. (1996). The relationship between social support and physiological processes: a review with emphasis on underlying mechanisms and implications for health. *Psychological Bulletin, 119*(3), 488–531.

van Harmelen, A. L., Gibson, J. L., St Clair, M. C., Owens, M., Brodbeck, J., Dunn, V., … & Goodyer, I. M. (2016). Friendships and family support reduce subsequent depressive symptoms in at-risk adolescents. *PloS One, 11*(5), e0153715.

Vaux, A., & Harrison, D. (1985). Support network characteristics associated with support satisfaction and perceived support. *American Journal of Community Psychology, 13*(3), 245–265.

Vaux, A., Phillips, J., Thomson, B., Holly, L., Williams, D., & Stewart, D. (1986). The social support perceptions (SSA) scale: Studies of reliability and validity. *American Journal of Community Psychology, 14*, 195–220.

Veit, C. T., & Ware, J. E. (1983). The structure of psychological distress and well-being in general populations. *Journal of Consulting and Clinical Psychology, 51*(5), 730.

Vogel, D. L., & Wei, M. (2005). Adult attachment and help-seeking intent: The mediating roles of psychological distress and perceived social support. *Journal of Counseling Psychology, 52*(3), 347–357.

Waldinger, R. J., & Schulz, M. S. (2006). Linking hearts and minds in couple interactions: Intentions, attributions, and overriding sentiments. *Journal of Family Psychology, 20*(3), 494–504.

Wasko, M. M., & Faraj, S. (2005). Why should I share? Examining social capital and knowledge contribution in electronic networks of practice. *MIS, quarterly*, 35–57.

Waters, L. E., & Moore, K. A. (2002). Predicting self-esteem during unemployment: The effect of gender, financial deprivation, alternate roles, and social support. *Journal of Employment Counseling, 39*(4), 171–189.

Watson, D., Clark, L. A., & Tellegen, A. (1988). Development and validation of brief measures of positive and negative affect: the PANAS scales. *Journal of Personality and Social Psychology, 54*(6), 1063–1070.

Watzlawick, P. (1984). *Self-fulfilling prophecies. The production of reality: Essays and readings on social interaction* (pp. 392–408).

Weinstein, N., & Ryan, R. M. (2010). When helping helps: Autonomous motivation for prosocial behavior and its influence on well-being for the helper and recipient. *Journal of Personality and Social Psychology, 98*(2), 222–244.

World Health Organization. (2017 April). *Mental disorders fact sheet*. Retrieved from http://www.who.int/mediacentre/factsheets/fs396/en/.

Wright, S. L., Perrone-McGovern, K. M., Boo, J. N., & White, A. V. (2014). Influential factors in academic and career self-efficacy: Attachment, supports, and career barriers. *Journal of Counseling & Development, 92*(1), 36–46.

Yeung, A. S., & Liu, W. P. (2007). *Workload and psychological wellbeing of Hong Kong teachers*. Fremantle: Paper presented at the Australian Association for Research in Education.

Young, R., & Collin, A. (2004). Introduction: constructivism and social constructionism in the career field. *Journal of Vocational Behaviour, 64*(3), 373–388.

Zimet, G. D., Dahlem, N. W., Zimet, S. G., & Farley, G. K. (1988). The multidimensional scale of perceived social support. *Journal of Personality Assessment, 52*(1), 30–41.

Chapter 3
Well-being, Psychological Adjustments and Effective Social Support Giving

Abstract As a popular research topic spanning a few decades, social support research has generated voluminous empirical findings which have shown the huge potential of utilising its benefits in different occupational fields apart from the fields of health psychology and medical health where this topic originated. The previous chapter clarifies the different conceptualisations of social support research and the instruments that measure the effects/outcomes, as well as methodological concerns. This chapter continues to establish the theoretical ground of social support research by elaborating the concepts related to psychological well-being and describing the psychological adjustment of people who need support. It then explores the conditions of effective social support giving. First, it describes the central concept—well-being—a concept being used to conceptualise its benefits for human beings. Second, based on the backdrop provided by the well-being literature, the chapter further discusses the emotional status of various groups of people in society who encounter life situations and experience critical circumstances which may cause them much effort to regulate their emotions and adjust themselves in living in their social environment. Finally, the conditions and factors that lead to effective social support are explored, addressing a list of parameters that describe effective social support giving. In sum, the chapter aims to achieve the following purposes: (1) to present a comprehensive definition of well-being and its associated psychological theories; (2) to discuss the inner self and emotional struggles of groups of needy people in society; (3) to identify facilitative conditions of social support and effective social support giving and (4) to discuss the implications of the theories of well-being and effective social support strategies to the situation of teaching in schools. The chapter ends with a list of suggestions about effective social support measures and some conditions that inhibit the effectiveness of social support. It suggests that the effectiveness of social support giving is dependent upon the nature of offering the support, types of support given at different times of need, support givers' relationship with the support recipient, support givers' experience, gender, common cultural traits and personalities of support receivers. The content of this chapter is planned in a way which leads readers to construct the knowledge of and appreciate the value of social support, the implications for application to the field of education are also discussed at the end.

© Springer Nature Singapore Pte Ltd. 2019
B. LAM, *Social Support, Well-being, and Teacher Development*,
https://doi.org/10.1007/978-981-13-3577-8_3

Well-being as an Outcome Measure of Social Support

This section explains the meaning of Well-being and the psychological processes that determine Well-being. As mentioned in the previous chapter, social support can influence an individual's health and well-being in a number of ways. Well-being is considered as an overarching theme to justify the importance of social support and it provides the theoretical underpinnings of this book. But the question is, how should we define health and/or well-being? According to the World Health Organization (WHO), 'health is a state of complete physical, mental and social well-being and not merely the absence of disease or infirmity' (WHO, 1948, p. 100). It implies that a healthy person should have a good integration of physical, mental and social domains and an absence of disease. Huber et al. (2011) further elaborated the idea based on WHO's definition which was formulated early in the last century. Since chronic disease is inevitable in modern society, Huber and his team proposed more a greater emphasis on an individual's ability to adapt and self-manage when he/she is facing physical, emotional and social difficulties (Huber et al. 2011). Viewed from this perspective, people are encouraged to accept and adjust to a situation in order to remain 'healthy', even when the situation is challenging and difficult.

One may raise the question of how to define the status of psychologically healthy? Psychological well-being typically refers to the positive status of psychological health that characterises individuals who feel optimistic about life and function well (Keyes & Annas, 2009), yet it is a complex idea (Ryan & Deci, 2001). Over decades of research, well-being has mainly been studied from two perspectives, namely hedonism and eudaimonism. The former considers well-being as pleasure or happiness, while the latter believes well-being consists of fulfilling or actualising oneself. Both of the explanations suggest a condition of relating one to others to gain happiness and support.

Determinants and Constituents of Well-being

Among various ways in *hedonism* to measure happiness, Wilson (1967) started to investigate the meaning of happiness and defined it as subjective well-being (SWB). SWB is 'a person's cognitive and affective evaluations of his or her life' (Diener, Lucas, & Oishi, 2002, p. 63). Life satisfaction, positive affect and negative affect are three core components of SWB; they are separate domains that have to be measured separately (Andrews & Withey, 1976; Lucas, Diener, & Suh, 1996), that is, as mentioned by Cacioppo and Berntson (1999), a person who lives with positive affect may also have negative affect. The three domains are usually measured with self-report questionnaires to elicit one's subjective feeling about their own life. A considerable amount of research has shown that a satisfying social life and social support from network members are strongly associated with SWB. For example, Diener and Seligman (2002) found that the happiest 10% of undergraduate students are those active ones in social activities and that social participation is strongly predictive of life satisfaction. It implies that interpersonal relationships play an important role in happiness, as evidence suggests that affiliation and relationship-enhancing traits are at the top of the list influencing SWB (DeNeve, 1999).

On the other hand, the *eudaimonic* concept of well-being encourages people to accept and live with their daimon (demon) or true self (Waterman, 1993). People would feel alive and authentic when they are allowed to live as who they really are (actual self). In support of eudaimonism, Ryan and Deci (2000a) defined three principal psychological needs that predict an individual's well-being with Self-Determination Theory (SDT). They are *autonomy, competence* and *relatedness*. Autonomy refers to the need of choices and volition in one's behavioural regulation; competence is an individual's self-efficacy in different situations; and relatedness refers to the feeling of being loved and connected to others. These three fundamental psychological needs are critical for the development of *intrinsic motivations* and psychological well-being (Kasser & Ryan, 1996). Motivation refers to the extent to which an individual is willing to invest time and energy into a certain goal. When a person is driven by *intrinsic* motivation to strive for a goal, he or she would be doing it for his/her own pleasure associated with the task itself. For instance, a musician keeps on practising musical instruments and hopes to improve purely because of his/her own pleasure without considering external factors such as wealth and fame. This is considered a kind of intrinsic motivation. Past research has found that people with more intrinsic motivation in general tend to demonstrate higher levels of persistence, invest more effort into their tasks, and show higher achievement (Ryan & Deci, 2000b; Deci & Ryan, 1985).

Perceived competence or *self-efficacy*, which is defined as the beliefs people hold about their own abilities to accomplish desired goals, is a crucial element in intrinsic motivation. It is influential in determining the amount of effort people invest into their work and is also related to accomplishments in life and mental health. In social cognitive theory, self-efficacy has an essential role in the regulation of emotional states (Bandura, 1997) by allowing people to appraise threatening situations as manageable (Bavojdan, Towhidi, & Rahmati, 2012). The reduction in negative affects regarding the stressors allows people with high self-efficacy to regulate their emotional states (Carr, 2011). Past research has revealed that individuals with a low level of self-efficacy are prone to poor mental health, such as anxiety and depression (Bandura, 1988; Muris, 2002). Thus, the more an individual believes in his/her own capability, the more motivated and healthy he/she is. Self-efficacy alone will not be able to enhance intrinsic motivation unless there is also the existence of a sense of autonomy (deCharms, 1968). The need for autonomy refers to people's innate desire of free will and the sense of choice when acting out one's own interests and values (Deci & Ryan, 2000). The availability of options, acknowledgment of feelings and opportunities for self-direction allows greater autonomy and thus increases intrinsic motivation (Deci & Ryan, 1985).

Although competence and autonomy seem to play important roles in determining an individual's intrinsic motivation, relatedness bears on its expression (Ryan & Deci, 2000a). Attachment and intimacy are two important concepts concerning relatedness. In Bowlby's (1980, 1982) Attachment Theory, human children are born with a tendency to engage in an evolutionary set of attachment behaviours such that a young child is proximate to figures who can protect him/her, in order to increase the child's chance of survival. Each person, after experiencing attachment in childhood, would develop concepts about what relationships are like. This is an unconscious process, the influence of which would extend to later adulthood (Mikulincer & Shaver, 2001). If a person fails to form a secure attachment with his/her caregiver in early life, he/she will be more likely to become emotionally unresponsive and avoidant in intimate and interdependent relationships (Mikulincer & Shaver, 2001). The fulfilment of the needs of autonomy, competence and relatedness mediates the relationship between intrinsic goals and well-being (Ryan, Huta, & Deci, 2008) as accomplishing intrinsic goals will satisfy an individual's psychological needs and then lead to better well-being. Therefore, the three basic psychological needs are important for personal growth and integration. This chapter will further elaborate attachment theory as the theoretical reason for looking at social support to students in the classroom.

In the field of positive psychology, with aims at building positive qualities in life and encouraging people to thrive and live meaningful lives (Seligman & Csikszentmihalyi, 2014), Seligman (2011) proposed the well-being theory to further emphasise the multifaceted nature of human *flourishing*. In his model, well-being consists of five core elements, including: Positive emotion, Engagement, Relationships, Meaning and Accomplishment (PERMA). The PERMA is considered 'the best approximation of what humans pursue for their own sake' (Seligman, 2011, p. 97) since these elements are intrinsically motivated by themselves, that is, individuals do not need other rewards in order to pursue them (e.g. it is not necessary to offer you rewards to stimulate you to pursue positive emotion, as positive emotion itself is a motivation). PERMA evaluates both hedonic and eudaimonic perspectives of well-being using both objective and subjective approaches so as to fully assess an individual's well-being. There is not a total score for well-being in Seligman's work because there should not be a single indicator of how well an individual is doing, since well-being is an integration of different attributes (Forgeard, Jayawickreme, Kern, & Seligman, 2011). Pursuing PERMA leads to personal well-being by integrating good feeling, meaningful life, close and supportive relationships, achievements and being fully engaged in life. These experiences help people go beyond surviving to flourishing and making an optimal life.

The economic value of well-being. There is a huge disparity between wealth and well-being. Subjective well-being can be divided into happiness (mood) and life satisfaction (evaluation). While life satisfaction may increase with income, happiness does not necessarily increase. As a matter of fact, people in the less abundant regions may lead happier lives despite their low gross domestic product. Therefore, Seligman (2011) suggests policymaking should change from using GDP to including well-being as the index of how well a nation is doing.

Well-being of children. Dunn and Layard (2009) proposed seven crucial elements for the well-being of children, including, loving families, friends, positive lifestyle, solid values, good schools, mental health and enough money. The development of children depends much on a warm, understanding, interesting and firm relationship with their parents. Children living in a harmonious family are less likely to exhibit antisocial and aggressive behaviours. Friendship affords children pleasure and joy, and better understanding of social relationships. Moreover, it can ease the stress from changes in their lives. Children who are rejected by their peers tend to become either aggressive or depressed (Arseneault et al. 2006). A positive lifestyle can help children to develop healthy interests and hobbies, and avoid exposure to excessive consumerism and unhealthy habits such as obesity, smoking, alcohol and illegal drugs. Such a lifestyle can only be built upon solid values which are imparted by parents, schools, media, political and faith affiliations. Mental health difficulties are one of the greatest barriers to a happy childhood. Enough financial support allows children to live without shame. An impoverished childhood tends to be correlated with poor mental health, academic achievements, substance abuse and teenage pregnancy; what is worse, their subsequent adulthood could also be negatively affected.

Self-actualisation and Life-Span Theory of Development

On the whole, the above-mentioned theories all agree on a point that health and well-being refers to a state of good integration of different domains in life. Health should be a state of having a complete (perceived wholeness) life. As suggested by Maslow's (1943) hierarchy of needs, human beings possess a set of motivation systems to achieve a certain need (see Fig. 3.1). Only when our lower level needs are satisfied will we be motivated to pursue our needs at the next stage as the upcoming needs become more salient. Physiological needs are our basic needs for survival. When these needs are fulfilled, we will move on to pursue safety, then belongingness and love and so on. This is what makes us grow and ultimately reach the highest level—self-actualisation, a state where an individual is fully realising his or her potentials and that is the meaning of life. Everyone is capable of self-actualisation, even those with mental illness. According to Maslow, a self-actualised person is able to resolve dichotomies in life such as id versus ego. However, life events (e.g. divorce, severe sickness) may frustrate people's certain needs and make them struggle between stages. Unmet needs may end up being expressed through difficult behaviour (e.g. antisocial behaviour) and affect an individual's well-being.

A similar idea is also reflected in Erikson's (1959) definition of life-span stages of development of human beings. He defined eight distinct stages in life, where human beings encounter a particular crisis of conflicting needs at each stage. According to this theory, successfully overcoming the crisis of each stage will result in a healthy personality and acquisition of a basic virtue (e.g. purpose, competency, love), which will be of use in resolving crises in the upcoming stages. In contrast, failure to overcome a stage successfully will result in reduced capability to resolve crises in the next stages and result in a less healthy personality and lower self-esteem. The last stage in this model is *integrity versus despair*, where if we have already completed our accomplishments and led a positive life, the sense of integrity will be developed in later life. However, if we perceive ourselves as a failure and feel

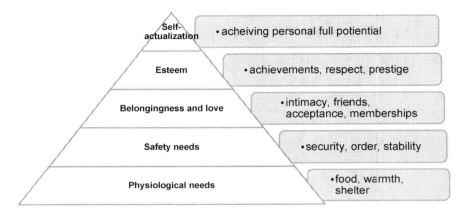

Fig. 3.1 Maslow's Hierarchy of needs as suggested by Maslow (1943)

guilty about not accomplishing any life goals, we will become discontented and develop despair which leads to depression and hopelessness. Success in this stage will allow an individual to gain *wisdom* to look back to their past life and feel a sense of completeness. However, debilitating social conditions in one's life may definitely undermine adolescents' fulfilment of basic needs, such as physiological needs for safety as well as psychological needs for emotional closeness and intimacy with peers and to be accepted by family and friends (Erikson, 1968).

Maslow and Erikson's theories points to a process in which our own selves take part in realising/establishing our own competence, emotions, relationships with others, autonomy and interest through the ongoing experience in life. They also implied the importance of adults being responsible for providing nourishing, growth-enhancing opportunities for children from the time they are young. This process of development is 'intergenerational' (Roeser, Eccles, & Sameroff, 2000) that involves both the students and the adults with whom the students are in contact.

Socio-emotional Development and Well-being

The above concepts and models can explain the conditions of psychological healthiness. emerging from the above theories, to enable human beings to achieve a healthy psychological status, one has to develop the socio-emotional capacity through their lifetime. One of the reasons why social support is important is that at times in life people become distressed and troubled because they cannot regulate their emotional state when facing difficulties; they experience a psychological adjustment process which is challenging for them (this process will be elaborated on in subsequent sections of this chapter). As we discussed in the psychological theories above, low efficacy, poor self-esteem, isolation, disengagement and disinterestedness undermine a per-

Well-being as an Outcome Measure of Social Support

son's growth and their ability to manage their own life. Socio-emotional development is crucial as it helps maintain a better condition in which to live with well-being.

Socio-emotional development is a crucial aspect of growth in human beings. It generally refers to the ability to regulate emotions, identify with the feelings of other persons (empathy), relate to others (social but not isolated), be actively involved in establishing a shared culture in an interaction or a community (synchronisation with others, intersubjectivity), and recognise that people have thoughts, feelings and beliefs that are different from one's own (theory of mind). Socio-emotional abilities can make a difference to one's life as one may perceive a more positive life, behave with altruistic behaviour, develop positive peer relationships, relate to others, achieve purposes in a thoughtful manner, and become socially productive. The ultimate goal of mankind apparently is to optimise our abilities to achieve personal goals so as to pursue a meaningful life. People who have more positive socio-emotional development have greater capacity to understand things and complete tasks in a collaborative manner with better problem-solving skills (Leary, 2007).

This part has explained the meaning of well-being and discussed the related concepts, it has described the benefits of social support and suggested how it could be used to enhance well-being. The research of social support therefore often suggests a change in one's perception and their psychological mechanisms, such as motivation, self-efficacy, self-esteem and self-worth etc., helping people to become more engaged and live fully and authentically with more positive energies, while eliminating people's difficulties by providing tangible and intangible support.

Who Needs Social Support?

Social support is deemed to protect people against a wide range of crises (Cobb, 1976) and different types of illness. However, the effects of social support may vary across different situations. The same way of support may not be useful to every individual. In this section, the circumstances of need for social support are described to address the psychological status which hinders one to develop a meaningful life or to achieve the status of well-being. To delimit the discussion, different groups of the needy are identified and their psychological states are discussed to provide a more comprehensive understanding of how difficult situations might affect an individual's well-being.

Cobb's (1976) suggestion of different categories of challenging life circumstances are referred to as a starting point. The resilience of a person determines whether they are able to successfully adapt in situations of social disadvantage or adverse conditions. In the cases of successful coping, people demonstrate competent functioning and optimal adjustment to adverse life incidents. In the cases where people fail to cope, they suffer from disturbances and negative feelings in their subjective self. They are brought down to a psychological status where they are emotionally disturbed, feel distressed, hurt, upset and emotionally uncontrollable to an extent that they cannot attain a state of well-being, which may persistently affect their behaviour, work and life, and eventually affect their well-being. The literature has described typical life circumstances, and suggests that different groups of people have need of social support.

Poor Health Conditions

Firstly, physically ill patients would definitely not be in good health conditions; many may also suffer from psychological stress since they are worried about their sickness, especially those who are diagnosed with life threatening diseases. Take heart failure as an example. Among hospitalised patients, depression occurs in 14–36.5% of patients whereas its occurrence is even higher in outpatients, up to 42% (for a review, see Luttik, Jaarsma, Moser, Sanderman, & van Veldhuisen, 2005). And in cancer patients, 10–30% suffer from anxiety disorder, and depression occurs in 10–25% of the patients (see also Brown, Kroenke, Theobald, Wu, & Tu, 2010). Their psychological burden may worsen their health condition and disrupt their recovery progress.

The case for mental illness patients may be more challenging. Recovery from mental illness has been defined as the 'personal experience of the individual as he or she moves out of illness into health and wholeness' (White, Boyle, & Loveland, 2004), which is not an easy task. On the one hand, the patients have to face difficulties during the process of recovery or encountering disabling symptoms (Jacobson & Greenley, 2001). On the other hand, they need to overcome negative labelling by society, which may be tougher than the recovery process itself as social stigmatisation may worsen their mental health condition (van Zelst, 2009). Powerlessness, injustice, abuse or 'social defeat' (hostile disputes among people) are major underlying social factors leading to difficulties in recovery (Tew, 2011). The stigmatisation along with poverty and social marginalisation will serve as huge barriers to the recovery progress. Fully recovery from mental illness, apart from medication, also requires social inclusion and positive self-concept of the patients (Markowitz, 2001; Social Care Institute for Excellence, Care Services Improvement Partnership, & Royal College of Psychiatrists, 2007). A supportive community is no doubt a catalyst for the recovery process and social engagement of the psychiatric patients.

Similar to mental illness patients, individuals with physical impairments (e.g. blindness, limb loss) also have to face discrimination. The impairments can deprive them of usual educational, social and economic activities in the community. For example, dropout rate of adolescents with disability is twice that of their healthy counterparts' (McFarland, Stark, & Cui, 2016). The attitudes to their 'illness' and the built environment in which society is organised may prevent this group from participating on an equal level with the normal others in their community. Discriminatory attitude, cultures, policies or institutional practices may also discourage people with physical impairments to participate in sociocultural contexts (Booth, 2000). Studies have found that children with impairment are at risk of social isolation since they are less likely to participate in interpersonal interactions. Even when they do, they receive few positive responses to their active participation. Therefore, they may lose interest in joining their peers and thus encounter social isolation (Celeste & Grum, 2010).

Nevertheless, caregivers of these patients or elderly people also are prone to a lot of health problems. The chronic stress of caregiving jobs affects caregivers' health in various dimensions (Son et al. 2007). Research has found that caregivers demonstrate more negative health symptoms after taking up caregiving duties (Shanks-McElroy & Strobino, 2001). They also use more prescription drugs than non-caregivers (Schulz et al., 1997). Prolonged experience of stress places caregivers at a higher risk of hypertension and cardiovascular diseases (Shaw et al., 1999; Mausbach, Patterson, Rabinowitz, Grant, & Schulz, 2007). One reason for caregivers' poor health condition in general is their irregular health behaviours. The job nature of caregivers is time and energy consuming as they have to be constantly alert to any emergencies. A stressful and demanding workload often makes them forget about their own health care, such as lack of sleep, having low levels of exercise and getting ill easily (Vitaliano, Zhang, & Scanlan, 2003) thus resulting in poor health.

Adjustment and Adaptation

Moreover, people experiencing major transitions in life may need social support to overcome the crises. Transition means 'an event or non-event, which results in a change in assumptions about oneself and the world and thus requires a corresponding change in one's behaviours and relationships' (Schlossberg, 1981, p. 5). It generally refers to retirement, graduating from college, becoming a parent, changing career, settling down into a country as an immigrant, ageing, loss of relatives and loved ones, etc. Transitions may affect an individual's well-being in different dimensions. For example, retirement may be considered as the beginning of enjoying life by many workers, yet studies have shown that it is actually distressing and this requires significant adjustment (e.g. Stambulova, 2003). Besides, during career transition, self-identity is the main issue influencing the time needed to adjust to the changes and to success in the new positions, especially those who were outstanding in their original fields (Park, Lavallee, & Tod, 2013; Warriner & Lavallee, 2008). Furthermore, for students, entering university is a source of strain and a critical stressor (Gall, Evans, & Bellerose, 2000). Attending university allows young adults to explore their roles and distinguish themselves as an individual apart from the role as a member of their families (Arnett, 2000). The new environment may however lead freshmen to experience higher levels of psychological disturbance, such as depression, obsession and absentmindedness (Fisher & Hood, 1987). Later in life, after getting married,, becoming a parent may cause anxiety due to the change of role, the new responsibilities for raising a baby (Warren, 2005) and the learning of new skills is needed to conquer such transition (Nelson, 2003). In the times of all these transitions in life, one must face identity crises and may need support to adjust to the new settings.

There are also some weaker members in our society who may suffer from various kinds of issues, which demand huge effort and resources in overcoming the hardships and adjusting themselves in the transitions. These include, for example, domestic violence victims, ethnic minorities and the poor. In the first nine months of 2016, there were 2471 reported cases of domestic abuse in Hong Kong (Social Welfare Department, 2016). A government report revealed that victims of domestic violence in general are lower in social desirability, self-esteem and social support but higher in domains like stress, depressive symptoms and substance abuse, compared to non-abused individuals (Chan, 2005). In general, the victims have poorer mental and physical health and thus need more health care than ordinary people (Constantino, Sekula, Rabin, & Stone, 2000). Besides, they are at risk of destructive behaviour such as self-injury and attempted suicide (Kernic, Wolf, & Holt, 2000). The traumatic consequences of domestic violence affect not only the victim but the whole family. Children who experienced battering between parents are found to be more prone to violence in later life and over 50 percent of the perpetrators had been involved in family violence (Chan, 2005). Domestic violence can have long-lasting devastating influences on the victim and the family. This minimises their life opportunities with the constraint borne by the consequences of problematic situations.

New immigrates and ethnic minority groups are often excluded in society in all countries and their source of stress is often related to adjustment (Levitt, Lane, & Levitt, 2005). Up till 2011, there were a total of 451,183 ethnic minorities (known as non-ethnic Chinese; NEC) living in Hong Kong, mainly Indonesians, Filipinos, Whites, Indians and Pakistanis, constituting 6.4% of the whole population (Census and Statistics Department, 2012). Ethnic discrimination is a major life stressor for ethnic minorities, which brings them adverse effects on adjustment to life and well-being (Lee, 2005). Research has shown that people from ethnic minority groups in general have lower income, live in poor and crowded accommodation, work in less desirable jobs and experience longer period of unemployment, compared with their local counterparts (Nazroo, 1998). Language barrier is another obstacle for NEC to integrate into the local society, not to mention their other needs, such as cultural and religious needs that may also be neglected by the system. Apart from these kinds of structural discrimination, they also have to face interpersonal discrimination, which is also known as racism. Evidence shows that there is a positive association between racism and both physical (e.g. respiratory illness) and psychological distress (e.g. depressive symptoms) (e.g. Karlsen & Nazroo, 2002; Pascoe & Richman, 2009). If local people show more positive attitude toward and interaction with people from ethnic minority groups, this will definitely provide them with a sense of belonging and support that facilitate them fitting into society (Phinney, Madden, & Santos, 1998).

Poor people comprise a substantial population of society and they may experience problems in living which weakens their well-being. Revealed in the Hong Kong Poverty Situation Report 2015 (Hong Kong SAR Government, 2016), there are 1.345 million poor people currently living under the poverty line. Poverty has been found associated with poor psychological (e.g. depression, anxiety) and physical health (e.g. heart disease, diabetes), as well as social problems (e.g. Miller, Chen, & Parker, 2011; Santiago, Wadsworth, & Stump, 2011) due to limited resources and a poor living environment. Poverty is a vicious cycle whereby poverty-related stressors lead to poor mental health, and the building up of chronic stress and poor health together make the situation more stressful and more difficult to deal with (Santiago et al., 2011). Children from low-income families in general have a higher risk of behavioural problems and academic difficulties at school (Becker & Luthar, 2002; Raver, Gershoff, & Aber, 2007), and their dropout rate is more than three times higher than that of children from high-income families (McFarland et al., 2016). As these poor children grow up, they tend to complete fewer years of school, and are three times more likely to live under poverty as adults (Heflin & Pattillo, 2006). Even after taking levels of education into account, college graduates from poor families earn less and have less desired occupations than their higher socioeconomic background counterparts, years after graduation (Walpole, 2003). Poverty can be a long-term problem influencing children's and adults' well-being from various perspectives and limiting poor people's upward mobility. Financial assistance alone may not completely help solve their difficulties. This stops them from proceeding to self-actualisation to achieve higher aspiration in terms of career development, and narrow opportunities undermine the feeling of autonomy in developing themselves.

Last but not least, when crises are treated badly, stress may bring along adverse effects on one's behaviours. If one continuously denies his/her problems and refuses to change or adjust, he/she may engage in maladaptive behaviour in response to the situation, such as substance abuse (e.g. tobacco, marijuana and drugs) or showing antisocial behaviour (e.g. criminality, aggressive behaviours, school dropout) to express or reduce their negative feelings. Ruminative individuals who tend to focus on the distress and negative consequences are more likely to drink or abuse substances to cope with their problems (Nolen-Hoeksema & Harrell, 2002). Health problems resulting from substance abuse are obvious, but what makes it even worse is that substance abuse and depression are usually comorbid (Wu, Hoven, Okezie, Fuller, & Cohen, 2008). This means that depressed individuals are more likely to abuse substances and at the same time, substance abusers are more likely to suffer from depression. Substance abusers often encounter other co-occurring problems such as unemployment, poverty, homelessness and low self-esteem (Center for Substance Abuse Treatment, 2005; Copeland & Hall, 1992). Therefore, if substance abuse is not treated, the negative effects will spread over different domains of a person's life and it is disastrous to the individual's overall well-being. They may find it very hard to integrate into life in schools and the normal settings of society. Furthermore, alcohol and illicit drug use often give rise to antisocial behaviour. Studies have found that a portion of teenagers have always been involved in antisocial behaviour under the influence of alcohol or drugs, including verbally insulting someone, damaging property and creating a public disturbance (Graham & Homel, 2008; McAllister & Makkai, 2003). Such behaviours do not only affect the well-being of the individual but also the well-being and harmony of society. As stressful life events and low level of support are strong predictors of antisocial behaviour (Windle, 1992), offering

96   3 Well-being, Psychological Adjustments and Effective Social …

social support to misbehaving individuals, especially youngsters will be essential, because adolescents' early-life problematic behaviours will become harder to change as they grow up (Tremblay, 2000).

According to the literature, well-being is subjective and people in adversity can create opportunities for themselves by enhancing their capacities for living, so that they can maintain a healthy status of well-being. The literature has proved the positive effect of social support in different circumstances and some situations have been discussed in Chap. 1. In the following section, a review of literature will be conducted to identify the conditions and concerns of effective social support applications, and some contrasting situations of social support provision failure are also described.

Social Support Is not Always Welcomed

While a voluminous amount of literature reports the benefits of social support on human well-being, recent research has also pointed out the adverse effect created by social support such as negative affect on support receivers (Shrout, Herman, & Bolger, 2006), depression (Eby, Buits, Lockwood, & Simon, 2004) and burnout (Ray & Miller, 1994). The effectiveness of social support actually depends on the situational fit and the support provider's characteristics (Uchino, 2009). Therefore, social support may not always be perceived as helpful (Kim, Sherman, & Taylor, 2008). Beehr, Bowling and Bennett (2010) suggested three reasons for failure in social support: (1) the support provided unintentionally draws the recipient's attention to the stressor (Beehr et al., 2010); (2) threat to self-esteem and lower self-efficacy (Bolger et al. 2000; Shrout et al. 2006) as the recipient may feel being negatively evaluated by the provider and incapable of dealing with the stress (Bolger et al., 2000); (3) the kind of support may not be wanted or needed by the recipient (Beehr et al., 2010). Support will be effective only if the support provided fits well with the recipient's need (Burleson, 2009; Cutrona & Cole, 2000; Dunkel-Schetter Blasband, Feinstein, & Herbert, 1992).

As visible support in each way can further intensify the stress response of the support recipient, reducing the recipient's awareness of the support provided may reduce the adverse effects brought about by visible support. Bolger and Amarel (2007) suggested that invisible support instead enhances the perceived availability of social support without drawing the recipient's attention to the stressor.

In one of their studies (Bolger and Amarel, Ibid), each of the 86 female undergraduate participants was paired up with a confederate. The participants were told to perform either a writing task or a speech that would be evaluated by teaching assistants (where all real participants were actually assigned to deliver a speech). Participants were also told that experimenters would be observing the students in pairs so the student who was assigned to the essay writing task (the confederate) could act as a practice audience during their preparation. The support provision occurred right after the practice period before the confederate left the room (supposedly to do the writing task). The experimenter asked the confederate if she had any questions. In

Social Support Is not Always Welcomed 97

Table 3.1 The three conditions in Bolger and Amarel's (2007) study

Condition	Confederate's response
Visible	'Not really. But I would like to say something to [Participant] if that's all right. Look, you've got nothing to worry about, you'll do fine. I'd understand if you were nervous, but I really think it's going to be okay.'
Invisible	'Yes, can you tell me more about what I'm doing? I mean, [Participant] is going to do fine, she's got nothing to worry about, but I still don't know what I'm supposed to do.'
Control	'Not really. Unless you're going to tell me more about what I'm supposed to do?'

the *visible* emotional support condition, the confederate told the participant directly she (the female student as participant) was doing fine. In the *invisible* condition, the confederate expressed it as part of the question to the experimenter about the task without any direct communication to the participant. In the *no support* control condition, the confederate did not directly or indirectly mention the participant. Examples of the responses are shown in Table 3.1.

It was found that the participants' distress level increased the least in invisible support condition, followed by no support condition and the increase in visible support condition was the greatest. The confederates' supportive acts without being noticed by the participants were the most effective in soothing emotional reactivity to a stressor. The effect of invisible support (and even no support) in this case outperformed that of visible support. As suggested by Howland and Simpson (2010), invisible support may be more likely to divert the recipient's attention from the stressful event and increase the perception of available support and therefore be more able to reduce negative affect. Aligned with the result, Shrout et al. (2006) also found that interactions that were considered by the support provider as support but not by the recipient enhanced adjustment better than visible support or no support.

In another study conducted by Deelstra et al. (2003) of imposed support with 48 administrative assistants, the participants were to perform administrative tasks in an office setting. There were three problematic conditions: (1) no problem; (2) solvable problem and (3) unsolvable problem. Both in no-problem condition and solvable-problem condition, participants had been told that they could look for information needed in a file in the office cabinet, before they started the task; while in unsolvable condition the file was not known about by the participants. In each condition, either imposed support or no support would be given to the participants by a confederate peer, who was thought to be a participant in the setting. In the imposed support condition, the confederate communicated with the participant in a friendly tone and offered help without seeking the participant's opinion of whether help is needed. The confederate took out the file from the cabinet and filled in the information needed for the participant before the participant returned to her own work. Later on, the participants were asked to evaluate the appropriateness of support received during the task and the 'sympathy for the support provider' (i.e. the confederate). It was found that the imposed support in the no-problem and solvable-problem condition was less appropriate compared to unsolvable-problem condition. Whereas the support provider was evaluated as less sympathetic as they imposed support in the no-problem and solvable-problem situation. Receiving imposed support was even found to be more stressful than facing an unsolvable problem as it threatens one's self-esteem, as Deelstra et al. (2003) concluded in the analysis of the study. It was perceived as less negative only when the participants were highly in need of support as imposed support in other cases harmed self-esteem and ignited negative affect.

The author has recently read about a case of unwanted help on the Internet which reveals the salient process of handling social support. An undergraduate student had been expressing her depressive emotions on her social media platform for a while due to some obstacles in life. Her friend B saw those posts and was worried about her, and therefore asked her out for lunch to chat with her. Knowing B's good intention, A felt free to tell B about her situation and the next day they met for lunch. Everything was fine until after lunch, B claimed he had to hand in an assignment to the department office and invited A to accompany him. When they arrived at the office, a professor had been waiting there for them. To A's surprise, actually B had told the professor about A's depressive symptoms and they would like to refer A to the counsellor as they thought A was at the risk of suicide. In the end, according to the counsellor's advice, A was sent to hospital. In this incident, A felt betrayed and her privacy was violated. She understood B's good intention but she did not feel helped at all. The hospitalisation even increased her mental burden as it was too sudden and it made her miss classes and deadlines. This incident affirms that help may be ineffective in the circumstances when the help offered by support givers may be given inappropriately, which would create mistrust and distress to those who are in a situation that needs help, making the situation even worse. The determination of the right time to help and the right move to help a person is a delicate process that should be considered with a broader spectrum of concerns that related to the persons' willingness to receive help, the problem status (such as psychological status of the person being helped), and the possible involvement of professional support such as positive intervention and clinical treatment.

Many schools and organisations have guidelines on how to deal with similar cases of psychological distress of young students as described in the case above. Teachers or supervisors may recommend the stressed student/employer to seek professional help from counsellor, clinical psychologist, however, prior consent has to be sought form the potential support receiver so as to protect personal information. Protecting clients' information is an ethical principle, it assumes a kind of respect for support receivers, and it has a crucial role to play to enable a successful positive intervention. The situations portrayed in the case also imply the need for general knowledge on social support giving as it can ensure that the efforts paid in supporting others are rewarding to the support givers and support receivers, since social support is aimed to help people to overcome stressful situations and improve their psychological well-being; such knowledge is useful in different situations such as in daily life and professional settings.

Support Offered by Similar Others Are More Effective

The literature has suggested that when people encounter difficult situations in life such as unemployment, breakup and bereavement, they may not always turn to their kin for comfort but instead to someone who has shared similar experiences because he/she has more understanding of the circumstances and thus can show greater empathy (Suitor & Pillemer, 2000).

The classical study of Suitor, Pillemer, Keeton and Robison's (1995) researched on experiential and structural similarity on social support and interpersonal stress. The participants comprised of 256 primary care givers of dementia parents and 56 returning students, whom did not have a bachelor's degree previously. The participants were asked to name and describe their network members who were their source of support or interpersonal stress, and who had been an obstacle for the participant to provide care to the dementia parent/return to school or made the participant feel bad about it. Experiential similarity was defined whether the associate had any experience in caring for an elderly relative as family caretakers and whether they had completed a 4-year degree for returning students.

It was found that having similar experiences in transition made someone a source of support for the participants immediately after the transition and a year later. At the same time, these associates were less likely a source of interpersonal stress to the participants, while structural similarity (e.g. gender and employment status) became saliently important in explaining patterns of support when experiential similarity was omitted. The importance of similarity in the effectiveness of social support has been confirmed by many studies (e.g. de Grood & Wallace, 2011; Suitor & Pillemer, 2000). People with similar experiences are good listeners to provide more support as they are less likely to reject people who seek support due to their distress (Suitor et al., 1995). They also tend to share similar values and knowledge of one another's situations and are therefore more empathic (Suitor & Pillemer, 2000). This facilitates communication and enhances effectiveness of support (de Grood & Wallace, 2011).

Besides the sharing of similar experience between the support givers and support receivers as a positive condition, friendship or a shared identity between the one giving help and the one receiving help is another factor of effective social support. People are more motivated to provide support to their in-group members of the same social category (Haslam, Reicher, & Levine, 2012). In Levine, Prosser, Evans, and Reicher's (2005) study of helping behaviours, 45 Manchester United FC (Man. Utd.) supporters were recruited as participants. In the beginning, they had to answer questions such as which was their favourite football team and how often they watched the team play, in order to prime them with their Man. Utd. Fans' identity. Then they were asked to proceed to another room alone, where on the way, they would witness a confederate fall and hurt his leg. The confederate was wearing either a Man Utd team shirt, a Liverpool FC (an opponent of Man Utd) shirt or an unbranded sports shirt. Not surprisingly, the confederate received the most help when he was wearing a Man Utd shirt but received the least help when he was wearing a Liverpool shirt, as his in-group identity was recognised in the prior condition. In the second part of the study, another 22 Man Utd supporters were recruited. The flow of the experiment was basically the same but this time, the participants had been primed with the identity of a football fan instead of a support of any team before they proceeded. All conditions remained unchanged but this time when the football fan identity was salient, participants were as willing to help a victim in a Man Utd shirt as they were to help someone in a Liverpool shirt, while in the plain shirt condition, the victim received the least help. The whole study shows that the membership of a social category significantly influences helping behaviours. In the first part of the study, the victim with a Liverpool shirt was classified as an out-group member by the Man. Utd. supporters since they disliked team Liverpool. And thus, they were less willing to offer help to their opponent. However, in the second part of the study, the participants recognised themselves as football fans; in this sense, the confederate was treated as an in-group member no matter which team's shirt he was wearing. In sum, it is apparent that people tend to offer help to people from the same group (i.e. in-group members).

As it is more likely for one to receive support from others who belong to the same group with a similar background, we also perceive support from these in-group members as useful and effective. This idea of similar others is also used as a tool for intervention, for example, forming a support group among substance abusers to help one another. Groh, Jason, Davis, Olson, and Ferrari (2007) studied the effect of social support on alcohol use, with 897 residents of Oxford House, which was a supportive abstinent communal-living setting for substance abuse in the U.S. Unlike hospitals and rehabilitation centres, Oxford House had no prescribed length of stay for residents and professional staff. Residents were expected to provide support to and develop strong bonds with people who had encountered the same experience, i.e. 'similar others', these people shared common abstinence goals, so as to maintain sobriety and reduce the chance of relapse. General support and specific support for alcohol use from family and friends were measured in the study. It was found that general support from friends had the strongest effect on decreasing drinking behaviours. Besides, the length of stay in Oxford House was also a strong predictor of less alcohol consumption. The importance of support from friends can be explained by the fact that Oxford House residents lived together with friends and not with family, in which 'fellowship with similar peers' was considered by the residents as the most important aspect of their living experience in Oxford House (Maton & Salem, 1995). This kind of mutual companionship effectively helped the residents to remain abstinent. In fact, the levels of friends' general support became less important to the change in drinking habits after a prolonged stay in Oxford House because the Oxford House experience was likely to cancel out the negative effect of low levels of general support. Therefore, the authors concluded that in such supportive settings general support from peers who shared similar experiences would be more effective than other sources of specific support as the support provided by experientially similar peers was more relevant to their recovery.

Relationships Determine the Effectiveness of Social Support

According to the relationship perspective of social support, relationship qualities simultaneously affect the perception and reception of social support (Cohen & Wills, 1985). The closer a relationship is, the more positive and effective the recipient would perceive the support provided by the partner (Collins & Feeney, 2000; Rini, Schetter, Hobel, Glynn, & Sandman, 2006). The closeness and intimacy within a relationship is many times developed and maintained through the partner's responsiveness of one another's need for support (Reis, Clark, & Holmes, 2004). However, on the one hand, support can increase relationship closeness; and on the other hand, it can increase personal distress at the same time. For instance, imagine you are working very hard on your assignment in order to meet the deadline. Seeing you being too stressed out, your partner suggests you have a break with him/her. You may appreciate his/her good intentions but meanwhile you feel bad about losing time to work. Despite the enhancement in relationship closeness, the imbalance in support provision and receipt between the couple would increase the support recipient's negative affect (Gleason, Iida, Bolger, & Shrout, 2003), as he/she may feel guilty and inferior for his/her unidirectional needs of support.

In a study by Shrout et al. (2010) with 293 law graduates, who were going sit a barrister exam, the participants and their partners were asked to indicate their emotional closeness and physical intimacy with their partner on a daily basis. Their negative emotions including anger, depressed mood and anxiety were measured with a standard questionnaire. The participants also reported whether they had provided/received any emotional support to/from their partner in the past 24 h. It confirmed the fact that receiving support simultaneously increased both 'relationship closeness' and 'negative emotions'. However, it happened only on the day when the participant received support from the partner but without providing support for him/her. When support was equally received and provided, the relationship increased and negative affect decreased, regardless of the stress level of the participants. This is in line with Gleason et al. (2003) finding that receiving support without reciprocation is more likely to trigger negative moods, while reciprocity in support provision correlates with positive affect. Therefore, it is beneficial to have more mutual support within a relationship. Providing support is beneficial in the sense that it repays our 'debts' or puts the support recipient in our debt (Uehara, 1995) and it is a proof of self-worth (Buunk & Schaufeli, 1999) as people who have the ability to help may have better self-esteem as they feel more competent and needed when they offer help (Fisher, Nadler, & Whitcher-Alagna, 1982). The discussion by authors on giving and providing support in a close relationship implies that consistent supportive responses in a close relationship are crucial as they can lead to better perceived partner support, which gives rise to greater trust and relationship satisfaction, and, eventually, better health outcomes (Cutrona et al., 2005).

The benefits of a good relationship can be widely applied as a means of intervention for family, marriage and children's developmental problems. In Murray and Malmgren's (2005) study of teacher–student relationship intervention on adjustment of children with emotional and behavioural problems, 48 primary school students and eight teachers were recruited. A teacher was assigned to each student in the beginning of the study. The intervention included (1) weekly meetings between each student and the teacher to facilitate communication and enhance involvement, (2) increased teacher praise to show positive feedback and expectation and (3) discussion on the phone between each student and the teacher about the student's school progress in a 5-month period. The aim of the intervention was to enhance involvement, communication and warmth within the teacher–student relationship, so as to alleviate the students' problems as a good relationship per se could lead to positive outcomes, including more perceived support. Early literature suggests that engagement, open communication and warmth between the teacher and the student is a key to the quality of the teacher–student relationship (Murray & Greenberg, 2001). It was found that positive teacher–student relationships effectively improved students' academic performance and school-related functioning, which is consistent with previous research (e.g. Hamre & Pianta, 2001; Malecki & Demaray, 2003).

The importance of relationships is also stressed in psychotherapy. Developing a trustful relationship between the therapist and the client is essential to positive therapeutic outcomes (Carlson, Watts, & Maniacci, 2006), especially in Roger's (1959) person-centred therapy, which emphasises a therapeutic relationship. The therapist him/herself acts as a catalyst for the client's change, has to demonstrate empathy, acceptance and unconditional positive regards, such that the client would be willing to remove his/her defences, come to accept what he/she has distorted and change their wrong perceptions in order to achieve personal growth. It is mainly the attitude of the therapist, rather than his/her knowledge or techniques, that guide the client's personality change (Rogers, 1961). In support of the significance of relationship, a meta-analysis of therapeutic effectiveness has shown that interpersonal elements are essential for effective psychotherapy, whereas skills are relatively less effective on therapeutic outcomes (Wampold, 2001).

Help at the Right Time by the Right Person

The composition and size of every individual's social network may vary, but we always turn to similar sources for support in a particular situation. For example, when we have difficulties with school work, it is more likely for us to seek help from our peers or teachers instead of our parents. But in some situations, we may prefer some personal space rather than receiving help from others. For instance, in the beginning, when we lose a loved one, we may want some time alone to calm ourselves down. In such situations, support offered may not be regarded as helpful or we might even feel annoyed. This section discusses how to help at the right time in a good position.

Dating back to the 80s, the idea of right timing for social support has been discussed. Coping with stress involves a series of processes with different kinds of support at different times (Jacobson, 1986). Weiss (1976) defined the time frame of a stressful event as (1) *crisis*, the onset of the event that threatens the individual's well-being, (2) *transition*, a period of a concurrence with that event which changes the person's assumption of the world and (3) *deficit state* following the event in which the person needs resources to encounter the change. He suggested that emotional support is needed mainly during the happening of the crisis. Then, in transition, the primary type of support is cognitive (informational) support in order to help the individual cope with the situation. Finally, in the deficit state, material (tangible) support is mostly needed to provide the sufferer with resources to solve the problem.

Arora, Finney Rutten, Gustafson, Moser, and Hawkins (2007) studied the helpfulness and effect of different types of support provided by family, friends and healthcare providers (doctors and other health professionals) to breast cancer patients. Social support and patient outcomes data were collected via surveys and medical records from 246 patients, who were newly diagnosed (on average less than two months) with breast cancer, at two time points: at baseline and at a follow-up after five months. It was found that at the beginning of the diagnosis, both family and healthcare providers were the major source of assistance to the patients, by providing decision-making support. Emotional and informational support from healthcare providers were additionally helpful. The data collected at the stage where the patient is newly diagnosed also shows that emotional support from friends was considered helpful. As time passed, family and friends continued to be sources of emotional support but healthcare providers would become the main sources of help in problem-solving coping by providing informational support. Malecki and Demaray (2003) found similar results in a study with 263 American elementary school students. Emotional support from parents was perceived to be the most important, whereas informational support from teachers and schools was also well regarded as important. As young adolescents' closest people, parents' overall support was significantly correlated to their children's personal well-being. Apart from informational support, teachers' emotional support could actually predict students' social skills and academic competence. Students who perceived more emotional support from their teachers (e.g. feel cared for and treated fairly) showed better social skills and academic achievements.

The above two studies indicate that people have evolving support needs at different time points. It is important for us to identify and respond appropriately to support recipients' needs in order to facilitate their stress coping and adjustment effectively. Provision of helpful support can have positive outcomes in various contexts such as mental and physical health (Thoits, 2011), school performance (Murray & Malmgren, 2005) and work satisfaction (Baruch-Feldman et al. 2002). As shown in much research, different kinds of support may be valued from different sources of provider (Taylor, 2011). For most of the time, emotional support from significant others would be useful but may be disliked when casual friends try to offer it, while informational support from experts is valued but that from well-intentioned family and friends is considered inappropriate as they have questionable expertise (e.g. Arora et al. 2007; Dakof & Taylor, 1990; Malecki & Demaray, 2003). Providing support that mismatches the recipient's needs may strengthen the recipient's distress (Itkowitz, Kerns, & Otis, 2003) or harm the relationship between the support provider and the

104　　　　　　　　3　Well-being, Psychological Adjustments and Effective Social …

recipient (Rini et al. 2006). Therefore, we should be aware of the type of support we are trying to provide in order to bring about a truly helpful impact for the support recipient.

The Dual Effect of Online Network

Online social networking sites are becoming more and more popular due to technological advances. We can interact with friends easily without geographical boundaries. As of 2015, 64% percent of Hongkongers held active social media accounts and the biggest social networking site Facebook has approximately 4.4 million users in Hong Kong, which is 1.5 times of the total population (GO-Globe Web Design Hong Kong, 2015). With the increasing number of users, the Internet has become a significant platform for the provision and reception of social support (Gemmill & Peterson, 2006). Whether these kinds of social network sites can enhance an individual's social support is still controversial (Frison & Eggermont, 2016). While some researchers claim that these sites have potential risk to the development of depressive symptoms among adolescents (e.g. Kross et al., 2013), some suggest that online social support may actually increase users' social capital and protect them from stress, depression and anxiety (Lin & Bhattacherjee, 2009).

Frison and Eggermont (2016) studied the relationships among habits of Facebook usage, perceived support and depressed mood with 910 adolescents. After detailing their habits of using Facebook (e.g. frequency of browsing, whether they post stuff on their timeline and interact with other users), the participants were classified into three groups: passive Facebook use, active private Facebook use and active public Facebook use. *Passive Facebook use* refers to users who only monitor others' lives by viewing their profile content. *Active private Facebook use* means communicating interactively with other Facebook users and friends in a private setting (e.g. private messaging) whereas *active public Facebook use* refers to communicating interactively with other users and friends in a public setting (e.g. status updating, posting of pictures). It was found that passive Facebook use positively predicted depressed mood as this type of users may compare their lives with their active counterparts when they viewed others' profile. Passive users may have negative self-image and feelings when they upward compared themselves with those they perceived to be having better lives (Haferkamp & Krämer, 2011), especially those who were low in narcissism (Qiu, Lin, Leung, & Tov, 2012). This is consistent with previous findings that mere consumption of Facebook content increases a user's feeling of loneliness (Burke, Marlow, & Lento, 2010).

Apart from gaining informal social support, the use of online social media sites has also been included in some interventions to replace typical face-to-face support groups, such as cancer (Hong, Pena-Purcell, & Ory, 2012), depression (Rice et al. 2014) and substance abuse (Rowe et al. 2007). Turner-McGrievy and Tate (2013) used online social networking known as Twitter as a tool that allows users to post messages and follow other people/organisations, for reading and responding to the others' posts regarding deliver weight loss intervention remotely. In an interventional study, two groups were set to assign 96 overweight adults in testing the use of online communication support group where one group uses podcast-only (Podcast) and the other group uses podcast in addition to enhanced mobile media intervention (Podcast + mobile) group in a random assignment. Both groups received the same content of podcast about nutrition and exercise, audio blog of people attempting to lose weight and goal setting activity, etc. The Podcast plus mobile group were additionally requested to download a specific diet and physical activity monitoring app and Twitter™ app to their mobile devices. They had to log on every day to read and post messages in order to receive the content distributed by a weight loss counsellor and other participants. The weight loss counsellor wrote two posts per day to reinforce messages from the podcasts and encourage discussion among the participants. Body weight of the participants was measured at three time points: at baseline, 3 months and 6 months. Participants had to fill out a questionnaire by week for evaluating the quantity of podcasts they had listened to and the use of Twitter (for Podcast plus mobile group only).

In the end, participants were categorised into (1) *active user*, who read and posted messages on Twitter, (2) *readers*, who did not frequently write but read posts and (3) *neither*. All Twitter posts written by the participants were recorded and categorised according to types of support. The posts were found to be mostly informational support for one another. Thus, online social media may be useful in delivering information and increase social support among users. Twitter use was found to be associated with weight loss; active participants were more successful in weight loss, which is consistent with other studies of traditional intervention that weight loss is due to increase provision of social support (Clarke, Freeland-Graves, Klohe-Lehman, & Bohman, 2007).

Online support groups have their pros and cons compared to traditional support groups. These virtual groups break geographical and temporal barriers, and participants can go online easily and anonymously, thus they are more willing to be open to talk about sensitive issues (Dosani, Harding, & Wilson, 2014). The benefits of online social support have been reported in numerous studies due to the increasing usage of the Internet. Online social platforms allow the sharing of multimedia (e.g. documents, pictures, videos) and enhance communications (Mehta & Atreja, 2015). In addition, Jones et al. (2011) suggested that users of online social networks found it easier to talk to strangers online than to family and friends and they prefer communicating online to on the phone. Having a friend available to message instantly online improves self-efficacy, lowers level of stress and increases support seeking behaviours (Feng & Hyun, 2012). However, one cannot go completely anonymous on the Internet; personal information and medical history might risk being collected and misused. Second, when an individual seeks support online but receives no response, it will have an adverse effect on his/her mental health (Mehta & Atreja, 2015). Also, as mentioned above, participating in online social networks may cause jealousy and depression (Kross et al., 2013). The consequences may be more harmful if an individual misuses healthcare-specific online support groups. Some extreme online groups encourage negative or self-harm behaviours (Haas, Irr, Jennings, & Wagner, 2011), for instance, some 'pro-suicide' and 'pro-amputation' self-harming communities were found in the current societies (Bell, 2007; Lewis & Michal, 2016). The quality of content, privacy issues and consumer fraud should also be made highlighted when joining online support groups or communities especially when it comes to health issues (Monteith, Glenn, & Bauer, 2013).

It is preferable to choose communities that include moderators who can monitor the discussion to avoid cyberbullying or misleading information that may bring traumatic consequences. Proper online support groups run by professionals may be a better choice when interventions are needed. Mehta & Atreja (2015) suggested that in order to produce positive outcomes from social support media, an ideal online social support network should be able to compromise between flexibility and security, anonymity and authenticity, openness and moderation. In sum, we should only join online groups that are well organised and managed, and be aware of the exposure of personal information when using these platforms.

Culture and Social Support

As discussed previously, relationships play an important role in the perception and effectiveness of social support. Culture is one key factor that determines an individual's view about the role of self and interpersonal relationships. As suggested by Markus & Kitayama (1991), in countries where their culture encourages them to be individualistic, such as the United States and western European countries, everyone is viewed as an independent individual, who is expected to decide and express one's personal beliefs and achieve personal goals. Relationships are assumed in independent form that is freely chosen by each individual with few obligations (Adams & Plaut, 2003). For people who live in collectivistic cultures, such as Asian countries (e.g. China, Japan, Korea, Vietnam), most people are interdependently connected and bound to one another by conforming themselves to a relational norm (Markus & Kitayama, 1991). Researchers have commonly suggested that people of Asian countries are oriented by group goals and this orientation develops as primary and personal beliefs (Kitayama & Uchida, 2005). The relationships in collectivist cultures take an interdependent form, in the sense that they are less voluntary than those in individualistic cultures (Adams, 2005; Nisbett, Peng, Choi, & Norenzayan, 2001). The cultural differences regarding relationships and social norms give rise to the differences in how people view and utilise social support.

Consistent across many studies, Asians and Asian Americans are generally identified as using less social support when they cope with stressors (e.g. Chu, Kim, & Sherman, 2008; Taylor et al., 2004). The differences are observed in both self-reported use of social support and support seeking behaviours in experimental settings (Sherman, Kim, & Taylor, 2009). Surprisingly, social support seeking is found to be associated with greater resolution of the stressor for European Americans but it is associated with less successful resolution for Asian Americans (Kim, Sherman, Ko, & Taylor, 2006). For example, in a study of implicit and explicit form of social support with Asian American and European American students by Taylor, Welch, Kim, & Sherman (2007), participants were primed with various forms of support and then they participated in a stressful task. Participants who are located in an implicit support condition were requested to write about a group to whom they thought they could develop a close connection with and write about the reasons why the group were important to them. This was to remind them of their support networks (i.e. implicit support). While in the explicit support condition, instead of writing about the group's importance, participants had to write a letter directly to ask the support groups to give advice and support for an impending task (i.e. elicit support). Saliva samples were collected from the participants for the measure of cortisol (a stress hormone) response, and they completed an assessment of post-task stress as well.

It is reported from the study that Asians and Asian Americans had higher levels of cortisol (i.e. feeling more stressed) in the explicit support condition than in the implicit support condition. In contrast, European Americans experienced less distress in the explicit support condition than in the implicit support condition. The results indicate that a culturally inappropriate form of social support may actually amplify stress (Taylor et al., 2007), such as explicit support for Asians and Asian Americans. In more individualistic cultures, free expression is a sign of autonomy and independent self. European Americans value verbal expression more than Asian Americans do (Kim & Sherman, 2007) and verbalisation of thoughts actually enhances cognitive performance of them but not that of Asian Americans (Kim, 2008). In contrast, Asian Americans prefer using suppression as a means of emotion regulation when they encounter stress (Gross & John, 2003) and therefore less frequently ask for support as they do not want to reveal their emotions.

The literature also reports that social support seeking is evaluated negatively by Asians and Asian Americans. In Chu et al. (2008) study, participants watched a video of a young woman who had experienced a stressful situation; when the woman explicitly sought help from others, she was evaluated more positively by European Americans and more negatively by Asian Americans, compared with the condition when she did not seek support. By relating to participants' own support seeking situations, it was found that for those who judged the support seeker in the video more negatively were less likely to seek social support to cope with their own stressors (Chu et al., 2008). In collectivistic cultures, people are expected to notice the needs of their close others before support is explicitly asked for; personal problem should be solved individually without bothering others as everyone is responsible for the solution to his/her own problems (Kim et al., 2008). As collectivists value group harmony, they seldom disclose their distress to minimise potential loss in relationships and losing face and tend not to seek support.

In a study of the effect of relational goals on social support seeking by the same research group (Kim et al., 2006), European American and Asian American students were primed with different relational goals: (1) *personal goals*, where students were requested to describe their most important personal goals, such as graduating from university, (2) *in-group goals* where they were requested to describe the most important goal of their in-group to which they were closely tied on paper, such as their family's goal to buy a flat, and (3) *out-group goals* where students were requested to describe the most important goal of a group they were not particularly close to, such as a random team's goal to win a game. These writing tasks drew participants' focus to different relationships, and then they reported their most stressful experience and how they would cope with it. It was found that Asian Americans reported 'less social support seeking' and their desire for support seeking was dependent on the salient relational goal (which they were primed with). Asian Americans in in-group goals condition were primed with the importance of relationships and they indeed were 'less willing' to seek support to cope with the stressor. Furthermore, according to Kim et al. (2006), when Asian Americans were primed with in-group goals, they perceived their family and friends as less helpful in assisting them to solve their stressful situations than when they were primed with personal goals.

The result indicates the cultural characteristics among cultures of social support seeking with reference to relationship closeness. People from a collective culture are more aware of the possible restrictions within their relationships with others. The more they value interpersonal relationships the less they are willing to seek social support and have reduced expectation of effectiveness of the support from their significant others. Another study by Sherman et al. (2008) further investigated this culturally significant feature. One member of each of a romantic couple was assigned a stressful task of delivering a speech whereas his/her partner would be given either an easy or difficult puzzle task while he or she was preparing for her speech. Asian Americans, who had to deliver a speech, showed higher sensitivity to the situational constraints on their partners than their European American counterparts. They sought less support when their partners were handling a difficult puzzle task than when their partners was doing an easy one. In contrast, European Americans sought support to an equal extent regardless of what their partners were working on. From the two studies, it can be implied that Asians Americans are generally more concerned about relationships than are European Americans and this leads to their reluctance to seek support from their close others, especially when the close others are occupied (Kim et al., 2008).

Another explanation for the difference between people from collectivistic and individualistic cultures in the use of social support can be viewed from a cognitive perspective. It is suggested there are cultural differences in whether people pay more attention to a focal event or to the social context (Sherman et al., 2009). For example, when you are in urgent need of money (the problem), you may think of borrowing from a friend (the solution). This is when you focus primarily on the problem and solution. However, if you choose to take up part-time jobs instead of asking a friend for help, you may be focusing more on the situational context facing your friends, as you may consider your friend's time, his/her financial status and so on. The differences in focusing on contextual factors may lead to cultural differences in the willingness of social support seeking. Research has shown that Asians and Asian Americans pay more attention to contextual factors than do European Americans as they are more attentive to the background of a focal object (an object that is intended to be focussed on) and social context of an event (Masuda & Nisbett, 2001). For instance, in Chua, Boland and Nisbett's (2005) study of eye movements, Americans fixated on the focal object, while Chinese made more eye movements towards the background.

The cultural significance of using support mainly shows that people from collectivistic cultures use social support to a lesser extent than do people from individualistic cultures (see Kim et al., 2008 for a review). Though, evidences also prove that people from different cultures can all benefit from social support, including social networks, coping with stressors and more (e.g. Morling, Kitayama, & Miyamoto, 2003). The discussion in this section only covers cultural differences in seeking and receiving support from social networks. It appears to be important that the current globalised society has brought people with different cultures together and that cultural differences have become more prominent in our daily life. When we try to provide support with good intentions, we should be aware of others' preferences of support needed, such as a friend from an Asian culture may prefer implicit and indirect support without discussing the issue directly, whereas a friend from a western culture may want more direct and explicit support from you, such as discussing the issue and providing advice or encouragement. Having said that, the influence of globalisation may also decrease the existing cultural differences among different cultures due to the pursuit of common goals and the values prevail in a globalised society. As a whole, the discussion of this section concludes that social support that is congruent with the needs of the recipient always brings about the best outcomes.

Personality May Limit the Amount of Social Support We Get

Increasingly, research literature has shown that tailoring social support is a key to making it more effective (Marigold, Cavallo, Holmes, & Wood, 2014). Social support that adapts to the recipient's personality may also enhance its effectiveness (Simpson et al., 2007). Since the mid-1980s, researchers have begun to recognise the role of personality in coping strategies in response to stress (Parkes, 1986). According to Cohen, Hettler, & Park (1997), personality refers to the individual difference variables, which are relatively stable, including characteristic thoughts, emotional responses and behaviours. Each characteristic is called a personality trait. Up until now, personality traits are believed to have a role in predicting social support (Swickert, Hittner, & Forester, 2010). Pierce, Lakey, Sarason, Sarason, and Joseph (1997) have acknowledged three mechanisms to explain the impact of personality on social support based on the models of personality–environment interactions (Scarr & McCartney, 1983).

The first mechanism, *reactive interaction*, suggests that personality may disturb how support is perceived and responded to. People who receive the same kind of support may perceive it differently. For example, discussing a stressful issue with a calm victim may give him/her rational advice on how to handle his/her problem but it may sound annoying to an emotional person. Actually, studies have demonstrated that emotional individuals are less likely to perceive their social network members to be supportive, compared with their emotionally stable counterparts (Dehle & Landers, 2005). Second, our manner generally evokes reactions from others (Scarr & McCartney, 1983). *Evocative interaction* asserts that it is an individual's personality that influences the way others respond to him/her. In everyday life, if an individual is always mad or hostile to people around, he/she would be viewed as a difficult person and as a result would receive less support from his/her friends (Dehle & Landers, 2005). Lastly, *the social network* of a person determines how much support one can receive and our personality influences the construction of our social network as every individual plays an active role in creating his/her social environment and networks, which in the end influences the sources of social support available to them.

The Big Five, i.e. five-factor model of personality is the general framework for studying relationships between personality traits and social support (Swickert, 2009). It contains five types of basic personality traits: *openness to experience, conscientiousness, extraversion, agreeableness and neuroticism.* According to Finch & Graziano (2001), Lakey & Dickinson (1994) and Swickert, Hittner, Kitos, & Cox-Fuenzalida (2004), people who are high in extraversion, high in agreeableness and low in neuroticism are suggested as the general type of people who perceive higher levels of social support. The characteristics of each of the five factors are discussed in the following.

The trait of *Extraversion* is associated with sociability, excitement-seeking and affection. Extraverts tend to be more outgoing, cheerful and outspoken (Costa & McCrae, 1985). As social support is highly dependent on a person's social network, it is logical to deduce that extraversion is a strong predictor of social support. Compared to introverts, extraverts are more likely to seek support from others when encountering stress (Ficková, 2001). In a study by Amirkhan, Risinger, and Swickert (1995), participants were assigned an unsolvable task and told that they would be allowed to ask for help from an assistant outside the room if it was needed. Results demonstrated that extraverts sought support much earlier than did introverts thus implying that extraverts are more willing to seek social support than introverts. Research has also proven that extraverts are more effective and active copers with stressful situations as they are more likely to make use of various ways, including support seeking, to solve their problems and therefore make coping strategies more effective (Lee-Baggley, Preece, & DeLongis, 2005; Newth & DeLongis, 2004). Aside from copying strategies, extraverts in general also have higher levels of perceived support and larger sizes of social networks. They also contact more often with network members than do introverts (Swickert, Rosentreter, Hittner, & Mushrush, 2002). As an important predictor of social support, extraversion and social support together might influence behavioural and health outcomes, such as having a lower level of depression (Finch & Graziano, 2001) and greater self-esteem (Swickert et al., 2004). In sum, extraverts seem to benefit more from social support than introverts. However, extraverts reveal more distress if they have lower levels of perceived support (Duckitt, 1984; Eastburg, Williamson, Gorsuch, & Ridley, 1994). Therefore, extraverted individuals would be more negatively affected if they do not receive an appropriate amount of support compared with the introverted.

People with high *neuroticism* are often described as emotional, insecure and self-conscious. Due to their high level of negative affect, they may react defensively or self-pitying when they face certain stressful situations. Neurotic individuals are poor copers with stress such that they are more likely to cope through emotional expressions (Newth & DeLongis, 2004). Neuroticism is negatively associated with social support seeking as individuals high in neuroticism are likely to be interpersonally withdrawing, avoidant and self-blaming during times of stress (Lee-Baggley et al., 2005). And not surprisingly, neurotic individuals generally are less satisfied with their social support network (Dehle & Landers, 2005) and neuroticism is found to be significantly associated with depression (Finch & Graziano, 2001). Although neuroticism does not directly predict social support, research has suggested that social support does play a modest mediating role between the relationship of neuroticism and negative outcomes such as depression (Finch & Graziano, 2001), bad quality of life (Burgess et al., 2000) and distress (Suurmeijer et al., 2005). It implies that neurotic individuals are easily stressed out and more physiologically reactive to stress (Suls & Martin, 2005). If they receive unsatisfied support or bad social interactions (such as having a quarrel with someone) when coping with stress, they will suffer from even more distress and negative mood outcomes.

The trait of *agreeableness* is related to trusting, generosity and soft-heartedness. People who are high in agreeableness are viewed as warm, helpful and kind. They are enthused to maintain good relationships with others (Jensen-Campbell & Graziano, 2001) and engage in social interactions that facilitate closeness (Branje, van Lieshout, & van Aken, 2005) such as providing more support to others (Bowling, Beehr, & Swader, 2005), compared with those who are low in agreeableness. Agreeableness is correlated with social support in a few ways. Apart from providing more support to others, agreeable individuals have a higher tendency to seek support when coping with stress (Ficková, 2001) and perceive higher levels of available social support to them (Branje et al., 2005; Finch & Graziano, 2001). Moreover, an interaction effect between agreeableness and social support was found to predict the change in depressive symptoms as shown in a longitudinal study with chronic kidney disease (Hoth, Christensen, Ehlers, Raichle, & Lawton, 2007). As reported from the study, after controlling the baseline levels of depressive symptoms of the patients, agreeableness significantly predicted the patients' depressive symptoms after 17 months, and social support moderated this relationship. It means that patients who were higher in agreeableness and at the same time received more support had a reduction of depressive symptoms at the end of the study. However, those who were low in agreeableness did not benefit in regard to the severity of their depressive symptoms even when they received high levels of social support.

The trait *conscientiousness* is associated with ambition, resourcefulness and determination. People who are high in conscientiousness are described as well organised, careful and self-disciplined. Not much work has been done on the relationship between conscientiousness and social support (Swickert, 2009). According to Asendorpf and Van Aken (2003), conscientious individuals perceive higher levels of available social support, however, other researchers suggest that they also receive little support (Dehle & Landers, 2005 they). Conscientious individuals are seen as competent therefore they are not thought to be people who need support from others (Swickert, 2009); when they receive support from people around, they are easily satisfied and are more satisfied with their support providers (Asendorpf & Van Aken, 2003; Dehle & Landers, 2005). For the trait *openness*, which is related to curiosity, imagination and adventures, its relationships with social support are inconclusive at the moment. It appears that more studies have to be carried out to determine the relationships that exist (Swickert, 2009).

Apart from the Big Five, the relationship between self-esteem and social support has also drawn researchers' attention recently. Self-esteem is described as the evaluation of our own worthiness and value (Neff, 2011). According to Rosenberg, Schooler, Schoenbach, and Rosenberg (1995), a higher self-esteem means more positive evaluation towards oneself. Self-esteem is suggested as a consequence of other processes (e.g. social support), rather than a driving force of other positive outcomes (e.g. health) (Baumeister, Campbell, Krueger, & Vohs, 2003, 2005). Therefore, in some studies of social support, self-esteem was used as a measure of health outcome (e.g. Maddy, Cannon, & Lichtenberger, 2015). Other studies have also shown that high self-esteem is associated with more perceived support (Lakey & Cassady, 1990; Sarason, Sarason, & Pierce, 1990) and more satisfying support from family and friends (Marigold et al., 2014). Therefore, there seem to be difficulties when people with good intentions want to provide effective support to low self-esteem individuals. In Marigold et al.'s (2014) series of study on the support provision to Low Self-esteem individuals (LSEs), the researchers found that support providing positive framing may be viewed as less satisfying and less responded to by LSEs and it was also harmful to their relationships with the LSEs. In contrast, validating their negative thoughts and feelings may be more effective to help them overcome stressors, as LSEs prefer social ties with those who verify their self-view (Marigold et al., 2014; Swann, De La Ronde, & Hixon, 1994) because this is helpful to their mood regulation goals.

In sum, it is important for support providers to understand the recipients' personalities and needs and adjust support attempts accordingly in order to maximise the effectiveness of support provided and not to destroy the relationship bonds between the providers and the recipients.

Gender Differences in the Perception and Utilisation of Social Support

Demographically defined subgroups (e.g. age, gender and ethnicity) often behave differently in social interactions and gender is always a variable being studied in social support research. Gender is often considered as a variable that determines human behaviour differences. According to Keller (1991), gender is a construct that differentiates between males and females in their roles, behaviour and psychological characteristics. Shettima (1998) elaborated that gender attributes roles and actions that distinguish males and females about who they are regarding the expectations of the society. Due to this gender role socialisation having existed in society for a long time in history, the feminine role of women and masculine role of men has resulted in different traits and personality differences as found in research in different disciplines. These differences have also been found to determine the types of support and levels of needs for support in social support research, and some common perceptions are reported in this section.

While gender is regarded as one of the key topics in social support study, it should be noted to readers that gender as a variable to determine differences between male and female on human beings has been challenged over the past few decades. The main argument is that people's gender identities are not only embedded in their physical and biological bodies but also in the intricate historical context (El-Bushra, 2000). The sex role division of male and female cannot be relied on as a valid determinant of behaviour differences due to the historical and cultural changes in societies. Additionally, people's sexual roles, perceptions and orientations have been shown in a wider variety, for example, some people may not even identify their physical sex; they are known as 'transsexuals'. Society's expectations of gender roles have been changed tremendously. Indeed, the fighting for gender equality and feminist studies have been shown in every domain of societal development, such as technology, economy, policy and even religiosity (Connell, 2014; Diehl, Koenig, & Ruckdeschel, 2014; Henwood, 2000; Kabeer, 2016); they have made changes to previously dominant gender role thinking. Therefore, scholars are encouraged not to simply regard gender as a variable of study (Ryan, 2014). In short, rather than being considered a valid concept, gender should be seen as an integral factor in a wider search to deeply comprehend human behaviour with physical and emotional needs, perceptions, motivations, relationships and structures (El-Bushra, 2000).

According to the study of gender influence reported in social support research, the literature has proven that women use more social support when they encounter stressors. In a meta-analysis (Tamres, Janicki, & Helgeson, 2002), the authors reviewed 50 studies of gender differences in using social support, and they significantly confirmed the fact men are less likely to seek support than women regardless of the type of stressor they are dealing with. The gender differences are more salient in emotional support seeking than other type of social support. Actually, men in general hold more negative attitudes towards support seeking behaviours than do women even when help is necessarily needed (Courtenay, 2003). They may rather deny their distress and avoid showing their difficulties or disability (Courtenay, 2000). In contrast, women value more emotional and expressive qualities within close relationships so they are more likely to disclose their distress to family and friends (Burleson, 2003). Since women are more devoted to close relationships with people around, they often receive more support in return (Luszczynska et al. 2007).

Men and women are also different in their views about support seeking behaviours and responsibility attribution. Men utilise more of an 'ethic of justice' kind of moral reasoning while women have a higher tendency to use an 'ethic of care' reasoning (Gilligan, 1982; MacGeorge, 2003). Justice-oriented reasoning focuses on an individual's contribution to one's own problems. Combined with masculine stereotypes about autonomy and self-determination (Auster & Ohm, 2000), men in general attribute more responsibility to the support seekers of the problems and think they should solve the problems themselves, whereas women's care-oriented reasoning places more attention on the support seekers' distress and needs and therefore women attribute less responsibility to the seekers (Jaffee & Hyde, 2000). Furthermore, MacGeorge (2003) continued working on the topic and interestingly found that men seem to attribute more responsibility to male than to female support seekers. They are also angrier at male support seekers who are supposed to be responsible for their own problems. So perhaps females do have an advantage in social support seeking.

Although women in general seek social support more than men do, it does not mean they benefit more from social support since women are more involved in both providing and receiving support (Thoits, 1995; Taylor, 2011). In Luszczynska et al's (2007) study of partners' support to cancer patients with 173 patients and their partners, patients' were interviewed and accessed about support they received from their partners at three time points: 1 week before surgery (Time 1), 1 month (Time 2) and 6 month post-surgery (Time 3). Questionnaires were sent to the partners at Time 1 and 2 to assess the degree of support they provided for the patients. It was found that men and women initially provided comparable amounts of support to their ill partners, however, as time went by, there was a significant decrease in emotional support provided by male partners while female caregivers were still providing the same degree of support to the patients. The results were also confirmed by the spousal support received by the patients throughout the study. Male patients received consistent support from their spouses but female patients received declining amounts of support from their partners. These differences in support provision between men and women are called the support gap (Belle, 1982), in which men receive more support and more helpful support from women than vice versa in marital relationships. In social support research, it has been consistently shown that men receive support mostly from their spouse, whereas women received more support from their female relatives and friends (Luszczynska et al., 2007; Nurullah, 2012).

Furthermore, as shown in a study (Wheeler, Reis, & Nezlek, 1983), women are also more effective support providers than men are. The study recruited undergraduate students who had to remain on campus during the December holidays to see whether they would feel depressed and lonely in such stressful situations. The students were told to keep records of how they spent the days and with whom. They also reported the emotions they came across during the holidays. Surprisingly, the students' loneliness was strongly predicted by how much contact they had with females each day. Regardless of gender, the more time a student stayed with females, the less lonely he/she felt. In contrast, time spent with males did not have any effects on the students' emotional status. Perhaps not only women are generally good support providers but their presence may already be a kind of support to both males and females.

Neff and Karney (2005) found that actually husbands and wives do not differ in the amount of support they provide to their spouses, but they differ in the timing of that support. When men suffer from great stress, they get the most support from their wives as women may adjust their ways of support to meet their partner's needs.

In contrast, when women are experiencing greater stress, their husbands do provide more support but as well show more perceived negative behaviours (e.g. argument, breaking a promise and criticism). These increased negative behaviours can easily undermine their positive supportive acts in women's perception and men are thus perceived as not responsive and less helpful. Previous research has suggested that men and women communicate their needs to their spouses differently, where women rely more frequently on indirect strategies (e.g. simply describing the problem) instead of direct ones (e.g. seeking for specific help) (Cutrona, 1996). And due to the fact that women in general are more empathic (Eagly & Crowley, 1986) and better at understanding nonverbal emotional expressions (Noller, 1980), women may be more capable of detecting their husbands' indirect signals of help requests and therefore able to provide the right kind of support to their stressed partners (Neff & Karney, 2005).

To account for the findings of gender differences in social support seeking and provision, several theoretical models have been proposed (Pierce, Sarason, & Sarason, 1996). Taylor et al. (2000) suggested that these gender differences in provision and reception of support may be due to the biological nature of the ways in which males and females cope with stress. During times of stress, typical 'fight or flight' response may only be applicable to men, whereas women might prefer a 'tend-and-befriend' approach. 'Tend' in this term refers to nurturing actions that may be used to protect oneself and her offspring from danger and stress, and 'befriend' means creating and maintaining social networks—better to include more women—would be helpful in tackling difficult situations. This model is developed on the basis of women's social role as caregivers and that they mainly use an emotion-focus strategy to cope with stress, and thus they prefer seeking social support. The authors argued that while fight and flight is to protect the well-being of an individual, tending the offspring and befriending others in social networks may be effective to protect both oneself and one's descendants.

Another model looks at the issue from the socialisation perspective, which is based on how males and females are socialised. It suggests men are naturally socialised to be independent and women are socialised to seek and make use of social support, and to provide support whenever necessary (Wallace & Jovanovic, 2011). Therefore, men would prefer active and problem-solving strategies whereas women would use more emotional coping strategies when dealing with stress (Brannon, 2011). Similarly, when support provision is needed, men provide less emotional support due to the independent and self-reliant focus of men's socialisation, compared to their female counterparts, who are more sensitive and better-socialised to provide care and emotional support, as well as more willing to be a source of support to others (de Grood & Wallace, 2011).

In sum, previous studies based on the segregated role shaping influences on men and women suggest the differences between male and female in seeking and providing social support to the others. However, as clarified earlier, gender differences may not be a reliable construct in social support research since previous perceptions of gender differences have been changed so that male and female may be expected to share quite common characteristics that are not predicted by traditional gender roles. The research findings outlined under this topic are subject to changes.

The Facilitative and Inhibitive Conditions of Social Support

The conditions under which social support can be positively received/perceived to benefit people, or it may create negative affect on receivers or it is ineffective are discussed to suggest a list of parameters that describe effective social giving. Although the information is not exhaustive, it has proposed some major effective social support measures and the variables that determine them. It describes that effective measures are dependent upon the nature of support, types of support given at different times of need, support givers' relationship with support recipients, support receivers' experience, gender, common cultural differences and personalities. The resultant framework as shown in Fig. 3.2 describes the facilitative and inhibitive conditions that affect the effectiveness of social support. It can be used as a guide to laypersons in providing social support in more thoughtful and appropriate ways; it can also guide professionals to construct intervention programmes in professional practice and help their clients more effectively to overcome the adjustment and adaptation problems they encounter.

Recommendations

Well-being as the Long-Term Goal of School Education

The chapter has identified the underpinnings of social support by relating the effect of social support to the idea of well-being. The concept of well-being illuminates different approaches of viewing human life satisfaction as important to human development. The concerns for psychological well-being in education have been considered by researchers in the past few decades. Researchers had started re-conceptualising education as helping students to attain a fulfilling and actualising self (Eccles & Roeser, 2009), instead of seeing students as failing who need help. The link of social support explored in this chapter has been inspired by the heightened concerns of positive psychology which emphasises students' well-being in the period of growth and development in schools (Niemiec & Ryan, 2009; Ryan & Deci, 2000a, 2000b; Seligman, 2011), and the group of researchers who explored teachers' emotional and social support in the classroom (Ahmed, Minnaert, van der Werf, & Kuyper, 2010; Hargreaves, 1999; Wentzel, 1994; Wentzel et al., 2010; Wilcox, Winn, & Fyvie-Gauld, 2005). The theoretical perspectives and research studies addressed by the authors have commonly suggested that teachers' concerns on learners' psychological functioning processes such as the work teachers do to enhance student motiva-

Invisible support is desirable as it diverts attention from stressful events and increase perception of available support, compared with visible support.	**Imposed support should be avoided** as it harms self-esteem & ignites negative affect, especially when it is mismatched with recipient's needs and may increase burden and cause distress, despite the provider's good intention.	**People tend to offer help to in-group members** or others whom they have close relationships with and less willing to offer help to opponents.	**Good relationships are essential** between support provider and recipient, the closer the relationship between support provider and recipient, the more positive and effective the support is perceived.	**Support from experientially similar peers is effective** because the support provider can show greater empathy due to more understanding of the circumstances.	**Providing support is beneficial to the support provider**. It is a proof of self-worth as those who have the ability to help may have better self-esteem when they feel more competent and needed.

Support from partners may simultaneously may drive positive/negative outcomes: ✓ Mutual support is beneficial when support is equally received/offered; it will enhance the relationship and reduce negative emotions; ✗ Imbalance in support between the couple would increase support receiver's negative affect.	**The Facilitative and Inhibitive Conditions of Social Support**	**People need different types of support at different stages of an event:** On set of an event: - Emotional support Transition: - Informational support Deficit (need resources): - Tangible support	**Different kinds of support valued from different support sources:** Emotional support is expected from kin, while informational support is preferably provided by experts.
Personality influences the receipt of social support Extroverts: • Are effective and active copers of stress • Are more likely to seek social support & perceive higher level of social support • Have a larger size of social support network • Have good relationships with others, actively engaged in social interaction and proactively provide support Neurotics: • Are poor copers of stress with higher negative affect • Are interpersonally withdrawing, avoidant & self-blamed in terms of stress • Are not easily satisfied with their social support network	**Men and women view social support differently:** **Men** in general use less social support as they hold more negative views about help seeking behaviors and they avoid showing their difficulties; **Women** are more caring and provide more effective support than men do and their companion is already a kind of social support regardless of the gender of the recipient.	**Support from Online networks is a double-edged sword:** ✓ Increase users' social capital as support can be acquired from a wider network ✓ Having at least a friend available online improves self-efficacy, lower stress, increase support seeking behaviours ✓ Active participants seek information to improve own problems (e.g. weight loss) ✗ Create negative self-image by upward comparison with others who have better lives ✗ Passive users are more likely to show negative emotions such as jealousy, depression and loneliness.	

Fig. 3.2 The Facilitative and Inhibitive Conditions of Social Support

tion, self-esteem and self-concept has been the consequence of teachers' supportive behaviour, such as interaction with learners and learner-centred teaching methods. This result has suggested a link to social support in health psychology which also concerns about the health and well-being of people in need in different life contexts.

Historically, education in schools received criticism suggesting the defects of an examination-oriented approach and teacher-control education implemented in different societies all over the world (OECD, 2011; Schweisfurth, 2015). The consequences inform us that, approaching the early twenty-first century, students in different countries find themselves as losers and live under academic pressure (Cheung & Chiu, 2016). The social support empirical literature reviewed in this chapter implies that students in school may come from different family backgrounds, who are diverse in terms of abilities, interests and personalities. Hence, education should create opportunities for all students to discover their potential in learning and identifying a more comprehensive and meaningful aim of education that benefit students' healthy development. In such a way it can help students to receive strength and provide the catalyst for students to flourish (Forgeard et al., 2011).

Apart from this, while support is given to students, teachers may consider its long-term outcomes and that support for students is well worth doing, as giving support to cater to the needs of students especially in taking care of individual aversive conditions may require a lot of effort. Feeney & Collins (2015) also proposed that social support occurs in different life contexts and plays different functions in people's lives; the help given to people can temporally precede the core thriving outcomes, similar to 'flourishing' as mentioned by Seligman (2002). This means that education is a process of cultivating the conditions for development for learners, it should be developed over time and accumulated to create positive effects on people's lives. With the insights of seeing education as a long-term goal, the effects of schools providing for students can be tremendous. The discussion also implies that educational support and resources given to students who experience averse life conditions should be more than those who live in advantageous conditions. The governments of different societies may have to design supportive measures, provide resources and train professionals in order to fully cover the needs in each school. For example, the recently promoted inclusive education policy in different countries over the world (integration of students of special educational needs to mainstream schools) and whole-school approach of catering for student differences (Carrington & Robinson, 2006; Forlin, 2010; Mittler, 2012) have to be supported by a vision of care for students and a fully fledged plan to help students of different circumstances to gain support and confidence.

As discussed earlier, the negative backwash effect of examinations (the influence that examinations have on the way students are taught in school where examinations may become the main aim of education) may create anxiety and pressure for both teachers and students. Government officials and policymakers who lead the direction of education should support the holistic development of students, by addressing students' well-being. If school education only focuses on developing the academic competence of students and only recognises academic outcomes, many students, especially those who encounter adjustment issues, and students with special educational needs and low academic achievement, may suffer from continuous frustration (Lam, 2011). In such cases, students would probably feel that they are not valued and supported, and develop low self-esteem. In fact, external demands from the social environment may dictate teachers' classroom practices in schools, because of the predominant achievement culture in society where some teachers may become more and more concerned about end results, giving less and less time to the detailed work of caring about students' growth. Practices such as creating positive experience, enhancing self-esteem and giving students opportunities to realise their own competence in areas that represent students' own strength and interest could be contradictory or time-consuming if the priority of education is to achieve short-term examination results. The evidence that students' mental health issues are growing in schools (Polanczyk, Salum, Sugaya, Caye, & Rohde, 2015; Storrie, Ahern, & Tuckett, 2010) could be the consequence of such an approach to education. In fact, satisfactory well-being can help students to achieve better results, unlike academic pressure which creates student disengagement in schooling. Concerted efforts in changing the examination culture and short-term goal in school education should be made in society in order to create opportunities for students and to enhance their sense of competence, self-esteem and motivation to learn and achieve.

Social Support as a Topic of Study for Teachers

Regarding professional support, teachers in the twenty-first century should equip themselves with a wide range of knowledge so that they can ensure that all learners are included and the learning environment suits every learner. Apart from subject knowledge and pedagogical knowledge, teachers should develop a stronger knowledge base related to multiculturalism and diversity of learners, and acquire a deeper understanding about the cause of emotional, deviant and antisocial behaviour problems of children and young adolescents. Social support is a topic that deals with human's innate needs for social bonds and belongingness, psychological well-being, social integration and the tactics and skills of social support; this topic can help teachers to contextualise their role in teaching and appreciate the humanistic nature of education by realising the psychological needs of learners and expanding the role of teachers in their care of students' well-being. The knowledge of social support and the supportive role of teachers should be included in teacher education programmes to prepare teachers for classroom teaching.

Furthermore, as academic results are supposed to be one of the many outcome measures of education, the insights developed from this chapter suggest that the outcomes social support aspires to, including self-esteem, self-worth, motivation, belongingness, competence and positive affect, can be largely adopted as indicators of success in terms of educational outcomes. Stronger emphasis on giving emotional support to learners inspires teachers to pay more attention in their interaction with students and in the delivery of instruction in the classroom. By considering the humanistic values in education as illustrated by the concept of social support and well-being, teachers can truly realise their professional role in the classroom, they are able to see teaching more as an art than a technical job; this can help teachers to develop the art of communication with students and generate learner-centred pedagogies which support the growth of students in an all-round manner.

The resource list of factors and parameters that guides effective social support as a result of the investigations described in this chapter implies the intricate and subtle nature of interaction between teachers and students. While teachers often assume a supportive role in the classroom and teachers' care is often valued, the nature and form of support teachers give to students in teaching is not systematically addressed in the teacher education literature because of its intangible nature. The parameters suggested in the findings regarding effective social support measures which take note of social support receivers' self-esteem, their relationship with the social support givers in the social environment, personality, gender and culture can be a guide for teachers to explore their supportive actions in the educational environment. For examples, while support should be given to low achievers in teaching, the types of support should not be often made visible to avoid specifying and labelling the weaknesses of these students; and support given to students should be monitored so that the changing needs can be taken care of.

The knowledge of social support is also important for every member of society. The effectiveness of social support giving and the appropriate strategies of giving social support as discussed in this chapter can be used as a guide to laypersons in giving social support to others in more thoughtful and appropriate ways. Social support is useful in almost all professional and organisational settings as mentoring, exchange and sharing of knowledge is an important part of knowledge management that can help individuals' professional and career development and support organisational growth. The growing needs for social support have also become more prominent in the twenty-first century as people encounter greater challenges in living; it is a catalyst to promote social support in different professional settings and for building up a healthy society.

Conclusion

The chapter provides both theoretical and empirical evidences to conceptualise well-being as the outcomes of social support. It illustrates how social support can help human beings overcome stress due to different life changes and circumstances, which lead them to better adjustment and integration into society. Social support can advance people's satisfaction in life. The chapter examines different constructs and theories related to the well-being of human beings. The concepts discussed include the subjective measure of well-being, economic value of well-being, positive and negative affect; self-determination, self-actualisation, social psychological development of human beings and socio-emotional development: they converge to provide readers with an exhaustive explanation of well-being and how they are related to social support. Furthermore, based on the backdrop provided by the well-being literature,

Conclusion 121

the chapter discusses the psychological status and adaptation processes of various groups of people in society who encounter life situations and experience critical circumstances which may cause them to pay a high price in regulating their emotions and adjusting their selves in living in the social environment. The conditions being discussed include poor health conditions (mental health and physical health), and people who experience transition such as retirement, transition to college, and immigration. Finally, a list of facilitative and inhibitive conditions to govern effective social support is compiled based on varied empirical sources reporting social support research results: the resultant picture can provide reliable knowledge to readers for understanding the nature of social support.

While the exploration of literature in this chapter has resulted in a picture that is composed of the general factors and parameters that define effective social support conditions and strategies and can be used as a guide for social support practice, the cultural specificity in the research that generalises such suggestions has not been attended to in fine-grained detail nor did the research sources provide such details for a thorough analysis. This limitation should be addressed; and such limitations can be overcome by verification based on further research based on the applications of such ideas in different cultural contexts. It might also be possible that the research findings regarding cultural studies and gender studies which were drawn for analysis in the report in this chapter contain suspected biases, as such results were not discussed extensively compared with diverse cultural settings. Also, due to the influence of globalisation in the twenty-first century, cultural boundaries between different countries might not have existed as clearly as before; this has decreased the cultural differences among people in different cultural contexts. The policy of accommodating cultural diversities in many societies in the current twenty-first century preserves cultural diversity; at the same time, this policy makes a deep-rooted division of cultural differences less distinctive, such as the typical cultural differences conceptualised in the countries of the east and west. The situation also makes cultural difference a less significant topic in social support studies. With regard to gender, since the nature of society has made tremendous changes to the culture and living of people over the past few decades, the gender-differentiated roles of people in societies may not generate differences as they are in the studies discussed in this chapter. Hence, some of and cases of social support giving describe in the chapter may be subject to changes. Further studies may be necessary to further enrich the ideas addressed in the current results in light of the social changes prompted by technological advancement and globalisation in the twenty-first century. Finally, this chapter identifies the potential of utilising social support and taking note of the concerns of giving social support in different professions, especially for those which involve human interaction such as the service profession, for example, the role of teachers in the teaching profession. The chapter also suggests social support tactics for applications in different social settings to benefit more people in the society.

Chapters 2 and 3 have explored the meaning, theoretical underpinnings and the application of social support to people in need in different circumstances. The chapters provide substantial background information regarding the theory and practice of social support that can be applied to view learning, teaching and teacher development in the field of education, and these topics will be discussed in forthcoming chapters of the book (Fig. 3.2).

References

Adams, G. (2005). The cultural grounding of personal relationship: Enemyship in North American and West African worlds. *Journal of Personality and Social Psychology, 88*(6), 948–968.

Adams, G., & Plaut, V. C. (2003). The cultural grounding of personal relationship: Friendship in North American and West African worlds. *Personal Relationships, 10*(3), 333–347.

Ahmed, W., Minnaert, A., van der Werf, G., & Kuyper, H. (2010). Perceived social support and early adolescents' achievement: The mediational roles of motivational beliefs and emotions. *Journal of Youth and Adolescence, 39*(1), 36.

Amirkhan, J. H., Risinger, R. T., & Swickert, R. J. (1995). Extraversion: A "hidden" personality factor in coping? *Journal of Personality, 63*(2), 189–212.

Andrews, F. M., & Withey, S. B. (1976). *Social indicators of well-being.* New York and London: Plenum.

Arnett, J. J. (2000). Emerging adulthood: A theory of development from the late teens through the twenties. *American Psychologist, 55,* 469–480.

Arora, N. K., Finney Rutten, L. J., Gustafson, D. H., Moser, R., & Hawkins, R. P. (2007). Perceived helpfulness and impact of social support provided by family, friends, and health care providers to women newly diagnosed with breast cancer. *Psycho-Oncology, 16*(5), 474–486.

Arseneault, L., Walsh, E., Trzesniewski, K., Newcombe, R., Caspi, A., & Moffitt, T. E. (2006). Bullying victimization uniquely contributes to adjustment problems in young children: A nationally representative cohort study. *Pediatrics, 118,* 130–138.

Asendorpf, J. B., & Van Aken, M. A. (2003). Personality–relationship transaction in adolescence: Core versus surface personality characteristics. *Journal of Personality, 71*(4), 629–666.

Auster, C. J., & Ohm, S. C. (2000). Masculinity and femininity in contemporary American society: A reevaluation using the Bem Sex-Role Inventory. *Sex roles, 43*(7), 499–528.

Bandura, A. (1988). Self-efficacy conception of anxiety. *Anxiety Research, 1*(2). 77–98.

Bandura, A. (1997). *Self-efficacy: The exercise of control.* New York: Freeman.

Baruch-Feldman, C., Brondolo, E., Ben-Dayan, D., & Schwartz, J. (2002). Sources of social support and burnout, job satisfaction, and productivity. *Journal of Occupational Health Psychology, 7*(1), 84–93.

Baumeister, R. F., Campbell, J. D., Krueger, J. I., & Vohs, K. D. (2003). Does high self-esteem cause better performance, interpersonal success, happiness, or healthier lifestyles? *Psychological Science in the Public Interest, 4*(1), 1–44.

Baumeister, R. F., Campbell, J. D., Krueger, J. I., & Vohs, K. D. (2005). Exploding the self-esteem myth. *Scientific American, 292*(1), 84–91.

Bavojdan, M. R., Towhidi, A., & Rahmati, A. (2012). The relationship between mental health and general self-efficacy beliefs, coping strategies and locus of control in male drug abusers. *Addiction and Health, 3*(3–4), 111–118.

Becker, B. B., & Luthar, S. S. (2002). Social-emotional factors affecting achievement outcomes among disadvantaged students: Closing the achievement gap. *Educational Psychologist, 37*(4), 197–214.

Beehr, T. A., Bowling, N. A., & Bennett, M. M. (2010). Occupational stress and failures of social support: When helping hurts. *Journal of Occupational Health Psychology, 15*(1), 45–59.

Bell, V. (2007). Online information, extreme communities and internet therapy: Is the internet good for our mental health? *Journal of Mental Health, 16*(4), 445–457.

References

Belle, D. (1982). The stress of caring: Women as providers of social support. In L. Goldberger & S. Breznitz (Eds.), *Handbook of stress: Theoretical and clinical aspects* (pp. 496–505). New York: Free Press.

Bolger, N., & Amarel, D. (2007). Effects of social support visibility on adjustment to stress: Experimental evidence. *Journal of Personality and Social Psychology, 92*(3), 458–475.

Bolger, N., Zuckerman, A., & Kessler, R. C. (2000). Invisible support and adjustment to stress. *Journal of Personality and Social Psychology, 79*(6), 953–961.

Booth, T. (2000). Inclusion and exclusion policy in England: Who controls the agenda? In F. Armstrong, D. Armstrong, & L. Barton (Eds.), *Inclusive education: Policy, contexts and comparative perspectives*. London: David Fulton.

Bowlby, J. (1980). *Attachment and loss: Vol. 3. Loss: Sadness and depression*. New York: Basic books.

Bowlby, J. (1982). Attachment and loss: Retrospect and prospect. *American Journal of Orthopsychiatry, 52*(4), 664–678.

Bowling, N. A., Beehr, T. A., & Swader, W. M. (2005). Giving and receiving social support at work: The roles of personality and reciprocity. *Journal of Vocational Behavior, 67*(3), 476–489.

Branje, S. J., van Lieshout, C. F., & van Aken, M. A. (2005). Relations between agreeableness and perceived support in family relationships: Why nice people are not always supportive. *International Journal of Behavioral Development, 29*(2), 120–128.

Brannon, L. (2011). *Gender: Psychological perspectives* (6th ed.). Boston: Allyn & Bacon.

Brown, L. F., Kroenke, K., Theobald, D. E., Wu, J., & Tu, W. (2010). The association of depression and anxiety with health-related quality of life in cancer patients with depression and/or pain. *Psycho-Oncology, 19*(7), 734–741.

Burgess, A. P., Carretero, M., Elkington, A., Pasqual-Marsettin, E., Lobaccaro, C., & Catalan, J. (2000). The role of personality, coping style and social support in health-related quality of life in HIV infection. *Quality of Life Research, 9*(4), 423–437.

Burke, M., Marlow, C., & Lento, T. (2010). Social network activity and social well-being. In *Proceedings of the SIGCHI Conference on Human Factors in Computing Systems, Atlanta, USA* (pp. 1909–1912).

Burleson, B. R. (2003). The experience and effects of emotional support: What the study of cultural and gender differences can tell us about close relationships, emotion, and interpersonal communication. *Personal Relationships, 10*(1), 1–23.

Burleson, B. R. (2009). Understanding the outcomes of supportive communication: A dual-process approach. *Journal of Social and Personal Relationships, 26*(1), 21–38.

Buunk, B. P., & Schaufeli, W. B. (1999). Reciprocity in interpersonal relationships: An evolutionary perspective on its importance for health and well-being. *European Review of Social Psychology, 10*(1), 259–291.

Cacioppo, J. T., & Berntson, G. G. (1999). The affect system architecture and operating characteristics. *Current Directions in Psychological Science, 8*(5), 133–137.

Carlson, J., Watts, R. E., & Maniacci, M. (2006). *Adlerian therapy: Theory and practice*. Washington, DC: American Psychological Association.

Carr, A. (2011). *Positive psychology: The science of happiness and human strengths*. London/New York: Routledge.

Carrington, S., & Robinson, R. (2006). Inclusive school community: Why is it so complex? *International Journal of Inclusive Education, 10*(4–5), 323–334.

Census and Statistics Department. (2012). *Hong Kong 2011 Population Census Thematic Report: Ethnic Minorities*. Retrieved from http://www.statistics.gov.hk/pub/B11200622012XXXXB0100.pdf.

Center for Substance Abuse Treatment. (2005). *Substance abuse treatment for persons with co-occurring disorders*. Treatment Improvement Protocol (TIP) Series 42. DHHS Publication No. (SMA) 05-3922. Rockville, MD: Substance Abuse and Mental Health Services Administration.

Celeste, M., & Grum, D. K. (2010). Social integration of children with visual impairment: A developmental model. *İlköğretim Online, 9*(1).

Chan, K. L. (2005). *Study on child abuse and spouse battering: Report on findings of household survey. [A consultancy study commissioned by the SWD of the HKSAR]*. Hong Kong: Department of Social Work & Social Administration, the University of Hong Kong.

Cheung, E. & Chiu, P. (2016, March 12). Students at breaking point: Hong Kong announces emergency measures after 22 suicides since the start of the academic year. *The South China Morning Post*. Retrieved from http://www.scmp.com/news/hong-kong/health-environment/article/1923465/students-breaking-point-hong-kong-announces.

Chu, T. Q., Kim, H. S., & Sherman, D. K. (2008, February). *Culture and the perceptions of implicit and explicit social support use*. Poster Presented at the Annual Meeting of the Society for Personality and Social Psychology, Albuquerque, NM.

Chua, H. F., Boland, J. E., & Nisbett, R. E. (2005). Cultural variation in eye movements during scene perception. *Proceedings of the National Academy of Sciences of the United States of America, 102*(35), 12629–12633.

Clarke, K. K., Freeland-Graves, J., Klohe-Lehman, D. M., & Bohman, T. M. (2007). Predictors of weight loss in low-income mothers of young children. *Journal of the American Dietetic Association, 107*(7), 1146–1154.

Cobb, S. (1976). Social support as a moderator of life stress. *Psychosomatic Medicine, 38*(5), 300–314.

Cohen, L. H., Hettler, T. R., & Park, C. L. (1997). Social support, personality, and life stress adjustment. In G. R. Pierce, B. Lakey, & I. G. Sarason (Eds.), *Sourcebook of social support and personality* (pp. 215–228). New York: Plenum.

Cohen, S., & Wills, T. A. (1985). Stress, social support, and the buffering hypothesis. *Psychological Bulletin, 98*(2), 310–357.

Collins, N. L., & Feeney, B. C. (2000). A safe haven: An attachment theory perspective on support seeking and caregiving in intimate relationships. *Journal of Personality and Social Psychology, 78*(6), 1053–1073.

Connell, R. (2014). Rethinking gender from the South. *Feminist Studies, 40*(3), 518–539.

Constantino, R. E., Sekula, L. K., Rabin, B., & Stone, C. (2000). Negative life experiences negative life experiences, depression, and immune function in abused and nonabused women. *Biological Research for Nursing, 1*(3), 190–198.

Copeland, J., & Hall, W. (1992). A comparison of women seeking drug and alcohol treatment in a specialist women's and two traditional mixed-sex treatment services. *British Journal of Addiction, 87*(9), 1293–1302.

Costa, P. T., & McCrae, R. R. (1985). *The NEO Personality Inventory manual*. Odessa, FL: Psychological Assessment Resources.

Courtenay, W. H. (2000). Behavioral factors associated with disease, injury, and death among men: Evidence and implications for prevention. *The Journal of Men's Studies, 9*(1), 81–142.

Courtenay, W. H. (2003). Key determinants of the health and well-being of men and boys. *International Journal of Men's Health, 2*(1), 1–30.

Cutrona, C. E. (1996). *Social support in couples: Marriage as a resource in times of stress* (Vol. 13). Thousand Oaks, CA: Sage Publications.

Cutrona, C. E., & Cole, V. (2000). Optimizing support in the natural network. In S. Cohen, L. G. Underwood, & B. H. Gottlieb (Eds.), *Social support measurement and intervention: A guide for health and social scientists* (pp. 278–308). New York: Oxford University Press.

Cutrona, C. E., Russell, D. W., Brown, P. A., Clark, L. A., Hessling, R. M., & Gardner, K. A. (2005). Neighborhood context, personality, and stressful life events as predictors of depression among African American women. *Journal of Abnormal Psychology, 114*(1), 3–15.

Dakof, G. A., & Taylor, S. E. (1990). Victims' perceptions of social support: What is helpful from whom? *Journal of Personality and Social Psychology, 58*(1), 80–89.

de Charms, R. (1968). *Personal causation*. New York: Academic Press.

de Grood, J. A., & Wallace, J. E. (2011). In sickness and in health: An exploration of spousal support and occupational similarity. *Work & Stress, 25*(3), 272–287.

References

Deci, E. L., & Ryan, R. M. (1985). *Intrinsic motivation and self-determination in human behaviour*. New York: Plenum.

Deci, E. L., & Ryan, R. M. (2000). The "what" and "why" of goal pursuits: Human needs and the self-determination of behavior. *Psychological Inquiry, 11*(4), 227–268.

Deelstra, J. T., Peeters, M. C., Schaufeli, W. B., Stroebe, W., Zijlstra, F. R., & van Doornen, L. P. (2003). Receiving instrumental support at work: When help is not welcome. *Journal of Applied Psychology, 88*(2), 324.

Dehle, C., & Landers, J. E. (2005). You can't always get what you want, but can you get what you need? Personality traits and social support in marriage. *Journal of Social and Clinical Psychology, 24*(7), 1051–1076.

DeNeve, K. M. (1999). Happy as an extraverted clam? The role of personality for subjective well-being. *Current Directions in Psychological Science, 8*(5), 141–144.

Diehl, C., Koenig, M., & Ruckdeschel, K. (2014). Religiosity and gender equality: Comparing natives and Muslim migrants in Germany. *Gender, Race and Religion*, 75–98.

Diener, E., Lucas, R. E., & Oishi, S. (2002). Subjective well-being. *Handbook of Positive Psychology, 16*(2), 63–73.

Diener, E., & Seligman, M. E. (2002). Very happy people. *Psychological Science, 13*(1), 81–84.

Dosani, S., Harding, C., & Wilson, S. (2014). Online groups and patient forums. *Current Psychiatry Reports, 16*(11), 1–6.

Duckitt, J. (1984). Social support, personality and the prediction of psychological distress: An interactionist approach. *Journal of Clinical Psychology, 40*(5), 1199–1205.

Dunkel-Schetter, C., Blasband, D. E., Feinstein, L. G., & Herbert, T. B. (1992). Elements of supportive interactions: When are attempts to help effective? In S. Spacapan & S. Oskamp (Eds.), *Helping and being helped: Naturalistic studies* (pp. 83–114). Thousand Oaks, CA, US: Sage Publications.

Dunn, J., & Layard, R. (2009). *A good childhood: Searching for values in a competitive age*. Penguin UK.

Eagly, A. H., & Crowley, M. (1986). Gender and helping behavior: A meta-analytic review of the social psychological literature. *Psychological Bulletin, 100*(3), 283–308.

Eastburg, M. C., Williamson, M., Gorsuch, R., & Ridley, C. (1994). Social support, personality, and burnout in nurses. *Journal of Applied Social Psychology, 24*(14), 1233–1250.

Eby, L., Buits, M., Lockwood, A., & Simon, S. A. (2004). Protégés negative mentoring experiences: Construct development and nomological validation. *Personnel Psychology, 57*(2), 411–447.

Eccles, J., & Roeser, R. (2009). Schools, academic motivation, and stageeenvironment fit. In R. M. Learner, & L. Steinberg (Eds.), *Handbook of adolescent psychology* (3rd ed.). (pp. 404–434). Hoboken, NJ: John Wiley & Sons.

El-Bushra, J. (2000). Rethinking gender and development practice for the twenty-first century. *Gender & Development, 8*(1), 55–62.

Erikson, E. H. (1959). Identity and the life cycle: Selected papers. *Psychological Issues, 1*, 1–71.

Erikson, E. H. (1968). *Youth: Identity and crisis*. New York: NY, WW.

Feeney, B. C., & Collins, N. L. (2015). A new look at social support: A theoretical perspective on thriving through relationships. *Personality and Social Psychology Review, 19*(2), 113–147.

Feng, B., & Hyun, M. J. (2012). The influence of friends' instant messenger status on individuals' coping and support-seeking. *Communication Studies, 63*(5), 536–553.

Ficková, E. (2001). Personality regulators of coping behavior in adolescents. *Studia Psychologica, 43*(4), 321–329.

Finch, J. F., & Graziano, W. G. (2001). Predicting depression from temperament, personality, and patterns of social relations. *Journal of Personality, 69*(1), 27–55.

Fisher, S., & Hood, B. (1987). The stress of the transition to university: A longitudinal study of psychological disturbance, absent-mindedness and vulnerability to homesickness. *British Journal of Psychology, 78*(4), 425–441.

Fisher, J. D., Nadler, A., & Whitcher-Alagna, S. (1982). Recipient reactions to aid. *Psychological Bulletin, 91*(1), 27–54.

Forgeard, M. J., Jayawickreme, E., Kern, M. L., & Seligman, M. E. (2011). Doing the right thing: Measuring wellbeing for public policy. *International Journal of Wellbeing, 1*(1), 79–106.

Forlin, C. (2010). Developing and implementing quality inclusive education in Hong Kong: Implications for teacher education. *Journal of Research in Special Educational Needs, 10,* 177–184.

Frison, E., & Eggermont, S. (2016). Exploring the relationships between different types of Facebook use, perceived online social support, and adolescents' depressed mood. *Social Science Computer Review, 34*(2), 153–171.

Gall, T. L., Evans, D. R., & Bellerose, S. (2000). Transition to first-year university: Patterns of change in adjustment across life domains and time. *Journal of Social and Clinical Psychology, 19*(4), 544–567.

Gemmill, E. L., & Peterson, M. (2006). Technology use among college students: Implications for student affairs professionals. *NASPA Journal, 43*(2), 280–300.

Gilligan, C. (1982). *In a different voice.* Cambridge, MA: Harvard University Press.

Gleason, M. E., Iida, M., Bolger, N., & Shrout, P. E. (2003). Daily supportive equity in close relationships. *Personality and Social Psychology Bulletin, 29*(8), 1036–1045.

GO-Globe Web Design Hong Kong. (2015, May 16). *Social media usage in Hong Kong—Statistics and trends* [Web log post]. Retrieved from http://www.go-globe.hk/blog/social-media-hong-kong/.

Graham, K., & Homel, R. (2008). *Raising the bar: Preventing violence in and around bars, pubs and clubs.* Oregon: Willan Publishing.

Groh, D. R., Jason, L. A., Davis, M. I., Olson, B. D., & Ferrari, J. R. (2007). Friends, family, and alcohol abuse: An examination of general and alcohol-specific social support. *American Journal on Addictions, 16*(1), 49–55.

Gross, J. J., & John, O. P. (2003). Individual differences in two emotion regulation processes: Implications for affect, relationships, and well-being. *Journal of Personality and Social Psychology, 85*(2), 348–362.

Haas, S. M., Irr, M. E., Jennings, N. A., & Wagner, L. M. (2011). Online negative enabling support groups. *New Media & Society, 13*(1), 40–57.

Haferkamp, N., & Krämer, N. C. (2011). Social comparison 2.0: Examining the effects of online profiles on social-networking sites. *Cyberpsychology, Behavior, and Social Networking, 14*(5), 309–314.

Hamre, B. K., & Pianta, R. C. (2001). Early teacher–child relationships and the trajectory of children's school outcomes through eighth grade. *Child Development, 72*(2), 625–638.

Hargreaves, A. (1999). The psychic rewards (and annoyances) of teaching. In M. Hammersley (Ed.), *Researching school experience: Ethnographic studies of teaching and learning* (pp. 85–104). London & New York: Falmer Press.

Haslam, S. A., Reicher, S. D., & Levine, M. (2012). When other people are heaven, when other people are hell: How social identity determines the nature and impact of social support. In J. Jetten, C. Haslam, & S. A. Haslam (Eds.), *The social cure: Identity, health, and wellbeing* (pp. 157–174). London & New York: Psychology Press.

Heflin, C. M., & Pattillo, M. (2006). Poverty in the family: Race, siblings, and socioeconomic heterogeneity. *Social Science Research, 35*(4), 804–822.

Henwood, F. (2000). From the woman question in technology to the technology question in feminism: Rethinking gender equality in IT education. *European Journal of Women's Studies, 7*(2), 209–227.

Hong Kong SAR Government. (2016). *Hong Kong Poverty Situation Report 2015.* Retrieved from http://www.povertyrelief.gov.hk/pdf/poverty_report_2015_e.pdf.

Hong, Y., Pena-Purcell, N. C., & Ory, M. G. (2012). Outcomes of online support and resources for cancer survivors: A systematic literature review. *Patient Education and Counseling, 86*(3), 288–296.

Hoth, K. F., Christensen, A. J., Ehlers, S. L., Raichle, K. A., & Lawton, W. J. (2007). A longitudinal examination of social support, agreeableness and depressive symptoms in chronic kidney disease. *Journal of Behavioral Medicine, 30*(1), 69–76.

References

Howland, M., & Simpson, J. A. (2010). Getting in under the radar a dyadic view of invisible support. *Psychological Science, 21*(12), 1878–1885.

Huber, M., Knottnerus, J. A., Green, L., van der Horst, H., Jadad, A. R., Kromhout, D., ... & Schnabel, P. (2011). How should we define health? *Bmj, 343*, d4163.

Itkowitz, N. I., Kerns, R. D., & Otis, J. D. (2003). Support and coronary heart disease: The importance of significant other responses. *Journal of Behavioral Medicine, 26*(1), 19–30.

Jacobson, D. E. (1986). Types and timing of social support. *Journal of Health and Social Behavior, 27*(3), 250–264.

Jacobson, N., & Greenley, D. (2001). What is recovery? A conceptual model and explication. *Psychiatric Services, 52*(4), 482–485.

Jaffee, S., & Hyde, J. S. (2000). Gender differences in moral orientation: A meta-analysis. *Psychological Bulletin, 126*(5), 703–726.

Jensen-Campbell, L. A., & Graziano, W. G. (2001). Agreeableness as a moderator of interpersonal conflict. *Journal of Personality, 69*(2), 323–362.

Jones, R., Sharkey, S., Ford, T., Emmens, T., Hewis, E., Smithson, J., ... & Owens, C. (2011). Online discussion forums for young people who self-harm: User views. *The Psychiatrist Online, 35*(10), 364–368.

Kabeer, N. (2016). Gender equality, economic growth, and women's agency: The "endless variety" and "monotonous similarity" of patriarchal constraints. *Feminist Economics, 22*(1), 295–321.

Karlsen, S., & Nazroo, J. Y. (2002). Relation between racial discrimination, social class, and health among ethnic minority groups. *American Journal of Public Health, 92*(4), 624–631.

Kasser, T., & Ryan, R. M. (1996). Further examining the American dream: Differential correlates of intrinsic and extrinsic goals. *Personality and Social Psychology Bulletin, 22*(3), 280–287.

Keller, E. F. (1991). Gender and science. In E. Thermey (Ed.), *Women's studies encyclopedia* (pp. 153–156). New York: Peter Beduck.

Kernic, M. A., Wolf, M. E., & Holt, V. L. (2000). Rates and relative risk of hospital admission among women in violent intimate partner relationships. *American Journal of Public Health, 90*(9), 1416–1420.

Keyes, C. L., & Annas, J. (2009). Feeling good and functioning well: Distinctive concepts in ancient philosophy and contemporary science. *The Journal of Positive Psychology, 4*(3), 197–201.

Kim, H. S. (2008). Culture and the cognitive and neuroendocrine responses to speech. *Journal of Personality and Social Psychology, 94*(1), 32–47.

Kim, H. S., & Sherman, D. K. (2007). "Express yourself": Culture and the effect of self-expression on choice. *Journal of Personality and Social Psychology, 92*(1), 1–11.

Kim, H. S., Sherman, D. K., Ko, D., & Taylor, S. E. (2006). Pursuit of comfort and pursuit of harmony: Culture, relationships, and social support seeking. *Personality and Social Psychology Bulletin, 32*(12), 1595–1607.

Kim, H. S., Sherman, D. K., & Taylor, S. E. (2008). Culture and social support. *American Psychologist, 63*(6), 518–526.

Kitayama, S., & Uchida, Y. (2005, March). Interdependent agency: An alternative system for action. In R. M. Sorrentino, D. Cohen, J. M. Olson, & M. P. Zanna (Eds.), *Cultural and social behavior: The Ontario symposium* (Vol. 10, pp. 137–164). Mahwah, NJ: Lawrence Erlbaum.

Kross, E., Verduyn, P., Demiralp, E., Park, J., Lee, D. S., Lin, N., ... & Ybarra, O. (2013). Facebook use predicts declines in subjective well-being in young adults. *PloS One, 8*(8), e69841.

Lakey, B., & Cassady, P. B. (1990). Cognitive processes in perceived social support. *Journal of Personality and Social Psychology, 59*(2), 337–343.

Lakey, B., & Dickinson, L. G. (1994). Antecedents of perceived support: Is perceived family environment generalized to new social relationships? *Cognitive Therapy and Research, 18*(1), 39–53.

Lam, B. H. (2011). A reflective account of a preservice teacher's effort to implement a progressive curriculum in field practice. *Schools, 8*(1), 22–39.

Leary, M. R. (2007). Motivational and emotional aspects of the self. *Annual Review of Psychology, 58*, 317–344.

Lee, R. M. (2005). Resilience against discrimination: Ethnic identity and other-group orientation as protective factors for Korean Americans. *Journal of Counseling Psychology, 52*(1), 36–44.

Lee-Baggley, D., Preece, M., & DeLongis, A. (2005). Coping with interpersonal stress: Role of Big Five traits. *Journal of Personality, 73*(5), 1141–1180.

Levine, R. M., Prosser, A., Evans, D., & Reicher, S. D. (2005). Identity and emergency intervention: How social group membership and inclusiveness of group boundaries shapes helping behavior. *Personality and Social Psychology Bulletin, 31,* 443–453.

Levitt, M. J., Lane, J. D., & Levitt, J. (2005). Immigration stress, social support, and adjustment in the first postmigration year: An intergenerational analysis. *Research in Human Development, 2*(4), 159–177.

Lewis, S. P., & Michal, N. J. (2016). Start, stop, and continue: Preliminary insight into the appeal of self-injury e-communities. *Journal of health psychology, 21*(2), 250–260.

Lin, C. P., & Bhattacherjee, A. (2009). Understanding online social support and its antecedents: A socio-cognitive model. *The Social Science Journal, 46*(4), 724–737.

Lucas, R. E., Diener, E., & Suh, E. (1996). Discriminant validity of well-being measures. *Journal of Personality and Social Psychology, 71*(3), 616–628.

Luszczynska, A., Boehmer, S., Knoll, N., Schulz, U., & Schwarzer, R. (2007). Emotional support for men and women with cancer: Do patients receive what their partners provide? *International Journal of Behavioral Medicine, 14*(3), 156–163.

Luttik, M. L., Jaarsma, T., Moser, D., Sanderman, R., & van Veldhuisen, D. J. (2005). The importance and impact of social support on outcomes in patients with heart failure: An overview of the literature. *Journal of Cardiovascular Nursing, 20*(3), 162–169.

MacGeorge, E. L. (2003). Gender differences in attributions and emotions in helping contexts. *Sex Roles, 48*(3), 175–182.

Maddy, L. M., Cannon, J. G., & Lichtenberger, E. J. (2015). The effects of social support on self-esteem, self-efficacy, and job search efficacy in the unemployed. *Journal of Employment Counseling, 52*(2), 87–95.

Malecki, C. K., & Demaray, M. K. (2003). What type of support do they need? Investigating student adjustment as related to emotional, informational, appraisal, and instrumental support. *School Psychology Quarterly, 18*(3), 231–252.

Marigold, D. C., Cavallo, J. V., Holmes, J. G., & Wood, J. V. (2014). You can't always give what you want: The challenge of providing social support to low self-esteem individuals. *Journal of Personality and Social Psychology, 107*(1), 56–80.

Markowitz, F. E. (2001). Modeling processes in recovery from mental illness: Relationships between symptoms, life satisfaction, and self-concept. *Journal of Health and Social Behavior,* 64–79.

Markus, H. R., & Kitayama, S. (1991). Culture and the self: Implications for cognition, emotion, and motivation. *Psychological Review, 98*(2), 224–253.

Maslow, A. H. (1943). A theory of human motivation. *Psychological Review, 50*(4), 370–396.

Masuda, T., & Nisbett, R. E. (2001). Attending holistically versus analytically: Comparing the context sensitivity of Japanese and Americans. *Journal of Personality and Social Psychology, 81*(5), 922–934.

Maton, K. I., & Salem, D. A. (1995). Organizational characteristics of empowering community settings: A multiple case study approach. *American Journal of Community Psychology, 23*(5), 631–656.

Mausbach, B. T., Patterson, T. L., Rabinowitz, Y. G., Grant, I., & Schulz, R. (2007). Depression and distress predict time to cardiovascular disease in dementia caregivers. *Health Psychology, 26*(5), 539–544.

McAllister, I., & Makkai, T. (2003). Antisocial behaviour among young Australians while under the influence of illicit drugs. *Australian & New Zealand Journal of Criminology, 36*(2), 211–222.

McFarland, J., Stark, P., and Cui, J. (2016). *Trends in High School Dropout and Completion Rates in the United States: 2013* (NCES 2016–117). U.S. Department of Education. Washington, DC: National Center for Education Statistics. Retrieved from http://nces.ed.gov/pubsearch.

References

Mehta, N., & Atreja, A. (2015). Online social support networks. *International Review of Psychiatry, 27*(2), 118–123.

Mikulincer, M., & Shaver, P. R. (2001). Attachment theory and intergroup bias: Evidence that priming the secure base schema attenuates negative reactions to out-groups. *Journal of Personality and Social Psychology, 81*(1), 97–115.

Miller, G. E., Chen, E., & Parker, K. J. (2011). Psychological stress in childhood and susceptibility to the chronic diseases of aging: Moving toward a model of behavioral and biological mechanisms. *Psychological Bulletin, 137*, 959–997.

Mittler, P. (2012). *Working towards inclusive education: Social contexts.* David Fulton Publishers.

Monteith, S., Glenn, T., & Bauer, M. (2013). Searching the internet for health information about bipolar disorder: Some cautionary issues. *International Journal of Bipolar Disorders, 1*(1), 22.

Morling, B., Kitayama, S., & Miyamoto, Y. (2003). American and Japanese women use different coping strategies during normal pregnancy. *Personality and Social Psychology Bulletin, 29*(12), 1533–1546.

Muris, P. (2002). Relationships between self-efficacy and symptoms of anxiety disorders and depression in a normal adolescent sample. *Personality and Individual Differences, 32*(2), 337–348.

Murray, C., & Greenberg, M. T. (2001). Relationships with teachers and bonds with school: Social emotional adjustment correlates for children with and without disabilities. *Psychology in the Schools, 38*(1), 25–41.

Murray, C., & Malmgren, K. (2005). Implementing a teacher–student relationship program in a high-poverty urban school: Effects on social, emotional, and academic adjustment and lessons learned. *Journal of School Psychology, 43*(2), 137–152.

Nazroo, J. Y. (1998). Genetic, cultural or socio-economic vulnerability? Explaining ethnic inequalities in health. *Sociology of Health & Illness, 20*(5), 710–730.

Neff, K. D. (2011). Self-compassion, self-esteem, and well-being. *Social and Personality Psychology Compass, 5*(1), 1–12.

Neff, L. A., & Karney, B. R. (2005). Gender differences in social support: A question of skill or responsiveness? *Journal of Personality and Social Psychology, 88*(1), 79–90.

Nelson, A. M. (2003). Transition to motherhood. *Journal of Obstetric, Gynecologic, and Neonatal Nursing, 32*(4), 465–477.

Newth, S., & DeLongis, A. (2004). Individual differences, mood, and coping with chronic pain in rheumatoid arthritis: A daily process analysis. *Psychology & Health, 19*(3), 283–305.

Niemiec, C. P., & Ryan, R. M. (2009). Autonomy, competence, and relatedness in the classroom: Applying self-determination theory to educational practice. *School Field, 7*(2), 133–144.

Nisbett, R. E., Peng, K., Choi, I., & Norenzayan, A. (2001). Culture and systems of thought: Holistic versus analytic cognition. *Psychological Review, 108*(2), 291–310.

Nolen-Hoeksema, S., & Harrell, Z. A. (2002). Rumination, depression, and alcohol use: Tests of gender differences. *Journal of Cognitive Psychotherapy, 16*(4), 391–403.

Noller, P. (1980). Misunderstandings in marital communication: A study of couples' nonverbal communication. *Journal of Personality and Social Psychology, 39*(6), 1135–1148.

Nurullah, A. S. (2012). Received and provided social support: A review of current evidence and future directions. *American Journal of Health Studies, 27*(3), 173–188.

OECD. (2011). *Lessons from PISA for the United States, strong performers and successful reformers in education.* OECD Publishing. Retrieved from http://dx.doi.org/10.1787/9789264096660-en.

Park, S., Lavallee, D., & Tod, D. (2013). Athletes' career transition out of sport: A systematic review. *International Review of Sport and Exercise Psychology, 6*(1), 22–53.

Parkes, K. R. (1986). Coping in stressful episodes: The role of individual differences, environmental factors, and situational characteristics. *Journal of Personality and Social Psychology, 51*(6), 1277–1292.

Pascoe, E. A., & Richman, L. S. (2009). Perceived discrimination and health: A meta-analytic review. *Psychological Bulletin, 135*(4), 531–554.

130

Phinney, J. S., Madden, T., & Santos, L. J. (1998). Psychological variables as predictors of perceived ethnic discrimination among minority and immigrant adolescents[1]. *Journal of Applied Social Psychology, 28*(11), 937–953.

Pierce, G. R., Lakey, B., Sarason, I. G., Sarason, B. R., & Joseph, H. J. (1997). Personality and social support processes. In G. R. In, B. Pierce, & I. G. Sarason Lakey (Eds.), *Sourcebook of social support and personality* (pp. 3–18). New York: Plenum.

Pierce, G. R., Sarason, B. R., & Sarason, I. G. (Eds.). (1996). *Handbook of social support and the family*. Springer Science & Business Media.

Polanczyk, G. V., Salum, G. A., Sugaya, L. S., Caye, A., & Rohde, L. A. (2015). Annual research review: A meta-analysis of the worldwide prevalence of mental disorders in children and adolescents. *Journal of Child Psychology and Psychiatry, 56*(3), 345–365.

Qiu, L., Lin, H., Leung, A. K., & Tov, W. (2012). Putting their best foot forward: Emotional disclosure on Facebook. *Cyberpsychology, Behavior, and Social Networking, 15*(10), 569–572.

Raver, C. C., Gershoff, E. T., & Aber, J. L. (2007). Testing equivalence of mediating models on income, parenting, and school readiness for white, black, and Hispanic children in a national sample. *Child Development, 78*(1), 96–115.

Ray, E. B., & Miller, K. I. (1994). Social support, home/work stress, and burnout: Who can help? *The Journal of Applied Behavioral Science, 30*(3), 357–373.

Reis, H. T., Clark, M. S., & Holmes, J. G. (2004). Perceived partner responsiveness as an organizing construct in the study of intimacy and closeness. In D. J. Mashek & A. Aron (Eds.), *Handbook of closeness and intimacy* (pp. 201–225). Mahwah, NJ: Lawrence Erlbaum.

Rice, S. M., Goodall, J., Hetrick, S. E., Parker, A. G., Gilbertson, T., Amminger, G. P., … & Alvarez-Jimenez, M. (2014). Online and social networking interventions for the treatment of depression in young people: A systematic review. *Journal of Medical Internet Research, 16*(9), e206.

Rini, C., Schetter, C. D., Hobel, C. J., Glynn, L. M., & Sandman, C. A. (2006). Effective social support: Antecedents and consequences of partner support during pregnancy. *Personal Relationships, 13*(2), 207–229.

Roeser, R. W., Eccles, J. S., & Sameroff, A. J. (2000). School as a context of early adolescents' academic and social-emotional development: A summary of research findings. *The Elementary School Journal, 100*(5), 443–471.

Rogers, C. R. (1959). A theory of therapy, personality and interpersonal relationships as developed in the client-centered framework. In S. In & S. Koch (Eds.), *Psychology: A study of a science. Vol. 3: Formulations of the person and the social context*. New York: McGraw Hill.

Rogers, C. R. (1961). *On becoming a person: A psychotherapist's view of psychotherapy*. London: Constable.

Rosenberg, M., Schooler, C., Schoenbach, C., & Rosenberg, F. (1995). Global self-esteem and specific self-esteem: Different concepts, different outcomes. *American Sociological Review*, 141–156.

Rowe, M., Bellamy, C., Baranoski, M., Wieland, M., O'connell, M. J., Benedict, P., … & Sells, D. (2007). A peer-support, group intervention to reduce substance use and criminality among persons with severe mental illness. *Psychiatric Services, 58*(7), 955–961.

Ryan, S. E. (2014). Rethinking gender and identity in energy studies. *Energy Research & Social Science, 1*, 96–105.

Ryan, R. M., & Deci, E. L. (2000a). Self-determination theory and the facilitation of intrinsic motivation, social development, and well-being. *American Psychologist, 55*(1), 68–78.

Ryan, R. M., & Deci, E. L. (2000b). Intrinsic and extrinsic motivations: Classic definitions and new directions. *Contemporary Educational Psychology, 25*(1), 54–67.

Ryan, R. M., & Deci, E. L. (2001). On happiness and human potentials: A review of research on hedonic and eudaimonic well-being. *Annual Review of Psychology, 52*(1), 141–166.

Ryan, R. M., Huta, V., & Deci, E. L. (2008). Living well: A self-determination theory perspective on eudaimonia. *Journal of Happiness Studies, 9*, 139–170.

References

Santiago, C. D., Wadsworth, M. E., & Stump, J. (2011). Socioeconomic status, neighborhood disadvantage, and poverty-related stress: Prospective effects on psychological syndromes among diverse low-income families. *Journal of Economic Psychology, 32*(2), 218–230.

Sarason, I. G., Sarason, B. R., & Pierce, G. R. (1990). Social support: The search for theory. *Journal of Social and Clinical Psychology, 9,* 133–147.

Scarr, S., & McCartney, K. (1983). How people make their own environments: A theory of genotype → environment effects. *Child Development, 54*(2), 424–435.

Schlossberg, N. K. (1981). Major contributions. *Counseling Psychologist, 9*(2), 2–15.

Schulz, R., Newsom, J., Mittelmark, M., Burton, L., Hirsch, C., & Jackson, S. (1997). Health effects of caregiving: The caregiver health effects study: An ancillary study of the Cardiovascular Health Study. *Annals of Behavioral Medicine, 19*(2), 110–116.

Schweisfurth, M. (2015). Learner-centred pedagogy: Towards a post-2015 agenda for teaching and learning. *International Journal of Educational Development, 40,* 259–266.

Seligman, M. E. (2002). Positive psychology, positive prevention, and positive therapy. *Handbook of positive psychology, 2*(2002), 3–12.

Seligman, M. (2011). *Flourish: A visionary new understanding of happiness and well-being*. New York: Free Press.

Seligman, M. E., & Csikszentmihalyi, M. (2014). Positive psychology: An introduction. In M. Csikszentmihalyi (Ed.), *Flow and the foundations of positive psychology: The collected works of Mihaly Csikszentmihalyi* (pp. 279–298). Netherlands: Springer.

Shanks-McElroy, H. A., & Strobino, J. (2001). Male caregivers of spouses with Alzheimer's disease: Risk factors and health status. *American Journal of Alzheimer's Disease and Other Dementias, 16*(3), 167–175.

Shaw, W. S., Patterson, T. L., Ziegler, M. G., Dimsdale, J. E., Semple, S. J., & Grant, I. (1999). Accelerated risk of hypertensive blood pressure recordings among Alzheimer caregivers. *Journal of Psychosomatic Research, 46*(3), 215–227.

Sherman, D. K., Kim, H. S., Pearson, D. M., Kane, H., Guichard, A., & Safarjan, E. (2008). *Culture and social support in couples: When social support seekers meet stressed support providers.* Manuscript in preparation.

Sherman, D. K., Kim, H. S., & Taylor, S. E. (2009). Culture and social support: Neural bases and biological impact. *Progress in Brain Research, 178,* 227–237.

Shettima, A. G. (1998). Gendered work patterns in the endangered Sahelian rural environment: Exploring three layers of exploitation. *Africa Development/Afrique et Développement, 22*(2), 163–183.

Shrout, P. E., Bolger, N., Iida, M., Burke, C., Gleason, M. E., & Lane, S. P. (2010). The effects of daily support transactions during acute stress: Results from a diary study of bar exam preparation. *Support Processes in Intimate Relationships*, 175–199.

Shrout, P. E., Herman, C. M., & Bolger, N. (2006). The costs and benefits of practical and emotional support on adjustment: A daily diary study of couples experiencing acute stress. *Personal Relationships, 13*(1), 115–134.

Simpson, J. A., Winterheld, H. A., Rholes, W. S., & Oriña, M. M. (2007). Working models of attachment and reactions to different forms of caregiving from romantic partners. *Journal of Personality and Social Psychology, 93*(3), 466–477.

Social Care Institute for Excellence, Care Services Improvement Partnership, & Royal College of Psychiatrists. (2007). *A common purpose: Recovery in future mental health services.* London: SCIE.

Social Welfare Department. (2016). *Statistics child abuse, spouse/cohabitant battering and sexual violence cases*. Retrieved from http://www.swd.gov.hk/vs/english/stat.html.

Son, J., Erno, A., Shea, D. G., Femia, E. E., Zarit, S. H., & Stephens, M. A. P. (2007). The caregiver stress process and health outcomes. *Journal of Aging and Health, 19*(6), 871–887.

Stambulova, N. (2003). Symptoms of a crisis-transition: A grounded theory study. In N. Hassmén (Ed.), *SIPF Yearbook 2003* (pp. 97–109). Örebro: Örebro University Press.

Storrie, K., Ahern, K., & Tuckett, A. (2010). A systematic review: Students with mental health problems—A growing problem. *International Journal of Nursing Practice, 16*(1), 1–6.

Suitor, J. J., & Pillemer, K. (2000). When experience counts most: Effects of experiential similarity on men's and women's receipt of support during bereavement. *Social Networks, 22*(4), 299–312.

Suitor, J. J., Pillemer, K., Keeton, S., & Robison, J. (1995). Aged parents and aging children: Determinants of relationship quality. In R. Blieszner & V. H. Bedford (Eds.), *Handbook of aging and the family* (pp. 223–242). Westport, CT, US: Greenwood Press/Greenwood Publishing Group.

Suls, J., & Martin, R. (2005). The daily life of the garden-variety neurotic: Reactivity, stressor exposure, mood spillover, and maladaptive coping. *Journal of Personality, 73*(6), 1485–1510.

Suurmeijer, T. P., Sonderen, F. V., Krol, B., Doeglas, D. M., Heuvel, W. V. D., & Sanderman, R. (2005). The relationship between personality, supportive transactions and support satisfaction, and mental health of patients with early rheumatoid arthritis. Results from the Dutch part of the EURIDISS study. *Social Indicators Research, 73*(2), 179–197.

Swann, W. B., Jr., De La Ronde, C., & Hixon, J. G. (1994). Authenticity and positivity strivings in marriage and courtship. *Journal of Personality and Social Psychology, 66*(5), 857–869.

Swickert, R. (2009). Personality and social support processes. In P. Corr & G. Mattews (Eds.), *The Cambridge handbook of personality psychology* (pp. 524–540). Cambridge, England: Cambridge University Press.

Swickert, R. J., Hittner, J. B., & Foster, A. (2010). Big Five traits interact to predict perceived social support. *Personality and Individual Differences, 48*(6), 736–741.

Swickert, R., Hittner, J. B., Kitos, N., & Cox-Fuenzalida, L. E. (2004). Direct or indirect, that is the question: A re-evaluation of extraversion's influence on self-esteem. *Personality and Individual Differences, 36*(1), 207–217.

Swickert, R. J., Rosentreter, C. J., Hittner, J. B., & Mushrush, J. E. (2002). Extraversion, social support processes, and stress. *Personality and Individual Differences, 32*(5), 877–891.

Tamres, L. K., Janicki, D., & Helgeson, V. S. (2002). Sex differences in coping behavior: A meta-analytic review and an examination of relative coping. *Personality and Social Psychology Review, 6*(1), 2–30.

Taylor, S. E. (2011). Social support: A review. In H. S. Friedman (Ed.), *The handbook of health psychology* (pp. 189–214). New York: Oxford University Press.

Taylor, S. E., Klein, L. C., Lewis, B. P., Gruenewald, T. L., Gurung, R. A., & Updegraff, J. A. (2000). Biobehavioral responses to stress in females: Tend-and-befriend, not fight-or-flight. *Psychological Review, 107*(3), 411–429.

Taylor, S. E., Sherman, D. K., Kim, H. S., Jarcho, J., Takagi, K., & Dunagan, M. S. (2004). Culture and social support: Who seeks it and why? *Journal of Personality and Social Psychology, 87,* 354–362.

Taylor, S. E., Welch, W. T., Kim, H. S., & Sherman, D. K. (2007). Cultural differences in the impact of social support on psychological and biological stress responses. *Psychological Science, 18*(9), 831–837.

Tew, J. (2011). *Social approaches to mental distress*. Basingstoke: Palgrave Macmillan.

Thoits, P. A. (1995). Stress, coping, and social support processes: Where are we? What next? *Journal of Health and Social Behavior, Forty Years of Medical Sociology: The State of the Art and Directions for the Future, 1995,* 53–79.

Thoits, P. A. (2011). Mechanisms linking social ties and support to physical and mental health. *Journal of Health and Social Behavior, 52*(2), 145–161.

Tremblay, R. E. (2000). The development of aggressive behavior during childhood: What have we learned in the past century? *International Journal of Behavioral Development, 24,* 129–141.

Turner-McGrievy, G. M., & Tate, D. F. (2013). Weight loss social support in 140 characters or less: Use of an online social network in a remotely delivered weight loss intervention. *Translational Behavioral Medicine, 3*(3), 287–294.

Uchino, B. N. (2009). Understanding the links between social support and physical health: A life-span perspective with emphasis on the separability of perceived and received support. *Perspectives on Psychological Science, 4*(3), 236–255.

References

Uehara, E. S. (1995). Reciprocity reconsidered: Gouldner's moral norm of reciprocity' and social support. *Journal of Social and Personal Relationships, 12*(4), 483–502.

van Zelst, C. (2009). Stigmatization as an environmental risk in schizophrenia: A user perspective. *Schizophrenia Bulletin, 35*(2), 293–296.

Vitaliano, P. P., Zhang, J., & Scanlan, J. M. (2003). Is caregiving hazardous to one's physical health? A meta-analysis. *Psychological Bulletin, 129*(6), 946–972.

Wallace, J. E., & Jovanovic, A. (2011). Occupational similarity and spousal support: A study of the importance of gender and Spouse's Occupation. *Relations Industrielles/Industrial Relations, 66*(2), 235–255.

Walpole, M. (2003). Socioeconomic status and college: How SES affects college experiences and outcomes. *The Review of Higher Education, 27*(1), 45–73.

Wampold, B. E. (2001). *The great psychotherapy debate: Models, methods, and findings*. Hillsdale, NJ: Erlbaum.

Warren, P. L. (2005). First-time mothers: Social support and confidence in infant care. *Journal of Advanced Nursing, 50,* 479–488.

Warriner, K., & Lavallee, D. (2008). The retirement experiences of elite female gymnasts: Self-identity and the physical self. *Journal of Applied Sport Psychology, 20*(3), 301–317.

Waterman, A. S. (1993). Two conceptions of happiness: Contrasts of personal expressiveness (eudaimonia) and hedonic enjoyment. *Journal of Personality and Social Psychology, 64*(4), 678–691.

Weiss, R. S. (1976). The emotional impact of marital separation. *Journal of Social Issues, 32*(1), 135–145.

Wentzel, K. R. (1994). Relations of social goal pursuit to social acceptance, classroom behavior, and perceived social support. *Journal of Educational Psychology, 86*(2), 173.

Wentzel, K. R., Battle, A., Russell, S. L., & Looney, L. B. (2010). Social supports from teachers and peers as predictors of academic and social motivation. *Contemporary Educational Psychology, 35*(3), 193–202.

Wheeler, L., Reis, H., & Nezlek, J. B. (1983). Loneliness, social interaction, and sex roles. *Journal of Personality and Social Psychology, 45*(4), 943–953.

White, W., Boyle, M., & Loveland, D. (2004). Recovery from addiction and recovery from mental illness: Shared and contrasting lessons. In R. Ralph & P. Corrigan (Eds.), *Recovery and mental illness: Consumer visions and research paradigms* (pp. 233–258). Washington, DC: American Psychological Association.

Wilcox, P., Winn, S., & Fyvie-Gauld, M. (2005). 'It was nothing to do with the university, it was just the people': The role of social support in the first-year experience of higher education. *Studies in Higher Education, 30*(6), 707–722.

Wilson, W. R. (1967). Correlates of avowed happiness. *Psychological Bulletin, 67*(4), 294–306.

Windle, M. (1992). A longitudinal study of stress buffering for adolescent problem behaviors. *Developmental Psychology, 28*(3), 522–530.

World Health Organization. (1948). *WHO definition of health*. Retrieved from http://www.who.int/about/definition/en/print.html.

Wu, P., Hoven, C. W., Okezie, N., Fuller, C. J., & Cohen, P. (2008). Alcohol abuse and depression in children and adolescents. *Journal of Child & Adolescent Substance Abuse, 17*(2), 51–69.

Chapter 4
Social Support, Student Outcomes and Teaching Strategies

Abstract Social support is a topic of study related to the link between psychological processes and health. Social support can be explained as the type of communication between support recipients and providers that reduces uncertainties, and enables relationships and functions that enhance support recipients' perception of personal control in their life experience (Adelman & Albrecht in Communicating social support. Sage Publications, 1987). Teaching is an interactional process between learners and teachers in the school environment. Teachers, as more knowledgeable others, give support to students in order to master a certain amount of content knowledge of a discipline, which demonstrates their role as a nurturer (Lam in There is no fear in love: The giving of social support to students enhances teachers' career development, 2017). In the classroom, student peers' scaffoldings and social interaction involve learners in a community for friendship and academic learning, and the school as a whole creates an environment to foster learners' social and academic development. Learning in school largely relies on different sources of social support. This chapter investigates the potential of social support in teaching and learning contexts. It attempts to explore teachers' supportive behaviours and other support sources in the classroom environment and the corresponding outcomes on student learning, to draw implications from theory and practice in teaching. The current chapter seeks to accomplish the following:

- Identify the theoretical reasons behind the link between social support and education, especially related to teaching and learning in the classroom;
- Explore the support documented in the literature mainly related to teacher social support, and generally about other support sources;
- Related to the above, what impact social support behaviours and practice from teachers and other support sources could have on students in terms of educational outcomes;
- Identify exemplary teaching strategies that utilise social support;
- Discuss implications from the above and further research directions.

The original version of this chapter was revised: Belated corrections have been incorporated. The correction to this chapter is available at https://doi.org/10.1007/978-981-13-3577-8_8

© Springer Nature Singapore Pte Ltd. 2019
B. LAM, *Social Support, Well-being, and Teacher Development*,
https://doi.org/10.1007/978-981-13-3577-8_4

Background

Perhaps no one would deny that school is a place created to support students' growth and development. The fact is, not every student can make a good life through education in schools. Before the dawn of the twenty-first century, the governments of different countries around the world implemented an array of education reform initiatives to prepare students for a changing society brought about by globalisation and its increasingly knowledge-based economies. These reform proposals have commonly recommended the use of more learner-oriented teaching approaches to fit the needs of the twenty-first century, such as inductive methods, project learning and experiential learning that encourage active construction of knowledge (OECD, 2011; Schweisfurth, 2015). However, in reality, education over the world has also become uniformly conformed to high-stake test-driven educational policies and practices (Au, 2007; Lee, 2008; Eckstein & Noah, 1993). As a result of keen competition for educational achievement measured at the world level in the twenty-first century, schools have become the place for intensive training for academic assessment grades for students (Jennings & Rentner, 2006). Training students to sit for examinations has become the key agenda in many schools. To guarantee achievement results, many teachers use drill and practice to train students to sit for examination. The emphasis on academic achievement becomes a dominant ideology that influences school policies in every aspects. The consequence is that it is not uncommon to find students who see themselves as losers (Bray, 2017) when they cannot meet up to the high academic requirement.

Academic pressure has been found as the main cause of student suicides in many countries (Arun & Chavan, 2009; Cheung & Chiu, 2016; Liu & Tein, 2005) and it is a rising trend (Centers for Disease Control, 2013; World Health Organization, 2017). To quote Hong Kong as an example, a citywide survey (Cheung, 2015) found that over half of the interviewed secondary school students showed symptoms of depression and 20% of them exhibited even moderate to severe levels of anxiety. Moreover, more than a quarter of students showed signs of anxiety mainly because of their worries about the future and not being competent enough. The overall declining mental health of school-aged children worldwide has been alarming (Polanczyk, Salum, Sugaya, Caye, & Rohde, 2015; Storrie, Ahern, & Tuckett, 2010) and it raises a warning signal to policymakers and practitioners in the field.

Substantial research literature has actually addressed the lack of motivation for academic activities as a major problem for school-aged students (Legault & Green-Demers, 2006). It has also been found that students' feelings of disconnection from school tend to cause serious problems of disengagement as students grow (Fredricks, Blumenfeld, Friedel, & Paris, 2005). Researchers have found that a narrow-focused emphasis on academic results in school education only serves particular areas of cognitive learning (Noddings, 2003). This type of education is likely to disvalue humanity in living, by engaging students in competition for extrinsic worth (McKenzie, Whitley, & Weich, 2002); as a result, the senses of feeling, human relatedness and affective learning are minimised. While

Background

137

more than half of the student population have been shown to suffer from negative emotions and pressure in school as in the case of Hong Kong, low achievers may probably be in a state of helplessness because of their unwitting self-defence reaction to protect the self from challenges and responsibilities (Lockett & Harrell, 2003; Banks & Woolfson, 2008). There are also students who come to schools with emotional and behaviourial problems, who have to deal with language, cultural integration and adaption issues, poverty, social and family problems.

If schools are to provide a proximal environment to prepare the future generation (National Education Association, 2015), the use of teaching-to-the-test approaches, tracked progress and mandated tests (Abrams, Pedulla, & Madaus, 2003; Christensen & Karp, 2003) are too narrowly focused to be appropriate for supporting students. It does not take account of the psychological processes of learning for learners who are diverse in terms of academic achievement, capabilities and potentialities. Practice and drill for examination results creates tension and anxiety for students (Barbara, 2004; Cohen, McCabe, Michelli, & Pickeral, 2009; Sacks, 2000), which has been shown by increasing mental health problems. Given the more challenging twenty-first century societal background, researchers have started to re-conceptualise education as supporting students to attain a fulfilling and actualising self (Gable & Haidt, 2005; McCombs, 2004). The process of learning, in the argument of this book, is enabled by teachers' social support behaviours and student peers' scaffoldings, and the school environment as a whole to foster meaningful learning.

As reviewed in Chap. 2, social support is an interaction that creates both long-term benefits (main effect) to enhance the overall well-being of people and immediate support for people in need (buffering effect). It is often related to affective traits, notably, coping, self-esteem, belonging, competence and exchange (Adelman & Albrecht, 1987) that help a person to develop their own capacities and to gain high-quality experience in life. As indicated in the conclusion of Chap. 2, social support can be a perspective from which to explore the salient features in teaching; it especially addresses the special relationships between learners and teachers and learners to learners in the interactional process, and the functions of such interactions on students. It is therefore crucial to identify teachers' supportive behaviours and social support sources in the classroom, as the desirable learning outcomes addressed in these support resources can inform classroom practice for teachers to learn from. As such, this chapter discusses relevant theories identified from the literature with an aim to justify how teaching is enacted as a form of social support. This support is found to include teacher's nurturance behaviours, peer support from students and the classroom environment. These support sources are also found to produce positive student outcomes. The chapter aims to achieve a cogent conceptualisation of teaching and learning, to raise implications for teaching practice and education improvement.

The investigation is based on a purposeful review of the research literature. For theory, the major categories of education theories related to human relationship and interaction that support learning are selected. To provide a broad base for discussion, the most updated empirical studies and materials published in the past three decades are included. The review also includes original authors' work and the most updated references. Although social support is not a common research construct in educational research, the use of global constructs in studies that implies its meaning is prolific. Hence, a list of major keywords is selected for managing a keyword search for the review, which include social support, emotional support, caring, relationship, teaching or learning strategies, classroom climate and other psychological outcome measures such as motivation, self-concept, self-esteem and well-being.

The Theoretical Reasons of Social Support on Students

Attachment Theory

As for teachers who provide social support for students, in the scenario of an expert adult who is responsible for students' growth in early childhood to young adulthood in general from school to university education, one of the theories which can relevantly explain the link is Bowlby's Attachment Theory (1980, 1982) (AT). This theory is among the most crucial psychological theories in the twentieth century, attracting attention from developmental, clinical and educational psychologists. This system postulates that there is an Attachment Behavioral System. This means that human children are born with the tendency to engage in a set of behaviours (*attachment behaviours*) that evolution designs to ensure that a young child is proximate to figures who could give protection to the child (*attachment figures*, usually but not necessarily, the parents). These attachment figures can defend the vulnerable child from threats such as predators. Therefore, this system enhances the child's chance of survival. This is especially pronounced in more advanced animals such as humans, whose young are generally born very immature and lacking the abilities of self-defence.

The AT is best illustrated in the Strange Situation (e.g. Ainsworth, Blehar, Waters, & Wall, 1978). In this experiment, a young child (usually an infant) first stays in a laboratory room in the presence of his/her caretaker (generally the mother) and a stranger. After a certain period, the mother is told to depart, leaving the child alone with the stranger. Usually, the child would start to show certain behaviours when he/she notices that his/her mother is missing. Often, he/she would begin to cry or otherwise engage in behaviours that may draw the attention of his/her mother or other adults (i.e. engage in attachment behaviours), until his/her mother appears in the laboratory room again. This demonstrates that attachment behaviours primarily function to ensure the child's proximity to their attachment figures.

During infancy, primary caretakers (usually the parents, but they can include grandparents, neighbours, older siblings and daycare workers) tend to assume the role of attachment figures. Ainsworth (1979) noted that infants tend to seek proximity to their attachment figures when they are tired, ill or otherwise discomforted, and they tend to be calmer when the caretakers are physically present (Heinicke & Westheimer, 1966). This is especially true for *secure attachment*—attachment bonds formed with caretakers who are consistent and available. Caretakers who are unre-

The Theoretical Reasons of Social Support on Students 139

sponsive to the child's needs tend to produce *avoidant* children, who are similarly unresponsive to their caretakers, while caretakers who are inconsistent (sometimes acting affectionately while sometimes acting cold) tend to produce *anxious* children, who tend to demonstrate hyperactive attachment behaviours. Children with secure attachment, in contrast, are known to be emotionally responsive without being anxious. It is thought that secure attachment fosters positive socio-emotional outcomes and corresponds to positive social support.

Though the AT was initially used to study infants, it has since been used to investigate the attachment behaviours of children, teenagers and adults (Bowlby, 1973, 1988). It is theorised that each person, after experience with attachment in infancy, develops an *internal working model* of what relationships are like. Secure children tend to expect the people around them (friends, teachers and for adults, spouses) to be emotionally available for support. Such a model can be summarised as 'If I encounter something distressing, I can approach a significant other for help; he/she will be supportive'. This largely unconscious process can extend its influence well into adulthood (Mikulincer & Shaver, 2001). For instance, it is known that infants whose caretakers have been unresponsive tend to favour 'deactivating' their Attachment Behavioral System—they prefer to avoid forming intimate and interdependent relationships (Mikulincer & Shaver, 2001).

The AT has been under frequent criticism and revision since its establishment due to advances in theory, data and other areas in psychology towards the end of the twentieth century (Mercer, 2011). To note but a few, researchers noted that later social interactions could have greater impact on later social behaviour than early experiences (Harris, 1998; Kagan, 1994). The experiments from which the AT had been generated are largely based on the interaction of the child with the primary caregiver (usually the mother), and the interaction being studied is controlled in a stressful situation, namely, the Strange Situation as described above. The design of this research approach creates two key methodological issues that affect the validity of research and thus the theory built upon it, as suggested by researchers (e.g. Holmes, 2014; Mace & Margison, 1997). First, it may be more appropriate that the study should also be based on the interaction of the child and the caretaker in an ordinary, non-stressful situation, as the ordinary interaction in normal daily situations can show better how the attachment model works saliently than in a stressful situation where the attachment figure creates another factor of tension. Second, the child's feelings of attachment towards the mother may not be the same as their feelings towards their playmate peers, hence, the complications of AT may extend beyond the current explanation which lay the focus on only the primary figure (i.e. mother) (Lee, 2003). The universality of the theory across different cultures is also in doubt (van IJzendoorn & Sagi-Schwartz, 2008). The development of cognitive neuroscience has brought new light to AT to constitute a subfield known as attachment neuroscience (Coan, 2008). It focuses on the power of the neurobiology of attachment in which early encounters of social relationships in infancy may create schemas that affect a person's relations with others, yet, the innate capacity of the human brain can grow new neurons that may change human relational experience in healthier ways. It is assumed that as children grow, the *internal working model* is open to amendment in later life (Baldwin, 1992; Shaver, Collins & Clark, 1996). Humans are constantly perceiving and evaluating the availability and emotional closeness of the people around them. Even if an infant fails to form secure attachments in early life, he/she could still change in later life—provided that in the said later life, there are significant others who are emotionally available. Thus, while teachers cannot alter their students' early life, this 'later life' is where teachers *can* intervene.

Broaden-and-Build Theory

It is widely known that attachment figures can serve as a 'secure base', through which the child obtains a sense of security because he/she believes that the attachment figures are here to give support should the need arise. This, in turn, brings us to another important theory related to how social support causes positive student outcomes—the Broaden-and-Build Theory of Positive Emotions. Proposed by Fredrickson (2003), this theory describes emotions as a set of biological functions that humans have developed to adapt over the course of evolution.

Negative emotions have been postulated to serve protective functions. Emotions such as fear, anger and anxiety are known to arise in response to potential dangers, and narrow peoples' scope of attention (Schmitz, De Rosa, & Anderson, 2009). The narrowing of scope of attention refers to the fact that people with negative emotions are known to be more focused on narrow sets of stimuli and thoughts, while ignoring information that is deemed irrelevant. They also tend to become defensive—any information which threatens to challenge their beliefs and views quickly provokes anger. Based on these findings, Fredrickson (2004) and other scholars (e.g. Frijda, 1988) theorised that negative emotions are evolutionarily designed to serve protective functions, prompting the individuals to engage in narrow behaviours such as fight, flight and freeze under the presence of dangers.

In contrast, positive emotions tend to arise in the absence of danger (Cacioppo, Gardner, & Berntson, 1999; Watson, Wiese, Vaidya, & Tellegen, 1999). They serve to facilitate 'approach behaviours', which function to prompt humans to grow to become more engaged with their surroundings and willing to participate in (intellectual or social) activities. Many of these activities are ultimately helpful for building the individual's resources and hence enhance future survival. For instance, engaging in social interactions fosters social bonds, which enables the individuals to seek help from their fellow humans in future situations; as a result, the ability to feel positive emotions is adaptive by evolution's standards. With the predisposition to experience positive emotions, people become more prone to exploring novel objects, people or situations, exposing themselves to a variety of stimuli and information, which in turn enhances their learning.

This central idea of the Broaden-and-Build Theory of Positive Emotions is also well-supported by evidence. First, there is ample evidence that positive emotions such as joy, interest, contentment and affection tend to broaden people's momentary thought repertoires—they tend to enable people to come up with new ideas and thoughts more readily (Fredrickson, 1998; Fredrickson & Branigan, 2001). They also tend to prompt people to be more interested in playing and leisure activities (Ellsworth & Smith, 1988). They make people more motivated to explore new information and experiences (Csikszentmihalyi, 1990; Seligman & Csikszentmihalyi, 2014). They make people more driven to engage in positive social interactions with each other (Lewis, 1993). All these action tendencies proposed (Fredrickson, 2003, 2004), serve in the long term to promote exploratory behaviours, which help build cognitive resources and enduring personal bonds, thus enhancing survival. As a result, positive emotions serve a survival-enhancing function and are favoured by natural selection.

Examples of positive emotions enhancing survival include: (1) contentment, a distinctive pleasant emotion, broadened by prompting the individual to savour and examine their current situations, prompting them to learn from the past (Izard, 1977); (2) pride, another pleasant emotion, arises from personal achievements and creates the urges to share the news about the said achievements with others, urging interpersonal interactions (Lewis, 1993); and (3) love, viewed as a distinct emotion, is experienced in the presence of a safe and close relationship and prompts the individual to cultivate relationships with the target loved ones (Fredrickson, 2000). These different types of positive emotions each prompt the individual to build personal resources, and this is the core idea of the Broaden-and-Build Theory of positive emotions.

Social Exchange Theory

The Social Exchange Theory (SET) originates from several academic disciplines with pioneers in earlier times including anthropology (e.g. Firth, 1967; Sahlins, 1972), psychology (e.g. Thibault & Kelley, 1959) and sociology (e.g. Blau, 1964; Homans, 1961). The social exchange theory explains 'social behaviour as exchange' in which people rationally seek for maximum profits and minimise costs in their interactions with others (Cook & Rice, 2006). According to SET, interactions among people are considered as interdependent and contingent on the responses from another person (Cropanzano & Mitchell, 2005; Blau, 1964). As such, our engagement in an interaction is driven by the rewards or punishments we expect to receive (either consciously or subconsciously) according to the equation first suggested by Homans (1961):

Behaviour (profits) = Rewards of interaction (approvals) − costs of interaction (disapprovals)

Social interdependence theory states two potential outcomes can be expected from such interaction, either positive ones that joint goals of all parties are promoted, or negative outcomes where each other's goals are obstructed (Redmond, 2015). Therefore, we can predict that the more rewards an individual receives within an interaction, the more he/she would like to keep the interaction going and get closer to that person (Sharan, 2010). Rewards can come in many ways, such as gifts, recognition or simply a smile; and costs may mean disrespect, insults, beating, etc. For example, if you ask someone out for a date and he/she agrees (a reward), you would be happy to invite him/her out again. However, if you get a direct—'No', you will be less likely to ask him/her out anymore to avoid further costs.

SET is assumed to be applicable in any interdependent interactions with anyone. In the educational settings, students are often encouraged to interact with their peers to train their interpersonal skills. For teaching, the method of cooperative learning correlates closely to the concept SET, since it aims at greater mutual benefits in learning by allowing students to work together in groups. Each student in the group is expected to make unique contributions so team members can rely on one another to achieve their common goal. In order to ensure positive outcomes, all group members must be responsible for contributing their own share of the work and mastering all the material to be learnt for the group's success (Choi, Johnson & Johnson, 2011). Moreover, group members have to give one another kind reactions and comments as rewards during such interaction, so as to maintain group bonding. All members are also rewarded through teaching, helping, applauding and encouraging one another (Slavin, 2011, 2014). Through the appropriate use of social, interpersonal and collaborative skills during the process when they work together, students are encouraged and helped to develop trust establishment, communication and conflict management skills, leadership and judgement.

Social Constructionist Learning Theory

Principles of social interaction are commonly involved in the field of education, such as Vygotsky's social constructionist learning theory of children's development. The psychologist Vygotsky proposed that the cognitive development of each individual, including thoughts, languages and reasoning processes, is a result of culture (Gallimore & Tharp, 1992), through social interactions with other people (especially significant adults such as parents and teachers). Therefore, a child's development represents the shared knowledge of a given culture. One important idea of his theory is that an individual's potential for cognitive development depends on his/her zone of proximal development (ZPD). This is 'the distance between the actual developmental level as determined by independent problem solving and the level of potential development as determined through problem solving under adult guidance, or in collaboration with more capable peers' (Vygotsky, 1978, p. 86). It means tasks that are too challenging for children to master alone may be learnt under adults' or more skilled others' guidance and assistance. The process in which the more knowledgeable person adjusts his/her support according to the child's guidance needs is called *scaffolding*, which refers to the support given to children in completing tasks that they are not capable of completing alone. As such, learning should be considered as a social process where children learn with others. The upper limit of ZPD cannot be broken through without social interactive support from teachers and peers, which illustrates that learning and development arise directly from social interaction (Gindis, 1996; Kim, 2001).

Wood, Bruner, and Ross (1976) described scaffolding as an adult-led instruction, which is effective when the instructions are contingent on the child's performance. The team provided early empirical evidence to Vygotsky's theory of ZPD and scaffolding in a series of work on mothers' tutoring strategies. For example, in Wood and Middleton (1975) experiment, 4-year-old children were asked to build a 3D model as shown in a picture with a set of blocks and pegs, which was extremely difficult for them to complete alone. Interactions between the mother and the child were observed and the types of support were categorised into three types (1) *general encouragement*, e.g. 'keep trying', (2) *specific instructions*, e.g. 'use the big block;' (3) *direct demonstration*, e.g. 'demonstrate to the child how to stack up the blocks'. The results showed that none of these strategies alone was the best for helping the children make headway. The most effective way was to vary the types of support strategies given according to the situation—give less specific instructions when the child was doing well independently, and be more specific when the child was facing difficulties until he/she started to make progress again. This study implies that scaffolding is most effective when the support provided matches the needs of the recipient. This process is known as *contingent shifting* (Gaskell, 2008; Wood, 1980). We also discussed in Chap. 3 that matched support is crucial to help in social support situation; it allows learners to achieve what they would not have been able to complete alone, and thus they can break through their own limit and push their ZPD to the next level. Recent literature suggests that this kind of adult-led contingent assistance is likely to be associated with children's later school success such as self-regulatory competence (Delen, Liew, & Willson, 2014; Neitzel & Stright, 2003), achievement motivation (Evans & Boucher, 2015; Grolnick, Gurland, DeCourcey, & Jacob, 2002) and executive function development (Blair & Raver, 2015; Hughes & Ensor, 2009).

Vygotsky's theory suggests that teachers and peers play important roles in children's developmental processes. For example, teachers provide directions and instructions to address students' ZPD and recognise their maturing knowledge and skills areas in order to help them reach their goals and move to higher levels. Teachers can also assess students' ZPD and give them feedback and suitable support that matches their needs. In addition, students are encouraged to work with their peers in handling exercises, projects and problems (Borich, 2004; Smith, Walker, Ainley, & McNay, 2012). Through the exchange of ideas and information, they interact with their peers and more knowledgeable others, by developing dialogues within the structure of activities, in which they learn new knowledge. According to Vygotsky, activity, i.e. 'doing', is essential since knowledge should be developed through active interaction in a social environment. In classroom settings, teachers can design meaningful activities that involve social interactions to allow students to learn in a culturally authentic context. Social Constructivist Learning implies a context of learning that utilises peer support and adult guidance, though its attention is focused on cognitive aspects of social support. It largely echoes the potentials generated from the social support literature as suggested in Chap. 2 that through interaction and the structure of scaffoldings set into the learning process, social referencing takes effect. Individuals tend to make reference to the norms within a social group and behave to meet such norms. This also means that individuals' positive changes in behaviour are the results of scaffolding supports of their peers, as the social norm is adopted to regulate ones' own behaviours. At this point, social support literature suggests the condition of human relationship norms for this cognitive learning process, which will be further discussed in a later section of the chapter.

Affective Learning Versus Cognitive Learning

The connection of human affect and cognition to support learning has been a key area in cognitive psychology and the field of neuroscience. These two functions in the human brain have suggested theoretical positions to guide education in schools over the history. The discussion in this section discusses the concerns of affective learning and cognitive learning, and their possible connections. This discussion is not directly about social support. However, since social support has an emotional basis, and is a crucial support for the overall development of a person, by discussing the connection of affect and cognition, this section can clarify the place of social support and imply whether it should be accounted for in the learning and teaching environment.

Several authors have discussed the positions of affective versus cognitive learning at different periods (see review by Lashari, Alias, Kesot, & Akasah, 2012; McCollum, 2014; Reigeluth, 2013; Willis, 2007). According to Reigeluth (2013), affect exists in different forms such as humanistic education, moral development and self-actualisation. Generally speaking, affect in education, also known as 'affective learning' or 'affective development', deals broadly with learning that is related to students' personal, social and spiritual development, covering concerns for human feelings, morals, ethics (Education & Mean, 2013), self-worth, relating to the others, world awareness, learning and spiritual life (Himsl & Lambert, 1993). It refers to a process of personal growth that leads to the ideal of a well-adjusted person to serve the best interest of individuals and society, and learning to become human (Beane, 1990; Reigeluth, 2013). In other words, affective learning comprises the virtues that represent the ideal of a supportive social environment, and it justifies the importance of social support. Cognition has a more straightforward definition. Cognitive learning is related to knowledge acquisition. Traditionally, cognition generally helps with the functions of perception, attention, memory, motor skills, language, verbal skills, spatial processing, and the application of these functions in problem situations, which require higher intellectual capabilities (Robertson, 2016; Michelon, 2011; Welsh, Nix, Blair, Bierman, & Nelson, 2010). The emergence of neuroscience as a new cognitive stream explains human cognition and behaviour as a functional system of the brain. It addresses the intersection of human emotions and cognition, and the specific functions of human nerves to advance our understanding of human intelligence and the interwovenness of human intelligences (e.g. Goleman, 2007) in different fields.

The Theoretical Reasons of Social Support on Students

Earlier work tended to minimise affect as an important tenet of human thinking as it did not have a clear operational definition and was difficult to measure (McCollum, 2014), until recently the affect has acquired a more prominent position (Ashby & Isen, 1999; Isen, Daubman, & Nowicki, 1987). The basic assumption is that thought and feeling are inseparable entities. Human emotions are expressed within reasoned actions and are found to exist in some forms of referent (Beane, 1990). Neuroscientists have reported that both the emotion and rational functions in human brain work in harmony, yet they operate separately, and emotion is found to function prior to cognition in a decision-making situation (Goleman, 1995). According to Strangeman (2007), the affective network in the human brain is responsible for the processing of emotional experience, social information and reward and punishment (McCollum, 2014). The emotional brain system works across the other brain networks to support cognitive functioning, such as when a person feels gratified, human emotions affect memory and brain function positively (LeDoux, 2000; Jensen, 2005), and otherwise lead to negative functions.

Neuroscience research findings have illustrated how human emotions affect cognitive learning. For example, fear conditioning is a type of brain function that determines people to predict averse events, which can deter one's learning cognitively. If one learns an averse stimulus (e.g. painful experience) from a particular natural stimulus (e.g. technical operation of a media network), it will result in the expression of fear responses to the supposed neutral stimulus and deter one's advanced understanding of it (e.g. avoid the use of technology but use other ways to get around the problem). For students, a painful learning experience in doing an experiment in chemistry or dealing with report writing may create a negative emotion for attending a science-related lesson. Furthermore, affective factors, such as motivation, confidence and anxiety, are associated with students' success in learning. As Krashen (1982) has found in students' acquisition of second language, students have to develop an optimal level of emotions should they be able to learn to master the subject. This implies that teachers should make use of pedagogies and support to students to prepare them emotionally for cognitive learning. In a way, this is different from the behaviourist model of learning by which learners are conditioned to exhibit desirable behaviours and students are set in lockstep in order to master the set syllabus content (Skinner, 2011).

Affective learning also cultivates socio-emotional intelligence or competence, which is a trait within the affective dimension in human cognition. Socio-emotional competence is related to the emotional functioning of the person in a problem situation in a social setting (Guerra et al. 2014). It contains self-awareness, self-management, relationship skills and responsible decision-making among its components (Collaborative for Academic, Social, and Emotional Learning [CASEL], 2005). As the way people behave and act does not only serve one's personal interest, people in the social environment should act by considering the welfare of others. Therefore, maintaining social relationships and developing social bonds with other human fellows is a virtue that every person should pursue, in order to create a better society. Individuals who work in a social setting may be involved in communications, collaborating with others, expressing views and giving opinions and making decisions. These circumstantial situations require the use of a person's intelligence and skills to manage emotions, consider the interest of other parties, and the public good. Socio-emotional competence is often categorised as 'soft skills' (Bowles & Gintis, 1976). These skills are generally in contrast with the perceptual performance of cognitive skills, and many of these skills have an affect component, such as socio-emotional skills that combine attitude, feeling for oneself, others and the public domain and rational thinking components. The non-cognitive skills have recently been found to predict educational attainment, labour market success, health and criminality (Jackson, 2012; Heckman & Kautz, 2012; Kautz, Heckman, Diris, Ter Weel, & Borghans, 2014). Furthermore, researchers suggest that socio-emotional competence is correlated with positive character traits, such as caring and empathy, agreeableness, conscientious and extravert personalities (e.g. Goroshit & Hen, 2016). Policy makers are now conscious about the agenda of including emotional and affective traits development for school students. Irrespective of the reason of promoting emotional traits in the twenty-first century, the above discussion on the connection of affective and cognitive learning underscores the human traits and social norms that are relevant to the emotional traits in social support, e.g. social support is related to altruistic acts, empathetic concerns, participation and civic virtues. They are a crucial part of learning which should be promoted in schools in various ways, such as cultivating norms and promoting relevant traits of social support through student–teacher interactions in schools.

The Meta-Theory Derived to Guide Learning and Teaching

The theories reviewed above suggest a strong connection to the assumptions of social support as discussed in Chaps. 2 and 3. The literature in health psychology and education both address human well-being as the prime importance, it values support to be given to human beings in different contexts. Special attention is paid on the psychological processes of achieving healthy development for human beings, to address the benefits people can gain by human interactions and the shaping of human cognition.

A meta-theory, as a theoretical perspective, is derived to guide learning and teaching. Generally, this theory proposes that human beings are influenced by their interaction with other human fellows. However, life experience, which is largely determined by the needs to satisfy social ties and good quality relationships, regulates and forms the perceptions and beliefs of human beings themselves. These interactive processes work to create the person's identity and self-esteem, and serve as social referencing that influences the positive attitude and behaviour of people. Positive influence is powerful as it creates a clear role for one to take so that the person would work to achieve the goal to move towards self-actualisation. If the experience is negative, it may generate antisocial behaviours, withdrawal actions, leading to mental illness. If the experience is positive, it will create positive emotions for these people and drive their social interaction with their fellow peers, building stronger resources and engaging in exploratory behaviours. Furthermore, satisfying social ties not only serves well-being, social learning, i.e. the exchange of ideas and scaffoldings provided to teach others between human peers but has an important role to play in advancing human intellect. In sum, education is to provide a supportive social environment for people who come from diverse backgrounds to learn. Since self-concept can be changed and people's perception on oneself is also changeable, teachers can develop the resources in the classroom and close relationship bonds to support every individual learner in schools.

Social Support Behaviours and the Corresponding Learning Outcomes

The above discussion provides the theoretical ground for promoting social support in schools. In education, social support has been argued as a crucial factor in helping students accomplish desired outcomes (Wentzel, Battle, Russell, & Looney, 2010a, 2010b) in affective, social and academic aspects. Several researchers who have published on social support in the education context or related themes (Russell, 2012a, 2012b; Wentzel, 2012; Wentzel, Barry, & Caldwell, 2004a, 2004b; Wentzel et al., 2010a, 2010b) have commonly suggested the multidimensionality of social support, which is similar to what has been discussed in the health psychology literature. It covers sources (i.e. network or persons), types (categorisation and classification schemes), and the effects and outcomes. Researchers in education have also borrowed ideas from social support literature to explain the teacher's nurturing role in the classroom (e.g. Ford, 1992; Malecki & Demaray, 2002; Wentzel, 1997), yet, a systematic organisation of this pool of literature has yet to be found.

The following section outlines social support in teaching mainly within the classroom context, focusing on teachers and students' social support behaviours, which may yield positive student learning outcomes The topics to be discussed are derived from the review of literature on emotional support, teacher–student and peer-to-peer relationships, various categories of teacher social support, teacher and student expectations, and environmental characteristics. Specific strategies that utilise social support for teaching in mainstream and special classrooms are also discussed to specify the core concepts and key concerns in order to highlight the focus of practice regarding social support in teaching and intervention programmes.

Emotional Support Enhances Self-esteem, Socio-emotional Competence and Academic Functioning

Wentzel et al., (2010a, 2010b) defined emotional support as the provision of care and value for students as persons. At the classroom level, NICHD Early

Child Care Research Network (2002) defined a classroom with positive emotion as characterised by warmth, child-centredness and teacher's sensitivity and responsiveness toward specific children (Hamre & Pianta, 2005). Emotional support is often presented as a form of teaching characterised by care (Noddings, 1984, 1992), and is described as relatedness and belongingness in the classroom context (Connell & Wellborn, 1991). It is positively associated with students' well-being, and has been found conducive to students' intrinsic motivation, social development and socio-emotional competence (e.g. Suldo, Shaffer, & Riley, 2008). It also supports students' adoption of cognitive strategies and benefits

Emotional Support as a Norm for Interaction. Teacher's emotional support for students has a role model effect on students for learning how to care for others, especially for students between 4 and 12 years of age when they develop their own views and ideas about proper interpersonal interactions (Denham, 1998). Similar to the assumption of a social interactionalist approach addressed in the social support literature, the social interactions with teachers serve as a reference for young children to understand other people's behaviours and emotions (i.e. social referencing), thus for them to better manage their own learning and behaviours. Teachers' responses allow children to learn about the consequences of their actions and the consequences of similar events in the future. Pianta, Hamre, & Stuhlman (2003) found that when teachers showed care for their students through providing social support, their students learnt and grew to be inclined to show such support to others. In contrast, if the teachers did not show social support (e.g. acting as emotionally cold, not conveying to students that they are valued members of the class), their students would behave in an isolated manner and only aim at self-achievement.

Many researchers have adopted socio-emotional development to evaluate the outcomes of emotional support in teaching. Marzano, Marzano, and Pickering (2003) found that warm relationships between teachers and students tended to render students demonstrating fewer behavioural problems and to foster prosocial behaviours. Birch and Ladd (1998) reported that young children who had less harmonious relationships with their teachers during kindergarten years tended to become less prosocial elementary school students (i.e. these students were less likely to be helpful towards others and were more aggressive), which predicts the social role of teachers in the classroom. Hughes, Cavell and Willson (2001) found that students who had less warm relationships with their teachers tended to demonstrate a higher level of aggression at school. As proved by a study of classroom dynamics by Hendrickx, Mainhard, Boor-Klip, Cillessen, and Brekelmans's (2016) with 58 classes of fifth grade Dutch students and teachers, in the class where a teacher showed more support, the students in the class reported more liking relationships with each other and showed more prosocial behaviours in the classroom. The findings evidence the positive effects of teachers' emotional support on students' social development, emotion and prosocial behaviours.

In Curby, Brock, and Hamre's (2013) study with 694 prekindergarten classroom observations, it was found that when the levels of emotional support were controlled, consistency of teacher support significantly predicted academic outcomes and social competence later when the preschoolers went to kindergarten. Emotional support is seen to be crucial for preschool education, according to the theory of AT; preschool teachers are generally regarded as a source of attachment for young children, who learn about social relationships and how to care for others from their ties with teachers, the process of which underpins their social competence (Copeland-Mitchell, Denham, & DeMulder, 1997). Besides, children learning in an emotionally consistent environment can avoid having their attention diverted. According to the resource depletion theory, attention grabbing stimuli in the classroom that are salient to the students' task in hand would cause distractions. When the interaction between teacher and student is inconsistent, young students would feel confused and have to pay more attention to monitor the emotional state of the teacher. Therefore, unpredictable responses from the teacher are likely to draw students' attention away from their task or from socialising with other peers, causing less cognitive resources being available for their learning (Kaplan & Berman, 2010). In contrast, an emotionally consistent classroom is more favourable for learning because students would understand what to expect and feel more secure and thus they can focus on learning without many distractions (Curby et al., 2013) and it is likely to produce better learning outcomes as students can concentrate on their study with relevant support from teachers. Hence, teachers' efforts in regulating their emotions in the classroom are crucial as teachers' positive emotion can ensure their care and support is offered consistently to students.

Emotional Work of Scaffoldings Enhances Academic Learning. Researchers also elaborate the effect of teacher's emotional support on students' academic development. Teachers who provide experience for students which involves crucial learning processes, that can help them master academic learning (Meyer & Turner, 2006), and teachers who interact with students and give them the feeling of responsiveness, sensitivity, and positivity, can make them more motivated in pursuing academic study (Gregory & Weinstein, 2004). These students tend to adopt a mastery goal of learning (Furrer & Skinner, 2003). The review by Hamre & Pianta (2005) mentions that teachers' emotional support can be demonstrated through their choice of teaching strategies, such as learner-centred teaching approaches that allows learner autonomy and encourages intrinsic interest, as well as students' perception of close connections with the teachers. These have resulted in greater motivation to learn and higher academic achievements.

The impact of teachers' emotional support in increasing students' academic achievement can partly be explained by the skills students adopt through teachers' emotional work of scaffolding, and partly because of the positive attitude of teachers who may have a positive influence on students. This suggests the dual effects of teacher's emotional support on student learning motivation and strategies. Stipek's (2002) study reported that students who felt supported by teachers were more willing to learn to master the subject matter (oriented with a mastery goal of learning) and more confident in managing school work, thus, they had lower levels of task engagement anxiety (Wang & Eccles, 2012). This implies that teachers' emotional support is crucial to boost students' non-academic and academic learning, instead of using controlling, drill and practice methods, as the latter methods have overlooked the most important part of learning for learners. As a whole, teachers' emotional scaffolding support in the classroom includes the interaction teachers maintain with their students that motivate students to learn as well as the pedagogical arrangement that teachers organise for students in order to engage students into their study in schools. Such behaviours may have a modelling effect on learners in developing their learning attitude and work approach that benefits their learning. As a result, the positive outcomes students achieved in such positive learning environment may create a sense of accomplishment for learners, and it is likely to generate civic responsibility for the learners who are contributing participants in the classroom as a learning community.

Peer Emotional Support Promotes Social Development and Prosocial Behaviours. The emotional support of student peers for each other is another source of support that benefits student learning. The needs of peer support are found to be growing during mid-adolescence (Hamre & Pianta, 2001). Therefore, approaching senior years of secondary schooling, social support from peers becomes critical for adolescents in proximal environment; some researchers suggested that the impact of peer support is even greater than teacher support (Davidson, Gest, & Welsh, 2010). According to the theory of self-determination (Ryan & Deci, 2017) discussed in Chap. 3, peer support fulfils an adolescent's need for relatedness that can enhance student's feeling of satisfaction. It also supports students' pursuit of social goals (Wang & Holcombe, 2010). Making friends with peers implies the disclosure of oneself. It is associated with prosocial behaviour and support (Wang & Eccles, 2012), and leads to better engagement in schools. Rejecting friendship and connection with peers will make young children become isolated, self-centred. This risks aggressive behaviour and delinquency in future (Chapple, 2005).

The need for developing strong bonds with social groups is seen as crucial in the classroom. Studies identified that students with weak academic ability, usually called low achievers, had low self-esteem and demonstrated at risk behaviours (Lee, 1997). Cheng & Lam (2007) found that students with weaker academic ability in a high-ability classroom could either 'feel bad about themselves' by comparing themselves with high-ability students or develop increased self-esteem by relaxing in the mirrored success of their peer significant others. The condition for the latter case is whether the weaker ability students have built a strong relationship with the social group in the classroom. Therefore, social support attributes, such as empathetic concerns and providing scaffoldings for other student peers should be cultivated among students in a mainstream school setting and an inclusive classroom setting with mixed ability students. As a whole, teachers' and peers' emotional support perceived by children and adolescents strongly influence their overall life satisfaction (Gilman, Huebner, & Laughlin, 2000). These social support sources are crucial for creating a low-conflict, harmonious classroom environment for learners, and the results, as suggested by numerous empirical evidences, are positive for the overall development of learners; academic learning outcomes are definitely a part that shows these positive outcomes.

Positive Relationships Protect Students from Negative Outcomes

Teacher Positive Relationship Buffers Stress and Increase Self-esteem. As relationships are discussed as examples of emotional support, teachers' relationships with students have been found to protect students from negative affective and anti-social outcomes (e.g. Barber & Olsen, 2004; Pössel, Rudasill, Sawyer, Spence, & Bjerg, 2013), i.e. helping students overcome certain difficult issues in life and sustaining the benefits over their life time. Youngsters frequently face stressors in common regarding academic performance, interpersonal relationships with parents and peers and self-identity. Teachers as outsiders may be more suitable to provide support and guidance for students by educating them with advice and values (Rhodes, Grossman, & Resch, 2000). Positive teacher–student relationships are proven to be an important means to buffer students from their stress. For example, Reddy, Rhodes, and Mulhall (2003a, 2003b) conducted a 3-year longitudinal study on the influence of teacher support on student adjustment with 2585 middle school students. Students' perception of teacher support, level of depressive symptoms, and self-esteem were assessed at the same time of each school year. It was found that regardless of gender and initial levels of depression and self-esteem, students who perceived a higher level of teacher support had a decrease in depressive symptoms and an increase in self-esteem. This shows the buffer effect of teacher's support. In contrast, those who perceived less teacher support had heightened depression and loss of self-esteem. The findings were consistent with earlier studies investigating other social problems experienced by school-aged students. For example, adolescents who had suffered from depression recovered more easily when they were provided with social support (Barrera & Garrison-Jones, 1992). Students who had been at risk (e.g. who suffered from poverty, familial problems, and poor relationships with peers) also tended to fare better when they were provided with social support from the school (e.g. Benard, 1991; Wang, Haertel, & Walberg, 1994). These studies highlight the importance of teacher support in predicting student well-being.

On the other hand, teacher support can also lead to positive student emotions via the main effect of social support, i.e. a long-term positive effect, such as well-being. For instance, students' feeling of closeness with teachers has been directly associated with their adjustment (Ryan, stiller, & Lynch, 1994). Positive teacher–student relationship also predicts better conduct and higher rates of retention (Pianta, Steinberg, & Rollins, 1995), and stronger academic engagement and competence among students (Hughes, Luo, Kwok, & Loyd, 2008; Roorda, 2012). Teachers' developing emotional bonds with students enable students to perceive support and care. In such situations, students are more likely to comply with teachers' expectations, act prosocially, and avoid engaging in deviant behaviours. It is therefore not surprising to see that the relationship between teachers and students outweighs that of family and peers, in its impact on students' well-being and academic performance at school

(Murray-Harvey, 2010). Teacher support even has a stronger impact on children at risk, who usually employ poorer coping strategies against stress (Reddy et al. 2003a, 2003b).

Sources of different social support are likely to prevent these jeopardised students from turning hostile and avoidant of challenges, and guide them to become more willing to interact with others (Buyse, Verschueren, Doumen, van Damme, & Maes, 2008). Apparently, teachers' social support giving is highly constructive to students' development and well-being from multiple aspects, and the beneficial outcomes have been confirmed as applicable across culture and ethnicity (Close & Solberg, 2008; Hughes & Kwok, 2007). Hence, fostering supportive teacher–student relationships is a key factor in educational intervention, especially in positive education programmes (Hughes, 2012; Midgley & Edelin, 1998; Pianta, Hamre, & Allen, 2012).

Positive Peer Relationship Promotes Social Goals. The benefits of peer relationship are found to be positively related to a broad range of outcomes including student's motivational orientation (i.e. goals and values), skills related to self-regulation, social skills, problem solving and academic outcomes (Becker & Luthar, 2002; Wentzel, 1997; Wentzel & Watkins, 2002). Though there is not full agreement in the research literature regarding the effects of peer relationships on academic outcomes, it is generally agreed that it does increase the learning motivation of students, enhance prosocial behaviours (such as helping, cooperating and sharing (Wentzel & Watkins, 2002), which affect academic outcomes positively. Being accepted by peers is considered a sign of popularity, and it increases students' interest in school and academic competence(Wentzel & Asher, 1995). Wentzel & Watkins (2002) described the mechanism of peer learning as a motivational resource, which refers to students' feeling of satisfaction and relatedness. With this feeling, students are more engaged in learning because they feel cared for and valued.

This situation can be explained by the social support literature, with two different approaches discussed in Chap. 2. From the relationship perspective, students' peer relationship has a crucial role to play in the proximal learning environment; this enhances the perceived support around the learning environment and gives them a higher sense of self-efficacy. Students are thus more competent and resilient in facing challenges and problems. In a social cognitive approach, Students' perception of supportiveness from their peers may impact on their behaviours, motivation and achievement (Goodenow, 1993; Wentzel, 1999). Supportiveness from the others can be regarded as the sources of establishing a person's self-esteem. Having peer standards to live up to for social comparison could serve as a self-monitoring mechanism for students in their attempt to improve their performance in the classroom. Peers as social support can therefore be seen as enablers (Lam, Cheng, & Yang, 2017), facilitating students to take prosocial action in the course of study in schools and improve academic outcomes. This discussion recommends the use of peers as resources for instructional strategies in the classroom to support learning; however, social learning does not only benefit students cognitively, as the theory of ZPD suggests, it has an implicit requirement that cultivation of social support is a prerequisite for making social learning a success.

Types of Social Support Teachers Give in Teaching

To find out which specific teacher behaviours could support students effectively, Suldo and colleagues (2009) interviewed 401 middle school students regarding teacher behaviours in classrooms and classified five themes of supportive acts that could effectively enhance students' well-being and academic achievement:

- *Emotional support* from teachers has robust positive effects on student life satisfaction, academic performance and social skills (Malecki & Demaray, 2003; Richman, Rosenfeld, & Bowen, 1998). Students reported feeling cared for when teachers showed concerns about their personal well-being, being respectful and giving rewards to them. Situations such as if the teacher 'comforts you and tells you they are on your side' and 'get you to think about your feelings' are examples of emotional support and emotional challenge support (Carter, Cushing, Clark & Kennedy, 2005).
- *Teaching method and attitude.* Teachers' classroom practices that ensure students' understanding and keeping everyone up to speed are perceived as supportive by students. Students found it helpful when teachers provided them with additional learning materials to ensure their mastery of content. Students also reported appreciating teachers' use of diverse teaching strategies, which might have direct positive impacts on students' learning and their interest in class. An autonomy-supportive teaching style, which encourages student to learning in their own way, is suggested to better motivate students (Reeve & Jang, 2006).
- *Instrumental support* given to students concerning their academic performance has been considered the most important type of teacher support by students (Malecki & Demaray, 2003). Specifically, students expect teachers to be keen on helping them achieve academic goals and recognise their accomplishments. It is noted that students appreciate teachers' feedback on their performance, as well as explaining to them their errors, in order to improve themselves.
- *Equity* should be present in teacher support, regardless of gender and classroom grades. Students perceive teachers as more supportive when teachers are consistently fair to all students in punishment and reward and use less punitive approaches. As reported in the literature, teachers who provide additional support to specific students are likely to create an unharmonious atmosphere in the classroom, such as peer disliking (Hendrickx et al., 2016) due to the teacher's pet effect (Babad, 2009).
- *Classroom climate* where questions are encouraged is valued by students. Positive responses from teachers are likely to encourage students to pose questions and learn intrinsically as a self-regulated learner.

Suldo and colleagues' study found that emotional and instrumental support from teachers is both important for student to perceive teachers' care. Especially, students who perceive more emotional support tend to have better well-being, perceive greater levels of school satisfaction, competence and social skills. It echoes the above discussion that teachers' emotional support can enhance student engagement (Roorda,

Table 4.1 Supportive teacher acts that could enhance student well-being and achievement

Theme of teacher support	Explanation
Emotional support	Showing concerns about students' well-being beyond academic performance
Teaching method and attitude	Ensuring every student's learning pace and teaching with a variety of strategies
Instrumental support	Offering sufficient support and feedback to students regarding their academic performance
Equity	Being fair in support, punishment and reward
Classroom climate	Creating an environment that encourages active learning

2012). The categories of support feature teachers' concern about clarifying students' doubt and engaging them in active learning in a warm and caring classroom climate (Table 4.1).

Correspondingly, Wentzel et al. (2010a, 2010b) also identified four forms of social support rendered by teachers in teaching, namely, emotional care, expectations, instrumental help and safety, and all these four forms predict students' interest in class. The 'expectation' of teachers and students are discussed in the following section as major sources of social support to students, while the other forms have been generally covered in this discussion.

Teacher and Student Expectations Shapes Students' Path to Success

Expectations are perceived through the interaction of students and teachers and students with their peers through social influencing. It is the guide to students on how they should act and the consequences of such actions can help to enhance their self-esteem and self-efficacy (Klem & Connell, 2004; Ryan & Patrick, 2001; Wentzel et al. 2004a, 2004b), as explained by social cognitive theory. Expectation is communicated by the embedded structure of learning in the classroom (Russell, 2012a), and it is how students can be helped to develop a clear sense about their role and identity. It is usually aimed at helping students to accomplish commendable behaviours, i.e. prosocial behaviours; it is often referred to as social goal pursuit. As early adolescents go through middle school years (generally defined as the age between primary and secondary school years), which are critical developmental stages, their relationships with teachers become important because they look for non-parental adults as role models and source of support (Lee, Smith, Perry, & Smylie, 1999). In schools, students' perception of teachers' level of support has been consistently found to be associated with their achievement motivation, academic success, social adjustment and subjective well-being (e.g. Roeser, Midgley, & Urdan, 1996; Verschueren,

Doumen, & Buyse, 2012). These positive outcomes are possibly the result of both teacher support and expectations, as perceived by learners, which is in line with teacher's self-fulfilling prophecy, which means having something come true in reality may be due to the strong belief held by oneself. When students believe in their teachers' expectations, they are motivated to keep up with these expectations and achieve their goals (Jussim, 1989).

As demonstrated by Murdock's (1999) study with seventh graders, teachers' appraisals and support are the most consistent and strongest predictors of students' achievement outcomes. It is also found that teachers' expectations about classroom structure predict students' engagement, if teachers' expectations are clear and their instructions are consistent, students will develop positive emotions and show support to the class (Skinner & Belmont, 1993). This finding aligns with the models of teacher expectation effects (Bronfenbrenner, 1977; Weinstein, 1989), which suggest that students' perception of teacher expectations is a significant predictor of behavioural and academic outcomes. Furthermore, expectation from peers also has an effect that governs student learning behaviours. Students' perceived expectations from their teacher and their peers for social behaviours (such as connecting to each other closely) affect students' feeling towards schooling.

Rosenthal and Jacobson's (1968) classical experiment of teacher expectation (Pygmalion) effect may better illustrate the impact of teachers' expectations on students' performance. The researchers distributed an intelligence test to students of an elementary school and claimed to their teachers that the result had revealed that some randomly picked students were gifted and were about to experience a dramatic intellectual bloom. It should be noted that this type of psychological experiment would not be accepted in modern society, such a controlled experiment has resulted in salient results that alert teachers to reflect on our own behaviours especially regarding differentiated treatment on students. After 2 years of follow-up, it was discovered that those 'gifted' students had gained more in IQ as the teachers had higher expectations of them. Teachers' expectation actually changed their interaction with the 'gifted' students unconsciously, and therefore they treated those students differently. Teachers were observed to spend more time answering 'gifted' students' questions, give them more specific feedback and give acts of appreciation such as nodding and smiling at the 'gifted' kids more frequently. Their findings implied teachers should not blindly apply expectations to students without the sensitivity to understand individual differences in ability, values and cultures (Weiner, 2000), as expectation did predict student behaviours as educational beliefs.

Generally, teachers' expectations correspond to students' achievements. Learners' perceptions of supportiveness from the learning environment may enhance their self-esteem and intrinsic interest in learning. The teachers' supportive role in the classroom is therefore a crucial factor that can better engage learners. While teachers are willing to provide scaffolding to students, it may also be important for them to vary the levels of support to students, as the decline of help at suitable time can support learners to acquire study skills and to learn independently. Considering the positive effect of perceived support from teachers and the anticipated expectation that teachers have of students, it may be useful for teachers to set reasonably challenging academic standards for learners while creating a supportive environment for learners so that they feel safe and confident to explore learning. Trying to push students by using drill and practice without a process of development would certainly create negative emotions for learners that destroy the intrinsic motivation of learning (Reeve, 2006). Therefore, another important role of teachers is to initiative ways to monitor (support) learner progress, such as formative assessment strategies, to ensure that learners are given relevant support and the learning progress made in a specific given timeframe during a learning process.

Researchers who studied motivational styles of teaching, particularly focuses on the study of self-determination (SDT), supplement the idea about teacher support regarding teacher expectations of students as has been realised in the structure teachers give to students (Deci & Ryan, 2008; Jang, Reeve, & Deci, 2010). These researchers proposed autonomy support and structure as inseparable in teaching to produce effective learning outcomes. The former can be explained by behaviour such as observing students' perspectives, providing rationales for students to explain teacher actions in managing the class, and using non-pressurised language; the latter is related to the guidelines and rules that teachers use to manage the class; that require students to comply with in order to facilitate learning (Reeve & Jang, 2006). According to SDT researchers, structure must be given with autonomy support, and the two can enable an autonomy-supportive style of teaching which would result in increased autonomous motivation of learners, who behaved in a more engaged manner in learning (Reeve, 2002). These researchers also mentioned that teachers who adopted a controlling style which is characterised by pressure-inducing language, asserting power and excess control (Deci & Ryan, 2008) may undermine students' motivation and interest in studying and fail to encourage students in higher levels of engagement in learning. Hence, while expectations of learners and a given structure to be organised in the classroom environment to support student learning have been proved to be essential, autonomy support to learners, which is realised in the giving of autonomy, relatedness and competency, as suggested by SDT researchers, should be taken into consideration in teaching. This theory enables a link to be built to the social support literature in considering education. If student learning can be seen as a process of growth of their self-esteem, learning the capacities, skills and strategies of achieving academic study may become a natural acquisition process in school that may lead to more favourable result of learning.

To summarise, teachers' expectations strongly influence students' perception of their own ability and chances of success. They could drive students to invest more effort in learning in order to achieve their goals. Teachers should have fair expectation according to students' strength in different areas and ensure students know about the availability of support to guarantee that students understand so that they may be able to achieve in certain fields.

School and Classroom Environment Characteristics as Social Support

Coordination of the Classroom and School Environment Works Well. A perception of social support influences the quality of student learning and the types of outcomes for students. Researchers have suggested another source of social support. This is a collective system known as the classroom environment and school environment (Ames, 1992; Bronfenbrenner 1995, 2005), which works to predict students' learning behaviours, attitude and emotions. Brophy (1988) postulated a list of school characteristics that support students for successful achievement outcomes. including (i) a safe climate, (ii) strong leadership, (iii) positive teacher attitudes and expectations, (iv) emphasis on instruction, (v) careful monitoring of student progress and staff evaluation, (vi) strong parent involvement and (vii) emphasis on the importance of academic achievement. Although this study laid its basis on the school effectiveness movement, which was a prevalent research approach in the later half of the twentieth century focused on the study of effectiveness mainly on the cognitive learning outcomes (Lezotte, 1989; Teddlie, & Reynolds, 2000). The resultant list of factors suggests the salient features of the school environment which are found to influence students' achievement motivation (e.g. Wigfield & Eccles, 2002) and mental health (e.g. Roeser & Eccles, 2000), indicating the importance of the role of social support in education. Cohen (2006) especially recognised emotional support as the core value of schooling, saying that 'interventions designed to create a safe, caring, participatory, and responsive school represent a systemic process that creates the optimal foundation for learning and development' (p. 209).

More recently, Russell (2012a, 2012b) theorised two forms of system functioning which were found to affect student perception of support in the classroom. 'Classroom cohesion' is one of the system aspects, which can be captured by students' perception of classroom relationship as a whole and involves different individual factors including involvement, affiliation, teacher support, belongingness and emotional support from teacher and peers (Olson, 2000; Wentzel, 1998). 'Structure' is a kind of support that affects student learning outcomes. A structure can be conceptually understood as the shared vision and the guide communicated at the structural level in the environment. A school with a clear vision and mission to guide its policies and practice affects student academic outcomes and behaviourial engagement (Church, Elliot, & Gable, 2001). If a clear structure of learning is established in the classroom, it will become the expectation of students and this expectation will guide students' behaviour (how to act) in the classroom and give them a sense of identity of self, and this is likely to give an orientation to students to proceed satisfactorily with their studies. Students may become committed to their role identity in the classroom and become motivated to act accordingly; in such a way students' self-esteem can be enhanced as their prosocial behaviour is developed and they develop higher sense of self-efficacy and accomplishment by the efforts they make. This is how social support is created in the classroom environment, according to Stryker (1994), where people make use of social interaction to evaluate and formulate their own self-concept, and roles become a point of reference for people to view themselves in their social environment.

School and Classroom Expectations Facilitate Student Engagement. Student engagement is also used to explain how classroom characteristics support students. It is based on the assumption that school education must help students to become genuinely interested in study and willing to invest time and energy to achieve success in it. Social support has been found to be a potent means of engaging students as shown from engagement models. For example, the 'contextual support structure' (Newmann, 1981) involves aspects such as student participation in school policymaking, maintaining clear and consistent educational goals, and encouraging student–teacher relationships. The model contains an expectation statement and emotional support measures. The 'self-system process model' is another model of student engagement which is based upon self-determination theory, i.e. focusing on student well-being, emphasising the intrapersonal dynamics which are based on human's basic needs for competence, autonomy and relatedness (Connell, 1990; Connell & Wellborn, 1991). These three ingredients of basic needs are believed to be the factors that drive learners to develop interest in the pursuit of learning, so that they can lead a fulfilling life (Connell, 1990; Skinner, Kindermann, Connell, & Wellborn, 2009). The 'participation-identification' model is a combination of the above contextual and intrapersonal models, which explains how the interaction between behaviour and emotion influences academic outcomes. It is hypothesised that students' behaviour in the early stages (participation) influences their connection with school (identification) in later stages, which in turn affects their participation again, and the cycle repeats itself (Finn, 1989; Finn & Zimmer, 2012). Successful academic outcomes can be driven when students show active participation (e.g. being responsive in class, and active participation in extracurricular activities) in the first place, and the school context allows students to build up a sense of identification and value at the same time. The construction of school and classroom environment alignment can therefore help students to achieve good performance, and the achievement in turn further reinforces participation and identification. Environmental support for learners gives insights to the governments if they aim at boosting the assessment results of school students; however, efforts should be made to track the development of students and cultivate the social support attributes in the learning environment. Therefore, professional development of teachers and the necessary resources to be given to education are essential.

From a micro-perspective, similar to teacher's expectation norms, the classroom environment influences students with behaviourial norms (Aber, Jones, Brown, Chaudry, & Samples, 1998); children conform to and adjust their behaviours in order to fit in the classroom context (Henry et al., 2000). Besides, teacher's behaviours would also be affected by classroom characteristics (such as student attributes), and this indirectly affects teaching effectiveness. For instance, previous research has revealed that teachers' expectations are biased due to particular students' background such as ethnicity and social-economic status (Murdock, 1996). Such lowered expectations towards and more negative appraisals of the disadvantaged students are often unrelated to their abilities (Weinstein, 2002). Another common example is that teachers may be harsher and more likely to adopt punitive discipline strategies to a class with more misbehaving children than to an obedient class. Hence, teachers themselves should also develop their commitment to teach students, and especially, the social support traits; they have to be responsive to students' needs and conscious about learner diversity. As in the case where teachers face a class with the majority of students having low morale in learning, students' resistance to class participation could be resistant to change. Teachers could change the classroom climate by considering involving student participation to construct a productive classroom at the classroom level. It appears that a stronger collaboration between school and class levels to cultivate the expectations for learners should be deemed necessary. According to Russell (2013), this collaboration could increase the learning outcomes tremendously. Therefore, it is appropriate for schools to set affective goals in their school policies, such as responsibility, social goal and self-management, so that misbehaving students can be guided by the rules and follow the school rules.

Student Features in the Classroom Environment Affect Learning. Student attributes can largely affect student attitude and learning behaviours in the classroom (Wentzel, Baker & Russell, 2009). Students' interest in academic study may affect positive student engagement, and the students' perception of peers as supportive predicts the learning behaviours and efforts individuals pay to tasks (Ryan, 2000; O'Donnell & O'Kelly, 1994). It has implications for implementing peer-learning tasks and collaborative learning in the classroom. This will be followed up and discussed later when focussing on teaching strategies.

Student demographics comprise a feature of classroom environment that are crucial for teachers to note in providing appropriate social support with reference to particular student variables. Gender and age characteristics are discussed by researchers; the results suggest that girls form more supportive relationships with teachers than boys (Russell, 2012a, 2012b; Wentzel et al., 2010a, 2010b; Rueger, Malecki, & Demaray, 2010), and girls tend to seek more emotional support and boys more instrumental support (Suldo et al, 2009). When perceiving the supportiveness of teachers, girls pay the most attention to whether teachers take care of students' emotions, while boys appreciate it more when teachers give sufficient instrumental support and manageable workloads, as well as being fair and creating an encouraging classroom environment. The reasons may be that girls have more salient experience as they proceed to puberty, and they are more expressive and tend to be more emotion-oriented, and girls are generally more mature than boys; therefore they may encounter problems at an earlier age (Reddy et al. 2003a). With regard to age, girls benefit early in mid-adolescence from adult social support, while boys benefit in late adolescence (Murberg & Bru, 2004; Reddy et al. 2003a, 2003b). Evidence shows that girls have stronger engagement than boys. Girls perceive academic study with greater interest and demonstrate less misbehaviour (Wang & Eccles, 2012). This gender difference regarding support is in line with the social support literature discussed in Chap. 3. While taking note of these gender differences, teachers should take note of the interaction with particular students to determine the right kind of social support, such as considering whether it is necessary, which should be the most relevant forms and whether certain forms may harm students' self-esteem. Regarding this, Chap. 3 may give us some insights in defining the right support.

With regard to grade level characteristics, Wentzel et al. (2010a, 2010b) suggest that teacher social support is prominent from early years to mid-adolescence. The engagement literature explains that students become less engaged in school as they progress from elementary school to high school (Marks, 2000). Correspondingly, the literature also finds that the linkage between teacher support and student engagement is more robust for secondary school students than for elementary school students (Klem & Connell, 2004), which can be explained by the reasons that adolescents may face more challenges in the current education environment. The situation implies that social support can be developed into the school curriculum and teaching strategies through early years and high school to benefit school-aged students, with special attention given to the transitional years during the milestones of the academic study path.

Teaching Strategies that Utilise Social Support

Social support can be more intrinsically designed in teaching strategies to benefit student learning. This section attempts to identify strategies that reflect teachers' use of social support sources in teaching. The following section introduces strategies that are commonly used in the mainstream classroom, including pedagogies that are characterised by emotional support, feeling and thinking, cooperative learning and formative feedback strategies.

Pedagogies Emphasises Emotional Support, Feeling and Thinking

To support student learning based on the theoretical underpinnings of social support, strategies that promote learning based on learner experience, feeling and practice are typical as these activities can encourage students sense-making and the realisation of one's own feeling and engaging them in thinking and responding. A number of authors have derived models that utilise the affective function of the human brain that facilitate learning effectively. Anderson et al. (2001) developed a taxonomy of affective learning with a hierarchy of affective domains that include receiving, responding, valuing, organising and characterising by value (Anderson et al., 2001). Receiving is to prepare students to be eager to learn and receive the information with awareness and willingness to deal with the learning content. Responding refers to students' active participation and giving responses in some small measures to suggest that they are participating in learning. Learners value particular learning objects by expressing their interest and commitment. Organising is to relate newly

Teaching Strategies that Utilise Social Support

acquired values to those that already exist in internal consistent logic in accomplished ways. Characterising is to act consistently with the same value as learnt in the lesson and to internalise the newly acquired value to consider ways of solving a problem. The teachers' role is to plan the learning activities based on such sequences so that students could personally value learning. In this model, the social support of teachers and the scaffoldings of students are considered important sources for learning.

Malikow (2006) proposed feel, listen and defend as the protocol for acknowledging human feeling in learning. The format bases learning upon perception, meaning-making and analytic thinking, which makes students feel that learning is authentic, personal and challenging, in order to enhance students' motivation to learn. Cultural Responsive Teaching is another model that utilises the cultural knowledge and experiences of diverse students to form a caring school environment (Vavrus, 2008). It advocates learner-centred pedagogies that highlight student active participation and use the learning community to engage learners in active acquisition of knowledge. Teachers use culturally relevant content and language that fit the diverse backgrounds of students as a strategy (Gay, 2002) and use students as cultural resources to acknowledge and empower every student about their cultural differences.

Not only can pedagogies enhance affective teaching but the manner, attitude and the traits of teachers. Caring practice appears to become a form of teaching based on the theory of ethnic care (Noddings, 1984). This form of practice accentuates moral values and human virtues in the interaction of teachers and students. Caring practice contains four components of teacher caring, namely, modelling, dialogue, practice and confirmation (Noddings, 2003). Modelling refers to the care of listening and appreciating each other's perspectives to cultivate respect in a shared space in the classroom. Dialogue refers to the conversation openly to create a trustworthy relationship with students to show that their voices are listened to practice is to provide chances for students to show care to others and give support to one another and to learn to become human. Confirmation means to assure students about their capabilities; teachers work with them and listen to them to achieve their own ideal goal of learning. In performing these roles, according to Noddings (2013, 2005), teachers have to exercise 'engrossment' and 'motivational displacement'. These two concepts outline the internal motivation and the flow of emotions towards helping students. Teachers have to take an open, non-selective attitude to students who are the one to be cared for (engrossment); they have to focus on the students and attend to the interaction with the students so that the motive energy is flowing towards the students who are the one to be cared for (motivational displacement). In this way, teachers are put in the position of students to feel about how they feel so that teachers can teach to cater for the interests and needs of students.

Cooperative Learning Utilises Social Support

As generated from the above discussion, positive social bonds and friendships among students benefit students as these qualities affect students' well-being in school life.

Relating to peers can also help to establish and maintain students' positive self-identity, which is a crucial support for student development, as argued in the social support literature.

Cooperative Learning (CL) is an instructional strategy assigning small groups of student to work together to complete tasks collectively; it is therefore a strategy that utilises social support, especially peer support. The primary aim of CL, however, is to operate an efficiency model, counting the costs and benefits of working together, i.e. in maximising the effectiveness of individual students own effort and each other's learning (Johnson et al. 2007). However, the basis of collaborative learning is largely based upon utilisation of social resources, and it has the benefit of promoting interpersonal relatedness in the social context (Wentzel & Watkins, 2002), which can facilitate students' intrinsic motivation (Law, 2011).

The traditional format of CL emphasises the belief that the effects of mutual support within a team can be enhanced when all group members are fairly equally participating (Gleason et al., 2003). Formats are therefore set for structured cooperative learning. For example, the jigsaw method developed by Aronson is a popular format of this approach and has been widely adopted in schools since the 1970s. In the jigsaw method, every student in the class will join in an expert group and a home group one after the other. In the expert group, every student studies a narrow topic which is a subtopic under a broad topic. The number of expert groups represents different subtopics of a broad theme, which should be the topic of investigation for the specific lesson. After studying in the expert groups, all students in the class will be allocated to a home group, who will produce a report on the broad topic. The membership of the home group contains one member of each of the expert groups, this result to the composition of experts from every subtopics in the home group. Then, with the combined expert knowledge individual expert members studied in the respective expert groups, each member in the home group has to teach everyone in the home group about the deep knowledge they learn in the expert group discussion they previously completed. With the combined expertise, the home group can therefore complete the investigation result of the broad topic with cooperative effort. This is how the jigsaw method is run and it becomes a popular method in schools (Slavin, 1983).

To ensure every member participates, CL also uses recognition and assessment to enhance the group's 'positive interdependence' (set in place mutual learning goals, joint rewards, shared resources, assigned roles) and 'individual accountability' (each group member should be responsible for a portion of the group work) (Johnson, Johnson, & Holubec, 1993). It is hoped that students have an equal share of responsibility among the group and that they develop the social skills to work collaboratively on the tasks. The Student Teams-Achievement Divisions (STAD) developed by Slavin (2008) uses a format to help students work towards a CL model, by having individuals responsible for a portion of the learning task where students are involved in peer tutoring and learn from one another. After learning the content collaboratively, students will take a test individually, with the individual assessment score aggregated as part of the overall group assessment scores. Slavin (1983), based on an earlier research, when rewards were given according to the summation of each member's performance rather than individual results, asserts that students would be encouraged to care about the learning progress of their group members, as it directly affected their own rewards.

CL creates an environment for students to work together instead of working individually; thus learners may gain through peer tutoring and peer assessment (Slavin, 2008) to achieve cognitive development; yet, CL encountered challenges in its use. Common problems include social loafing or free riding (Felder & Brent, 2007), and the problems of working in a group (Cheng, Lam and Chan, 2008), such as the use of peer pressure and the division of a fair share of work to determine collaboration (Russell, 2012a, 2012b).

Reasons for the problems may be related to student characteristics. For example, students' perception of whether members in the class are emotionally supportive determines the classroom behaviour of individual members of the class (Wentzel et al., 2010a, 2010b). A classroom with low-conflict, high social bonds and high student well-being may work wellto implement CL. Furthermore, the processes of working in a team is also a crucial condition. Research has found that group collaboration is dependent on the socialisation skills among peers, which creates positive peer influencing in the team (Hawley, Little, & Pasupathi, 2002). This idea is further elaborated in Cheng, Lam and Chan's (2008) study where the research team found that positive interdependence, personal accountability, social skills and equal participation are elements that determine high-quality group processes. They also found that if the quality of group processes was low, students were more likely to have lower collective efficacy than self-efficacy; in contrast, if the quality of group processes was high, student would have higher collective efficacy than self-efficacy, irrespective of academic abilities.

The study by Law (2011) illustrates an exemplary case of CL, which can provide insights to create a supportive social environment for peer learning. He adopted an intervention study and examined its effect mainly on students' mastery goals, autonomous motivation, and study scores, in a reading programme. 279 fifth graders from three different schools in Hong Kong participated in the study. Jigsaw and drama, which involved team collaboration, were used as cooperative strategies. Other than the chances of collaboration, these two strategies encouraged students to contribute towards group performance instead of individual performance, and it eliminated social comparison among individuals which was possibly harmful to self-image and feelings (Haferkamp & Kramer, 2011). Besides promoting scaffoldings among peers, teachers' efforts in scaffolding students was designed to facilitate learning in two key aspects—this is where social support giving of teachers works. On the one hand, students' metacognitive skills were enhanced as they had to handle the tasks assigned to them by working with group members and complete it by the set deadlines, including the follow-up of the teacher's feedback during the process. On the other hand, ongoing cognitive intervention from the teacher was given throughout the process to enhance the cognitive outcomes of learning, such as explaining issues to the whole class when issues were identified from a specific team, and asking students prompting questions to stimulate higher order thinking. This two-part support of the teacher in the cooperative learning intervention was recognised as a source of cognitive autonomy support. When teacher guidance was given, the enhanced abilities to handle the work further increased the autonomy of learners in exploring challenging issues in learning.

The outcomes of the intervention reported favourable results (Law, 2011). Students were found to acquire a mastery goal of learning, reflecting the desire to improve one's ability, understand tasks, master skills and acquire new knowledge; students in the experimental group also attained higher autonomous motivation as a result of studying in an autonomous support environment where embedded scaffoldings were provided. In terms of academic outcomes, i.e. higher order reading proficiency and reading scores, the experimental group outperformed the control group who learned in the traditional teacher-led approach without the scaffolding supports. The effects were substantial for at least three months, as reported by the researcher. The social support that was structured in a cooperative learning setting in the case echoes benefits that social support has on human beings on their perception of their own ability and the actual enhancement of abilities (Cacioppo & Patrick, 2008). Students tend to behave and meet up with social expectations and social norms (Slavin, 2014).

In CL, students who provide scaffolds to peers may also benefit personally. As suggested by the literature, support providers' ability is recognised when they are needed for help, and as such, people who try to help others benefit from increased self-esteem and a sense of self-worth (Fisher, Nadler, & Whitcher-Alagna, 1982). Through constant mutual support, a trusting relationship can be built among the group members and lead to the well-being of all students (Cutrona et al., 2005). Social support from classmates during the learning process promotes effective learning and the sense of achievement students gain via group work will then reinforce further learning (Danielsen et al. 2009). To sum up, regardless of student gender or ethnicity (Cabrera, Nora, Crissman, & Terenzini, 2002; Tinto, 1997), such reciprocal social support provided in CL effectively fosters students' academic performance, personal growth and ultimately enhances their well-being. Due to these beneficial effects, CL has been considered the most promising teaching practice by educators (Cockrell, Caplow, & Donaldson, 2000), which offers both academic and social experiences to student (Tinto, 1997).

As a whole, CL is a recommended strategy to promote higher quality learning. In practice, teachers may consider the appropriateness of lesson design and attractiveness of instructional tasks to add a crucial element of how social support in classroom can afford a successful experience for students, as it may interest learners by engendering their internal locus of control instead of relying on external assessment as the major incentive of learning. A caution may be that in a cooperative learning setting, social support is used instrumentally for achieving positive learning outcomes. Yet, cooperative learning has a value-added strength added to the strategy, which is to establish humanistic virtues in the classroom, creating a sharing and supportive environment, which can enhance young learners' well-being.

Feedback Strategies as Support to Drive Learning Motivation

Feedback giving is related closely to social support as teacher and student peers actively involved in receiving and giving feedback can help students of different abilities to learn. A qualitative study by Burnett and Mandel (2010) reveals that teachers on average give 40 times positive feedback to students per hour when they conduct lessons. Continuous feedback to diagnose learning problems and support learning is called formative feedback. Black and Wiliam's (2009) definition of formative assessment pointed out the extent to which evidence about 'student achievement is elicited, interpreted, and used by teachers, learners, or their peers, to make decisions about the next steps in instruction that are likely to be better' (p. 9). Their interpretation highlights the 'regulating learning processes' in which constant feedback can improve learner's self-reflection in learning. Effective formative assessments enable teachers to recognise what a student might achieve in his/her zone of proximal development (ZPD) (Vygotsky's idea, see theory). The role of the teacher is to identify and develop students' immature but maturing qualities, in order to facilitate cognitive growth through guidance and scaffolding, so as to minimise the distance between the student's current state of learning and the desired outcome (Heritage, 2007).

Similar to CL, feedback has become a popular strategy in twenty-first-century school education. The discussion of feedback in the literature used to focus on its cognitive aspect. However, viewing feedback from the perspective of social support can make this strategy even more beneficial for learners, as it serves to support learners emotionally and cognitively. Similar to coping, learners may experience learning anxiety when learning due to challenging learning situations and learning difficulties, especially when learners find that they are lagging behind compared with their classroom peers. The act of feedback giving is itself a support action, and it is inseparable from the job of teaching. It plays a role in monitoring the progress of learning, and more importantly, it helps learners gradually develop an internal mechanism to self-monitor learning and learn with intrinsic interest (Lam, Cheng, & Yang, 2017). Establishing social support in the processes of giving feedback is useful in building a classroom environment to facilitate students' independent learning; it can begin with developing the traits of receiving feedback on learners. Some of the examples of using feedback by incorporating social support are discussed below; some of the examples are from higher education settings and are based on research-based experiments.

Wingate (2010) studied formative feedback in academic writing tasks of a first-year undergraduate course. Students were required to submit three writing assignments, which were an ungraded Exploratory Essay (EE) in week 5, first graded assignment (A1) in week 6 and the final assignment (A2) in week 12, respectively. Upon the submission of EE, tutors provided extensive written comments, spent about 10 min with each student to discuss their work, and provided verbal advice. A1 was also returned to students with grades and detailed comments two weeks before the deadline for A2, so the students could make use of the feedback for the EE and A1 to do better in A2. The interview results with some of the students suggested that students who were able to utilise feedback they had received previously did improve in the criticised areas, and they did not make the same mistakes in the next assignment. Those students who had the same problems persisting had paid little attention to the comments they received. The success of this intervention is dependent on the conditions that extra effort from teachers can be made through a concentrated and timely feedback process, their patience and supportive gestures, and the part that students have to play to digest the feedback received, reflecting on their own performance, and deriving personal meaning from what they have learnt in class.

Wingate's (2010) study demonstrates a self-regulating process in which learners have to regulate internally their thinking, motivation and behaviours proactively (Pintrich & Zusho, 2002), and come up with better approaches to learn. Therefore, the essence of formative assessment is to engage students in a metacognitive process, in which learners are involved in goal setting and self-managing their own learning progress, with informed evaluative judgements provided by peers and teachers from time to time (Sadler, 2010). An effective formative feedback situation should be a reciprocal process between the teacher and the learner. If learners are unable to self-evaluate their own learning, it is unlikely that they would make any improvement because receiving feedback per se is not enough to facilitate learning (Maclellan, 2001). On the other hand, if the giving of formative feedback can change students' attitudes and outcomes of learning, as the increased amount of feedback information they receive from teachers equips them to be more competent (Brookhart, 1997), it can enhance their positive emotions and intrinsic motivation to study. Therefore, following up teacher feedback may not be expected of every individual; it depends on what types of learner they are. However, it is believed that teachers could change students' attitude and learning behaviour by creating an environment utilising feedback as a means of support for student learning, by peer influencing and scaffolding support, hopefully to help students to become self-regulated and motivated in learning.

In a study by Lam, Cheng and Yang (2017), participants were 127 undergraduate students from six courses who were undergoing teacher education training. Three classes (68 students) were assigned to the control group and the other three (59 students) to the experimental group, where formative feedback practices were employed in class. The strategies included (i) setting study goals, (ii) students' self-reflection on the intended learning outcomes, (iii) teacher comments on in-process drafts and (iv) verbal feedback on group outputs. Descriptions and rationales of the formative feedback strategies are summarised in Table 4.2.

Student motivation and affect were measured. All students completed a questionnaire before the first lesson and in their final lessons, which assessed their extrinsic and intrinsic motivation to attend the courses, and their experiences of positive affect over the weeks before they filled in the questionnaires. Results showed that formative feedback practices increased students' intrinsic motivation in attending the courses and prevented them from losing their extrinsic motivation. In addition, formative feedback practices gave rise to more positive emotional experiences of students. The

Table 4.2 Formative feedback strategies employed in the Lam et al. (2017) study

Strategies	Description
Setting study goals	Students were told to write down five study goals of their own in priority order at the beginning of the course
Students' self-reflection of the intended learning outcomes	Students self-rated their level of achievement of the given lessons' intended learning outcomes on a 4-point scale upon completion of lessons on the same theme. The teacher would discuss and follow up the overall self-reflection of outcomes with students either individually or in class
Teacher comments on in-process draft	Student could submit in-progress drafts of their interim and final assignment voluntarily for teacher's comments. This is to assist students to troubleshoot their performance and self-correct
Verbal feedback on group outputs	Teacher gave verbal feedback on students' ideas and outputs during in-class group tasks

study indicates that consistent support of feedback in the classroom creates a positive emotion towards learning for participants, which is the key for them to engage better in studying the course.

Pat-EI, Tillema, Segers, & Vedder, (2013) reported a study of the use of formative feedback by teachers on 558 Dutch students of different ethnicities, which measured two aspects: (1) monitoring, which provides students with feedback information on learning progress, and (2) scaffolding that supports learners to move on by giving direction and advice. Students' intrinsic motivation and motivational needs (i.e. relatedness, competence and autonomy) were also assessed. It was found that teachers' formative feedback (i.e. monitoring and scaffolding) had a positive effect on students' interest in learning. Specifically, monitoring positively influenced students' relatedness towards the teacher, while scaffolding satisfied all of the three basic needs of students. Another noticeable observation was that students valued teacher's proximity as this had facilitated them to accept the feedback received in the classroom. These positive effects of formative feedback in promoting students' intrinsic motivation worked equally among different ethnic student groups. The findings echoed Suldo et al's. (2009) last theme concerning classroom atmosphere—positive effects on motivation and learning can only be achieved when the classroom, where formative assessment is practiced, has a supportive and trusting atmosphere (Cauley & McMillan, 2010).

Formative assessment works complementarily with other teaching strategies, such as CL where they can produce more rewarding educational learning experiences. Salend, Whittaker, and Reeder (1992) examined the efficacy of a group evaluation system with a sample of students with either learning disabilities or emotional disturbance. In the beginning, students were given training on the group evaluation system and inappropriate classroom behaviours were pinpointed for them. During the experiment, the students were divided into groups of four and they had to reach consensus within the group on common ratings for the group's behaviour during a fixed time period in class. Each group's rating was then compared with that of the teacher's. Rewards were given to the groups regarding their behaviour in class, and bonus points would be given to the group whose rating accurately matched the teacher's rating. The results indicated that students' inappropriate bahaviours significantly decreased after the intervention as they were more aware of their misbehaviour and such peer assessment could effectively modify classroom behaviour. A follow-up satisfaction survey also showed that the students cooperated well during the intervention and they enjoyed the peer assessment.

To sum up, feedback is a promising strategy that utilises support for learners and the teacher to help build a social learning environment to support student learning. Teachers' support and students' peer learning have proved positive effects on students' self-efficacy, motivation needs and self-regulated learning strategies via feedback instructions. The support from student peers and teachers is crucial to enhance students' positive emotions and cultivate the attributes of social learning in the classroom, which may result to pro-social behaviour and positive learning outcomes.

Strategies to Support Students with Special Educational Needs

The concept of social support has been commonly applied in schools with students who have special educational needs and who need support for transition due to different life circumstances. A few common strategies, including nurture groups, circle time and a restorative justice approach are introduced to indicate the features of social support in integrated school or special programme settings.

Nurture groups and their effectiveness on children with social, emotional and behavioural difficulties. In response to the growing number of children who have social, emotional and behavioural difficulties (SEBD) and could not bridge the gap between home and school, the educational psychologist Marjorie Boxall proposed and implemented Nurture Groups (NGs) in London in the 1960s to cater for these impaired children whose needs were not easily addressed in the mainstream class (Boxall, 2002). The rationale for nurture groups is grounded in the AT (Bowlby, 1980, 1982). The children with SEBD tend to be subject to family stress and missing or distorted nurturing care in their early years, which from the perspective of cognitive neuroscience could permanently impede hippocampus-dependent learning (Karten, Olariu, & Cameron, 2005). Children who have experienced intense and lasting stressful events in their lives have been found to be deficient in spatial working memory and short-term memory. It is hypothesised that effective intervention and sufficient nurture and support from adults can help children to return to tolerable stress levels (Middlebrooks & Audage, 2008), and eliminate the negative effects of their impoverished early experience on executive functioning (McDermott, Westerlund, Zeanah, Nelson, & Fox, 2012). During the nurture group intervention, the process of early learning is re-created; a supportive and secure environment is fostered to bring about close attachment, a trusting relationship and emotionally relevant and reassuring experiences (Boxall, 2002). The assumption is that when children's attachment needs are addressed, their emotional well-being would improve, thus allowing them to improve their behaviour in class and make the most of the available opportunities to learn and develop friendships (Hughes & Schlösser, 2014).

Nurture groups have gained widespread adoption worldwide. By 2016, over 2100 groups had been established in UK and others in Australia, New Zealand, Canada and Malta (The Nurture Group Network, 2016). The classic nurture groups usually consist of 10–12 children aged from 4–8 with a teacher and a teaching assistant (Boxall, 2002). The teacher and the assistant work collaboratively to model constructive interaction with the teacher directing and controlling children's experiences. Being an integral part of a supportive school, nurture groups are tightly structured and routinised, and provide opportunities for academic skills, social activities, free play and a shared dining experience. The children usually attend NGs for 4.5 days per week and join their mainstream peers in the remaining time. This usually lasts for two school terms before they return to their mainstream class on a full-time basis.

A growing number of empirical studies have reported the effectiveness of nurture groups on children's emotional well-being and academic outcomes. Hughes and Schlösser (2014) conducted a comprehensive review of 11 articles on NGs and provided useful insights for the type, age group and communication styles that can be used in NG intervention. There is a consensus in the literature that NGs have a positive impact on children's social and emotional development (e.g. Binnie & Allen, 2008; Cooper, Arnold, & Boyd, 2001; Cooper & Whitebread, 2007; Doyle, 2005; O'Connor & Colwell, 2002a, 2002b; Sanders, 2007; Scott & Lee, 2009). More specifically, the greatest improvements in social and emotional functioning tend to occur within the first two terms of the intervention, whereas cognitive development is likely to improve within the third and fourth terms (Cooper & Whitebread, 2007). NGs could also lead to increased self-management, self-awareness and confidence in children (Cooper & Tiknaz, 2005). Their prosocial behaviour and social skills such as sharing, turn taking and recognising feelings are also found to have progressed significantly in some studies (Cooper & Tiknaz, 2005; Seth-Smith, Levi, Pratt, Jaffey, & Fonagy, 2010).

Although there is limited research on the effectiveness of NGs on academic skills, several studies have revealed more consistent though not significantly greater academic achievements in NG children when compared with those not receiving the intervention (Cooper et al., 2001; Scott & Lee, 2009; Seth-Smith et al. 2010). As Binnie and Allen (2008) argue, the first and foremost mission of NGs is to support the emotional needs of child, after which, hopefully, academic progression will follow.

Circle Time and Circle of Friends to Enhance Social Development. Circle Time was first proposed by Murray White in the 1980s, and was further developed by Jenny Mosley to be integrated in school settings. It is currently in widespread use in schools across the UK, the USA and a number of countries in Europe. It is an active teaching and learning strategy that employs well-structured and purposeful lessons plans to facilitate children's personal, social and emotional development (Mosley, 2005). During the period of Circle Time, the participants sit in a circle together with a teacher to discuss a social, emotional or curricular issue and share ideas and feelings about it (Lown, 2002; Mary, 2014; Mosley, 2005). It should be noted that the enhancement of self-esteem is central to the learning process (Lown, 2002; Mosley, 1993) and the relationship between the teacher and the students is non-hierarchical whereby the teacher is a facilitator rather than a leader and each person's contribution is equally valued (Canney & Byrne,2006). The activities are suggested to be structured and involve a range of forms such as games, role play, etc. (Mosley, 2005). This can take place on a weekly basis in the children's own classroom (Mosley, 1996).

The Circle Time approach has been found to have a positive impact on improving children's self-esteem and social skills (Canney & Byrne, 2006; Cefai et al., 2014; Miller & Moran, 2007; Kelly, 1999; Mary, 2014; Tominey & McClelland, 2011). Circle time can provide an enjoyable learning experience and create an atmosphere whereby individual pupils' are respected and valued, their confidence is therefore increased and they are able to develop a sense of self-worth and the ability to express feelings and ideas. Furthermore, their self-regulation skills can be improved. Through well-structured and purposeful activities, students learn to sit attentively and listen to others in the class. As they become more socially accepted and gain more under-standing of other students, their ability to cooperate and get along with others will increase. As a result, their cognitive ability such as letter-word identification and problem-solving skills may increase (Tominey & McClelland, 2011; Mosley, 2005).

Circle of Friends (CoF) is an approach to mobilise young peers to provide assis-tance to and enhance inclusion of individuals experiencing difficulties because of disability, social rejection or isolation (Goldstein, 2013; Taylor, 1996, 1997). Orig-inating in Canada, the circle of friends approach encourages the development of friendships around the focus child who is experiencing difficulties in social relation-ships. The underlying rationale of CoF is the conceptualisation of the concentric circles that are made up of a variety of people giving support to the individual at the centre (Goldstein, 2013).

There are a number of variants of this intervention approach. The intervention typically initiates with a discussion among the class in the absence of the focus child about the focus child's strengths and difficulties and the importance of giving friendship and support to the focus child. Then volunteers are encouraged to form a circle to help the focus child to carry out activities and tackle their peer relationship problems. This is often conducted on a weekly basis with the teacher as a facilitator monitoring the process. It can be adapted to involve the focus child in the initial class discussion and use the circle of friends as a way to help all circle members to get to know one another more and become better friends. More recently, Barrett and Randall (2004) used a new model to establish several circles around two or more isolated children in a class.

Despite the limited empirical research on CoF, there has been some evidence to suggest that this approach is beneficial to the children involved in it. It is powerful to enhance the inclusion of the targeted children with social, emotional and behavioural difficulties into the mainstream setting. On the one hand, research has shown that the intervention plays a favourable role in their listening skills and problem-solving skills (Newton, Taylor, & Wilson, 1996) and can improve the communication skills of preschool-aged children with autism (Kalyva & Avramidis, 2005), thus facilitating their interaction with other kids. The focus pupil can experience less bullying, greater happiness and exhibit desirable behaviours (James, 2011; O'Connor, 2016; Schlieder, Maldonado, & Baltes, 2014), which provides a much needed network of social support for them to integrate into the mainstream settings.

On the other hand, the group members' understanding and empathy for the focus child increases as a result of the intervention (Newton et al., 1996; Schlieder et al., 2014). Positive impact has been found on focus child's peer acceptance and rejection, especially after the whole-class meeting, though this might not be maintained throughout the whole CoF process (Frederickson, Warren, & Turner, 2005; James, 2011). They become more accepting and respectful of others (Calabrese et al., 2008). This impact might also expand to those who do not take part in the intervention (Barrett & Randall, 2004; Schlieder et al., 2014). The proponents maintain that children's social skills can be enhanced and true friendship can be fostered through the intervention.

Encouraging results have also been observed with school staff and parents involved in the process. While it provides teachers with a new approach to handling class ethos and improving class cohesion (Barrett & Randall, 2004), it can also reduce the level of alienation for the parents. The CoF is able to alleviate parents' sense of powerlessness and isolation as the intervention provides a path for their children to be integrated into mainstream school settings (Calabrese et al., 2008). Therefore, it is also suggested that the impact of CoF be extended to the whole school and the community.

Restorative Justice Approach that Nurtures Respect and Relationships. As a form of conflict resolution, Restorative Justice (RJ) focuses on repairing harm and setting things right by reintegrating those who are affected by offending or challenging behaviour in a community (Hopkins, 2002; Morrison, 2002). The underpinning tenet is that human beings are relational and social relationships are important for regulating social life. Individuals can learn to become socially responsible and resilient when they are respected and well integrated into a social network (Morrison, 2002, 2003; Morrison & Vaandering, 2012). As a community, schools have the skills and opportunities to adopt RJ to resolve conflicts and nurture favourable relationships.

Acknowledging that students should be valued as human beings instead of objects to be controlled, this practice embodies a paradigmatic shift from retribution to restoration. Rather than applying external punitive systems, RJ is intended to find a mutually acceptable solution from relational ecologies (Zehr, 2002, cited by Morrison & Vaandering, 2012, p. 140). A set of processes and approaches are involved, including all formal and informal interventions that require a range of skills which are underpinned by a distinctive ethos and philosophy. The interventions may include various collaborative social activities such as peer mediation or reconciliation, meetings and conferencing, and peacemaking or healing circles at all levels from small group, class, to whole school (Hopkins, 2002; Macready, 2009; Morrison & Vaandering, 2012). Everyone affected by the wrongdoing joins the process on a voluntary basis and explains what happened from their own perspectives to express their feelings about the incident and then to be invited to explore a mutually acceptable solution to the incident.

There have been a number of studies to investigate the effect of RJ in schools since its emergence in the 1990s (Morrison, 2007). Prior research has, overall, shown participant satisfaction with the process and outcomes achieved, especially in terms of the decrease in challenging behaviours at school (Cameron & Thorsborne, 2001; Miers, 2001). RJs have also been found to offer numerous learning opportunities with regard to dialogue, respect and collaboration, which finally contributes to an improvement in social relationships, mutual engagement and perceived respect among the participants (Gregory, Clawson, Davis, & Gerewitz, 2016). School culture change brings about a more positive atmosphere and climate and can help to cultivate conflict resolution skills among students (McCluskey, Lloyd, Kane, Riddell, & Stead, 2008; Shaw, 2007). The implementation of RJs is useful for developing a restorative ethos to address aggressive behaviours in schools (McCluskey et al. 2008). However, there have also been concerns about the sustained development of institutional praxis and call for the systematic implementation and evaluation of the approach (Gregory et al., 2016; Morrison & Vaandering, 2012; Vaandering, 2014). It is also suggested that the local contexts, including the families and the community groups be recognised as important sources of support during the process (Wearmouth, McKinney, & Glynn, 2007).

Implications and Recommendations

This chapter investigates the theoretical framework of social support in educational settings, by referring to educational theories, empirical literature and teaching strategies that reflect social support assumptions and behaviours.

The results suggest different levels of support sources that include teacher, students and the school and classroom environment. Various types of teacher support, and especially emotional support, have appeared to be crucial for making intrapsychic influences on students' motivation, such as self-esteem, interest, intrinsic motivation, cognitive/learning strategies and social goal (prosocial behaviour), as well as attitude, social skills, behaviours and academic outcomes, as shown from the discussion. The review also identifies a range of teaching strategies that utilise social support as the means to support student learning, reflecting the theoretical underpinnings examined in part one. They include several developed instructional approaches such as strategies that promote feeling and thinking, caring practice, cultural responsive teaching, cooperative learning and formative feedback strategies, as well as several intervention strategies that are commonly applied in integrated education settings, i.e. circle time, nurture group and a restorative justice approach. As suggestions are discussed on specific themes in earlier sections, this part discusses the main implications and suggestions, addressing both the theory and practice.

Implications and Recommendations

A Theoretical Framework that Guides Learning and Teaching

The chapter proposes a meta-theory to explain human learning, to justify the relevance of social support in education. It asserts that human beings are intrinsically influenced by the experience of relating to other human beings. The nature and quality of interaction with other human beings, including the experience of the past and present, determines emotional well-being and engagement behaviour, such as learning. Antisocial behaviour, self-handicapping behaviour and mental health issues can be explained by having some form of negative emotions when individuals interact with people and the world; but positive interaction, as a basic human need, can help people to change behaviours in healthier ways.

The theory suggests that humans have an innate tendency towards social bonds and relatedness, and they benefit emotionally from them. Humans also learn in a social learning community where they interact, communicate and solve problems in a social constructivist manner that contributes to the intellect. Furthermore, the experience of each individual member in society forms one's own beliefs about the supportiveness of the social environment, and their perception affects their action, roles to take and their living and satisfaction in life. Therefore, developing the attributes of supportiveness, empathy and care in the educational environment is the key to achieve positive educational outcomes for learners. The theoretical assumptions of social support as discussed in Chap. 2, such as stress buffering, social cognition, social capital and relationship, are echoed in the educational theories and teaching strategies as discussed in this chapter. Teachers' pedagogical practice and personal interaction with students that enable students to perceive supportiveness, relatedness and autonomy may be the most crucial part of learning in schools. The investigation on the topic of social support in the context of learning and teaching in this chapter has provided strong evidence to suggest that making students feel that they are emotionally connected and that they are given support in the learning environment are the most important areas teachers should try to work on in their role in teaching. Such a learning environment can develop positive self-esteem in learners that can ensure their greater success in life, echoing the benefits of social support that have been discussed in Chaps. 2 and 3.

Teacher Professionalism Regarding Commitment, Traits and Knowledge

One of the significant findings of this review is a more in-depth understanding of teachers' emotional support and how it is related to cognitive learning to help student achievement in schools. Emotional support is obviously one of the most popular forms of support that features the teacher's role (Rogers, 1961; Brophy, 1986; Hargreaves, 1999; Day, 2004). This chapter hinted at a more elaborated understanding of emotional support. First, emotional support is not simply offering a gesture such as a smile or an emotional role that teachers should perform; it is an attitude towards teaching, which can be a prerequisite for teaching. As discussed, the various types of emotional support are underlined by value traits such as equity (sensitivity and responsiveness), empathy (care about other's feeling and feeling about other's emotions), diversity (understand individual learning pace and teaching with a variety of methods), positivity (positive emotions and attitude) and well-being (relatedness, competence, autonomy). Furthermore, emotional support also comprises a skill component, i.e. modelling, consistency, coaching and scaffolding. All of these, including values and skills, underlie the 'emotional work' of the teacher (Isenbarger & Zembylas, 2006). This means teachers are constantly paying attention to learners while they manage to deliver the lesson, and respond to students' problems and offer different scaffoldings and support to make sure that students are motivated to move on, learn and achieve in the lesson. This performance, i.e. behaving to be a caring, supportive and knowledgeable teacher, requires teachers to acquire a spectrum of professional knowledge, skills and attitude, and be involved in constant reflection as a practitioner in teaching continuously in their teaching careers.

Teacher education providers might wish to strengthen the emotional traits in the training programmes to enable teachers to explore the skills of performing as a caring teacher. This part of the skills set is procedural (should be developed by enacting) and character related (as a dispositional trait), hence it implicates the need for practice and supervision throughout pre-service and in-service teacher development programmes in order to acquire it proficiently. It is assumed that the traits and values behind social support, such as connecting to students, empathic understanding on students and respect for students with differences, are generated from teachers' intrinsic interest in teaching (Hargreaves, 1999, 2001; Jennings & Greenberg, 2009). The review therefore recommends that teachers' commitment to teaching should be the prerequisite requirement of teaching. The strengthening of teachers' knowledge of psychological foundations appears to be an essential topic in teacher education programmes; this foundation knowledge can support teachers to inquire about the psychological processes of learners and their own supportive actions. This suggestion complements the views of other authors in arguing that teaching is emotional work (Isenbarger & Zembylas, 2006; Sutton & Wheatley, 2003). The concerns for social support to learners echo this area of interest. They are popular topics within the background of increasing mental health problems and the affective and emotional aspects of handling teaching are marginalised against cognitive development in the twenty-first century (McCollum, 2014; Reigeluth, 2013).

A Social Support Approach to Education Planning and Teaching

The discussion points out that a test-driven approach to education adopted by schools in the twenty-first century is in an inappropriate direction. It provides evidence to argue the disadvantages of reinforcing an examination-oriented teaching approach

Implications and Recommendations 175

in schools, showing the negative effects on students such as creating learning anxiety, and the lack of education for learners in their self-development, such as identity formation, developing self-esteem and belongingness in the learning environment so that their intrinsic interest in learning cannot be developed. As the chapter discusses, these qualities can promote learners' social goals, prosocial behaviour and learning outcomes, which serve to increase students' well-being. The inadequacy of education in these parts seems to be a huge deficit of the present state of education in schools. Since social support at the school environmental level is seen as the most effective means of support that determines educational success, schools can develop a set of succinct values that echo social support in the school environment, and have them expressed through school mottos and school policies. Schools should design the school timetable to allow more opportunities for student-teacher interaction and for students to take part in organising school events. The time students are involved in communicating with teachers and their peers, taking part and taking up responsibilities in schools are helpful for students in cultivating a sense of belongingness to school, which is the prerequisite of a supportive learning environment.

The vision of giving social support should be targeted as a long-term goal—which is to support learners to develop motivation, self-esteem and self-efficacy as well as to acquire various learning skills, so that students can become autonomous learners. Therefore, teachers should develop a long-term vision for the students and classes they teach, and set a plan of how to teach to help students develop these psychological resources for learners themselves and create the environment to help them attain a healthy psychological functioning so as to achieve well-being. The present teaching environment seems to revert teachers to engage in short-term planning as demands on results are so intense that they cause teachers to develop the mentality of making things 'perfect in a day', thus giving them less time to construct the environment and involve themselves more with students in helping and arranging a supportive environment for them. Therefore, schools may need to allow time for teachers to investigate ways of supporting learners, and arrange professional development activities to enable teachers to work together to improve teaching to serve the target shared by the school. As long-term planning and development is necessary, and given that the focus of giving support is in building the environment by the whole school team, with teachers as a part of the team, teachers would feel more comfortable about offering support to students.

With regard to teaching, teachers should also consider that social support is not only a moment of support for students but that teachers should think broadly about the strategies they develop in order to help students become self-regulated learners. Any support to learners should entail a purpose of helping them to learn. According to Vygotsky's social constructivist learning (Gaskell, 2008), scaffoldings (as social support) should be given by considering learners' different situations; less specific support should be given once students are able to master knowledge on their own. This is so-called contingency shifting to decline support once learners are able to handle the learning on their own. Therefore, social support must be strategic, serving to develop independent learners, as in the case of social support in the discipline of health psychology where social support is aimed to have long-term effects on people, improving their capacities in coping with challenges and stressful situations.

The discussion of the chapter therefore can supplement a view towards education as a combination of support of affective (engage students in learning with positive emotions) and cognitive learning (including non-cognitive strategies and academic outcomes). That means that while teachers offer social support, the support teachers giving carries a purpose of supporting students' cognitive learning strategies and developing relationships and positive emotions for learners. The analysis of the literature predicts that social support may be most useful in enhancing students' self-regulating strategies, as students may model teachers' behaviour and adopt the strategies they use in different situations that help them advance in learning. It ultimately helps learners to become independent both emotionally and psychologically. Furthermore, self-regulation is not only related to learners' attribution of their own success and failure, it is also related to self-appraisal and help-seeking behaviours; therefore learners can manage to use appropriate strategies, and seek resources and support for handling learning. Social support resources are meant to help learners to approach learning as a life-long endeavour, i.e. to develop interests and skills in mastering knowledge, thus gaining experience of learning, so that learners learn more and better. This approach is not the same as preparing learners for a specific test or examination. Social support actually helps learners to strengthen learning capacities and be more resilient in managing difficulties in learning; teachers should develop these traits for children and young adolescent in preparing them for the twenty-first century's environment.

Designing Pedagogies to Promote Change Noting the Cultural Context

Similarly, in the choice of pedagogies, teachers may be able to consider pedagogies based on the cultivation of social values, attributes of learners, and design methods and mechanisms to engage learners in a process of learning that stimulate their feelings, thinking and reflection, individually and collaboratively, as inspired by the various methods discussed in the chapter. The use of peers as resources and involving learners in constructing knowledge and producing outputs are the key principles of lesson design. Standard exemplars and the format of specific teaching strategies should not be the straitjacket for implementing teaching strategies. Teachers should examine the ideas they have for introducing the strategies, therefore students can benefit from the learning opportunities teachers create for them. Teachers may have to carefully consider the use of teaching strategies in a specific cultural context, and identify the possible issues in applying any new teaching strategies and approach the issues by using one's professional judgement. For example, the dominance of examination-oriented culture in some countries such as Hong Kong (e.g. Brown, Kennedy, Fok, Chan, & Yu, 2009) may cause students to think that any assess-

Implications and Recommendations 177

ment should converge in a final summative grade. The use of formative assessment, which originally was meant to support students continuously at different stages of the learning journey, may create pressure to students as continuous feedback to students' work may be seen as frequent testing and assessment to students. Similarly to CL, a competitive learning culture would cause barriers for teachers in carrying out CL, if students are forced to take part in CL because their participation is counted as a form of assessment; it will create an assessment backwash effect on learners and it is contradictory to the spirit of CL in promoting collaboration and self-regulated learning. It would also induce passive learning attitudes instead of intrinsic interest in learning. The disadvantage is that the encouragement of assessment will further damage students' motivation and restrain them from taking a mastery approach to learning; therefore, they could become even more externally regulated and passive in learning. Hence, identifying supportive teaching strategies and modifying standard prototypes of some strategies to the way that suits the cultural environment should be the direction for reflective practitioners in the field to aim at.

Further Research and Limitations

While this chapter has largely fulfilled its purposes, it cannot be claimed to be an exhaustive one because of the huge database of studies on the affective, motivational outcomes existing in education, with almost every study related to certain types of support for teachers. Our location of the empirical literature in the discussion might overlook some research that has a close link with social support, however, without clear identifiers in the name. On the other hand, the focus of the review is to draw insights based on this area of research, the results provide a set of potential ideas that confirm the importance of social support in education and its link to health and well-being. However, due to the use of different constructs used by authors across the studies and that a consistent operationalisation of the terms has yet to be consolidated in the literature, the sets of potential ideas provided in the results are subject to further research to confirm, refine and enrich its content. In addition, because many of the studies are quantitatively based, salient descriptions of some of the sources of social support are not extensively elaborated, hence, parts of the description may not be sufficiently elaborated. As the review laid the focus largely on school-aged students, while the results have come up with a cogent explanation for the specific target, its content may not be generalised across settings such as university students due to cohort characteristics.

Specific to the interest of different stakeholders, data described in this chapter has claimed that teachers' emotional support influenced students' engagement that it has intrapsychic influences on students' psychological mechanisms such as self-esteem, self-efficacy, interest, intrinsic motivation and social goal; it has a positive effect on students' engagement in learning, academic outcomes and well-being. However, further research on social support is needed as social support is a potential topic for improving some of the issues identified in education as suggested in the societal background. At present, research to fully utilise the benefits in educational research is still scant. The use of this concept can identify results to inform the usefulness of promoting social support and the use of it to develop innovative pedagogies. The research findings might provide useful content for teacher training if this area is going to be adopted in the teacher training curriculum.

The discussion of teaching strategies in this chapter suggests the current limitations of research and innovation on teaching strategies, which are largely focused on effectiveness based on learning outcomes and short-term achievement goals. Social support as a pedagogical idea can bring about a wide range of positive student outcomes, which can be incorporated in the planning and design of typical teaching strategies, such as CL and feedback, to create innovative pedagogies to support student learning and development and contribute to the scholarship of teaching. It may also be useful to look at the support of these strategies on the needs of both high achiever and those who are weak in ability. As the latter type of student has a low self-image and self-efficacy, therefore research to address particular needs of this group by using social support of teachers and student peers would be useful to provide further insights in constructing feedback strategies.

Regarding methodologies, qualitative studies of teachers' social support is limited, and it emerged as having potential needs to supplement the current quantitative research dominant results. Based on the review, students as social support sources have emerged as a topic that has huge potential for research, and it will provide insights to supplement the current literature which largely bases the effectiveness of student cooperative learning on academic outcomes. The social support perspective may enrich the current literature by providing a perspective which emphasises human development. The study of the variables such as gender and grade, and the identification of social support sources on learners of different needs, academic status and cultural differences are topics that can yield important ideas for application at the classroom level; the salient features resulted from these topics can take research on social support in teaching to the next level.

References

Aber, J. L., Jones, S. M., Brown, J. L., Chaudry, N., & Samples, F. (1998). Resolving conflict creatively: Evaluating the developmental effects of a school-based violence prevention program in neighborhood and classroom context. *Development and Psychopathology, 10*(2), 187–213.

Abrams, L. M., Pedulla, J. J., & Madaus, G. F. (2003). Views from the classroom: Teachers' opinions of statewide testing programs. *Theory into Practice, 42*(1), 18–29.

Adelman, M. B., & Albrecht, T. L. (1987). Communicating social support. Sage Publications.

Ainsworth, M. D. S. (1979). Infant–mother attachment. *American Psychologist, 34*(10), 932–937.

Ainsworth, M. D. S., Blehar, M. C., Waters, E., & Wall, S. (1978). *Patterns of attachment: A psychological study of the strange situation*. Hillsdale, NJ: Erlbaum.

Ames, C. (1992). Classrooms: Goals, structures, and student motivation. *Journal of Educational Psychology, 84*(3), 261.

References

Anderson, L. W., Krathwohl, D. R., Airasian, P. W., Cruikshank, K. A., Mayer, R. E., Pintrich, P. R., ..., & Wittrock, M. C. (2001). *A taxonomy for learning, teaching, and assessing: A revision of Bloom's taxonomy of educational objectives, abridged edition*. White Plains, NY: Longman.

Arun, P., & Chavan, B. (2009). Stress and suicidal ideas in adolescent students in Chandigarh. *Indian Journal of Medical Sciences, 63*(7), 281.

Ashby, F. G., & Isen, A. M. (1999). A neuropsychological theory of positive affect and its influence on cognition. *Psychological Review, 106*(3), 529.

Au, W. (2007). High-stakes testing and curricular control: A qualitative metasynthesis. *Educational Researcher, 36*(5), 258–267.

Babad, E. (2009). *The social psychology of the classroom*. New York: Routledge.

Baldwin, M. W. (1992). Relational schemas and the processing of social information. *Psychological Bulletin, 112,* 461–484.

Banks, M., & Woolfson, L. (2008). RESEARCH SECTION: Why do students think they fail? The relationship between attributions and academic self-perceptions. *British Journal of Special Education, 35*(1), 49–56.

Barbara, L. M. (2004). The learner-centered psychological principles: A framework for balancing academic achievement and social-emotional learning outcomes. In E. Z. Joseph, R. W. Roger, C. W. Margaret, & J. W. Herbert (Eds.), *Building academic success on social and emotional learning: What does the research say?* (pp. 23–39). New York: Teachers College Press.

Barber, B. K., & Olsen, J. A. (2004). Assessing the transitions to middle and high school. *Journal of Adolescent Research, 19*(1), 3–30.

Barrera, M., & Garrison-Jones, C. (1992). Family and peer social support as specific correlates of depressive symptoms. *Journal of Abnormal Clinical Psychology, 20*(1), 1–16.

Barrett, W., & Randall, L. (2004). Investigating the circle of friends approach: Adaptations and implications for practice. *Educational Psychology in Practice, 20*(4), 353–368.

Beane, J. A. (1990). *Affect in the curriculum: Toward democracy, dignity, and diversity*. Columbia: Teachers College Press.

Becker, B. E., & Luthar, S. S. (2002). Social-emotional factors affecting achievement outcomes among disadvantaged students: Closing the achievement gap. *Educational Psychologist, 37*(4), 197–214.

Benard, B. (1991). *Fostering resiliency in kids: Protective factors in the family, school, and community (Northwest Regional Educational Laboratory)*. Portland, OR: Western Center for Drug-Free Schools and Communities.

Binnie, L. M., & Allen, K. (2008). Whole school support for vulnerable children: The evaluation of a part-time nurture group. *Emotional and Behavioural Difficulties, 13*(3), 201–216.

Birch, S. H., & Ladd, G. W. (1998). Children's interpersonal behaviors and the teacher-child relationship. *Developmental Psychology, 34,* 934–946.

Black, P., & Wiliam, D. (2009). Developing the theory of formative assessment. Educational assessment, evaluation and accountability (formerly: Journal of Personnel Evaluation in Education), *21*(1), 5–31.

Blair, C., & Raver, C. C. (2015). School readiness and self-regulation: A developmental psychobiological approach. *Annual Review of Psychology, 66,* 711–731.

Blau, P. M. (1964). *Exchange and power in social life*. New Brunswick, NJ: Transaction Publishers.

Borich, G. D. (2004). *Vital impressions: The KPM approach to children*. KPM Institute.

Bowlby, J. (1973). Attachment and loss. *Separation: Anxiety and anger* (Vol. 2). New York: Basic Books.

Bowlby, J. (1980). *Attachment and loss: Vol. 3. Loss: Sadness and depression*. New York: Basic books.

Bowlby, J. (1982). Attachment and loss: Retrospect and prospect. *American Journal of Orthopsychiatry, 52*(4), 664–678.

Bowlby, J. (1988). *A secure base: Parent–child attachment and healthy human development*. New York: Basic Books.

Bowles, S., & Gintis, H. (1976). *Schooling in capitalist America* (Vol. 57). New York: Basic Books.

Boxall, M. (2002). *Nurture groups in school: Principles & practice*. Sage.

Bray, M. (2017). Hong Kong education in an international context: The impact of external forces. In *Education and society in Hong Kong: toward one country and two systems* (pp. 83–94). Routledge.

Bronfenbrenner, U. (1977). Toward an experimental ecology of human development. *American Psychologist, 32*(7), 513–531.

Bronfenbrenner, U. (1995). *Developmental ecology through space and time: A future perspective*.

Bronfenbrenner, U. (2005). *Making human beings human: Bioecological perspectives on human development*. Sage.

Brookhart, S. M. (1997). A theoretical framework for the role of classroom assessment in motivating student effort and achievement. *Applied Measurement in Education, 10*(2), 161–180.

Brophy, J. (1986). Teacher influences on student achievement. *American Psychologist, 41*(10), 1069.

Brophy, J. (1988). Educating teachers about managing classrooms and students. *Teaching and Teacher Education, 4*(1), 1–18.

Brown, G. T., Kennedy, K. J., Fok, P. K., Chan, J. K. S., & Yu, W. M. (2009). Assessment for student improvement: Understanding Hong Kong teachers' conceptions and practices of assessment. *Assessment in Education: Principles, Policy & Practice, 16*(3), 347–363.

Burnett, P. C., & Mandel, V. (2010). Praise and feedback in the primary classroom: Teachers' and students' perspectives. *Australian Journal of Educational & Developmental Psychology, 10*, 145–154.

Buyse, E., Verschueren, K., Doumen, S., Van Damme, J., & Maes, F. (2008). Classroom problem behavior and teacher-child relationships in kindergarten: The moderating role of classroom climate. *Journal of School Psychology, 46*(4), 367–391.

Cabrera, A. F., Nora, A., Crissman, J. L., & Terenzini, P. T. (2002). Collaborative learning: Its impact on college students' development and diversity. *Journal of College Student Development, 43*(1), 20–34.

Cacioppo, J. T., & Patrick, W. (2008). *Loneliness: Human nature and the need for social connection*. New York: W. W.slavin Norton & Company.

Cacioppo, J. T., Gardner, W. L., & Berntson, G. G. (1999). The affect system has parallel and integrative processing components: Form follows function. *Journal of Personality and Social Psychology, 76*, 839–855.

Calabrese, R., Patterson, J., Liu, F., Goodvin, S., Hummel, C., & Nance, E. (2008). An appreciative inquiry into the circle of friends program: The benefits of social inclusion of students with disabilities. *International Journal of Whole Schooling, 4*(2), 20.

Cameron, L., & Thorsborne, M. (2001). Restorative justice and school discipline: Mutually exclusive? *Restorative Justice and Civil Society, 180*, 194.

Canney, C., & Byrne, A. (2006). Evaluating circle time as a support to social skills development—Reflections on a journey in school-based research. *British Journal of Special Education, 33*(1), 19–24. https://doi.org/10.1111/j.1467-8578.2006.00407.x.

Carter, E. W., Cushing, L. S., Clark, N. M., & Kennedy, C. H. (2005). Effects of peer support interventions on students' access to the general curriculum and social interactions. *Research and Practice for Persons with Severe Disabilities, 30*(1), 15–25.

Cauley, K. M., & McMillan, J. H. (2010). Formative assessment techniques to support student motivation and achievement. *The Clearing House: A Journal of Educational Strategies, Issues and Ideas, 83*(1), 1–6.

Cefai, C., Ferrario, E., Cavioni, V., Carter, A., & Grech, T. (2014). Circle time for social and emotional learning in primary school. *Pastoral Care in Education, 32*(2), 116–130.

Centers for Disease Control. (2013). *Make a Difference at Your School*. Chronic Disease. Paper 31. Retrieved from: http://digitalcommons.hsc.unt.edu/disease/31.

Chapple, C. L. (2005). Self-control, peer relations, and delinquency. *Justice Quarterly, 22*(1), 89–106.

Cheng, R. W. Y., & Lam, S. F. (2007). Self-construal and social comparison effects. *British Journal of Educational Psychology, 77*(1), 197–211.

References

Cheng, W. Y., Lam, S. F., & Chan, C. Y. (2008). When high achievers and low achievers work in the same group: The roles of group heterogeneity and processes in project-based learning. *British Journal of Educational Psychology, 78*(2), 205–221.

Cheung, E., & Chiu, P. (2016, March 12). Students at breaking point: Hong Kong announces emergency measures after 22 suicides since the start of the academic year. *The South China Morning Post*. Retrieved from http://www.scmp.com/news/hong-kong/health-environment/article/1923465/students-breaking-point-hong-kong-announces.

Cheung, E. (2015, August 31). Depression hits half of Hong Kong secondary pupils and a quarter have considered suicide, study finds. *The South China Morning Post*. Retrieved from http://www.scmp.com/news/hong-kong/health-environment/article/1853967/depression-hits-just-over-half-hong-kong-secondary.

Choi, J., Johnson, D. W., & Johnson, R. (2011). Relationships among cooperative learning experiences, social interdependence, children's aggression, victimization, and prosocial behaviors. *Journal of Applied Social Psychology, 41*(4), 976–1003.

Christensen, L., & Karp, S. (Eds.). (2003). *Rethinking school reform*. Rethinking Schools.

Church, M. A., Elliot, A. J., & Gable, S. L. (2001). Perceptions of classroom environment, achievement goals, and achievement outcomes. *Journal of Educational Psychology, 93*, 43–54.

Close, W., & Solberg, S. (2008). Predicting achievement, distress, and retention among lower-income Latino youth. *Journal of Vocational Behavior, 72*(1), 31–42.

Coan, J. A. (2008). Toward a neuroscience of attachment. In J. Cassidy & P. R. Shaver (Eds.), *Handbook of attachment: Theory, research, and clinical applications* (2nd ed., pp. 241–265). New York: The Guilford Press.

Cockrell, K. S., Caplow, J. A. H., & Donaldson, J. F. (2000). A context for learning: Collaborative groups in the problem-based learning environment. *The Review of Higher Education, 23*(3), 347–363.

Cohen, J. (2006). Social, emotional, ethical, and academic education: Creating a climate for learning, participation in democracy, and well-being. *Harvard Educational Review, 76*(2), 201–237.

Cohen, J., McCabe, L., Michelli, N. M., & Pickeral, T. (2009). School climate: Research, policy, practice, and teacher education. *Teachers College Record, 111*(1), 180–213.

Collaborative for Academic, Social, and Emotional Learning. (2005). *Safe and sound: An educational leader's guide to evidence-based social and emotional learning programs—Illinois edition*. Chicago: Author.

Connell, J. P. (1990). Context, self, and action: A motivational analysis of self-system processes across the life-span. In D. Cicchetti & M. Beeghly (Eds.), *The self in transition: From infancy to childhood* (pp. 61–97). Chicago: University of Chicago Press.

Connell, J. P., & Wellborn, J. G. (1991). Competence, autonomy, and relatedness: A motivational analysis of self-system processes. In M. R. Gunnar & L. A. Sroufe (Eds.), *The Minnesota symposia on child psychology* (Vol. 23, pp. 43–77)., Self-processes and development Hillsdale, NJ, US: Lawrence Erlbaum Associates Inc.

Cook, K. S., & Rice, E. (2006). Social exchange theory. In J. Delamater (Ed.), *Handbook of social psychology* (pp. 53–76). New York: Springer.

Cooper, P., & Tiknaz, Y. (2005). Progress and challenge in nurture groups: Evidence from three case studies. *British Journal of Special Education, 32*(4), 211–222.

Cooper, P., & Whitebread, D. (2007). The effectiveness of nurture groups on student progress: Evidence from a national research study. *Emotional and Behavioural Difficulties, 12*(3), 171–190.

Cooper, P., Arnold, R., & Boyd, E. (2001). *Evaluation of nurture group provision in an English LEA* (Unpublished research report edn). University of Leicester.

Copeland-Mitchell, J., Denham, S. A., & DeMulder, E. K. (1997). Q-sort assessment of child—teacher attachment relationships and social competence in the preschool. *Early Education and Development, 8*, 27–39.

Cropanzano, R., & Mitchell, M. S. (2005). Social exchange theory: An interdisciplinary review. *Journal of Management, 31*(6), 874-900.

Csikszentmihalyi, M. (1990). *Flow: The psychology of optimal experience*. New York: Harper Perennial.

Curby, T. W., Brock, L. L., & Hamre, B. K. (2013). Teachers' emotional support consistency predicts children's achievement gains and social skills. *Early Education & Development, 24*(3), 292–309.

Cutrona, C. E., Russell, D. W., Brown, P. A., Clark, L. A., Hessling, R. M., & Gardner, K. A. (2005). Neighborhood context, personality, and stressful life events as predictors of depression among African American women. *Journal of Abnormal Psychology, 114*(1), 3–15.

Danielsen, A. G., Samdal, O., Hetland, J., & Wold, B. (2009). School-related social support and students' perceived life satisfaction. *The Journal of Educational Research, 102*(4), 303–320.

Davidson, A. J., Gest, S. D., & Welsh, J. A. (2010). Relatedness with teachers and peers during early adolescence: An integrated variable-oriented and person-oriented approach. *Journal of School Psychology, 48*(6), 483–510.

Day, C. (2004). The passion of successful leadership. *School Leadership & Management, 24*(4), 425–437.

Deci, E. L., & Ryan, R. M. (2008). Self-determination theory: A macrotheory of human motivation, development, and health. *Canadian Psychology/Psychologie Canadienne, 49*(3), 182–185.

Delen, E., Liew, J., & Willson, V. (2014). Effects of interactivity and instructional scaffolding on learning: Self-regulation in online video-based environments. *Computers & Education, 78*, 312–320.

Denham, S. (1998). *Emotional development in young children*. New York: Guilford Press.

Eckstein, M., & Noah, H. (1993). *Secondary school examinations. International perspectives on policies and practices*. New Haven, CT: Yale University Press.

Education, A., & Mean, W. D. I. (2013). Affective education and the affective domain: Implications for instructional-design theories and models. *Instructional-Design Theories And Models: A New Paradigm of Instructional Theory, 2*(1992), 485.

Ellsworth, P. C., & Smith, C. A. (1988). Shades of joy: Patterns of appraisal differentiating pleasant emotions. *Cognition and Emotion, 2*, 301–331.

Evans, M., & Boucher, A. R. (2015). Optimizing the power of choice: Supporting student autonomy to foster motivation and engagement in learning. *Mind, Brain, and Education, 9*(2), 87–91.

Felder, R. M., & Brent, R. (2007). Cooperative learning. In *Active learning: Models from the analytical sciences, ACS Symposium Series* (Vol. 970, pp. 34–53).

Finn, J. D. (1989). Withdrawing from school. *Review of Educational Research, 59*(2), 117–142.

Finn, J. D., & Zimmer, K. S. (2012). Student engagement: What is it? Why does it matter? *Handbook of research on student engagement* (pp. 97–131). US: Springer.

Firth, R. (1967). Themes in economic anthropology: A general comment. *Themes in Economic Anthropology, 6*, 1–28.

Fisher, J. D., Nadler, A., & Whitcher-Alagna, S. (1982). Recipient reactions to aid. *Psychological Bulletin, 91*(1), 27–54.

Ford, M. E. (1992). *Motivating humans: Goals, emotions, and personal agency beliefs*. California: Sage Publications.

Frederickson, N., Warren, L., & Turner, J. (2005). "Circle of Friends"—An exploration of impact over time. *Educational Psychology in Practice, 21*(3), 197–217.

Fredricks, J., Blumenfeld, P., Friedel, J., & Paris, A. (2005). School engagement. In K. A. Moore & L. H. Lippman (Eds.), *What do children need to flourish?* (pp. 305–321). New York: Springer.

Fredrickson, B. L. (1998). What good are positive emotions? *Review of General Psychology, 2*, 300–319.

Fredrickson, B. L. (2000). Cultivating positive emotions to optimize health and well-being. *Prevention & Treatment, 3*(1), 1a.

Fredrickson, B. L. (2003). The value of positive emotions: The emerging science of positive psychology is coming to understand why it's good to feel good. *American Scientist, 91*(4), 330–335.

Fredrickson, B. L. (2004). The broaden-and-build theory of positive emotions. *Philosophical Transactions of the Royal Society B: Biological Sciences, 359*(1449), 1367–1377. https://doi.org/10.1098/rstb.2004.1512.

References

Fredrickson, B. L., & Branigan, C. (2001). Positive emotions. In T. J. Mayne & G. A. Bonnano (Eds.), *Emotion: Current issues and future directions* (pp. 123–151). New York: Guilford Press.

Frijda, N. H. (1988). The laws of emotion. *American Psychologist, 43*(5), 349–358.

Furrer, C., & Skinner, E. (2003). Sense of relatedness as a factor in children's academic engagement and performance. *Journal of Educational Psychology, 95*(1), 148.

Gable, S. L., & Haidt, J. (2005). What (and why) is positive psychology? *Review of General Psychology, 9*(2), 103–110.

Gallimore, R., & Tharp, R. G. (1992). Teaching mind in society: Teaching, schooling, and literature discourse. In L. C. Moll (Ed.), *Vygotsky and education: Instructional implications and applications of sociohistorical psychology* (pp. 175–205). New York: Cambridge University Press.

Gaskell, J. (2008). Learning from the women's movement about educational change. *Discourse: Studies in the Cultural Politics of Education, 29*(4), 437–449.

Gay, G. (2002). Preparing for culturally responsive teaching. *Journal of Teacher Education, 53*(2), 106–116.

Gilman, R., Huebner, E. S., & Laughlin, J. E. (2000). A first study of the Multidimensional Students' Life Satisfaction Scale with adolescents. *Social Indicators Research, 52*(2), 135–160.

Gindis, B. (1996). Psychology applied to education: L. S. Vygotsky's approach. NASP. *Communique, 25*(2), 12–13.

Gleason, M. E., Iida, M., Bolger, N., & Shrout, P. E. (2003). Daily supportive equity in close relationships. *Personality and Social Psychology Bulletin, 29*(8), 1036–1045.

Goldstein, H. (2013). Circle of friends. In *Encyclopedia of autism spectrum disorders* (pp. 641–645). Springer New York.

Goleman, D. P. (1995). *Emotional intelligence: Why it can matter more than IQ for character, health and lifelong achievement.*

Goleman, D. (2007). *Social intelligence.* New York: Random house.

Goodenow, C. (1993). Classroom belonging among early adolescent students: Relationships to motivation and achievement. *The Journal of Early Adolescence, 13*(1), 21–43.

Goroshit, M., & Hen, M. (2016). Teachers' empathy: Can it be predicted by self-efficacy? *Teachers and Teaching, 22*(7), 805–818.

Gregory, A., & Weinstein, R. S. (2004). Connection and regulation at home and in school: Predicting growth in achievement for adolescents. *Journal of Adolescent Research, 19*(4), 405–427.

Gregory, A., Clawson, K., Davis, A., & Gerewitz, J. (2016). The promise of restorative practices to transform teacher-student relationships and achieve equity in school discipline. *Journal of Educational and Psychological Consultation, 26*(4), 325–353.

Grolnick, W. S., Gurland, S. T., DeCourcey, W., & Jacob, K. (2002). Antecedents and consequences of mothers' autonomy support: An experimental investigation. *Developmental Psychology, 38,* 143–155.

Guerra, N., Modecki, K., & Cunningham, W. (2014). Social-emotional Skills Development across the Life Span: PRACTICE. *Policy Research Working Paper, 7123.*

Haferkamp, N., & Krämer, N. C. (2011). Social comparison 2.0: Examining the effects of online profiles on social-networking sites. *Cyberpsychology, Behavior, and Social Networking, 14*(5), 309–314.

Hamre, B. K., & Pianta, R. C. (2005). Can instructional and emotional support in the first-grade classroom make a difference for children at risk of school failure? *Child Development, 76*(5), 949–967.

Hamre, B., & Pianta, R. C. (2001). Early teacher-child relationships and trajectory of school outcomes through eighth grade. *Child Development, 72,* 625–638.

Hargreaves, A. (1999). The psychic rewards (and annoyances) of teaching. In M. Hammersley (Ed.), *Researching school experience: Ethnographic studies of teaching and learning* (pp. 85–104). London & New York: Falmer Press.

Hargreaves, D. H. (2001). A capital theory of school effectiveness and improvement. *British Educational Research Journal, 27*(4), 487–503.

Harris, J. R. (1998). *The nurture assumption: Why children turn out the way they do*. New York: Free Press.

Hawley, P. H., Little, T. D., & Pasupathi, M. (2002). Winning friends and influencing peers: Strategies of peer influence in late childhood. *International Journal of Behavioral Development, 26*(5), 466–474.

Heckman, J. J., & Kautz, T. (2012). Hard evidence on soft skills. *Labour Economics, 19*(4), 451–464.

Heinicke, C. M., & Westheimer, I. (1966). *Brief separations*. Oxford, England: International U. Press.

Hendrickx, M. M., Mainhard, M. T., Boor-Klip, H. J., Cillessen, A. H., & Brekelmans, M. (2016). Social dynamics in the classroom: Teacher support and conflict and the peer ecology. *Teaching and Teacher Education, 53*, 30–40.

Henry, D., Guerra, N., Huesmann, R., Tolan, P., VanAcker, R., & Eron, L. (2000). Normative influences on aggression in urban elementary school classrooms. *American Journal of Community Psychology, 28*(1), 59–81.

Heritage, M. (2007). Formative assessment: What do teachers need to know and do? *Phi Delta Kappan, 89*(2), 140–145.

Himsl, R., & Lambert, E. (1993). Signs of learning in the affective domain. *Alberta Journal of Educational Research, 39*(2), 257–73.

Homans, G. C. (1961). *Human behavior: Its elementary forms*. New York: Harcourt Brace.

Holmes, J. (2014). *John Bowlby and attachment theory*. London: Routledge.

Hopkins, B. (2002). Restorative justice in schools. *Support for Learning, 17*(3), 144–149.

Hughes, C. H., & Ensor, R. A. (2009). How do families help or hinder the emergence of early executive function? In C. Lewis & J. I. M. Carpendale (Eds.), *New directions in child and adolescent development: No. 123. Social interaction and the development of executive function* (pp. 35–50). New York, NY: Wiley.

Hughes, J. N. (2012). Teacher–student relationships and school adjustment: Progress and remaining challenges. *Attachment & Human Development, 14*(3), 319–327.

Hughes, J. N., & Kwok, O. M. (2007). Influence of student-teacher and parent-teacher relationships on lower achieving readers' engagement and achievement in the primary grades. *Journal of Educational Psychology, 99*(1), 39–51.

Hughes, J. N., Cavell, T. A., & Willson, V. (2001). Further support for the developmental significance of the quality of the teacher-student relationship. *Journal of School Psychology, 39*, 289–301.

Hughes, J. N., Luo, W., Kwok, O. M., & Loyd, L. K. (2008). Teacher-student support, effortful engagement, and achievement: A 3-year longitudinal study. *Journal of Educational Psychology, 100*(1), 1–14.

Hughes, N. K., & Schlösser, A. (2014). The effectiveness of nurture groups: a systematic review. *Emotional and Behavioural Difficulties, 19*(4), 386–409.

Isen, A. M., Daubman, K. A., & Nowicki, G. P. (1987). Positive affect facilitates creative problem solving. *Journal of Personality and Social Psychology, 52*(6), 1122.

Isenbarger, L., & Zembylas, M. (2006). The emotional labour of caring in teaching. *Teaching and Teacher Education, 22*(1), 120–134.

Izard, C. E. (1977). *Human emotions*. New York: Plenum.

Jackson, C. K. (2012). *Non-cognitive ability, test scores, and teacher quality: Evidence from 9th grade teachers in North Carolina (No. w18624)*. Cambridge, MA: National Bureau of Economic Research.

James, R. (2011). *An evaluation of the 'Circle of Friends' intervention used to support pupils with autism in their mainstream classrooms* (Doctoral dissertation, University of Nottingham).

Jang, H., Reeve, J., & Deci, E. L. (2010). Engaging students in learning activities: It is not autonomy support or structure but autonomy support and structure. *Journal of Edu-cational Psychology, 102*(3), 588–600.

Jennings, J., & Rentner, D. S. (2006). Ten big effects of the No Child Left Behind Act on public schools. *Phi Delta Kappan, 88*(2), 110–113.

References

Jennings, P. A., & Greenberg, M. T. (2009). The prosocial classroom: Teacher social and emotional competence in relation to student and classroom outcomes. *Review of Educational Research, 79*(1), 491–525.

Jensen, E. (2005). *Teaching with the brain in mind*. ASCD.

Johnson, D. W., Johnson, R. T., & Holubec, E. J. (1993). *Circles of learning*. Edina, MN: Interaction Book Company.

Johnson, D. W., Johnson, R. T., & Smith, K. A. (1991). *Cooperative learning: increasing college faculty instructional productivity. ASHE-ERIC Higher Education Report No. 4*. Washington, DC: School of Education and Human Development, The George Washington University.

Johnson, D. W., Johnson, R. T., & Smith, K. (2007). The state of cooperative learning in postsecondary and professional settings. *Educational Psychology Review, 19*(1), 15–29.

Jussim, L. (1989). Teacher expectations: Self-fulfilling prophecies, perceptual biases, and accuracy. *Journal of Personality and Social Psychology, 57*(3), 469–480.

Kagan, J. (1994). *Three seductive ideas*. Cambridge, MA: Harvard University.

Kalyva, E., & Avramidis, E. (2005). Improving communication between children with autism and their peers through the 'circle of friends': A small-scale intervention study. *Journal of Applied Research in Intellectual Disabilities, 18*(3), 253–261.

Kaplan, S., & Berman, M. G. (2010). Directed attention as a common resource for executive functioning and self-regulation. *Perspectives on Psychological Science, 5*(1), 43–57.

Karten, Y. J., Olariu, A., & Cameron, H. A. (2005). Stress in early life inhibits neurogenesis in adulthood. *Trends in Neurosciences, 28*(4), 171–172.

Kautz, T., Heckman, J. J., Diris, R., Ter Weel, B., & Borghans, L. (2014). *Fostering and measuring skills: Improving cognitive and non-cognitive skills to promote lifetime success (No. w20749)*. Cambridge, MA: National Bureau of Economic Research.

Kelly, B. (1999). Circle time. *Educational Psychology in Practice, 15*(1), 40–44. https://doi.org/10.1080/0266736990150107.

Kim, Y. Y. (2001). *Becoming intercultural: An integrative theory of communication and cross-cultural adaptation*. Sage.

Klem, A. M., & Connell, J. P. (2004). Relationships matter: Linking teacher support to student engagement and achievement. *Journal of School Health, 74*(7), 262–273.

Krashen, S. (1982). *Principles and practice in second language acquisition*. (Vol. 47, Jyvaeskylae studies in education, psychology and social research). Oxford u.a.: Pergamon.

Lam, B. H. (2017, June). *There is no fear in love: The giving of social support to students enhances teachers' career development*. Paper presented at the Education and Cognitive Development Lab research seminar series of National Institute of Education, Singapore.

Lam, B. H., Cheng, R. W. Y., & Yang, M. (2017). Formative feedback as a global facilitator: Impact on intrinsic and extrinsic motivation and positive affect. In S. C. Kong, T. L. Wong, M. Yang, C. F. Chow, & K. H. Tse (Eds.), *Emerging practices in scholarship of learning and teaching in a digital era* (pp. 265–288). Singapore: Springer.

Lashari, T. A., Alias, M., Kesot, M. J., & Akasah, Z. A. (2012). *The effect of integrated affective-cognitive learning approach on classroom behavioral engagement of engineering students*.

Law, Y. K. (2011). The effects of cooperative learning on enhancing Hong Kong fifth graders' achievement goals, autonomous motivation and reading proficiency. *Journal of Research in Reading, 34*(4), 402–425.

LeDoux, J. E. (2000). Emotion circuits in the brain. *Annual Review of Neuroscience, 23*(1), 155–184.

Lee, C. (1997). Social context, depression and the transition to motherhood. *British Journal of Health Psychology, 2*(2), 93–108.

Lee, E. J. (2003). *The attachment system throughout the life course: Review and criticisms of attachment theory*. Rochester, NY: Rochester Institute of Technology. http://www.personalityresearch.org/papers/lee.html(Erişim: 29/01/2012).

Lee, J. (2008). Is test-driven external accountability effective? Synthesizing the evidence from cross-state causal-comparative and correlational studies. *Review of Educational Research, 78*(3), 608–644.

Lee, V. E., Smith, J. B., Perry, T. E., & Smylie, M. A. (1999). *Social support, Academic Press, and student achievement: A view from the middle grades in Chicago. Improving Chicago's Schools.* A Report of the Chicago Annenberg Research Project. Retrived from https://files.eric.ed.gov/fulltext/ED439213.pdf.

Legault, L., & Green-Demers, I. (2006). Why do high school students lack motivation in the classroom? Toward an understanding of academic motivation and the role of social support. *Journal of Education Psychology, 28*(1), 567–582.

Lewis, M. (1993). Self-conscious emotions: Embarrassment, pride, shame, and guilt. In M. Lewis & J. M. Haviland (Eds.), *Handbook of emotions* (pp. 563–573). New York: Guilford Press.

Lezotte, L. W. (1989). School improvement based on the effective schools research. *International Journal of Educational Research, 13*(7), 815–825.

Liu, X., & Tein, J. Y. (2005). Life events, psychopathology, and suicidal behavior in Chinese adolescents. *Journal of Affective Disorders, 86*(2), 195–203.

Lockett, C. T., & Harrell, J. P. (2003). Racial identity, self-esteem, and academic achievement: Too much interpretation, too little supporting data. *Journal of Black Psychology, 29*(3), 325–336.

Lown, J. (2002). Circle time: The perceptions of teachers and pupils. *Educational Psychology in Practice, 18*(2), 93–102.

Mace, C., & Margison, F. (1997). Attachment and psychotherapy: An overview. *British Journal of Medical Psychology, 70*(3), 209–215.

Maclellan, E. (2001). Assessment for learning: The differing perceptions of tutors and students. *Assessment & Evaluation in Higher Education, 26*(4), 307–318.

Macready, T. (2009). Learning social responsibility in schools: A restorative practice. *Educational Psychology in Practice, 25*(3), 211–220. https://doi.org/10.1080/02667360903151767.

Malecki, C. K., & Demaray, M. K. (2003). What type of support do they need? Investigating student adjustment as related to emotional, informational, appraisal, and instrumental support. *School Psychology Quarterly, 18*(3), 231–252.

Malecki, C. K., & Demaray, M. K. (2002). The relationship between perceived social support and maladjustment for students at risk. *Psychology in the Schools, 39*(3), 305–316.

Malikow, M. (2006). Teaching in the affective domain: Turning a crier into a crier. *Kappa Delta Pi Record, 43*(1), 36–38.

Marks, H. M. (2000). Student engagement in instructional activity: Patterns in the elementary, middle, and high school years. *American Educational Research Journal, 37*(1), 153–184.

Mary, L. (2014). Fostering positive peer relations in the primary classroom through circle time and co-operative games. *Education 3–13, 42*(2), 125–137.

Marzano, R. J., Marzano, J. S., & Pickering, D. (2003). *Classroom management that works: Research-based strategies for every teacher*. Alexandra, VA: ASCD.

McCluskey, G., Lloyd, G., Kane, J., Riddell, S., Stead, J., & Weedon, E. (2008). Can restorative practices in schools make a difference? *Educational Review, 60*(4), 405–417.

McCollum, B. D. (2014). *The caring beliefs and practices of effective teachers*. Electronic Theses & Dissertations, 1186. Retrieved from https://digitalcommons.georgiasouthern.edu/etd/1186/.

McCombs, B. (2004). The learner-centered psychological principles: A framework for balancing academic achievement and social-emotional learning outcomes. In J. Zins, M. Bloodworth, R. Weissberg, & H. Walberg (Eds.), *Building academic success in social and emotional learning* (pp. 23–29). New York: Teachers College Press.

McDermott, J. M., Westerlund, A., Zeanah, C. H., Nelson, C. A., & Fox, N. A. (2012). Early adversity and neural correlates of executive function: Implications for academic adjustment. *Developmental Cognitive Neuroscience, 2,* S59–S66.

McKenzie, K., Whitley, R., & Weich, S. (2002). Social capital and mental health. *British Journal of Psychiatry, 181*(4).

Mercer, J. (2011). Attachment theory and tis vicissitudes: Toward an updated theory. *Theory & Psychology, 21*(1), 25–45.

Meyer, D. K., & Turner, J. C. (2006). Re-conceptualizing emotion and motivation to learn in classroom contexts. *Educational Psychology Review, 18*(4), 377–390.

References

Michelon, G. (2011). Sustainability disclosure and reputation: A comparative study. *Corporate Reputation Review, 14*(2), 79–96.

Middlebrooks, J. S., & Audage, N. C. (2008). *The effects of childhood stress on health across the lifespan.* Project Report. National Center for Injury Prevention and Control of the Centers for Disease Control and Prevention.

Midgley, C., & Edelin, K. C. (1998). Middle school reform and early adolescent well-being: The good news and the bad. *Educational Psychologist, 33*(4), 195–106.

Miers, D. R. (2001). *An International Review of restorative justice* (No. 10). Home Office.

Mikulincer, M., & Shaver, P. R. (2001). Attachment Theory and intergroup bias: Evidence that priming the secure base schema attenuates negative reactions to out-groups. *Journal of Personality and Social Psychology, 81,* 97–115.

Miller, D., & Moran, T. (2007). Theory and practice in self-esteem enhancement: Circle-Time and efficacy-based approaches—a controlled evaluation. *Teachers and Teaching: Theory and Practice, 13*(6), 601–615.

Morrison, B. (2002). Bullying and victimisation in schools: A restorative justice approach. In *Australian Institute of Criminology: Trends & issues in crime and criminal justice*, 219. Retrieved from http://www.aic.gov.au.

Morrison, B. E. (2003). Regulating safe school communities: Being responsive and restorative. *Journal of Educational Administration, 41*(6), 690–704.

Morrison, B. (2007). *Restoring safe school communities.* Sydney: Fedreation.

Morrison, B. E., & Vaandering, D. (2012). Restorative justice: Pedagogy, praxis, and discipline. *Journal of School Violence, 11*(2), 138–155.

Mosley, J. (1993). *Turn your school round: A circle-time approach to the development of self-esteem and positive behaviour in the primary staffroom, classroom and playground.* Lda.

Mosley, J. (1996). *Quality circle time in the primary classroom: Your essential guide to enhancing self-esteem, self-discipline and positive relationships.* Lda.

Mosley, J. (2005). *Circle time for young children.* Routledge.

Murberg, T. A., & Bru, E. (2004). School-related stress and psychosomatic symptoms among Norwegian adolescents. *School Psychology International, 25*(3), 317–332.

Murdock, T. B. (1996, April). *Expectations, achievement and academic self-concept: The continuing significance of race.* Paper presented at the annual meeting of the American Educational Research Association, New York.

Murdock, T. B. (1999). The social context of risk: Status and motivational predictors of alienation in middle school. *Journal of Educational Psychology, 91,* 62–75.

Murray-Harvey, R. (2010). Relationship influences on students' academic achievement, psychological health and well-being at school. *Educational and Child Psychology, 27*(1), 104–115.

National Education Association (2015). *Preparing 21st century students for a global society.* Retrieved from http://www.nea.org/assets/docs/A-Guide-to-Four-Cs.pdf.

Neitzel, C., & Stright, A. D. (2003). Mothers' scaffolding of children's problem solving: Establishing a foundation of academic self-regulatory competence. *Journal of Family Psychology, 17*(1), 147.

Newmann, F. (1981). Reducing student alienation in high schools: Implications of theory. *Harvard Educational Review, 51*(4), 546–564.

Newton, C., Taylor, G., & Wilson, D. (1996). Circles of friends: An inclusive approach to meeting emotional and behavioural needs. *Educational Psychology in Practice, 11*(4), 41–48.

Noddings, N. (1984). *Caring: A feminine approach to ethics and moral education.* Berkeley and Los Angeles: University of California Press.

Noddings, N. (1992). *The challenge to care in schools.* New York: Teachers College Press.

Noddings, N. (2003). *Happiness and education.* Cambridge, UK: Cambridge University Press.

Noddings, N. (2013). *Caring: A relational approach to ethics and moral education.* Berkeley and Los Angeles, California: University of California Press.

Noddings, N. (2005). *The challenge to care in schools.* New York: Teachers College Press.

O'Connor, T., & Colwell, J. (2002a). Research section: The effectiveness and rationale of the 'nurture group' approach to helping children with emotional and behavioural difficulties remain within mainstream education. *British Journal of Special Education, 29*(2), 96–100.

O'Connor, T., & Colwell, J. (2002b). Research section: The effectiveness and rationale of the 'nurture group' approach to helping children with emotional and behavioural difficulties remain within mainstream education. *British Journal of Special Education, 29*(2), 96–100.

O'Donnell, A. M., & O'Kelly, J. (1994). Learning from peers: Beyond the rhetoric of positive results. *Educational Psychology Review, 6*(4), 321–349.

O'Connor, E. (2016). The use of 'Circle of Friends' strategy to improve social interactions and social acceptance: A case study of a child with Asperger's syndrome and other associated needs. *Support for Learning, 31*(2), 138–147.

OECD. (2011). *Lessons from PISA for the United States, strong performers and successful reformers in education*. OECD Publishing. Retrieved from http://dx.doi.org/10.1787/9789264096660-en.

Olson, D. H. (2000). Circumplex model of marital and family systems. *Journal of Family Therapy, 22*(2), 144–167.

Pat-El, R. J., Tillema, H., Segers, M., & Vedder, P. (2013). Validation of assessment for learning questionnaires for teachers and students. *British Journal of Educational Psychology, 83*(1), 98–113.

Pianta, R. C., Hamre, B. K., & Allen, J. P. (2012). Teacher-student relationships and engagement: Conceptualizing, measuring, and improving the capacity of classroom interactions. *Handbook of research on student engagement* (pp. 365–386). Boston, MA: Springer.

Pianta, R. C., Hamre, B., & Stuhlman, M. (2003). Relationships between teachers and children. In W. M. Reynolds & G. E. Miller (Eds.), *Comprehensive handbook of psychology* (Vol. 7, pp. 199–234). New York: Wiley.

Pianta, R. C., Steinberg, M. S., & Rollins, K. B. (1995). The first two years of school: Teacher-child relationships and deflections in children's classroom adjustment. *Development and Psychopathology, 7*(2), 295–312.

Pintrich, P. R., & Zusho, A. (2002). The development of academic self-regulation: The role of cognitive and motivational factors. In A. Wigfield & J.S. Eccles, Jacquelynne (Eds.), *Development of achievement motivation* (pp. 249–284). San Diego, CA: Academic Press.

Polanczyk, G. V., Salum, G. A., Sugaya, L. S., Caye, A., & Rohde, L. A. (2015). Annual research review: A meta-analysis of the worldwide prevalence of mental disorders in children and adolescents. *Journal of Child Psychology and Psychiatry, 56*(3), 345–365.

Pössel, P., Rudasill, K. M., Sawyer, M. G., Spence, S. H., & Bjerg, A. C. (2013). Associations between teacher emotional support and depressive symptoms in Australian adolescents: A 5-year longitudinal study. *Developmental Psychology, 49*(11), 2135–2146.

Reddy, R., Rhodes, J. E., & Mulhall, P. (2003a). The influence of teacher support on student adjustment in the middle school years: A latent growth curve study. *Development and Psychopathology, 15*(1), 119–138.

Reddy, R., Rhodes, J. E., & Mulhall, P. (2003b). The influence of teacher support on student adjustment in the middle school years: A latent growth curve study. *Development and Psychopathology, 15*(1), 119–138.

Redmond, M. V. (2015). *Social exchange theory*. English Technical Reports and White Papers, 5. Retrieved from http://lib.dr.iastate.edu/engl_reports/5.

Reeve, J. (2002). Self-determination theory applied to educational settings. In E. L. Deci & R. M. Ryan (Eds.), *Handbook of self-determination research* (pp. 183–203). Rochester, NY, US: University of Rochester Press.

Reeve, J. (2006). Teachers as facilitators: What autonomy-supportive teachers do and why their students benefit. *The Elementary School Journal, 106*(3), 225–236.

Reeve, J., & Jang, H. (2006). What teachers say and do to support students' autonomy during a learning activity. *Journal of Educational Psychology, 98*(1), 209–218.

Reigeluth, C. M. (2013). *Instructional-design theories and models: A new paradigm of instructional theory*, Volume II. Routledge.

References

Rhodes, J. E., Grossman, J. B., & Resch, N. L. (2000). Agents of change: Pathways through which mentoring relationships influence adolescents' academic adjustment. *Child Development, 71*(6), 1662–1671.

Richman, J. M., Rosenfeld, L. B., & Bowen, G. L. (1998). Social support for adolescents at risk of school failure. *Social Work, 43*(4), 309–323.

Robertson, S. I. (2016). *Problem solving: perspectives from cognition and neuroscience.* Psychology Press.

Roeser, R. W., & Eccles, J. S. (2000). Schooling and mental health. In *Handbook of developmental psychopathology* (pp. 135–156). Springer US.

Roeser, R. W., Midgley, C., & Urdan, T. C. (1996). Perceptions of the school psychological environment and early adolescents' psychological and behavioral functioning in school: The mediating role of goals and belonging. *Journal of Educational Psychology, 88*(3), 408.

Rogers, M. E. (1961). *Educational revolution in nursing.* New York: Macmillan.

Roorda, D. L. (2012). *Teacher-child relationships and interaction processes: Effects on students' learning behaviors and reciprocal influences between teacher and child* (Doctoral dissertation, Universiteit van Amsterdam [Host]).

Rosenthal, R., & Jacobson, L. (1968). Pygmalion in the classroom. *The Urban Review, 3*(1), 16–20.

Rueger, S. Y., Malecki, C. K., & Demaray, M. K. (2010). Relationship between multiple sources of perceived social support and psychological and academic adjustment in early adolescence: Comparisons across gender. *Journal of Youth and Adolescence, 39*(1), 47.

Russell, S. L. (2012a). *Individual- and classroom-level social support and classroom behaviour in the middle school* (Unpublished dissertation for the degree of Doctor of Philosophy). University of Maryland, College Park.

Russell, S. L. (2012b). *Individual-and classroom-level social support and classroom behavior in middle school* (Ph.D. dissertation). University of Maryland, College Park, ProQuest Dissertations Publishing.

Ryan, A. M. (2000). Peer groups as a context for the socialization of adolescents' motivation, engagement, and achievement in school. *Educational Psychologist, 35*(2), 101–111.

Ryan, A. M., & Patrick, H. (2001). The classroom social environment and changes in adolescents' motivation and engagement during middle school. *American Educational Research Journal, 38*(2), 437–460.

Ryan, R. M., & Deci, E. L. (2017). *Self-determination theory: Basic psychological needs in motivation, development, and wellness.* New York: Guilford Publications.

Ryan, R. M., Stiller, J. D., & Lynch, J. H. (1994). Representations of relationships to teachers, parents, and friends as predictors of academic motivation and self-esteem. *The Journal of Early Adolescence, 14*(2), 226–249.

Sacks, P. (2000). Predictable losers in testing schemes. *School Administrator, 57*(11), 6–9.

Sadler, D. R. (2010). Beyond feedback: Developing student capability in complex appraisal. *Assessment & Evaluation in Higher Education, 35*(5), 535–550.

Sahlins, M. (1972). *Stone age economy.* Chicago: Aldine.

Salend, S. J., Whittaker, C. R., & Reeder, E. (1992). Group evaluation: A collaborative, peer-mediated behavior management system. *Exceptional Children, 59*(3), 203–209.

Sanders, T. (2007). Helping children thrive at school: The effectiveness of nurture groups. *Educational Psychology in Practice, 23*(1), 45–61.

Schlieder, M., Maldonado, N., & Baltes, B. (2014). An investigation of "Circle of Friends" peer-mediated intervention for students with autism. *Journal of Social Change, 6*(1).

Schmitz, T. W., De Rosa, E., & Anderson, A. K. (2009). Opposing influences of affective state valence on visual cortical encoding. *Journal of Neuroscience, 29*(22), 7199–7207.

Schweisfurth, M. (2015). Learner-centred pedagogy: Towards a post-2015 agenda for teaching and learning. *International Journal of Educational Development, 40,* 259–266.

Scott, K., & Lee, A. (2009). Beyond the 'classic'nurture group model: An evaluation of part-time and cross-age nurture groups in a Scottish local authority. *Support for Learning, 24*(1), 5–10.

Seligman, M. E., & Csikszentmihalyi, M. (2014). Positive psychology: An introduction. *Flow and the foundations of positive psychology* (pp. 279–298). Netherlands: Springer.

Seth-Smith, F., Levi, N., Pratt, R., Jaffey, D., & Fonagy, P. (2010). Do nurture groups improve the social, emotional and behavioural functioning of at risk children? *Educational & Child Psychology, 27*, 21–34.

Sharan, Y. (2010). Cooperative learning for academic and social gains: Valued pedagogy, problematic practice. *European Journal of Education, 45*, 300–313.

Shaver, P. R., Collins, N., & Clark, C. L. (1996). Attachment styles and internal working models of self and relationship partners. In G. J. O. Fletcher & J. Fitness (Eds.), *Knowledge structures in close relationships: A social psychological approach* (pp. 25–61). Hillsdale, NJ: Erlbaum.

Shaw, G. (2007). Restorative practices in Australian schools: Changing relationships, changing culture. *Conflict Resolution Quarterly, 25*(1), 127–135.

Skinner, B. F. (2011). *About behaviorism*. New York: Vintage.

Skinner, E. A., & Belmont, M. J. (1993). Motivation in the classroom: Reciprocal effects of teacher behavior and student engagement across the school year. *Journal of Educational Psychology, 85*(4), 571.

Skinner, E. A., Kindermann, T. A., Connell, J. P., & Wellborn, J. G. (2009). Engagement and disaffection as organizational constructs in the dynamics of motivational development. In K. R. Wentzel & A. Wigfield (Eds.), *Handbook of motivation at school* (pp. 223–245). London: Routledge.

Slavin, R. E. (1983). When does cooperative learning increase student achievement? *Psychological Bulletin, 94*(3), 429–445.

Slavin, R. E. (2008). Cooperative learning, success for all, and evidence-based reform in education. *Éducation et didactique, 2*(2), 149–157.

Slavin, R. E. (2011). Cooperative learning. In V. G. Aukrust (Ed.), *Learning and cognition in education* (pp. 160–166). Boston: Elsevier Academic Press.

Slavin, R. E. (2014). Cooperative learning and academic achievement: Why does groupwork work? *Anales de Psicología/Annals of Psychology, 30*(3), 785–791.

Smith, K., Walker, S., Ainley, P., & McNay, I. (2012). From the editors. *Compass: Journal of Learning and Teaching, 3*(4).

Stipek, D. (2002). Good instruction is motivating. In A. Wigfield & J. S. Eccles (Eds.), *Development of achievement motivation: A volume in the educational psychology series* (pp. 309–332). San Diego, CA: Academic Press.

Storrie, K., Ahern, K., & Tuckett, A. (2010). A systematic review: Students with mental health problems—A growing problem. *International Journal of Nursing Practice, 16*(1), 1–6.

Strangeman, C. C. (2007). *Strange allies?*. English Catholicism and the Enlightenment: Southern Illinois University at Carbondale.

Stryker, R. (1994). Rules, resources, and legitimacy processes: Some implications for social conflict, order, and change. *American Journal of Sociology, 99*(4), 847–910.

Suldo, S. M., Friedrich, A. A., White, T., Farmer, J., Minch, D., & Michalowski, J. (2009). Teacher support and adolescents' subjective well-being: A mixed-methods investigation. *School Psychology Review, 38*(1), 67–85.

Suldo, S. M., Shaffer, E. J., & Riley, K. N. (2008). A social-cognitive-behavioral model of academic predictors of adolescents' life satisfaction. *School Psychology Quarterly, 23*(1). 56–69.

Sutton, R. E., & Wheatley, K. F. (2003). Teachers' emotions and teaching: A review of the literature and directions for future research. *Educational Psychology Review, 15*(4), 327–358.

Taylor, G. (1996). *Creating a circle of friends: A case study*. Peer counselling in school, 73–86.

Taylor, G. (1997). Community building in schools: Developing a circle of friends. *Educational and Child Psychology, 14*, 45–50.

Teddlie, C., & Reynolds, D. (2000). *The international handbook of school effectiveness research*. Psychology Press.

The Nurture Group Network. (2016). *What is a nurture group?* Retrieved from https://www.nurturegroups.org/introducing-nurture/what-nurture-group-0.

References

Thibault, J. W., & Kelley, H. H. (1959). *The social psychology of groups*. New York: Wiley.

Tinto, V. (1997). Classrooms as communities: Exploring the educational character of student persistence. *The Journal of Higher Education, 68*(6), 599–623.

Tominey, S. L., & McClelland, M. M. (2011). Red light, purple light: Findings from a randomized trial using circle time games to improve behavioral self-regulation in preschool. *Early Education and Development, 22*(3), 489–519. https://doi.org/10.1080/10409289.2011.574258.

Vaandering, D. (2014). Implementing restorative justice practice in schools: What pedagogy reveals. *Journal of Peace Education, 11*(1), 64–80.

van IJzendoorn MH, & Sagi-Schwartz, A. (2008). Cross-cultural patterns of attachment: Universal and contextual dimensions. In J. Cassidy, & P. R., Shaver (Eds.), *Handbook of attachment: Theory, research and clinical applications* (pp. 880–905). New York and London: Guilford Press.

Vavrus, M. (2008). Culturally responsive teaching. *21st Century Education: A Reference Handbook, 2*, 49–57. Retrieved from https://static1.squarespace.com/static/55a68b71e4b075daf6b2aa0b/t/55a7322ae4b0a573ba71de46/1437020714535/CulturallyResponsiveTeaching.pdf.

Verschueren, K., Doumen, S., & Buyse, E. (2012). Relationships with mother, teacher, and peers: Unique and joint effects on young children's self-concept. *Attachment & Human Development, 14*(3), 233–248.

Vygotsky, L. S. (1978). *Mind in society: The development of higher psychological processes*. Cambridge, MA: Harvard University Press.

Wang, M. C., Haertel, G. D., & Walberg, H. J. (1994). Educational resilience in inner cities. In M. C. Wang & E. W. Gordon (Eds.), *Educational resilience in inner-city America: Challenges and prospects* (pp. 45–72). Hillsdale, NJ: Lawrence Erlbaum.

Wang, M. T., & Eccles, J. S. (2012). Social support matters: Longitudinal effects of social support on three dimensions of school engagement from middle to high school. *Child Development, 83*(3), 877–895.

Wang, M. T., & Holcombe, R. (2010). Adolescents' perceptions of school environment, engagement, and academic achievement in middle school. *American Educational Research Journal, 47*(3), 633–662.

Watson, D., Wiese, D., Vaidya, J., & Tellegen, A. (1999). The two general activation systems of affect: Structural findings, evolutionary considerations, and psychobiological evidence. *Journal of Personality and Social Psychology, 76*, 820–838.

Wearmouth, J., McKinney, R., & Glynn, T. (2007). Restorative justice: Two examples from New Zealand schools. *British Journal of Special Education, 34*(4), 196–203.

Weiner, L. (2000). Research in the 90s: Implications for urban teacher preparation. *Review of Educational Research, 70*(3), 369–406.

Weinstein, R. S. (1989). Perceptions of classroom processes and student motivation: Children's views of self-fulfilling prophecies. *Research on Motivation in Education, 3*, 187–221.

Weinstein, R. S. (2002). Overcoming inequality in schooling: A call to action for community psychology. *American Journal of Community Psychology, 30*(1), 21–42.

Welsh, J. A., Nix, R. L., Blair, C., Bierman, K. L., & Nelson, K. E. (2010). The development of cognitive skills and gains in academic school readiness for children from low-income families. *Journal of Educational Psychology, 102*(1), 43.

Wentzel, K. R. (1997). Student motivation in middle school: The role of perceived pedagogical caring. *Journal of Educational Psychology, 89*(3), 411.

Wentzel, K. R. (1998). Social relationships and motivation in middle school: The role of parents, teachers, and peers. *Journal of Educational Psychology, 90*(2), 202.

Wentzel, K. R. (1999). Social-motivational processes and interpersonal relationships: Implications for understanding motivation at school. *Journal of Educational Psychology, 91*(1), 76.

Wentzel, K. R. (2012). Socio-cultural contexts, social competence, and engagement at school. In S. Christenson, A. Reschly, & C. Wylie (Eds.), *Handbook of research on student engagement* (pp. 479–488). New York: Springer.

Wentzel, K. R., & Asher, S. R. (1995). The academic lives of neglected, rejected, popular, and controversial children. *Child Development, 66*(3), 754–763.

Wentzel, K. R., & Watkins, D. E. (2002). Peer relationships and collaborative learning as contexts for academic enablers. *School Psychology Review, 31*(3), 366.

Wentzel, K. R., Barry, C. M., & Caldwell, K. A. (2004a). Friendships in middle school: Influences on motivation and school adjustment. *Journal of Educational Psychology, 96*(2), 195.

Wentzel, K. R., Barry, C. M., & Caldwell, K. A. (2004b). Friendships in middle school: Influences on motivation and school adjustment. *Journal of Educational Psychology, 96*(2), 195.

Wentzel, K. R., Battle, A., Russell, S. L., & Looney, L. B. (2010a). Social supports from teachers and peers as predictors of academic and social motivation. *Contemporary Educational Psychology, 35*(3), 193–202.

Wentzel, K. R., Battle, A., Russell, S. L., & Looney, L. B. (2010b). Social supports from teachers and peers as predictors of academic and social motivation. *Contemporary Educational Psychology, 35*(3), 193–202.

Wentzel, K., Baker, S. A. N. D. R. A., & Russell, S. (2009). Peer relationships and positive adjustment at school. *Handbook of positive psychology in schools*, 229–243.

Wigfield, A., & Eccles, J. S. (2002). *The development of competence beliefs, expectancies for success, and achievement values from childhood through adolescence.*

Willis, J. (2007). The neuroscience of joyful education. *Educational Leadership, 64*(9). Retrieved from http://www.district287.org/uploaded/A_Better_Way/ME_PrereadingJudyWillisEdLeadArt.pdf.

Wingate, U. (2010). The impact of formative feedback on the development of academic writing. *Assessment & Evaluation in Higher Education, 35*(5), 519–533.

Wood, D. J. (1980). Teaching the young child: Some relationships between social interaction, language, and thought. In D. R. Olsen (Ed.), *The social foundations of language and thought* (pp. 280–296). New York, NY: Norton.

Wood, D., & Middleton, D. (1975). A study of assisted problem-solving. *British Journal of Psychology, 66*(2), 181–191.

Wood, D., Bruner, J. S., & Ross, G. (1976). The role of tutoring in problem solving. *Journal of Child Psychology and Psychiatry, 17*, 89–100.

World Health Organization. (2017 April). *Mental disorders fact sheet*. Retrieved from http://www.who.int/mediacentre/factsheets/fs396/en/.

Zehr, P. E. (2002). Considerations for use of the Hoffmann reflex in exercise studies. *European Journal of Applied Physiology, 86*(6), 455–468.

Chapter 5
Expert Teachers' Social Support Behaviours—A Humanised Classroom Characterised by Productive Learning

Abstract The discussion of social support sources for students in educational settings in Chap. 4 recommends the need for understanding teachers' classroom behaviours. This chapter continues to explore teachers' social support behaviours by expert teachers at the classroom level. Since expert teachers are often suggested as effective teachers who can benefit students in both the cognitive and affective aspects, and their teaching is found to be characterised by relationship qualities and teacher attitudinal qualities, they are a relevant target for study in order to identify social support behaviours. The chapter seeks to accomplish the following purposes:

- To identify social support behaviours of the four expert teachers in classroom teaching and conceptualise the expertise these behaviour features
- To identify the motivation for learning of students who study in the classes taught by the four teachers
- To make implications and suggestions regarding theory and practice in learning and teaching.

This chapter reports on a qualitative study based on classroom observations and interviews of 4 teachers regarding their teaching, and a questionnaire survey on a total of 144 junior form students on their motivation for learning, in a secondary school in Hong Kong. The analysis of teachers' instructional behaviour shows a particular style of teaching among the four teachers. In delivering the lessons, the teachers engaged students into a series of dialogic discourse which engaged students in metacognitive learning. Such dialogic discourse led students to take part in exchanging views in the classroom which was safe, encouraging and challenging. Students were highly motivated under the four teachers' guidance and instruction. The findings of the study resulted in a 'triad of teaching expertise' as a theoretical framework that conceptualises teachers' teaching expertise. This triad includes teacher commitment, communication skills and metacognitive teaching skills. The study argues that teachers' genuine care is an underlying trait which is significant in producing outstanding teaching, as teachers' care prompts them to render meticulous support in guiding students through the learning process, which results in better learning outcomes for students. Recommendations for teacher education and training, and school leadership to promote high-quality teaching are made. Limitations of the study and future research directions are discussed.

© Springer Nature Singapore Pte Ltd. 2019
B. LAM, *Social Support, Well-being, and Teacher Development*,
https://doi.org/10.1007/978-981-13-3577-8_5

Background of Studying Teacher Behaviours

The assumption that teaching quality is the most important factor at the classroom level (Kyriakides, Creemers, & Antoniou, 2009; Meyer & Turner, 2002) makes teacher behaviour a timeless topic of investigation in the education literature (Emmer, Sabornie, Evertson, & Weinstein, 2013; Hargreaves, 2000a). Studies of teachers' teaching behaviour have gained recurrent interest in the twenty-first century, due also to the higher expectation given to teachers in preparing students for the challenges facing our globalised society (Stein, 2000). To gain an understanding of social support at the classroom level, this chapter discusses a study of four expert teachers' behaviour at the classroom level, to shed light on further directions for teacher education.

In the literature, teacher behaviours are studied in terms of different organising constructs, such as effective teaching (Ko, Sammons, & Bakkum, 2013), expert teaching (Berliner, 2001) and teaching styles (Harris, 1998). As a form of social support, giving leads to favourable educational outcomes, exploring teachers' practice of social support in the classroom (what teachers actually do in the classroom suggests social support) becomes a prominent topic for investigation. In the literature, qualitative studies of teachers' social support behaviour have been scant. To investigate 'how are expert teachers' behaviours expressed in teaching' and 'what are teachers' views towards their enacted practice' can further answer 'how' social support is related to teaching in the education setting, and this is one of the topics this book pursues. The chapter begins with a discussion of the background literature on expert teachers' behaviours, effective teaching and other related themes.

Studying Teacher Cognition and Teaching Expertise

The literature has suggested that expert teachers practise good teaching behaviours for novices to learn from. One major issue with studying expert teachers is the relative lack of an objective definition of expert teachers. Fenstermacher and Richardson (2000) suggested that successful teaching does not mean good teaching, as the judgement of the former is concerned with the achievement of the intended purpose of teaching for example, to make sure that students are able to 'write superlative adjectives in correct form' or 'perform multiplication of two-digit numbers', but not necessarily with the professional behaviour of teachers in teaching the topic in class (Berliner, 2001). Hence, students' academic results cannot be a sufficiently reliable index to determine expert teaching behaviours (Hattie & Clinton, 2008) although it is also believed that expert teachers must demonstrate success in terms of achieving the intended outcomes to prove their expertise. One condition of expert teachers is that they must go through deliberate practice as professionals (Ericsson, 2000), which means that expert teachers are engaged in practice to make their practice become perfect—i.e. seek for improvement and high-quality performance.

The reason is that expert teachers are committed to the profession; therefore, they are engaged in the pursuit of expert-level performance. One of the prerequisites of expert teachers is therefore about their length of practice (teaching experience) (Berliner, 2001), and a minimum of 10,000 h or 7–10 years of experience is proposed in identifying expert teachers (Anderson, 1982; Ericsson & Lehmann, 1996). Other methods of selecting expert teachers include social recognition or nomination, professional or social group membership and performance-based criteria (Palmer, Stough, Burdenski, & Gonzales, 2005). Based on a vigorous review, Palmer, Stough, Burdenski, and Gonzales (2005) suggested that there is a huge variability in student populations and their associated instructional contexts (such as differences between life skills training versus academic knowledge for students with severe disabilities and college-bound high school students), and a range of possible student outcomes (e.g. high-stakes testing performance, social outcomes as well as thinking skills); hence, it is difficult to pin down a definition of expert teaching. The recommendation is that researchers should look into the unique knowledge, skills and outcomes that are relevant to the context of a particular setting, to investigate teacher behaviours. However, for teachers who are accorded the status of high-level expertise, it is reasonable to believe that some common traits may be found to characterise their teaching even within different contexts and environments.

Over the past decades, researchers have reported important findings to explain the classroom behaviours of expert teachers. Teacher cognition, which emerged in the 1970s, resembles the developing stage of researching expertise in the field of education (see reviews by Berliner, 1994, 2001; Freeman, 2002; Hogan, Rabinowitz, & Craven, 2003). Taking a cognitive psychological stance, the initial studies on teacher cognition inquired into the interactive nature of teacher decision-making within the processes of teaching in the classroom (e.g. Calderhead, 1996; Shavelson & Stern, 1981), attempting to understand how the knowledge of teaching possessed by teachers is retrieved/processed in the planning and interactive phase of teaching (Harris, 1998; Hogan, Rabinowitz, & Craven, 2003). Early efforts generally agreed that teacher expertise is identified in a teacher's role in their ability to modify instruction in an ongoing manner, give instructions involving a mental processes; and that it relies on teacher beliefs, judgement and decision-making (Berliner, 2001; Clark & Peterson, 1986; Harris, 1998).

The studies on teaching expertise or expert teachers' behaviours are aimed at comparing the teaching performance of experts with novices to identify and contrast differences between them. For example, authentic classroom studies have reported that expert teachers apply internalised mental scripts in conducting teaching; they perform fluently and demonstrate a higher capacity to recall details about students in lessons (Borko & Putnam, 1996). Expert teachers also teach with higher flexibility and more improvisation (Bereiter & Scardamalia, 1993). They are better at monitoring individual students and adjusting their lessons to students' needs accordingly (e.g. Borko & Livingston, 1989). While a non-expert teacher is likely to stick to his/her lesson plan, an expert is inclined to seek to understand students' problems and guide them back to the lesson. The instructional practice of novices was commented as vulnerable to student questions and disruptions (Emmer & Stough, 2001) as it is rigid and unable to fit the changing situations of the classroom. Hence, a distinct feature of expert teaching may be that expert teachers provide continuous, flexible guidance to students that lead them to learn through the lesson.

Later, research on expert teachers adopted a prototype approach that summarised the key qualities of an expert teacher (Berliner, 2001). Bond, Smith, Baker, and Hattie (2000) created a summary of 13 prototypical features of expert teachers, which started to include the affective ones, such as that expert teachers show a higher level of respect towards students (Hattie, 1999, 2003). Hattie's (2003) meta-review proposed five major dimensions of expertise in common. In addition to teachers' subject content knowledge, four of the other aspects underscore a supportive, guiding process of learning for students, including (i) guiding learning through classroom interactions, (ii) monitoring learning and providing feedback, (iii) attending to affective attributes and (iv) influencing student outcomes. These features are highly relevant to teacher's social support-giving behaviour discussed in Chap. 4. Recent studies on expert teachers have revealed ways in which expert teachers perform differently from novices in the affective domain. Using a survey, Bond et al. (2000) found that the classrooms taught by expert teachers tended to have a more positive climate (the teachers smiled more often, etc.) and had respect for students (the teachers gave students more say in the classes, etc.) than those taught by novices, as echoed by other researchers (e.g. Hattie, 2003; Meyer & Turner, 2002; Tan, Heng & Tan, 2013). This further reinforces the emotional figure of the teacher, from whom students receive respect and psychological support, making a difference from an authoritative image of novice teachers who often exercise control (Emmer & Stough, 2001).

Democratic Classroom Management

Studies comparing effective and non-effective teachers also point to teachers' supportive behaviours in guiding student learning, motivational strategies and relationship quality with students. Bohn, Roehrig, and Pressley (2004) observed six primary-grade teachers during their first 3 days in school. They eventually identified two of them as effective teachers with behaviours of more engaging activities (meaningful learning tasks), more enthusiastically introducing reading and writing, higher expectations of students, recognition of students and encouragement of self-regulated learning (monitoring and providing scaffoldings).

Opdenakker and Van Damme (2006) studied a sample of 132 mathematics classes in 47 Belgian secondary schools. By using multilevel analysis on student and teacher surveys, they concluded that the presence of effective classroom practice could be explained by a learner-centred teaching style which emphasised instructional support of teachers, suggesting features including provision of a variety of activities and differentiated materials, support to student specific needs, regular communication with students and concern with student development, which led to high-level participation and engagement of students in class. Both the research led by Bohn and Opdenakker (Bohn, Roehrig, & Pressley, 2004; Opdenakker & Van Damme, 2006) found that effective teachers' classroom management approach focused on student control in the learning process and how the teachers made students understand the established rules for desired behaviours. Other studies also suggested that effective teachers made efforts to accustom students to behavioural expectations and consequences. Instead of exercising harsh control to achieve classroom management, these teachers managed to structure the classroom environment by allowing flexibility. They attempted to cultivate trust and respect in the classroom and they were concerned about building positive student–teacher relationships to facilitate a pleasant classroom environment to support student learning (Emmer & Stough, 2001; Stough, Palmer, & Leyva, 1998).

Effective teachers tend to use preventive measures (Stough et al., 1998) in managing the classroom as they help to detect and correct problems before they emerge (Emmer & Stough, 2001). Instead of being rigid, effective teachers also make decisions in response to changing factors in classroom teaching to ensure progress (Jennings & Greenberg, 2009). This ongoing decision-making process has been found to distinguish expertise in teaching (Berliner, 2001). Jennings and Greenberg (2009) elaborated a prosocial classroom with an accent on producing positive experience and autonomous motivation for students. In a prosocial classroom, teachers use strategies to maintain a supportive and encouraging relationship with students, designing lessons that build on students' strengths and abilities, establishing behaviour guidelines in ways which promote intrinsic motivation, coaching students through conflict situations, encouraging cooperation among students and shaping prosocial behaviour (Jennings & Greenberg, 2009). This type of classroom provides positive emotions and fulfilling experiences for students and reinforces the learning of desirable behaviours.

In terms of effective classroom management, Djigic and Stojiljkovic (2011) researched a sample of teachers and students by asking them to rate their agreement on a set of scales which measured three styles of classroom management, i.e. interventionalist, non-interventionist and interactionalist, according to three domains, i.e. personality, teaching and discipline. The results suggested that an interactionalist classroom management style focuses on a shared control of the classroom environment, featuring cooperation between students and teachers in safeguarding discipline and positive relationships in the classroom, goal-oriented activities, effective discipline management procedures, self-control and the responsibilities of students. Compared with the non-interventional approach and interventional approach, where teachers give little control or complete control in managing the classroom, the interactionalist classroom management approach emphasises the motivation and engagement of student learning (Martin & Baldwin, 1993). The interactionalist approach is believed to enhance conflict management and avoid conflict between students and teachers (Bru, Stephens & Torsheim, 2002); it thus can generate positive student–teacher relationships and productive learning for students (Adelman & Taylor, 2005) on the basis of mutual respect (Miler & Pedro, 2006).

Autonomy-Supportive Teaching Styles

As addressed in Chap. 4, teachers who engage students in a supportive classroom are conceived as sharing the concerns of self-actualization and human flourishing as their prime goal of teaching, hoping to support students' well-being (Deci & Ryan, 2002). Specific to classroom instruction, the self-determination theory also proposes a framework of teaching styles (Reeve, 2009) which identifies teaching behaviours that promote student development. The framework is presented in a continuum of two poles, with one representing an autonomy-supportive style while the other a controlling style (Deci, Schwartz, Sheinman, & Ryan, 1981; Ryan & Deci, 2017). The autonomy-supportive teaching style means making students motivated to act on their own internal locus of control, specifying a learning condition which engenders autonomy, competence and relatedness (Ryan & Deci, 2017; Vansteenkiste, Niemiec, & Soenens, 2010) (for a detailed explanation of self-determination theory, please refer to Chap. 3). Deci, Schwartz, Sheinman and Ryan (1981) identified the autonomy-supportive behaviours that can create a driving force of engagement for learners, including asking what students want, allowing time for students to work in their own way, arranging seating to benefit more motivating interactions, offering encouragement and hints, being responsive to student-generated questions and using empathetic statements to acknowledge student perspective or experience (Reeve, Bolt, & Cai, 1999). Students taught by an autonomy-supportive teacher would achieve positive outcomes such as classroom engagement, emotionality, creativity, intrinsic motivation and psychological well-being (Reeve, Deci, & Ryan, 2004). This teaching style echoes the emotional attributes of creating positive affect and promoting the internal interest of learners, in which learners use volitional resources that produce the drive of learning for themselves; therefore, learners are engaged energetically in learning. Such motivational status of learners is known as 'autonomous motivation' (Deci & Ryan, 2008).

Compared with autonomy-supportive styles, controlling teaching styles tend to manipulate students' ways of thinking, feeling and behaving which create negative affect for learners (Reeve, Jang, Carrell, Jeon, & Barch, 2004), characterised by behaviours such as commanding language, criticising students, asking controlling questions, making 'ought-to' statements, as well as depreciating the opportunities for performing thinking or higher order thinking such as providing answers and solutions (Deci et al., 1981). In fact, research at different times has suggested that novice teachers take a custodian orientation in classroom management, aligning with an oppressive management style which is characterised by impersonality, mistrust and pessimism towards students (Emmer & Stough, 2001; Hoy, 1968).

Productive Classroom Discourse and Monitoring Student Learning

Viewing teaching as a process of interaction is synonymous with viewing teaching as social support. It implies a classroom discourse through which interaction of the class and the teacher takes place. Nystrand, Wu, Gamoran, Zeiser, and Long (2003) offered a conceptualization of the classroom as a dialogic discourse versus a monologic discourse. The latter presents to students a script that processes the teachers' prepared knowledge, whereas the former involves students' genuine dialogues with teachers to expand or modify the topic by mutual contribution. The dialogic discourse suggests a discourse that involves positive reinforcement and draws on students' experience (Hadfield, 1992). By doing so, teachers have to pay attention to students by observing them and listening to them (Walshaw & Anthony, 2008). In fact, dialogic discourse reflects an epistemological belief that suggests the 'construction of knowledge', therefore, teachers conversing with students with a dialogic discourse may also involve more scaffoldings and feedback with students with productive learning results. Teachers' generation of dialogues in different formats creates social support sources, which is consistent with an autonomy-supportive style of teaching that recommends the spirit of meaningful pedagogies that help learners construct knowledge and develop learning capabilities.

Dialogic discourse created by teachers in the classroom enhances the engagement of learners. The authors researching effective teaching suggested that teachers' use of prompting questions, uptake or flow of questions and follow-up answers in response to students' response and time for discussion as the characteristics of dialogic discourse (Lam, 2015; Nystrand, Gamoran, Kachur, & Prendergast, 1997). Dialogic discourse also suggests the concerns of student diversity and differences, taking into account students' differing points of views and encouraging participation. Some of the authors also developed protocols for practice that encourage learner engagement, such as Krathwohl & Anderson's (2001) taxonomy of affective learning that suggests receiving, responding, valuing, organising and characterising by value as layers of learning levels, and Malikow's (2006) proposal to feel, listen and defend, as described in Chap. 4. This type of instruction, organised by dialogic discourse as well as group discussion, requires the attention of teachers to monitoring students' exchange of ideas, and giving a lot of formative assessment to students' points of view (Lam, 2015). It is also known as a scaffold discussion (Cazden, 1983).

In addition to the role of keeping the conversation or learning activities going in the classroom, teachers who create dialogic interaction with students and take part in it to monitor student learning and knowledge construction also demonstrate their metacognitive teaching strategies. These strategies are related to teachers' 'awareness of the learning process' (Flavell, 1970, p. 232). More specifically, teachers performing metacognitive teaching are aware of the learning process and the factors that influence students' learning. They help learners to make use of available resources and make the best use of strategies to learn (knowledge of cognition); they also help learners to set goals, reflect and evaluate (regulation of cognition) learning with direction (Balcikanli, 2011; Schraw, 2001). The regulated learning strategies and formative assessment strategies, and dialogic conversation with students are exemplary instructional practices commonly suggested in the literature. In fact, metacognitive learning is a developing area in the education literature. As a whole, teachers who are inclined to involve students in constructivist learning are more likely to introduce teaching by considering students metacognitive learning, interaction with students and giving opportunities to students to master their own learning. Expert teachers' are characterised by their improvisation in the classroom, their interest in individual learners' progress and their caring attitude (Borko & Livingston, 1989) which also suggest the features of metacognitive thinking in teaching.

As a whole, effective classroom practice has been seen to shift from one which was measured by student academic gain (Harris, 1998) to motivating students to learn (Ryan & Deci, 2017). Similarly, research on expert teachers has also revealed a pattern in which expert teachers are more inclined to be concerned about students' personal well-being (Agne, 1999). This turns the attention of researchers to the dispositional aspects of teaching to seek understanding of expert teaching.

Caring, Empathetic and Virtuous Personality Traits Underlie Teacher Behaviours

Caring is a disposition or a gesture describing how teachers relate to students (McAllister & Irvine, 2002). In Chap. 4, Noddings' (2013) caring practice is discussed—it is a form of teaching that supports learners to respect others, become involved in exchange of ideas, recognise each other's ideas and achieve learning with intrinsic interest; therefore learners learn to care about each other as a form of ethnic care. Viewing it as one of the traits in teaching, the researchers have found that when teachers use affinity-seeking strategies, such as non-verbal immediacy (Anderson, Evertson, & Brophy, 1979; Asad & Hassan, 2013) with the use of gesture, relaxed body position, smiling, vocal expressiveness, movement and proximity etc., students perceive these teachers as caring and these teachers' teaching is better received. These behaviours are also found to cause enhanced outcomes of motivation for students (as cited in Teven & Hanson, 2004), students' trust in teachers (Teven & Hanson, 2004), increased learning (e.g. Richmond, 1990; So & Brush, 2008) and positive classroom environments (Asad & Hassan, 2013). Studies have further proved that teachers who have high immediacy and verbal caring are perceived as significantly more competent than teachers with low scores in these aspects (Teven & Hanson's, 2004), although some authors suggested that it also depends on the characteristics of students (Richmond, Gorham, & McCroskey, 1987). Verbal and non-verbal immediacy, as behaviourial expressions, suggest the importance of how teachers relate to students in the classroom, which is generated from the emotional attributes that teachers possess.

As an emotional attribute, empathy is regarded as a necessary condition for caring behaviours (Tettegah & Anderson, 2007). In simple terms, empathy means 'entering the other person's frame of reference' (Aspy, 1975, p. 12). It refers to an affective expression of understanding another person's situation (Nickerson, Butler, & Carlin, 2009), in the state of 'feeling with' the person in a non-judgemental fashion, to experience to some degree the emotions that the other is experiencing, as an altruistic act in service of the other's needs (Noddings, 1984). Teacher empathy works as an attitude and an ability to express concern for students, to feel about what the student feels (Tettegah & Anderson, 2007). This character trait is important for teachers to manage a diverse population in classrooms. Empathy is found to promote prosocial classroom behaviours (Garaigordobil, 2009). It generates the desire of helping others (affective response), understanding others, and the giving of helping behaviour (Tettegah & Anderson, 2007). Being empathetic also means that teachers attach themselves mentally and emotionally to students and generate supportive responses/behaviours in return (Cooper, 2004). Research has proved that empathetic teachers' practices are conducive to student learning and achievement (Peck, Maude, & Brotherson, 2015). They boost students' confidence (Cooper, 2004) and demonstrate a positive attitude towards students who need special attention (such as at-risk students and ethnic minorities) (Hen & Goroshit, 2016). Empathetic teachers are found to enhance students' sense of belonging and their relationships with teachers and peers (Schutz & DeCuir, 2002). These teachers create psychological resources for students that benefit their well-being.

As also mentioned in Chap. 4, socio-emotional competence is a non-cognitive skill correlated with caring and empathy, agreeableness, conscientiousness and extroverted personalities and other positive character traits that can form supportive relationships with students (Garaigordobil, 2009; Hen & Goroshit, 2016). Teachers high in socio-emotional competence are keen to use emotional cues and verbal support to guide students, making them more participative in learning (Elias, 2009).

Judging from a moral conduct perspective, 'manner of teaching' is used to explain individual teachers' instructional practice as inseparable from the skills and methods teachers use in teaching (Richardson & Fallona, 2001). Fenstermacher (2001) pointed out that virtuous conduct, which carries positive character traits such as justice and fairness, forms the manner of teaching that at the same time helps students learn to perform virtuous behaviours.

It is regarded as the moral basis for teacher professionalism (Sockett, 1993). Narvaez & Lapsley (2008) postulated that effective teaching promotes moral and academic excellence, specifying that good teaching should lead to student character development. These emotional characteristics can also be observed in more clearly described classroom settings.

The person-centred approach to education proposed by Rogers also suggests similar traits of teachers, which includes teacher empathy, unconditional positive regard (warmth), genuineness, non-directivity (student-initiated and student-regulated activities) and encouragement of critical thinking (Cornelius-White, 2007; Rogers, 1983). Similar to the literature which advocates teacher empathy and care, Roger's recommended approach of teaching is largely based on the development of the person, but it serves to benefit learners emotionally and cognitively. The results of this study demonstrate the effectiveness of a learner-centred approach in education.

To summarise, good teachers make use of emotional attributes, attitudinal qualities, and character traits as important resources in teaching that often lead to beneficial student learning outcomes such as autonomous motivation, prosocial behaviours, engagement and cognitive development, as well as a positive classroom environment. Behind technical expertise, affective variables of teachers affect their pedagogical reasoning, which makes their teaching different. Understanding about expert teachers' behaviours can help infer these variables, and know how they work in classroom practice. As discussed in Chap. 4, these behaviours resemble teachers' social support in the education setting, which is a theoretical perspective useful to explain teaching, and it is found to underline expert teachers' behaviour. At present, discussion of the affective dimension of teaching or social support behaviours in the classroom is scant, and teacher behaviour related to these aspects is described as learner-centred teaching orientation (O'Neill & McMahon, 2005), as an idiosyncratic term. The study into expert teachers' behaviours and understanding the behaviours to look at the affective variables can fill this research gap.

Four Expert Teachers' Teaching Behaviours in the Classroom

The Study Background

Aim. A study of four expert teachers is reported in this section. As one aim of this book is to identify teachers' social support-giving behaviour, this empirical study identifies expert teachers' behaviours and examines the emotional attributes that guide expert teachers' actions. It seeks to understand how teachers relate to students during classroom instruction, in aspects including their relationship, their expectations and attitudinal qualities of perceiving students while teaching. There are two focuses to guide the study: (1) the behaviours of teachers demonstrated in managing the overall classroom climate, instructional format and behaviour management, (2) the interpretation of behaviours and analysis of behaviours related to the attitude components and emotional attributes. As an auxiliary focus, the motivation level for learning of the students who studied in the class of teacher participants is also evaluated.

To be able to capture teachers' general behaviours in classroom teaching, the domains of teacher behaviour were selected based on Pianta, La Paro, & Hamre's (2008) research instrument which was designed to capture teachers' prosocial behaviour in classrooms, and Newmann's (1992) suggestion of critical aspects of teaching which could increase student achievement, i.e. classroom management and instructional practice. Student perceptions about the lesson were included as they could provide student perspectives (Chen & Hoshower, 2003) which were deemed important to support the findings generated from the side of the teachers.

Participants. The study was conducted in 2014 in the context of a local secondary school in Hong Kong. The participating school was recruited for study by invitation through the project's principal supervisor who approached a few local secondary schools who were known to researchers in the research team. The school was a local aided school, thus representing the most common type of secondary school in Hong Kong. The school had an average to low-academic standing in the region. The selection of school was by criterion sampling (Palinkas et al., 2015), which is to select information-rich cases related to the study of a phenomenon of interest as a research focus. The selection of teachers for the study was through nomination by the school principal. The school selected four teachers based on the standard evaluation results of teaching the school had administered in the last 2 academic years when the study was initiated, i.e. 2012–2013 and 2013–2014. The standard evaluation form used by the school was largely accommodative to the common criteria of assessing teaching, which covered personal dispositions (e.g. having a professional teaching attitude, enthusiasm and being communicative), effective teaching and classroom management skills (e.g. classroom atmosphere and discipline, smooth delivery, appropriate selection of teaching methods and assessment strategies to support learning) and student receptiveness. Each of the four teachers had at least 7 years teaching experience at the time they joined the study. All the teacher and student participants consented to participate in the study. The study on teachers' teaching behaviour was general domain-independent teaching behaviours rather than subject domain-specific. However, as the study sought to cover different subject teachers as an additional factor in sample selection, finally, four subject specialists were selected representing English Language, Chinese Language, Mathematics and Liberal Studies, respectively. All of these subjects are core subjects in secondary schools.

Methods

Teacher Observation Schedule. The four teachers were observed for a total of four lessons with a total time of 150 min, in either one single lesson or a double lesson (two single lessons run consecutively). Two researchers were involved in the observation in each of the sessions. They referred to a guided observation schedule to take note of teacher behaviours, echoing the guiding research questions. The observation schedule was modified from the Classroom Assessment Scoring System (CLASS) (Pianta, La Paro, & Hamre, 2008) and included suggestions from Newmann (1992) to identify teachers' classroom prosocial behaviours and aspects of teaching which lead to students' learning and development. The framework behind CLASS addresses teachers' emotional supports, classroom organisation and instructional supports which echo the social support of teachers throughout the lesson. The researchers used an ethnographic study approach (Berg, 2004; Spradley, 2016); however, they referred to the schedule as a starting point to look for teachers' elaborated behaviours.

The domains designed for observation include (a) *Classroom Climate* to identify the emotions displayed mainly by the students and the teacher behaviours which cause the emotions (Is positive affect characteristic of the lessons? How does the teacher do it? For example, how does the teacher maintain relationships with students, how does the teacher involve students in the learning setting?) (b) *Behaviour Management* to identify what teachers do to encourage prosocial behaviours (What behaviours does the teacher regard as appropriate for his/her classroom? What strategies does the teacher use to deal with misbehaviour?) and (c) *Instructional Learning Formats* to identify the strategies teachers use in teaching (What are the learning activities used for? What are the expected outcomes and consequential outcomes for students?)

In the observation, the researchers jotted down field notes according to the flow of the lesson. They noted down the questions and issues about which they would like to ask the teachers in order to gain a deeper understanding of the teaching style of each teacher. Their understanding of the teachers' teaching behaviours was incremental, moving towards the end of the field study.

Teacher Interview. Semi-structured interviews (Bryman, 2012) were conducted after each of the observed lessons, in the mother tongue of the teachers. The aims of the interviews were to gain an understanding of teachers' personal views regarding planning and teaching the lesson(s), and especially any events where they would like to supplement explanation. The researchers would ask questions which were related to their observation to gain more understanding of teachers' behaviour with respect to the domains of observation, such as how they relate to students, their preferred format of interaction and their approach to handling students that drives/explains their actions. In the final session of observation, the teachers were interviewed more conclusively with a focus on their views and their other concerns about teaching in the school context. The interview questions revolved around how teachers saw their students, themselves as teachers, contextual requirements and any other comments related to their teaching. Content analysis (Krippendorff, 2004) was done on the interview transcripts through coding and identifying emerging themes. A sample of the observation schedule and interview sample questions is provided in Tables 5.1 and 5.2.

Analysis of Teacher Behaviour and Student Motivation

The project team included five members who are specialists in curriculum and teaching. They were teachers before becoming academics. Two team members were paired for field study for each of the four teacher participants. The principal investigator took part in every session of field study. In each lesson, the principal investigator was paired with a member of the research team who is a subject specialist relevant to the lessons being observed, i.e. Chinese Language, English Language, Mathematics and Liberal Studies. Before the actual classroom studies, the observation protocol were discussed to analyse the first 15 min of a sample video on a mathematics teaching session borrowed from the library. The research team clarified the domains and the

Table 5.1 Guiding protocol for teacher behaviour analysis

Domains	Sub-domains	Prompts
Classroom climate (emotional)	**Affect** – How does the teacher engage learners from the outset? What are the kinds of emotions demonstrated by the students during their class activities? (e.g. positive or negative, happiness, anger or fear)	– Teacher behaviour/strategies: What does teacher do to relate the learners in the learning context? (e.g. giving them a sense of relatedness, supporting community, etc.) – Expression of positive affect: Is positive affect generally characteristic of the lessons? If yes, under what moments is it dominant? – Expression of negative affect: is negative affect generally characteristic of the lessons? If yes, under what moments is it dominant?
Behaviour management	**Behaviour expectations** – What behaviours does the teacher regard as appropriate for his/her classroom? How does he/she convey the said rules to the students (e.g. explicitly stating it, or posting it on the wall)?	– Expectations: What expectations does the teacher convey to his/her students? Are they positive or negative? – Rules setting: How does the teacher inform his/her students about the rules of his/her classroom? Does he/she explicitly state them?
	Behaviour control – What strategies does the teacher use to control students behaviour? When students misbehave, does he/she use coercive, shaming or some other ways to manage them?	– Reinforcement: Does the teacher use reinforcements, such as praise, in order to encourage appropriate behaviours? – Punishment: Does the teacher use punishments to discourage inappropriate behaviours? – Positive control: Does the teacher deal with students' misbehaviour by talking in calm and warm tones?
Instructional learning format	**Motivational strategies** – What are the strategies /learning activities teacher use in teaching? – Is the teaching and learning activities stimulating? – Do the students enjoy/engage into the learning activities?	– Opportunities: What is the learning activities introduced in the lessons? – Outcomes: What are the expected outcomes of learning? – Choices: What choices are students encouraged to make regarding their learning activities? (e.g. being instructed to write about a certain theme, rather than presented with a few themes to choose from.) Are the choices presented in a positive manner?

Table 5.2 Sample Interview Questions

– In your teaching philosophy, what do you think a 'student' is? [Prompts: a reason to be committed to the job? A target to be served? Or what?]
– How do you expect students to perform during the lesson for example, in the last two lessons when we did the observation?
– If you are asked to tell me the two outstanding features of your teaching, what do you think you would tell?

procedure of data collection. As two researchers would participate in the observation and post-lesson interviews, two researchers' perspectives were included in the analysis. The follow-up interview questions also covered the questions of the two researchers to make sure that relevant concerns and issues were discussed and clarified. This process strengthened the reliability and validity of the data and was an important process of data analysis embedded in the data collection process (Cohen, Manion, & Morrison, 2000).

The interview scripts and video scripts were transcribed verbatim. The completed interview transcripts were sent back to teacher participants for review as a process of member checking (Mays & Pope, 2000). This step was to check if any misunderstanding had been made to the record of the data. While the teacher participants have agreed to obtain the meaningfulness of the data as generated from the research (Sandelowski, 1993), opportunities for feedback were granted to the teachers if they would like to elaborate on the teaching and learning situations in their position as teacher-practitioners in this classroom study; questions for clarification were also initiated by the researchers if they would like to check understanding particular situations based on the data (Harper & Cole, 2012). Each teacher's teaching behaviour profiles were dealt with individually based on the transcribed data set. This included two key stages.

Individual Profile Analysis. An individual profile for each teacher was compiled based on constant comparisons (Dye, Schatz, Rosenberg, & Coleman, 2000) on the data gathered on each of the analysis domains one by one. Common themes, patterns of behaviour and categories of ideas were generated from the episodes observed and the views of teachers as recorded in the post-lesson interviews. The process of coding involves reading the content of each observation domain thoroughly and going back and forth from the observation data and interview data to verify the themes to be developed as the preliminary results. The results of each profile were consolidated at the end by compare and contrast with each other, therefore, the profiles as a whole can systematically report the findings along with a set of meaningful themes drawn from the study.

Composite Analysis. The researchers attempted to further conduct constant comparisons across each of the other teacher profiles as the second stage analysis, one against the others, until all the teacher profiles were dealt with. At this stage, the researchers reduced the themes by giving conceptual labels to explain each of the domains within a teacher's profile. Quotes and episodes were selected to illustrate the findings of each profile with reference to the others. In this way, themes and sub-themes were drawn to address similarities and differences across the four teachers' profiles, which ended up with a composite report of the main ways in which the teachers duplicated each other or differed. The results were sent to the teachers for comments after the analysis was completed to ensure trustworthiness (Shenton, 2004). The results were further consolidated, explained and discussed, and theoretical and practical implications were suggested.

Student motivation questionnaire and analysis. Students' learning motivation was measured in five aspects: (1) student relationship with teacher (measured by Teacher Involvement Scale by Skinner, Wellborn, & Connell, 1990); (2) perceived self-efficacy (measured by Academic Efficacy Scale by Midgley et al., 2000); (3) learning goals (measured by Mastery Goal Orientation scale by Midgley et al., 2000); and (4) self-handicapping behaviour (measured by Academic Self-Handicapping Strategies by Midgley et al., 2000). These aspects are selected with reference to the outcomes of social support in forming relationships, enhancing self-competence and encouraging prosocial behaviours in order to enable a person to manage their work and life. These measures explain students' motivation as assessed by students' relationship with the teacher, their perceived confidence about learning in the class, their drive to master knowledge taught and their avoidance of impending failure therefore creating impediments to performance. As expert teachers have been commonly found to teach in a way that engages learners, helping learners to solve problems and enhance skills by boosting their confidence to explore and learn. The selected measures are therefore relevant to explore the anticipated consequence of students. Altogether, there were 26 items in the questionnaire for students to fill in. All items were rated on a 7-point Likert scale from 1 (strongly disagree) to 7 (strongly agree). The students completed the Chinese version of the questionnaire. The internal reliability and the sample item for each scale are displayed in Table 5.3. A series of one-way ANOVAs were conducted to investigate whether there were significant differences in student motivation across the four classes.

Discussion of Findings

Teacher Behaviours

In this report, the four teachers are named A, B, C and D to denote the teacher who taught English, Chinese, Math and Liberal Studies. The lessons observed are listed in Table 5.4. The following sections of discussion highlight the major findings.

Table 5.3 Scales of student motivation

Scale	Number of items	Cronbach's Alpha	sample item
1. Student relationship with teacher	8	.87	My (subject) teacher really cares about me
2. Perceived self-efficacy	5	.83	I'm certain I can master the skills taught in (subject) class this year
3. Learning goals	5	.81	One of my goals in (subject) class is to learn as much as I can
4. Self-handicapping behaviour	6	.85	Some students purposely get involved in lots of activities. Then if they don't do well on their (subject) work, they can say it is because they were involved with other things. How true is this of you?

The Key Instructional Formats Adopted by Expert Teachers

As a whole, the lessons conducted by the four teachers progressed smoothly. Although the four teachers were found to exercise some forms of control in managing classroom discipline, the classroom climate created by the teachers was characterised by positive affect. The findings conclusively suggested that expert teachers' enacted behaviours were entirely built on the interests and abilities of learners. All the teachers had developed a distinct instructional format which supported learners to achieve some desirable learning goals, emphasising self-regulation, self-discipline and student development. The teachers made efforts to balance the environmental constraints with learners' needs and interest, trying to lessen academic pressure and motivate students' learning.

A variety of activities were used in the lessons. In particular, the classroom format was set in a flow of dialogic feedback, and the lesson was planned to provide a process of constructing knowledge. Therefore, social resources were often used, such as peer assistance and cooperative learning, and student diversity was often carefully addressed so that each of the students was encouraged to participate in the construction of knowledge.

Cooperative Learning, Questioning and Dialogical Feedback. Teacher A and D both developed their own curriculum materials for students, and both of them used cooperative learning as a key instructional format. Typically, they started teaching a lesson by offering opportunities for learners to explore the topic, equipping students with a basic understanding of the topic. They used questioning facilitated by enriched teaching resources to aid student understanding of the topic of study. They spoke with fairly user-friendly vocabularies in conducting the lesson, using prompting questions, and different forms of reinforcements and recognitions in the initial session. It was followed by interesting group work activity for learners to construct, advance and consolidate the topic of learning in an investigative manner, with a debriefing bringing up the end of the session.

Discussion of Findings 209

Table 5.4 Content of the observed lessons

Subject/teacher	Topics of each session	Length (min)	Objectives of lessons
English Language/A	Vowel sound practice	60	– pronounce the five short vowels in words: a, e, i, o, u – change the pronunciation of words with the same vowels but different consonants – recognise vowel sounds from spelling – guess meanings of vocabularies from a context
	Identifying characters in a story	30	– identify phrasal verbs from a story text (set off, look for and tear off) – extract specific information about the characters from reading a story – use a graphic organiser to take notes on characters – identify the emotions of the characters
	Describing emotions of characters	60	– identify and memorise vocabularies about people at school – identify and memorise vocabularies of emotions – recognise the hyponyms of emotions – identify the use of subject pronouns
Chinese Language/B	The history of styles in Chinese traditions	60	– distinguish methods of exposition – identify the skills of different methods of writing exposition – identify the cultural changes in Chinese traditions – identify layers in writing exposition
		30	– reinforce the methods of description explanation, classification explanation, example explanation and definition explanation – identify the hierarchy of explanation and explanation sequence order – identify several cultural traditions of the Chinese
	Writing skills practice—exposition	60	– explanatory memorandum's features and function – write an explanatory memorandum to give clear instructions to users on folding paper into objects

(continued)

Table 5.4 (continued)

Subject/teacher	Topics of each session	Length (min)	Objectives of lessons
Mathematics/C	Volume and surface area of upright pyramid and frustum	60	– calculate the total surface area of frustum – calculate the volume of frustum – calculate the total surface area of pyramid – calculate the volume of pyramid
	Circular Cone—Volume and Surface Area	30	– identify the formula to calculate the volume of a circular cone – apply the formula to calculate the circular cone – identify frustum of a cone – calculate the volume of a frustum
	Circular cones and sectors	30	– identify the formula to calculate curved surface area – apply the formula to calculate curved surface area and total surface of right circular cones
	Calculating the volume of spheres	30	– identify the formula to calculate application questions of a cone – identify the different part of sphere – identify the formula to calculate sphere's volume
Liberal studies/D	Contradiction of commercialised and culture conservation	60	– identify the advantages and disadvantages of commercialised culture conservation – practice the skills of integration in presenting the conclusion of an investigation result – practice reflection and evaluation of a given social topic
	Gender stereotyping I	30	– identify the traditional gender role in societies – identify the situation of gender role switch nowadays
	Gender stereotyping II	60	– inquire on gender role changes in the society of Hong Kong – analyse the reason of gender role switch – summarise the investigation result by the use of a mind map

Discussion of Findings

For example, teacher A showed 'a chain' of such dialogue which showed her patience to guide student engagement into the lesson. In her English Language lesson, each group of students had to stand up and do sight reading of some vocabulary with a group of vowel sounds.

Teacher: You may find it is not easy, because it is something new to you, but it is ok. Are you ready? I would like you to tell me how to pronounce the words on the screen. So look at set one, tell me, which group got this word, this group? Do you have this word with you?

Teacher:No. Which group has this word with you? Which group? Group 2, is it? How about we invite group 2 to try first, ok? Can we give group 2 a big hand?

(Applause from the whole class)

Teacher:Ok, group 2, are you ready? We will listen...group 4. I want you to listen, group 2 you tell us the pronunciation of this word. The first one is? Whole group together, 1, 2, 3.

Teacher:Ok, group 2, are you ready? We will listen...group 4. I want you to listen, group 2 you tell us the pronunciation of this word. The first one is? Whole group together, 1, 2, 3.

Student:Bottle.

Teacher:Ok...can we do it better? We don't say bot-tle, bottle.

Student:Bottle.

Teacher:Ok, the first one is bottle. And?

Student:Little/settle/cattle/battle/send/lend/tend

Teacher:Oh, this is difficult.

Student:Tenderly.

Teacher:Yes, you have three sounds, tenderly, very good.

Student:upset/handset

Teacher:Ok, thank you group 2. Well done. Now we have to let other groups to try. Which group got the word rock? Ok, group 6. Everybody, listen to group 6. Can we give a big hand to group 6?

(Applause from the whole class)

(Lesson 1, Teacher A)

Her emotional scaffoldings in this dialogue show the details she attended to in the content accuracy as well as her concerns about student learning and giving ongoing feedback to them.

In discussing the issue of gender stereotyping, Teacher D used films, PPT notes and current statistics to involve students into a discussion. She provides her students with a variety of resources to develop their critical thinking. In the dialogue below, she followed up with students by a conversation after watching a short video to enhance their understanding:

Teacher: Men are in charge of internal matters while women are responsible for external matters. Then what do the fathers do?

Student: ...

Teacher: Yes, fathers stay at home taking care of the kids and mothers ...

Student: work.

Teacher: Yes, work. Well, I'd like to ask: does the dad in the video enjoy this kind of life?

Student: Yes, he does.

Teacher: Enjoy? How do you know he enjoys this change, rather than be forced to or feel sorry?

Student: Seems when he ate the dessert at his friend's he found the recipe right away that night.

Teacher: All right. Do you think if he likes cooking? Likes. Did you see that women asked him, "What are the books on the shelf behind the Christmas tree?"

Student: Recipe.

Teacher: Yes. You can see this father is really competent. He does not care staying at home and cooking; instead, he tries his best to do the cooking, learn from his friends and buy recipes to follow.

Teacher B also used dialogue throughout the whole lesson as the instructional format. Though the content of teaching was largely based on a textbook, she redesigned the content materials in note form and showed them to the class while she conducted the dialogical discussion. She also designed one to several individual exercises for students in each session. She broke the lesson into short sessions to engage the full attention of the class because of the relatively low-academic abilities of students in the class.

Teacher C, who taught Mathematics—a subject which is more rationally governed by formula and rules, used flows of dialogue with the students in teaching Mathematics, accompanied by demonstrations of mathematic calculation exercises by herself or the students. A similar scene was also captured in Teacher C's class in using dialogues to guide students to recognise the concepts behind the volume of spheres. The episode showed Teacher C's patience of leading students to grasp the concepts and articulate them:

Teacher: Isosceles triangle, right, all the four are isosceles triangles. Anything else, Ahua?

Student: …

Teacher: Don't know… Then how many triangles do you think we need to count?

Student: Two.

Teacher: Zifang said two, any other answers? You think four different? Four different on the side, then counting from the start, how many altogether?

Student: …

Teacher: Ok, Wenle said a lot but with a low voice. Because it is a rectangular pyramid, this is 30, this is 14, then the other side are 30 and 14 too, right? Then he said, the slant edges are equal, because it is a regular pyramid, all the edges are the same. Ok? (Lesson 1, Teacher C)

By using dialogues and questioning in class, the teachers' concern was to make students feel ease in participating.

Actually sometimes I give them the freedom to talk aloud voluntarily, that is, they just say the answers while seated. Actually I do this deliberately to give as many answers as possible, so that a discussion is advanced. If you choose the most confident one, you know he knows the answer, then you get the right answer. But sometimes I want a wrong answer, then I ask those (who are not so sure about the answer) (Post-lesson interview, Lesson 1, Teacher C).

They were typically giving prompts, hints and constructive feedback to students in an ongoing manner, at the time students made a mistake or in the cases that

Discussion of Findings 213

students were not confident enough to give an answer, hoping that students would self-correct and think out the answers by themselves, or by the support of other students' answers. While teachers conducted the lessons, they encouraged students to express their views. Verbal appreciations were given to students' efforts even when their answers were not complete, thus reinforcing students' participation. Apart from the instructional strategies, the teachers also created an established norm in the classroom for maintaining a close relationship with the students, through self-disclosure, (e.g. showing personal preference and personal stories), intimacy (talking informally, using varied vocal expression and relaxed posture) and recognition (praise, rewards and called students by name). These aspects supplement details for the dialogic discourse as discussed earlier (Nystrand, Wu, Gamoran, Zeiser, & Long, 2003), which also echoes the literature suggesting that good teaching is a highly creative, improvised activity (Borko & Livingston, 1989; Borko & Putnam, 1996).

Adopting a Constructivist Teaching Approach. In conducting teaching, all the teachers seemed to apply some form of constructivist learning in the classroom. Instead of direct teaching and deductive teaching, teachers wanted students to seek answers through working on tasks and in group work. In addition, the teachers had commonly used authentic materials in presenting the content to students; this makes the lesson user-friendly for students and as a result, students participated in the lessons with concentration and they were engaged during the lessons. Experiential learning was also introduced in the classes of the teachers to help students to learn by feeling and experiencing before they learn the technical content of the subject knowledge. For example, in teaching Chinese composition in a lesson by Teacher B, students were asked to make their own origami. After they produced their own origami product, students were asked to write a guiding instruction to teach other users to follow step by step in making an origami. In the case of Teacher C who teaches mathematics, students were asked to work out a three-dimensional model to learn the formula of calculating the total surface of a pyramid, by analysing the slant edges.

Teacher A and D also used cooperative learning widely in teaching students, while Teacher B and C did not explicitly use group activities because of the factors including student ability and the nature of the subject matter. Both of them involved students in peer comment and review of class exercise outputs. These group-oriented strategies can help students practice social learning (Panadero & Järvelä, 2015), and realise personal accountability (responsiveness in learning) and positive interdependence in learning in a group, which can help develop a supportive learning environment and a learning community. In this way, students could also learn to develop the skills of learning, both the cognitive and non-cognitive strategies (Brookhart, 2010) such as integration of knowledge and self-regulated learning (Azevedo, Behnagh, Duffy, Harley & Trevors, 2012). Teacher A's meticulous arrangement in balancing support in the group and individual participation can be observed in the following teaching scene:

Teacher:Ok, now what I want you to do is…listen, listen very carefully, 1E, listen. I will give each group one set of this, there will be 12 cards, with this ring. Now I would give it to you, and I want you to look at these words…Ling, listen to me. I want you to look at these words with your group members, then I will read a word, what you have to do is look at the word, and then pick up the word I just read. Put it up and show me the word I have just read, do you understand? For example if I say orange, then you have to find out orange and raise it. Understand?

(Lesson 2, Teacher A)

In order to engage all students to work together, I will particularly ask a student to answer a particular question, instead of let them do a question together. That's why one of the activities is that I ask students to recognize the word and then put up the card, and then I will specify like: student A you have to do this question, student B you have to do this question, in order to make sure they all have the chance to answer my question. Interview 1 (279–288)

Catering for Diversity. The teachers generally reflected the difficulties of students' extreme ability performance and differences, within a very tight teaching schedule and relatively large class size. They expressed the challenges to take care of diverse populations. Instead of seeing low-ability students as limitations, teachers found ways to ascertain that low achievers in their class could take part in the lesson—they cared about easing their discomfort, encouraging their participation and attempts, while they also cared about high achievers to enhance their sense of accomplishment.

Teacher B had an averagely low-ability class and mentioned that within the class, the differences among the students were huge. As she stated, she introduced a range of media and used students as resources to help one another and made use of the strength of each student to complement the others, so that they learnt from each other.

Researcher: Then you have a clear idea who are good at reading...

Teacher: Yes, Li Chun-Hon, Auyang Ki-Man, Chan Siu-Tung, these students are okay in reading.

Researcher: But there are some who cannot do reading well, or can only read one or two sentences...

Teacher: Lee Man-Hong, he can't. Those like A-Bing can't. I know which students have to rely on pictures, like Yip Wing-Lan. She's very obvious, because I've checked with her... She's literate but better in Art.

Some students are articulate like Lee Man-Hong. He's good at logic, so better in maths, but poorer in Chinese. So I have him think first and then tell me why he thinks this is the answer, because he uses logical thinking to learn. But in terms of logic, some are ... like Chan Siu-Tung whose logic is poor, so sometimes I might ask Lee Man-Hong to explain, and then ask if Chan Siu-Tung gets the idea. (Interview 3, Teacher B)

The problem of diversity also existed in the Mathematics class. Teacher C also capitalised on the differences of the class. She used to ask the students to do peer review of students' work done on the blackboard or in their individual classwork book. Students took part in discussing the content. Some high-ability students also played the role of tutor to explain the topic in class, making the lesson more challenging for the more talented students.

Researcher: Actually you know this class is smarter than that one now that it's one month ever since the term commenced, don't you?

Teacher: Yes, because we've already done a quiz. You might find some who can't even do fractions in equation, and mistakenly do addition and subtraction with parentheses.

Researcher: Is 3E the strongest in maths?

Discussion of Findings

Teacher: No, it's the overall score, that is, the overall ranking among the whole grade, not just one particular subject. So to some degree there are huge differences in mathematics ability in this class. (Interview 3, Teacher C)

The teachers were willing to offer extra time to support students who had learning problems. Teacher B used the lunch break to approach students who may need help, quite informally,

> For example, after class I will stay with them during their lunch time and ask, "hey, is there anything you don't really understand from that lesson today?" For those poorer like Bin-Tsoi, I would ask them what they didn't get. You need to follow up in the after-class time. You have to do it without their notice, like during lunch time. (Lesson 2, Teacher B)

Teacher C claimed a more structured remedial plan for her students and mentioned:

> For those who failed in the quiz, I would give them a detention and give them extra work to do. I told them explicitly, I do not hide to avoid you, but sit here to assist you. If you have anything you don't understand, you should raise it. This period of time is devoted to their questions, they need to ask questions in relation to what they need to do regularly. I told them, you cannot accumulate all your questions until the last day before the examination, so I specifically spend some sitting in the classroom for these questions, usually one or two days a week. (Interview 3, Teacher C)

> As I'm used to sitting in the classroom during lunch time, no matter whether there are questions from the students. I just take one of the seats rather than the teacher's seat, because it is kind of discouraging them to approach you if you are in the teacher's seat. So usually I just sit there, doing nothing, marking the exercise, or sneakily hearing their conversations… I try to give them encouragement continuously, like, "Raise your questions if you don't know how to do the exercise." (Interview 2, Teacher C)

She did not only offer remedial help to the low achieving students, but also assigned more advanced materials for the high achievers to enhance their achievement:

> For those able students you need to spend time making them more competent…. Therefore, I give them extra tutoring during lunch time or after school. Sometimes in the morning reading session, when he shows me the notebook of reading, I would find some concepts wrong or something, I would immediately give him an explanation. (Interview 3, Teacher B)

In fact, the teachers did have high expectation of their students, however, none of them exercised force and drilling on students which are said to be typical in a Chinese classroom (Hue, 2008; Lam, 2011). They were encouraging and supportive to low-ability students and committed to helping them even sacrificing their own time over the only break in a day, in informal ways, as illustrated in the description above, in order to make the process also friendly to the students. Table 5.5 summarised the key features of the instructional practice of the teachers.

On the whole, the teachers' instructional format reflects their caring and empathetic concerns for learners. These teachers did not teach to urge students to get the correct answers, but used emotional scaffoldings to mentor students and involve students in making sense of the content of learning, therefore they could learn the knowledge through their own discovery. Moreover, the scaffoldings in teaching are the most demanding part of teaching. Teachers concentrated on the students' responses

Table 5.5 Key features of the instructional format of the four teachers

Engaging Activities	Meaningful to learners, leading to discovery, gains in cognitive and non-cognitive skills, including recalling and extracting information, analysis, self-regulation, participation and reflection
Key Features	
Authentic	Taking from real-life experience or drawing inner resources of the students
Experiential	Learning by first-hand experience, going through processes of meaning making, reasoning, evaluation, reflection and creation
Constructivist	Learning by doing and discovering knowledge based on guided exploration
Cooperative learning	Emphasising personal accountability, positive interdependence between learners, scaffolding and support given by teachers and peers
Dialogical discourse	Using questioning and formative feedback by involving the whole class
Formative assessment	Continuously giving feedback, verbal corrections, and hints to encourage student uptakes to self-correct and peer-correct mistakes
Catering for diversity	Offering remedial support in informal ways, developing curriculum materials and differentiated materials in group activities

throughout the lesson, and made meaningful and challenging responses to students. While they observed the schedule of the lessons and the class discipline, they also used skills to prompt and encourage students to take part and correct their answers, and arranged activities for students with well-managed administration and organisation. As they had made their expectations known to students, students tried to follow and meet their expectations, hence, the whole class behaved to be participative and highly engaged in their lessons.

Building the Positive Classroom Climate—Positive Affect, Relatedness, and Autonomous Motivation

The instructional format presented by the teachers indicated their attempts to secure student learning. Although it is suggested that expert teachers teach with a learner-centred orientation, the literature does not elaborate their behaviours with regard to the learner-centred model of teaching of expert teachers. This study provides some evidence of learner-centredness in expert teachers' instructional practice.

Create relatedness and attached feelings among students. The concern about building relationships and nurturing relatedness in the classroom environment is partly due to the background of students, for many students came from a single-parent family, or the students lacked love in their family environment. The teachers showed great empathy to the students.

> Perhaps in their (students') home there was no figure, that means a father's figure or a mother's figure; hence, they would look for compensation from you (teacher), therefore, I

Discussion of Findings 217

> should make them feel that I am approachable and can let them follow me as a figure to be relied on, and I will have to act as a model to guide them (interview 1, Teacher A)

> I was the class teacher of form one in the last academic year. Among all the students in the class, less than ten of them have a complete family, others are incomplete. It is similar in this class, around a dozen. (Interview 2, Teacher B)

For these reasons, all the teachers were caring and considerate about their students' feelings. Apart from building relationships in the instructional format drawing upon scaffoldings in a give-and-take social supportive environment, Teacher B was successful in connecting students' to each other and making them feel that they were contributing to one another. When she taught, she automatically drew students' answers and point of views in a networked structure, and presented to the class as the teaching points. She often asked students to respond to others' answers. For example, in her class, these sentence patterns were constantly used: 'Fong-fong, could you comment on Fai-wong's answer?' or 'Yiu-tung, could you explain to Kiu-fong about the symbol of omega as she seemed to have some doubts about it'. The same connection can be created by Teacher C's practice of utilising peer review in the class as described above.

This social network and relationships in the social environment are important for one to develop self-worth. As has been discussed in Chaps. 1 and 2, in the school context, social support can protect students from struggling with academic matters, developing a sense of belonging and harmony in the classroom. A selected scene below portrays how Teacher A built relatedness in the classroom environment.

> In your group, if some of your classmates cannot do it, what should you do? If your classmates say "I can't do it, I can't do it", what can you do?
>
> Student: Help him.
>
> Teacher: Help him. So the whole group helps your classmate together. Can you do this, 1E?
>
> Student: Yes.
>
> (Lesson 1, Teacher A)

Verbal Immediacy. Another distinct feature is that the teachers' effective use of communication facilitated the relationship between students and teacher. According to the literature, teacher language can enhance the perceived trustworthiness and care on the teacher and this creates a number of positive gains, including and cognitive and non-cognitive aspects. Generally speaking, the four teachers' communication behaviours encouraged student participation, enhanced confidence and promoted friendship. Their way of communication projected the eagerness of students in making responses to the teachers; it also created positive affect as shown from the flow of dialogues in the classroom. The dialogues, which were ongoing, are exceptionally effective in forming students' identity in the classroom, such as in building rapport, for feedback purposes such as correcting errors and mistakes, and prompting students to self-correct and directing students to help each other (see the topic related to feedback above). The internal value and empathy of the teachers' personality can be one of the reasons to explain how this can be done.

Though the four teachers showed different communication styles, ranging within a continuum from a warm and affinity-seeking style (speaking more softly and sharing more personal feelings) towards a confident and leadership model (speaking more firmly and a little bit more assertive in the case), they had an encouraging manner and spoke logically, providing reasons for their decisions. Students showed cooperation with the requests and instructions of the teachers, which enabled smooth lesson transition as the time for organisation was kept to a minimum.

It can be said that the teachers played a successful leadership role in the classroom. Their communication with students' could erase students' anxiety and fear about making mistakes in the classroom. For example, on one occasion Teacher A found that all the groups had given the right answer but one group, she mentioned 'hey, group 6 has a different answer for us, let us study their answer. What do you think? This is…ok, do you know this one? Let us conclude the answer together'. Teacher B also avoided giving negative comments to wrong answers. When she heard a wrong answer, she responded typically such as 'are you sure about this answer? If you want to think it over and tell me again? I will ask you in a moment.' Among the four teachers, slightly more than one-fifth of the students would volunteer to give answers, except Teacher C's class who were comparatively less voluntary and less active in responding to teacher's request for responses. The teacher suggested the reason was that the majority of the students in her class were of high ability and seemed to be more reserved in answering questions. Yet, as discussed above, Teacher C did encourage them by asking 'would you like to share your answers with us?' or 'could you tell me if you have got the same answer as Wing-yin?' In this way, she earned more enthusiastic responses, as the students were eager to play the role as an expert to comment on others' work.

While authenticity is suggested as adding value to the instructional format, using examples of common experience can work on the affective aspect in the classroom. For example, when Teacher A introduced emotional words in a lesson, she aroused students' interest in talking about some common situations in daily life:

> Teacher: They feel what? When Miss Tsang give everyone a five-hundred dollar note except them. Except means I give everyone 500, but I do not give these 3 students. Everybody got one, but not Tang, Ka-kit and Sze-sze. They will feel happy? (Lesson 3, Teacher A)

This kind of communication increased intimacy and intensity to the student-teacher relationship since common experience could arouse empathy and shared feeling (Redmond, 1985).

Recognition and Reinforcement. Whenever students made a response, teachers would commonly recognise their effort, and most of the time the teachers showed a genuine appreciation for students by specifying their names or giving a specific comment. For example,

> "Very good, well done." (Teacher D, Lesson 2) and "Right, Thank you for your answer, Benji (student's name)." (Teacher C, Lesson 1)

In one of the sessions of Teacher D's class, she showed to the whole class the good work done by a student, which was the best in the class. She suggested in the follow-up interview that she would like to give confidence to students,

Discussion of Findings

> I found a student did very well in the last homework, to which I gave a full grade 10. You might take a look at his work. Why is he so good? What are the good features? He first discussed the advantages of the commercialization of preserving culture, and then used Researcher Temple (A Chinese Temple under the government's protection) as an example......Well, you'd better read his work after class before doing your own lessons, ok? (Lesson 3, Teacher D)

The case of Teacher D above shows that the teachers aimed to create more successful learning experiences for students, therefore they offered recognition to students in different ways. For example, on one occasion, Teacher B jotted down students' names on the board to record their outstanding responses in the class. She rewarded students with drinks during the recess as a form of acknowledgement. Teacher A issued a point-earning scheme to recognise group effort and cooperative attitudes. All four teachers used verbal recognition such as 'smart idea', 'good work', 'excellent idea', and 'well done' when they found students presented a brilliant idea. The way teachers encouraged students to take part was seen to be reinforced by the appreciation of students and their willingness to try and make responses in class, especially the less active students.

Non-verbal Immediacy. The teachers also used non-verbal immediacy to communicate with students and cultivate a sense of positive affect in the classroom climate. They used eye contact evenly across the classroom when they spoke, and they addressed every student by name. They spoke with enthusiasm and used non-verbal gestures in communication with students. Their conversation was characterised by warmth ('you have given a fantastic answer by making the wild guess!' says Teacher A), cheerfulness ('How are you getting on this a.m.? The table seems to be untidy after a day's work, I will give you two minutes to get ready for our LS lesson' says Teacher D), consideration ('you all look tired, let's stand up and we do a two-minute mediation exercise' Teacher A) and a sense of humour (Teacher B teased herself that she had a big body because she was more easily visible to every student, to make everyone in class become more attentive when she stood in the classroom). Sometimes, the classroom was filled with joy and laughter, and relaxing moments.

Teacher B was a passionate teacher who sometimes presented with high self-disclosure with the students as the subject matter content was related to personal hobbies, preference and history. She shared with the students her personal hobbies when talking about the traditional Chinese cultural activities related to people's life in society. She showed the picture of her pet when she was in senior primary school. While students were very interested about their teacher's story, the teacher also referred to the students' own personal feelings.

Similar to Teacher A, Teacher C mentioned that in fact, she intended to give freedom to students to express their views, and that she hoped that by longing to openly raise their opinions students could move one step forward to debate and discuss the right answers. She mentioned that she would like to cultivate the atmosphere of open discussion to promote student learning, i.e. through critical thinking, which is the ability that helps in learning mathematics and the teaching methods of mathematics.

> Some people think this way, then what do you think? They would realise through others' answer, "Well, right, I can think this way too." I believe, if I tell them everything, they don't

need to think. But if it is from the student's mouth, or I tell them the answer at a later stage, at least they will have to think a bit, "Which of the answers is correct?" At least there is a bit of thinking in it that should be the way mathematics is taught. (Post-lesson interview, Lesson 1, Teacher C)

The teachers also made themselves accessible to students outside formal lesson time to offer additional support to low achievers, which reveal their concerns for diversity—especially to give support to low achievers to relieve their anxiety of lagging behind and help them achieve success. The teachers hoped that the environment they created in the classroom could encourage students to take part in learning actively and through participating in the activities students could be developed as thinking persons. The teachers would like to make sure that students could experience satisfaction in learning—instead of failure and frustration. As a long-term goal, the teachers aspired to better prepare students for adulthood. Behind the behaviours, the teachers' high expectation for themselves and the students can be observed, and this point was also mentioned in the previous literature (Good & Brophy, 1994; Rubie-Davies, Hattie, & Hamilton, 2006).

Making Learning User-friendly. Selecting content materials that fit the interest of students is crucial. Presenting the case to students that can attract their participation and does not scare them away is also another skill that the teachers are concerned about. Teacher A suggested that

Actually to give them a happy experience, we need to come up with some easy words to make them feel "this is actually easy, I got the answer." We need to give them more experience of success. This is what I believe this subject is in great need of. I don't give them difficult words, such as 'pronunciation' or 'context', because you have to explain these words. Like 'context', they don't really understand what it means, it's too abstract. So I can only say, "you know the meaning from the story, you guess the meaning from the story". (Lesson 2, A)

Teacher D also echoed that,

Yes. First, you cannot give them complex things, if it's too complex, he will not be able to figure it out, so he will ignore it. Therefore generally I just ask simple questions piece by piece for those low ability students, and repeat many times, that'd be better. (Lesson 1, Teacher D)

You have to tune the questions more straightforward, and to the point. (Interview 3, Teacher D)

Generally speaking, the four teachers' teaching behaviour has highlighted that communication is the key for effective teaching. This communication not only means delivering teachers' messages accurately and clearly, but the emotional tone and manner of communication with students, as well as their attention to make themselves approachable, warm and accessible to students. The verbal and non-verbal immediacy employed by teachers has been shown to be effective. Table 5.6 summarised teachers' immediacy identified from the study. As shown from the dialogues, students were feeling comfortable when interacting with teachers, and they were also willing to speak. They did not feel intimidated when teachers gave a comment to their response. This relationship is desirable as it would support students to learn and seek support from teachers. Furthermore, the teachers were able to arrange the content materials

Discussion of Findings

Table 5.6 Teacher immediacy identified from the study

Themes	Descriptions	Shown/not shown on teachers			
		A	B	C	D
Verbal communication	warm and affinity seeking	√	√	√	√
	speaking in a gentle manner	√	√	√	√
	assertive, confident and strong sense of leadership	√	√	√	√
Reinforcement	use of rewards consistently for desirable behaviours,	–	√	–	–
	use of praise for desirable behaviours,	√	√	√	√
Self-disclosure	share personal stories	–	√	–	–
	show positive/negative feelings in personal ways	√	√	√	√
	Refer to common experience of teacher and students	√	√	–	√
Recognition	call students by name	√	√	√	√
	give visual attention via gestures and eye contact	√	√	√	√
Posture	Relaxed, walk around and attract attention	√	√	√	√

Shown by the teacher is denoted by '√'; not shown by '–'

that fit the learners' level. This metacognitive teaching arrangement was mentioned as an important skill of supporting students to receive the lesson topics well. Hence, emotional support-giving behaviours can actually help learners to gain cognitively and academically, and it establishes a treasured relationship as described by the teachers.

Classroom Management Features: Self-discipline, Learning-Focused and Respectfulness

It is suggested that effective teachers also have high behaviour expectations of students (Babbage, 2002). With regard to classroom management, all four teachers had a high expectation of students in following the classroom management rules. Each of the classrooms was arranged in a traditional setting and it appeared that the teachers managed discipline well. Researchers did not see any personalised posting of rules but individual teachers stated their expectations very explicitly when some students broke the rules. Since students were in junior secondary school level (F1 and F2), they were very active and easily distracted during the lesson (except teacher C's class which was a high-ability class), and varying degrees of intervention was used by the teachers such as asking students to keep quiet, listen and calling student by name or giving a warning to a particular student.

> Ok, now what I want you to do is…listen, listen very carefully, 1E, listen, sit properly. Lesson 1 (626)
>
> 1E, listen, 1E, group 4, look at me. Group 2, look at me. Lesson 1 (700)
>
> Sit properly. Ok, 1E, look at me…
>
> I don't like this. When your classmates are reading to us, what should you do? Sit properly first, and then you have to listen, don't laugh, can you do it?
>
> (Lesson 1, Teacher A)
>
> Student sit straight, otherwise go to the toilet for a face wash?
>
> Well, those still in your seats, keep quiet. What's wrong with you guys at the back? Do you have anything delightful to share with us? Be well seated.
>
> (Lesson 1, Teacher D)

In consistently maintaining a classroom climate with positive affect in Teacher A, B and D's classrooms which appeared to have developed some slight discipline problems from time to time, their disapproval was always limited to gestures and non-verbal messages. On a few occasions, Teacher A and D gave verbal advice with articulated reasons to stop students' misbehaviour to eliminate possible chain effects. Another example from Teacher A:

> Teacher: Ok, because you have a lot of argument, I do not want to continue the game. Do you want to continue the game?
>
> Student: Yes.
>
> Teacher: But if you argue in this way, we cannot continue the game, do you understand me?
>
> Student: Yes.
>
> Teacher: Can you be an honest student? What is honest?
>
> Student: Sincerity (in Cantonese, a dialect of China)
>
> Teacher: Be an honest student, don't change the answer, can you do it?
>
> Student: Yes
>
> Teacher: So group 2, tell me honestly did you change the answer.
>
> Student: No.
>
> Teacher: Ok, I trust you.
>
> (Lesson 3, Teacher A)

None of the teachers paid too much attention to ruling the students and using coercive methods. The lessons generally ran at a brisk pace. In the classes, students were expected to listen when teachers were explaining, be attentive and follow their

Discussion of Findings

teachers' instructions. All the teachers mentioned that they wanted to cultivate a strong sense of respect among students in the class—a norm which the school put up as the ethos. This was very useful, as students noticed that they were respected and that they should also learn to respect the teacher and support the activities running in the lesson.

> We set some rules at the very beginning of the term, among which keeping the classroom tidy and clean is basic. Some are highlighted, for example, we emphasise respect in class. I constantly tell them to be respectful. I think our school does a good job in moral education, because the principal and VP are concerned about it. (Interview 3, Teacher A)

As a result, it is reasonable that the students would, in turn, regard their teachers as somewhat understanding and caring. This, as predicted by Self-Determination Theory (Ryan & Deci, 2000), is likely to motivate them to do what the teachers want them to do, which would consequently produce students adherence to their teachers' teaching philosophies. In the classroom of Teacher C where discipline was not the focus, she mentioned that the management was focused on how to cultivate an atmosphere for learning, so that everyone should take part. This theme appeared to be very clear in the analysis.

Classroom management also refers to teachers' sensitivity to learners' needs and reactions. On one occasion, Teacher A used a hypothetical example to suggest the word 'embarrassed', and said that 'Richard' (a student's name in the class) had gone to the female toilet and he felt embarrassed. Then, the teacher immediately realised that the other students laughed, however, Richard cried because of the situation. Teacher A then said 'I apologise for using your name in making this example and make you feel unhappy'. Although Richard was still crying and the other students also told the teacher he was crying, the teacher mentioned to Richard that 'I did not intend to make you unhappy and would you please accept my apology, I will talk to you after the class, ok?' Then the teacher continued to teach. In the interview, the teacher explained to the researcher that she had explained to the students about this incident and she thought it was a lesson in life for both herself and Richard, the student. Instead of thinking of this as an issue and the negative impact, the teacher was very positive to regard this as a learning experience that she would be more careful as students may not really like their names to be mentioned in teachers' examples in public.

As a whole, the classroom management behaviour of the teachers consistently showed that respect is the key to successful classroom management. They believed that students could do well if they understand that classroom is a place for learning, therefore they did not focus on classroom rules but the academic content of the lesson, and tried to engage learners in the lessons so that they can become autonomous learners who are competent and enthusiastic in the pursuit of knowledge.

Contextual Influences on Teaching Styles

As far as discipline is concerned, Teacher D was the one who was found to give relatively more reminders about student behaviour. On average, the times she spent dealing with behaviour intervention amounted to 8 in each session, compared with 4 times as the average for the other teachers. There are three key reasons to explain this. Teacher D's class was a low-ability one. Students were easily distracted and they became very noisy because of the instructional context factor—group discussion. Some students were off task during the group activities. Also, by nature, LS requires critical thinking abilities and when students move to senior forms they would be required to work on a project to sit for the public examination. Therefore, Teacher D had to train students' examination skills in advance. In fact, other teachers also clearly mentioned that the focus of teaching in schools in Hong Kong was examination base. They regarded preparing students for examinations as the main job of teachers. However, all the teachers showed commitment to fulfilling the job both to serve the responsibility they had for academic matters and also address their concerns about student development and care for the affect in the learning environment in schools.

As a school with a high proportion of students with low-academic achievement and social economic status, teachers knew that they had to make greater efforts for their students. The teachers saw their job as meaningful and they developed high morale in serving the school. The teachers mentioned that the lessons observed in the study were typical of their ordinary practice, however, in higher forms, their practice would revert to the training of examination skills and practice of examination papers. These findings echo the suggestion of social support created by the classroom environment. If the examination-oriented culture in the school becomes over-demanding, these expert teachers' work may fail or they might have to change their teaching approaches and sacrifice the time they spend in scaffolding students and the activities that aim to stimulate their interest, and use a controlling style to teach. Therefore, it is believed that teachers in the current education environment might somehow experience the conflict between their ideal of creating autonomous support for learners and the reality of examination demand on students' external examination result, as suggested in the case of Hong Kong and elsewhere.

Student Motivation

Results indicated that student motivation was almost equally high in all four classes taught by the four different teachers. As seen in Table 5.7, there were no significant differences across the four classes in the students' relationship with their teachers $[F(3, 139) = 1.62, p = .19]$, perceived self-efficacy $[F(3, 139) = .45, p = .72]$, learning goals $[F(3, 139) = .83, p = .48]$ and self-handicapping behaviour $[F(3, 139) = 2.04, p = .11]$. In general, students reported a good relationship with teachers $(M = 4.55)$, high self-efficacy $(M = 4.55)$, high learning goals $(M = 5.14)$ and low self-handicapping behaviour $(M = 2.62)$. These findings aligned with the effect of social support as discussed in Chaps. 2–4; students who are surrounded by social support are shown to be motivated, they relate to teachers closely, adopt social goals (i.e. prosocial behaviour) and have a high sense of perceived competence (self-efficacy).

Conceptualisation of the Results

Table 5.7 Student motivation in four classes

Student motivation	Class			
	Chinese ($n = 30$)	English ($n = 37$)	Mathematics ($n = 38$)	LS ($n = 38$)
Student relationship with teacher	4.23 (1.14)	4.70 (1.16)	4.73 (.98)	4.48 (.93)
Perceived self-efficacy	4.48 (1.20)	4.41 (1.24)	4.61 (1.02)	4.69 (.99)
Learning goals	4.95 (1.31)	5.16 (1.07)	5.34 (.98)	5.05 (.95)
Self-handicapping behaviour	2.49 (1.25)	2.68 (1.28)	2.33 (.95)	2.94 (1.01)

Note Numbers in parentheses are standard deviations. Means with differing subscripts are significantly different at $p < .05$ based on LSD post hoc paired comparison

Conceptualisation of the Results

Good Teachers Humanise Students

The behaviours identified from this study address a fundamental value that underlies expert teachers' teaching performance, which is to see every student as an individual who has the potential to learn, grow and pursue a fulfilling life. The teachers understand that students are situated in a competitive environment, therefore, they do not reject the idea that students should keep meeting higher expectations, however, they see education as a means of developing the person; therefore, an important goal of academic learning is to develop the person. The teachers all use relationship building to engage learners. The warm relationship between teachers and students echoes the meta-theory discussed in Chap. 4. It suggests that secure and reciprocal relationships with teachers, peers and subject matter in the learning environment help develop healthy self-concepts for young students (Cornelius-White, 2013), and the positive affect and sense of well-being actually help one to pursue goals in life.

Consistent with previous findings that expert teachers have a higher level of respect for students (Hattie, 1999, 2003), the results of expert teachers' behaviours in this study adds further evidence to suggest expert teachers by describing their social support-giving behaviours. The expert teachers in the study used positive emotional cues, dialogic discourse and continuous scaffoldings as strategies to support learners to achieve learning while they developed their metacognitive and cognitive skills. They focused on giving continuous support to students to relieve their tension during the learning process, since they were students of average ability. Yet, what these teachers aimed at was to enhance students' skills and capabilities as a long-term goal; therefore, instead of preparing students for examinations, they implemented constructivist learning pedagogies. This marks the characteristics of the behaviours of expert teachers, and such teaching behaviours cannot be enabled without the attitude of accepting students genuinely as a human being. Haslam's (2006) humanness model can be used to conceptualise the behaviour of expert teachers. It is a social psychology theoretical model that seeks to understand how humans ascribe 'humanness' to each other—how they come to grant each other moral status (e.g. are the others deserving of help? Or, are they deserving of punishment?). The tendency not to distance oneself from others through power is a sign that one is ascribing humanness traits to others (Lammers & Stapel, 2011). In the case of expert teachers in this study, their various behaviours demonstrated that they treated students with nurturance (emotional warmth) and that these teachers were more inclined to ascribe humanness traits to their students, thinking that human individuals are valuable beings and that every individual should respect and relate to each other and offer support to one another in the learning environment. Instead of exerting disciplines to control students because of perceiving them as potential rule breakers, teachers empowered students and triggered the students to have a good attitude towards learning and develop their skills for mastery of knowledge. Furthermore, as also discussed earlier, teachers who ascribe humanness to students (humanised teachers) are likely to implement an autonomy-supportive style of teaching that encourages students' self-determination and promotes their intrinsic interest and internal drive (volition resources) for learning. This humanness trait is essential to teachers in playing their role in education, as the guide to students in many important aspects of their growth in life. The four teachers demonstrated to us how they could do this as a real case of learner-centred education.

The humanised context of learning that teachers created for students can be observed in areas including instructional formats, classroom climate and classroom management. This context can be illustrated by an Emotional Design of Instruction (EDI) framework (Astleitner, 2000). The EDI suggests that fear (a threatening situation), envy (being anxious to get something that is possessed by others) and anger (being hindered to reach a desired goal and forced into an action) should be reduced during instruction, while sympathy (feelings of other people who are in need of help) and pleasure (mastering the situation with a deep devotion to an action) should be increased as an experience for learners. The EDI is concerned about the environmental support that can establish one's self-worth and value. Humanised teachers would aim at creating this setting for students as they would like students' potential to be developed through education. Because of this, humanised teachers are sensitive in planning and delivering the lesson based on the consideration of how learners receive the content, what the possible difficulties of learning on such topics for learners will be and how to make the learning interesting, rewarding and productive. Teachers are also able to handle challenging situations related to classroom discipline and student behaviour that need attention. Therefore, teachers, such as the teachers' in the study, who have a learner-centred perspective may be more likely to achieve higher levels of teaching and a more organised and better managed classroom. This conceptualization aligns closely with the social support literature as discussed in Chap. 4, highlighting the connections between environmental support sources and human development, and targeting the outcomes towards positive emotions and well-being.

Conceptualisation of the Results

Affective-and-Cognitive Scaffoldings as an Area of Teaching Expertise

The analysis shows that continuous efforts in scaffolding and guiding students in mastering the skills and knowledge of the topic of lesson appear to be the outstanding features found among the four teachers. As a result, we can see that students were motivated in learning as shown from the quantitative data. This approach to teaching demonstrates teachers' 'emotional work' of teaching (Isenbarger & Zembylas, 2006); this kind of scaffolding is also called emotional scaffolding, which marks the detailed work of the teachers in considering learners' emotions, shaping learners' attitude and providing feedback and support to learners so they can approach learning with greater interest and cognitive resources. By engaging in the emotional work of teaching, teachers do not only play an affective role, they function to support cognitive learning that helps the learner to advance in learning as a whole.

As observed, the four teachers turn learning into a series of moments where the students are prompted to engage in metacognition. It is an approach of involving learners to reflect upon the work they have done or the ideas they have given, and engaging learners into a series of inquiries and thought-provoking situations; therefore learners can proceed with learning the content of the lesson based on a clear expectation given to the students in the lesson. Being able to do this, teachers have to monitor the process of teacher's own knowledge about teaching to facilitate the process of learning for students at different stages. It refers to the 'knowledge of cognition' such as the awareness of factors that influence students' learning, the strategies students can use in their own learning and the ability to choose appropriate strategies for a specific topic or situation; as well as the 'regulation of cognition', that is to set expectation targets, control learning processes and evaluate learning outcomes (Ambrose, Bridges, DiPietro, Lovett, & Norman, 2010; Pintrich, 2002; Wilson & Cole, 1991). For example, in the study, teachers would do pre-assessment of the content of teaching with reference to the level of students. They suggested delivering some specific content in more user-friendly ways (teacher's awareness of difficulties). Teacher C used a hands-on activity to help students to appreciate the formula of calculating the volume of a sphere and Teacher B asked students to do an origami exercise and then, write a guiding instruction to tell other people how to do the origami step by step in a composition format (choosing strategies for a specific teaching purpose that fit learners). As described in the findings, the examples given above are related to teachers' design of content and the appropriate choice of strategies that can help learners engage in introspection; therefore learners think about how to learn and adopt relevant strategies to achieve learning effectively and efficiently.

In order to help students' become aware of the cognitive process of learning, the four teachers exercised another skill in teaching which is known as dialogic discourse. They initiated continuous dialogue with learners and facilitated learners to attend to a detailed process of learning. This discourse enables learners to be willing to seek advice, share ideas and experience, and also be willing to give comments, ask questions and make suggestions, so that each individual can take part, seek help and be willing to help others. In the study, for example, the verbal and non-verbal immediacy adopted by the teachers has suggested some forms of communication skills that can help to build such a discourse. Teachers' questioning dialogues, their feedback giving publicly and individually with students throughout the lessons are important skills that are embedded in the dialogic discourse in the classroom. They are the skills to continuously 'assess' students' performance and communicate with students about their mistakes, areas for improvement and work habits that may help learners to self-correct and support learners to move forward in their own learning. To develop a specific learner and teacher discourse in the classroom setting is a higher level of professional learning for teachers, which makes teachers' communication different from or more than an attractive, monologic public speech. Although variation across subjects may exist, for example, language teaching may use more dialogic bids within a lesson, the portrayal of teachers' dialogue in this study suggest the skills of teachers in implementing formative assessment fluently in the classroom through flows of continuous dialogue.

The discourse presented in the class is pleasant, dialogic and socially engaging. As shown from the results, students are found to have high motivation towards learning, and the high engagement in learning can help learners develop belongingness and a personal identity as a member of the class.

This echoes the relationship perspective of the social support literature, and its application in education is found to be effective as discussed in Chap. 4. This study shows clearly how teachers' work in the classroom can promote relationships while also considering cognitive learning in the classroom.

Implications and Recommendations

Based on the above conceptualization, two important implications are made for teacher education and discussed below. It may be more appropriate to see them as two interrelated aspects, which may provide a point of view to address the professionalism of teaching.

The Triad of Teaching Expertise for Learning to Teach

The three elements the topic refers to include teachers' commitment to teaching, the skills of managing classroom communication with learners and monitoring student learning to develop their metacognitive learning. These skills are seen as combined to form teachers' teaching expertise.

Implications and Recommendations

Traditionally, teacher training covers lesson planning, teaching strategies and assessment strategies to prepare must-have skills for teachers, and theories related to learning and teaching. Classroom communication is a general aspect which focuses on technical aspects of presentation, such as speaking accurately, effectively and audibly with rising and falling tones to engage learners. There has been long-standing criticism that teacher education has an excessive emphasis on 'methods and skills' (Popham & Greenberg, 1958) and that teaching have been treated as a purely skill-based business (e.g. Hegarty, 2000). This study illustrates examples of good teaching by teachers' demonstration of metacognitive teaching in class. It suggests the awareness of teachers about using the best suitable methods for learning, monitoring the learning process, setting goals and focusing students on achieving and evaluating outcomes of learning. In fact, with the advancement of technology, the teachers' role in facilitating learners is seen to be even more important, and their role in guiding learners to develop an interest in learning and being able to self-regulate one's own learning becomes significant. The expertise presented by the teachers demonstrates two key skills, including the skills of facilitating students through planning and guiding learners to explore the concept of achieving metacognitive learning and teachers' communication skills in prompting learners to engage in a cognitive learning process.

Since teaching is essentially an interactive process, it relies very much on interaction with learners. Teachers' keen interest in every learner as an individual, and their professional attitude to making efforts to facilitate learning and engaging learners to learn the skills of learning are the areas that distinguish the professionalism of teaching. It is believed that teachers' care and empathy are the core traits that can generate a genuine respect for learners, which enable teachers to see student development as a valuable target in their teaching career. The attitude may prompt teachers to provide more scaffoldings and guidance to students in their classroom instruction; it may also allow them to invest time to initiate detailed plan and invest quality effort in conducting teaching in the classroom.

To enhance teacher training and development beyond the skill-based level, the results of this study argue that teacher training should be placed on developing teachers' intrinsic interest in learners, and concentrating on supporting learners with a clear direction of playing the role of scaffolding learners in the classroom. It seems that genuine interest in learners underlies the triad of teaching expertise.

In fact, for beginning teachers without experience, the questions such as 'how should teachers relate to their students in different aspects of classroom teaching?' and 'what could teachers do to support learners?' should be the inquiry for them in the beginning years. This theme has consistently emerged as crucial to teaching and essential for classroom practice as discovered from the study. In fact, increasing evidence suggests that affective factors play a huge role in teaching (Berliner, 2004), and the attitude of teachers is seen as inseparable from good teaching as the literature review shows earlier in this chapter. The study confirms the importance of viewing teaching as a socially situated practice that relies heavily on frequent human interactions (Hargreaves, 2000b; O'Connor, 2008), therefore, the nurturance role of teachers in social support giving in the classroom should be learnt and enhanced.

According to the evidence discussed, the other two elements that can generate teachers' expertise in teaching is the abilities and skills of establishing a dialogic discourse or a communication pattern with students in the classroom, and the thoughtful consideration of the teaching content and selection of activities to enable learners to learn the content with understanding through a meaningful inquiry process to enhance their self-regulated learning. At present, metacognitive learning is still a developing area in education; however, researchers have started to address the use of techniques for teaching, such as formative feedback (Black & William, 2009), self-explanation (Aleven & Koedinger, 2002), monitoring learning outcomes (1990), the use of hypermedia in prompting, supporting and modelling students self-regulation in learning (Azevedo, 2005), and suggested quite encouraging results in specific skills, such as self-monitoring, decision-making and declarative knowledge. Suggestions in the literature also support the notion that such advanced teaching skills can move teacher education to the next level such as through engaging in the approach of reflective practice (Graham & Phelps, 2003). Examples of how learning these skills can be made through video analysis of teaching, classroom observation and discussion in a community of practice are recommended ways of doing this (Bakkenes, Vermunt & Wubbels, 2010; Kiemer, Gröschner, Pehmer, & Seidel, 2015; Kovalainen & Kumpulainen, 2005). Teacher education providers can also reconsider the format of block practice supervision such as peer evaluation and peer observation, and assessment of teaching practicums focused on exploring the skills of establishing interaction and a learning and teaching discourse to guide student learning to strengthen these aspects of skill training.

Specifying Social Support as the Rationale of Learner-Centred Education

The study also suggests that school contextual factors may undermine teachers' nurturance behaviour. Due to examination demands, time in the classroom is limited; teachers may have no choice but to shift to behaviour intervention by using controlling straighter classroom management rules. They may use more teacher-centred methods to teach which is regarded as more efficient to achieve the measureable outcomes of learning of students, in order to fulfil the expectations of the other stakeholders. Pelletier and colleagues (2002) found that the more teachers perceive pressure from above (in situations such as complying with a curriculum, compromising with colleagues, and with performance standards) and pressures from below (in cases such as perceiving their students as non-self-determined, e.g. students are not responsible for their own feeling and rely on others to decide for them), the less they are self-determined towards teaching. The result is that the less they are self-determined towards teaching, the more they become controlling with students. Also, schools which require teachers to teach for higher academic outcomes may shape the behaviours of teachers towards negativity. Teachers would become more critical of students and use more directive language, more hints and more controlling if they are told to be responsible for a student performing up to high standards (Deci, Spiegel, Ryan, Koestner, & Kauffman, 1982). However, studies have also proved that teachers' autonomous motivation for teaching (i.e. motivation that is drawn on volitional resources, which means it is self-determined and would drive teachers to work with sustained effort) is associated with students autonomous motivation for learning (Roth, Assor, Kanat-Maymon, & Kaplan, 2007). The implication for governments is that they should elaborate currently promoted learner-centred orientation by emphasising teachers' social support and social support sources in the education setting, as proved by the positive evidences discussed in this chapter. Schools should set up policies that create curriculum space and instructional time to support the development of expert model of teaching (Barrow, 1999; Deci et al., 1982; Lam, 2006, 2011, 2014), and to encourage teachers' motivation to grow in the profession, so as to benefit student learning. It has been discussed above that the affective aspects such as motivation, positive affect and socio-emotional traits are the conditions for cognitive and higher level learning. Placing examinations as the goal of education should be considered a defect that leads to academic pressure and depression for learners. The growing mental health issues of young students evidence such negative impacts (Cheung & Chiu, 2016; World Health Organization, 2017).

Conclusion, Major Limitations and Future Studies

In conclusion, the findings of this study echoes the literature regarding the affective traits and emotional support of expert teachers and the characteristics these traits and supportive teaching behaviour guided their teaching practices in the classroom. The emotional support of expert teachers has been demonstrated in maintaining a relationship with students in such a way students feel ease to express their feelings, have higher control in their own learning by taking responsibilities in learning and are motivated to take part in class activities with positive emotions. The classroom teaching practices also illustrate active and frequent interactions among the students with the teachers in dialogical exchange of ideas and feedback, to continuously promote students' metacognitive learning and support students to be self-regulated in their learning. The teachers' work in the classroom illustrates social support giving in the teachers' role to play in supporting students' study that concerns with students' cognitive development. However, the study illustrates to us that sophisticated and delicate work in cultivating students' motivation, self-efficacy and self-esteem, and building up a cooperative learning environment to help students to be engaged in a social supportive network should be done together with the role of supporting students' learning of the school subject. This emotional and affective aspects comprises an essential area of teaching expertise. Thus, guided by the insights of social support, this study has further generated analysis at the theoretical level to propose a framework regarding teacher's teaching expertise, in a model known as the triad of teachers' expertise. This model specifies teacher commitment, skills of managing classroom communication with learners, and monitoring student learning to develop their metacognitive learning. The implications of the study are drawn which have made a number of important implications regarding teacher training and development, and the leadership role of schools in cultivating an environment which prepares teachers to advance their expertise in such a way that meaningful learning can be promoted to benefit student learning.

The current study was carried out in the context of Hong Kong in a secondary school which has a lower academic ranking. The findings may represent the eastern culture where expression of relationship and relationship-oriented attitudes may be strong, therefore, studies in other countries on this topic may provide evidence to substantiate the preliminary ideas drawn from the current findings. Studies on a wider population including students of a wide spectrum of academic abilities may contribute to a more comprehensive understanding of teaching skills related to teachers' social support giving. A second limitation is that the analysis of the study was focused on teachers' expressed behaviour in the classroom. As the narrative of the study develops, a thesis regarding teachers' affective aspect of teaching and the various skills related to teaching in the classroom, the analysis did not consider the academic achievement of students, therefore, a comprehensive understanding of teachers' effectiveness could not be reached. The study also focused more on teacher behaviour, and observation of student behaviour might yield more fruitful results, especially on the learning behaviour corresponding to teachers' methods of teaching. These are the aspects which the current study could not address and certainly would be useful research directions for further study.

Furthermore, studies of teachers' behaviours in a qualitative research approach are recommended to understand the salient features of teaching. Specific focuses of research such as teacher's character traits in relation to teachers' dialogic discourse and teacher–student, and metacognitive teaching are recommended as potential topics (Balcikanli, 2011) that can provide further implications for the focus of training of such skills and character traits this study addressed. These two areas appear to be new areas of interest where, at present, empirical studies are scant, and further studies can also help strengthen the dialogue initiated in this chapter.

The study has identified that the interaction of teachers' personal beliefs may be in conflict with the school which focuses on external examination results. Further studies on teacher's classroom practice and teachers' teaching practice in relation to aspects beyond classroom level are worth investigating to problematise the situation of carrying out humanised teaching in different environments. It is believed that the results drawn from this topic will shed light in the twenty-first century as many countries have been drawn to examination-oriented education.

References

Adelman, H. S., & Taylor, L. (2005). School-wide approaches to addressing barriers to learning and teaching. In B. Doll & J. A. Cummings (Eds.), *Transforming school mental health service: Population-based approaches to promoting the competency and wellness of children* (pp. 277–306). Thousand Oaks: Corwin Press.

Agne, K. J. (1999). Caring: The way of the master teacher. In R. P. Lipka & T. M. Brinthaupt (Eds.), *The role of self in teacher development* (pp. 165–188). Albany: State University of New York Press.

Aleven, V. A., & Koedinger, K. R. (2002). An effective metacognitive strategy: Learning by doing and explaining with a computer-based Cognitive Tutor. *Cognitive science, 26*(2), 147–179.

Ambrose, S. A., Bridges, M. W., DiPietro, M., Lovett, M. C., & Norman, M. K. (2010). *How learning works: Seven research-based principles for smart teaching*. Wiley.

Anderson, L. M., Evertson, C. M., & Brophy, J. E. (1979). An experimental study of effective teaching in first-grade reading groups. *The Elementary School Journal, 79*(4), 193–223.

Anderson, J. R. (1982). Acquisition of cognitive skill. *Psychological Review, 89*(4), 369.

Asad, E. M. M., & Hassan, R. B. (2013). The characteristics of an ideal technical teacher in this modern era. *International Journal of Social Science and Humanities Research, 1*(1), 1–6.

Aspy, D. N. (1975). Empathy: Let's get the hell on with it. *The Counseling Psychologist, 5*(2), 10–14.

Astleitner, H. (2000). Designing emotionally sound instruction: *The FEASP-approach. Instructional Science, 28*(3), 169–198.

Azevedo, R. (2005). Using hypermedia as a metacognitive tool for enhancing student learning? The role of self-regulated learning. *Educational Psychologist, 40*(4), 199–209.

Azevedo, R., Behnagh, R., Duffy, M., Harley, J., & Trevors, G. (2012). Metacognition and self-regulated learning in student-centered leaning environments. In D. Jonassen & S. Land (Eds.), *Theoretical foundations of student-centered learning environment* (pp. 171–197). New York and London: Routledge.

Babbage, K. (2002). *Extreme teaching*. Lanham, MD: Scarecrow Press.

Bakkenes, I., Vermunt, J. D., & Wubbels, T. (2010). Teacher learning in the context of educational innovation: Learning activities and learning outcomes of experienced teachers. *Learning and Instruction, 20*(6), 533–548.

Balcikanli, C. (2011). Metacognitive awareness inventory for teachers (MAIT). *Electronic Journal of Research in Educational Psychology, 9*(3), 1309–1332.

Barrow, C. J. (1999). *Environmental management: Principles and practice*. London: Routledge.

Bereiter, C., & Scardamalia, M. (1993). *Surpassing ourselves. An inquiry into the nature and implications of expertise*. Chicago: Open Court. Retrieved from http://ikit.org/fulltext/1993surpassing/preface.pdf.

Berg, B. L. (2004). *Methods for the social sciences*. USA: Pearson Education Inc.

Berliner, D. C. (1994). Expertise: The wonder of exemplary performances. In J. N. Mangieri & C. C. Block (Eds.), *Creating powerful thinking in teachers and students* (pp. 141–186). Ft. Worth, TX: Holt, Rinehart and Winston.

Berliner, D. C. (2001). Learning about and learning from expert teachers. *International Journal of Educational Research, 35*(5), 463–482.

Berliner, D. C. (2004). Describing the behavior and documenting the accomplishments of expert teachers. *Bulletin of Science, Technology & Society, 24*(3), 200–212.

Black, P., & Wiliam, D. (2009). Developing the theory of formative assessment. Educational Assessment, Evaluation and Accountability (*formerly: Journal of Personnel Evaluation in Education*), *21*(1), 5.

Bohn, C. M., Roehrig, A. D., & Pressley, M. (2004). The first days of school in the classrooms of two more effective and four less effective primary-grades teachers. *The Elementary School Journal, 104*(4), 269–287.

Bond, L., Smith, T., Baker, W. K., & Hattie, J. A. (2000). *The certification system of the national board for professional teaching standards: A construct and consequential validity study*. Greensboro, NC: Greensboro Center for Educational Research and Evaluation, University of North Carolina at Greensboro.

Borko, H., & Livingston, C. (1989). Cognition and improvisation: Differences in mathematics instruction by expert and novice teachers. *American Educational Research Journal, 26*(4), 473–498.

Borko, H., Putnam, R. T. (1996). Learning to teach. In D. C. Berliner & R. C. Calfee (Eds.), *Handbook of educational psychology* (pp. 673–708). New York, NY, US: Macmillan Library Reference USA; London, England: Prentice Hall International.

Brookhart, S. M. (2010). *How to assess higher-order thinking skills in your classroom*. Alexandria, VA: ASCD.

Bru, E., Stephens, P., & Torsheim, T. (2002). Students' perceptions of class management and reports of their own misbehavior. *Journal of School Psychology, 40*(4), 287–307.

Bryman, A. (2012). *Social research methods* (4th ed.). New York: Oxford University Press.

Calderhead, J. (1996). Teachers: Beliefs and knowledge. In D. C. Berliner & R. C. Calfee (Eds.), *Handbook of education psychology* (pp. 709–725). New York: Macmillan.

Cazden, C. (1983). Adult assistance to language development: Scaffolds, models, and direct instruction. *Developing literacy: Young children's use of language* (pp. 3–18).

Chen, Y., & Hoshower, L. B. (2003). Student evaluation of teaching effectiveness: An assessment of student perception and motivation. *Assessment & Evaluation in Higher Education, 28*(1), 71–88.

Cheung, E., & Chiu, P. (2016, March 12). Students at breaking point: Hong Kong announces emergency measures after 22 suicides since the start of the academic year. *The South China Morning Post*. Retrieved from http://www.scmp.com/news/hong-kong/health-environment/article/1923465/students-breaking-point-hong-kong-announces.

Clark, C. M., & Peterson, P. L. (1986). Teachers' thought processes. In M. C. Wittrock (Ed.), *Handbook of research on teaching* (pp. 255–296). New York: Macmillan.

Cohen, L., Manion, L., & Morrison. K. (2000). *Research methods in education* (5th ed.). Routledge.

Cooper, B. (2004). Empathy, interaction and caring: Teachers' roles in a constrained environment. *Pastoral Care in Education, 22*(3), 12–21.

Cornelius-White, J. (2007). Learner-centered teacher-student relationships are effective: A meta-analysis. *Review of Educational Research, 77*(1), 113–143.

Cornelius-White, J. H. (2013). Environmental responsibility: A social justice mandate for counseling. *Journal of Border Educational Research, 6*(1), 5–15.

Deci, E. L., & Ryan, R. M. (Eds.). (2002). *Handbook of self-determination research*. Rochester, NY: University Rochester Press.

Deci, E. L., & Ryan, R. M. (2008). Self-determination theory: A macrotheory of human motivation, development, and health. *Canadian Psychology/Psychologie Canadienne, 49*(3), 182.

Deci, E., Schwartz, A., Sheinman, L., & Ryan, R. (1981). An instrument to assess adults' orientations toward control versus autonomy with children: Reflections on intrinsic motivation and perceived competence. *Journal of Educational Psychology, 73*, 642–650.

Deci, E. L., Spiegel, N. H., Ryan, R. M., Koestner, R., & Kauffman, M. (1982). Effects of performance standards on teaching styles: Behavior of controlling teachers. *Journal of Educational Psychology, 74*(6), 852–859.

Djigic, G., & Stojiljkovic, S. (2011). Classroom management styles, classroom climate and school achievement. *Procedia-Social and Behavioral Sciences, 29*, 819–828.

Dye, J. F., Schatz, I. M., Rosenberg, B. A., & Coleman, S. T. (2000). Constant comparison method: A kaleidoscope of data. *The Qualitative Report, 4*(1), 1–10.

Elias, M. J. (2009). Social-emotional and character development and academics as a dual focus of educational policy. *Educational Policy, 23*(6), 831–846.

Emmer, E., Sabornie, E., Evertson, C. M., & Weinstein, C. S. (Eds.). (2013). *Handbook of classroom management: Research, practice, and contemporary issues*. Routledge.

References

Emmer, E. T., & Stough, L. M. (2001). Classroom management: A critical part of educational psychology, with implications for teacher education. *Educational Psychologist, 36*(2), 103–112.

Ericsson, K. A. (2000). *Expert performance and deliberate practice: An updated excerpt.* Retrieved from www.psy.fsu.edu/faculty/ericsson/ericsson.exp.perf.html.

Ericsson, K. A., & Lehmann, A. C. (1996). Expert and exceptional performance: Evidence of maximal adaptation to task constraints. *Annual Review of Psychology, 47*(1), 273–305.

Fenstermacher, G. D. (2001). On the concept of manner and its visibility in teaching practice. *Journal of Curriculum Studies, 33*(6), 639–653.

Fenstermacher, G. D., & Richardson, V. (2000, July). *On making determinations of quality in teaching.* A paper prepared at the request of the Board on International Comparative Studies in Education of the National Academy of Sciences. July 11, 2000.

Flavell, J. H. (1970). Developmental studies of mediated memory. In H. W. Reese & L. P. Lipsitt (Eds.), *Advances in child development and behavior* (Vol. 5). New York: Academic Press.

Freeman, D. (2002). The hidden side of the work: Teacher knowledge and learning to teach. A perspective from North American educational research on teacher education in English language teaching. *Language Teaching, 35*(1), 1–13.

Garaigordobil, M. (2009). A comparative analysis of empathy in childhood and adolescence: Gender differences and associated socio-emotional variables. *International Journal of Psychology and Psychological Therapy, 9*(2), 217–235.

Good, T., & Brophy, J. (1994). *Looking in classrooms* (6th ed.). New York: HarperCollins.

Graham, A., & Phelps, R. (2003). 'Being a teacher': Developing teacher identity and enhancing practice through metacognitive and reflective learning processes. *Australian Journal of Teacher Education, 27*(2), 2.

Hadfield, J. (1992). *Classroom dynamics.* Oxford: Oxford University Press.

Hargreaves, A. (2000a). Mixed emotions: Teachers' perceptions of their interactions with students. *Teaching and Teacher Education, 16*(8), 811–826.

Hargreaves, A. (2000b). Mixed emotions: Teachers' perceptions of their interactions with students. *Teaching and Teacher Education, 16*(8), 811–826.

Harper, M., & Cole, P. (2012). Member checking: Can benefits be gained similar to group therapy? *The qualitative report, 17*(2), 510–517.

Harris, A. (1998). Effective teaching: A review of the literature. *School Leadership & Management, 18*(2), 169–183.

Haslam, N. (2006). Dehumanization: An integrative review. *Personality and Social Psychology Review, 10*(3), 252–264.

Hattie, J. (1999, August 2). *Influences on student learning.* Inaugural Lecture: Professor of Education, University of Auckland.

Hattie, J. (2003, October). *Teachers make a difference: What is the research evidence?* Paper presented at the Australian Council for Educational Research Annual Conference on Building Teacher Quality, Melbourne.

Hattie, J., & Clinton, J. (2008). Identifying Accomplished Teachers: A validation study In L. Ingvarson & J. Hattie (Eds.), *Assessing Teachers for Professional Certification: The first decade of the national board for professional teaching standards* (Vol. Advances in Program Evaluation, pp. 313–344). Oxford: JAI Press.

Hegarty, S. (2000). Teaching as a knowledge-based activity. *Oxford Review of Education, 26*(3–4), 451–465.

Hen, M., & Goroshit, M. (2016). Social–emotional competencies among teachers: An examination of interrelationships. *Cogent Education, 3*(1), 1151996.

Hogan, T., Rabinowitz, M., & Craven, J. A., III. (2003). Representation in teaching: Inferences from research of expert and novice teachers. *Educational Psychologist, 38*(4), 235–247.

Hoy, W. K. (1968). The influence of experience on the beginning teacher. *The School Review, 76*(3), 312–323.

Hue, M. T. (2008). The influence of Confucianism: A narrative study of Hong Kong teachers' understanding and practices of school guidance and counselling. *British Journal of Guidance and Counselling, 36*(3), 303–316.

Isenbarger, L., & Zembylas, M. (2006). The emotional labour of caring in teaching. *Teaching and Teacher Education, 22*(1), 120–134.

Jennings, P. A., & Greenberg, M. T. (2009). The prosocial classroom: Teacher social and emotional competence in relation to student and classroom outcomes. *Review of Educational Research, 79*(1), 491–525.

Kiemer, K., Gröschner, A., Pehmer, A. K., & Seidel, T. (2015). Effects of a classroom discourse intervention on teachers' practice and students' motivation to learn mathematics and science. *Learning and Instruction, 35*, 94–103.

Ko, J., Sammons, P., & Bakkum, L. (2013). *Effective Teaching: a review of research and evidence.* CfBT Education Trust.

Kovalainen, M., & Kumpulainen, K. (2005). The discursive practice of participation in an elementary classroom community. *Instructional Science, 33*(3), 213–250.

Krathwohl, D. R., & Anderson, L. W. (2001). *A taxonomy for learning, teaching, and assessing.* New York: David McKay Company.

Krippendorff, K. (2004). *Content analysis: An introduction to its methodology.* Thousand Oaks, CA: Sage.

Kyriakides, L., Creemers, B. P., & Antoniou, P. (2009). Teacher behaviour and student outcomes: Suggestions for research on teacher training and professional development. *Teaching and Teacher Education, 25*(1), 12–23.

Lam, B. H. (2006). An analysis of the curriculum development of the Hong Kong visual arts. *Contemporary Educational Research Quarterly, 14*(1), 147–167.

Lam, B. H. (2011). A reflective account of a pre-service teacher's effort to implement progressive curriculum in field practice. *Schools: Studies in Education, 8*(1), 22–39.

Lam, B. H. (2014). Challenges beginning teachers face. *Schools: Studies in Education, 11*(1), 156–169.

Lam, B. H. (2015). There is no fear in love: The giving of social support to students enhances teachers' career development. In R. Osbourne (Ed.), *Job satisfaction: Determinants, workplace implications and impacts on psychological well-being* (pp. 97–111). New York: Nova Science Publishers.

Lammers, J., & Stapel, D. A. (2011). Power increases dehumanization. *Group Processes & Intergroup Relations, 14*(1), 113–126.

Linley, P. A., Joseph, S., Harrington, S., & Wood, A. M. (2006). Positive psychology: Past, present, and (possible) future. *The Journal of Positive Psychology, 1*(1), 3–16.

Malikow, M. (2006). Teaching in the affective domain: Turning a crier into a crier. *Kappa Delta Pi Record, 43*(1), 36–38.

Martin, N. K., & Baldwin, B. (1993, April). *Validation of an inventory of classroom management style: Differences between novice and experienced teachers.* Paper presented at the Annual Meeting of the American Educational Research Association. Atlanta, GA. April 12–16, 1993.

Mays, N., & Pope, C. (2000). Assessing quality in qualitative research. *BMJ, 320*(7226), 50–52.

McAllister, G., & Irvine, J. J. (2002). The role of empathy in teaching culturally diverse students: A qualitative study of teachers' beliefs. *Journal of Teacher Education, 53*(5), 433–443.

Meyer, D. K., & Turner, J. C. (2002). Discovering emotion in classroom motivation research. *Educational Psychologist, 37*(2), 107–114.

Midgley, C., Maehr, M. L., Hruda, L. Z., Anderman, E., Anderman, L., Freeman. K. E., … , Urdan, T. (2000). *Manual for the patterns of adaptive learning scales* (PALS). Ann Arbor, MI: University of Michigan.

Miller, R., & Pedro, J. (2006). Creating respectful classroom environments. *Early Childhood Education Journal, 33*(5), 293–299.

Narvaez, D., & Lapsley, D. K. (2008). Teaching moral character: Two alternatives for teacher education. *The Teacher Educator, 43*(2), 156–172.

References

237

Newmann, F. M. (1992). *Student engagement and achievement in American secondary schools*. New York: Teachers College Press.

Nickerson, R., Butler, S. F., & Carlin, M. (2009). Empathy and knowledge projection. In J. Decety & W. Ickes (Eds.), *The social neuroscience of empathy* (pp. 44–56). Cambridge, MA: The MIT Press.

Noddings, N. (1984). *Caring: a feminine approach to ethics and moral education*. Berkeley: University of California Press.

Noddings, N. (2013). *Caring: A relational approach to ethics and moral education*. Berkeley and Los Angeles, CA: University of California Press.

Nystrand, M., Wu, L. L., Gamoran, A., Zeiser, S., & Long, D. A. (2003). Questions in time: Investigating the structure and dynamics of unfolding classroom discourse. *Discourse Processes, 35*(2), 135–198.

Nystrand, M., Gamoran, A., Kachur, R., & Prendergast, C. (1997). *Opening dialogue*. Teachers College, Columbia University, New York and London.

O'Connor, K. E. (2008). "You choose to care": Teachers, emotions and professional identity. *Teaching and Teacher Education, 24*(1), 117–126.

O'Neill, G., & McMahon, T. (2005). Student-centred learning: What does it mean for students and lecturers. In G. O'neil, S. Moore, & B. McMullin (Eds.), *Emerging issues in the practice of university learning and teaching* (pp. 27–36). Dublin: AISHE.

Opdenakker, M. C., & Van Damme, J. (2006). Teacher characteristics and teaching styles as effectiveness enhancing factors of classroom practice. *Teaching and Teacher Education, 22*(1), 1–21.

Palinkas, L. A., Horwitz, S. M., Green, C. A., Wisdom, J. P., Duan, N., & Hoagwood, K. (2015). Purposeful sampling for qualitative data collection and analysis in mixed method implementation research. *Administration and Policy in Mental Health, 42*(5), 533–544. https://doi.org/10.1007/s10488-013-0528-y.

Palmer, D. J., Stough, L. M., Burdenski, T. K., Jr., & Gonzales, M. (2005). Identifying teacher expertise: An examination of researchers' decision making. *Educational Psychologist, 40*(1), 13–25.

Panadero, E., & Järvelä, S. (2015). Socially shared regulation of learning: A review. *European Psychologist, 20*, 190–203.

Peck, N. F., Maude, S. P., & Brotherson, M. J. (2015). Understanding preschool teachers' perspectives on empathy: A qualitative inquiry. *Early Childhood Education Journal, 43*(3), 169–179.

Pelletier, L. G., Séguin-Lévesque, C., & Legault, L. (2002). Pressure from above and pressure from below as determinants of teachers' motivation and teaching behaviors. *Journal of Educational Psychology, 94*(1), 186–196.

Pianta, R. C., La Paro, K. M., & Hamre, B. K. (2008). *Classroom assessment scoring system manual: Pre-K*. Baltimore: Brookes.

Pintrich, P. R. (2002). The role of metacognitive knowledge in learning, teaching, and assessing. *Theory into Practice, 41*(4), 219–225.

Popham, W. J., & Greenberg, S. W. (1958). Teacher education: A decade of criticism. *The Phi Delta Kappan, 40*(3), 118–120.

Redmond, M. V. (1985). The relationship between perceived communication competence and perceived empathy. *Communications Monographs, 52*(4), 377–382.

Reeve, J. (2009). Why teachers adopt a controlling motivating style toward students and how they can become more autonomy supportive. *Educational Psychologist, 44*(3), 159–175.

Reeve, J., Bolt, E., & Cai, Y. (1999). Autonomy-supportive teachers: How they teach and motivate students. *Journal of Educational Psychology, 91*(3), 537–548.

Reeve, J., Deci, E. L., & Ryan, R. M. (2004a). Self-determination theory: A dialectical framework for understanding socio-cultural influences on student motivation. In D. McInerney & S. Van Etten (Eds.), *Big theories revisited* (Vol. 4, pp. 31–60)., Research on sociocultural influences on motivation and learning Greenwich, CT: Information Age Publishing.

Reeve, J., Jang, H., Carrell, D., Jeon, S., & Barch, J. (2004b). Enhancing students' engagement by increasing teachers' autonomy support. *Motivation and Emotion, 28*(2), 147–169.

Richardson, V., & Fallona, C. (2001). Classroom management as method and manner. *Journal of Curriculum Studies, 33*(6), 705–728.

Richmond, V. P. (1990). Communication in the classroom: Power and motivation. *Communication Education, 39,* 181–195.

Richmond, V. P., Gorham, J. S., & McCroskey, J. C. (1987). The relationship between selected immediacy behaviors and cognitive learning. *Annals of the International Communication Association, 10*(1), 574–590.

Rogers, C. R. (1983). *Freedom to learn for the 80's.* Columbus: Charles E. Merrill Publishing Company.

Roth, G., Assor, A., Kanat-Maymon, Y., & Kaplan, H. (2007). Autonomous motivation for teaching: How self-determined teaching may lead to self-determined learning. *Journal of Educational Psychology, 99*(4), 761.

Rubie-Davies, C., Hattie, J., & Hamilton, R. (2006). Expecting the best for students: Teacher expectations and academic outcomes. *British Journal of Educational Psychology, 76*(3), 429–444.

Ryan, R. M., & Deci, E. L. (2000). Intrinsic and extrinsic motivations: Classic definitions and new directions. *Contemporary Educational Psychology, 25*(1), 54–67.

Ryan, R. M., & Deci, E. L. (2017). *Self-determination theory: Basic psychological needs in motivation, development, and wellness.* New York: Guilford Publications.

Sandelowski, M. (1993). Rigor or rigor mortis: The problem of rigor in qualitative research revisited. *ANS. Advances in Nursing Science, 16*(2), 1–8.

Schraw, G. (2001). Promoting general metacognitive awareness. In H. J. Hartman (Ed.), *Metacognition in learning and instruction: Theory, research and practice* (pp. 3–16). Dordrecht: Springer.

Schutz, P. A., & DeCuir, J. T. (2002). Inquiry on emotions in education. *Educational Psychologist, 37*(2), 125–134.

Shavelson, R. J., & Stern, P. (1981). Research on teachers' pedagogical thoughts, judgments, decisions, and behavior. *Review of Educational Research, 51*(4), 455–498.

Shenton, A. K. (2004). Strategies for ensuring trustworthiness in qualitative research projects. *Education for Information, 22*(2), 63–75.

Skinner, E. A., Wellborn, J. G., & Connell, J. P. (1990). What it takes to do well in school and whether I've got it: The role of perceived control in children's engagement and school achievement. *Journal of Educational Psychology, 82,* 22–32.

So, H. J., & Brush, T. A. (2008). Student perceptions of collaborative learning, social presence and satisfaction in a blended learning environment: Relationships and critical factors. *Computers & Education, 51*(1), 318–336.

Sockett, H. (1993). *The moral base for teacher professionalism.* New York: Teachers College Press.

Spradley, J. P. (2016). *The ethnographic interview.* Waveland Press.

Stein, S. (2000). *Equipped for the future content standards. What adults need to know and be able to do in the 21st century.* Washington DC: National Institute for Literacy.

Stough, L. M., Palmer, D. J., & Leyva, C. (1998, April). *Listening to voices of experience in special education.* Paper presented at the Annual Meeting of the American Educational Research Association. San Diego, CA.

Tan, K. S., Heng, C. Y., & Tan, S. (2013). Teaching school science within the cognitive and affective domains. *Asia-Pacific Forum on Science Learning and Teaching, 14*(1), Article 3.

Tettegah, S., & Anderson, C. J. (2007). Pre-service teachers' empathy and cognitions: Statistical analysis of text data by graphical models. *Contemporary Educational Psychology, 32*(1), 48–82.

Teven, J. J., & Hanson, T. L. (2004). The impact of teacher immediacy and perceived caring on teacher competence and trustworthiness. *Communication Quarterly, 52*(1), 39–53.

References

Vansteenkiste, M., Niemiec, C. P., & Soenens, B. (2010). The development of the five mini-theories of self-determination theory: An historical overview, emerging trends, and future directions. In T. C. Urdan & S. A. Karabenick (Eds.), *The decade ahead: Theoretical perspectives on motivation and achievement* (pp. 105–165). Emerald Group Publishing Limited.

Walshaw, M., & Anthony, G. (2008). Creating productive learning communities in the mathematics classroom: an international literature review. *Pedagogies: An International Journal, 3*(3), 133–149.

Wilson, B., & Cole, P. (1991). A review of cognitive teaching models. *Educational Technology Research and Development, 39*(4), 47–64.

World Health Organization. (2017, April). *Mental disorders fact sheet*. Retrieved from http://www.who.int/mediacentre/factsheets/fs396/en/.

Chapter 6
Social Support Giving and Teacher Development

Abstract The investigation of social support in learning and teaching in Chaps. 4 and 5 informs a form of practice that illustrates the characteristics of social support. This chapter continues to explore the benefits of social support giving for support givers in the role of teachers. It seeks to accomplish the following objectives:

- How is social support giving related to teachers' satisfaction?
- Is providing social support to students related positively to teacher development?
- What are the attributes that determine teachers' positive development in the teaching profession?
- Do mental health issues have anything to do with teachers' lack of satisfaction in teaching? If so, why?

The chapter begins with a discussion that 'love for students' has emerged as a common reason in the literature to explain teachers' motivation to join the teaching profession. This is also the reason that keeps teachers in the profession despite the challenges they face in the education environment, across cultures over time. The chapter discusses evidence of the claim that teachers' social support behaviour can drive teachers to advance their teaching strategies and also support them in their attempts to negotiate with the social environment to achieve their personal goals of teaching, which eventually help teachers to experience a satisfying and fulfilling career. The link regarding teachers' career satisfaction to teachers' self-efficacy has been demonstrated, whereby self-efficacy could be enhanced by social support giving. The chapter continues to explore the attributes that determine teachers' positive engagement with the teaching profession. This part of the discussion elucidates the nature of teaching, teacher satisfaction, teacher's personality traits, and the emotional work of teaching, which explain how teachers can proceed with a more satisfying career and advance in the profession. The chapter also discusses the detrimental effects of the performative culture that dominates current educational environments and has changed learning and teaching to a consumerism relationship instead of a human caring relationship, thus harming both teacher development and the teaching profession. A number of recommendations for teacher education and teacher development are suggested. The chapter concludes with a framework for viewing the link between teacher altruistic motivation (satisfaction), teacher development and teacher

© Springer Nature Singapore Pte Ltd. 2019
B. LAM, *Social Support, Well-being, and Teacher Development,*
https://doi.org/10.1007/978-981-13-3577-8_6

practice. It suggests that social support is an underlying trait of good teaching and a perspective for interpreting teaching, and emphasises that the well-being of students and teachers should be valued in the scholarship of the education discipline.

The Nature of the Teaching Profession and Self-generating Rewards of Teaching

Teaching is a multifaceted profession. One of the unique features of the teaching profession is the guidance and support teachers give to students beyond the classroom, which may enlighten young people's personal future lives—making a difference to students. A famous Chinese scholar-teacher in the Tang dynasty (768–824 AD), Han Yu specified teachers' influence on students' life in terms of multiple domains, which is, "teacher is one who could propagate the doctrine, impart professional knowledge, and resolve doubts" (師者, 所以傳道、 受業、 解惑也) (Han, 819, cited in Zeng, 2005). In traditional Confucian values, education is considered a pursuit of personal moral perfection (Lee, 2000). This is also echoed in the literature of western culture. Socrates (469–399 B.C.), who is believed to be one of the greatest philosophers of education in the West once said, "I cannot teach anybody anything. I can only make them think" (Denson, 2009). In his view, teachers are to lead and guide students to discover knowledge and the wonders of life. In line with Aristotle's philosophy, "those who educate children well are more to be honoured than parents, for these gave only life, those the art of living well" (Ngcwele, 2016). Teachers, apart from transmitting knowledge, play a more important role in teaching students how to discover knowledge and find the meaning of their life.

Traditional concepts endorse the respected role of teachers in cultivating a person, suggesting the concept of social support giving to students through the psychological, social and emotional development in the lives of children to adolescents, in pursuit of their future adult life. Correspondingly, teachers who chose to enter the teaching profession also expressed the view that they cherish the satisfaction they received in guiding students. In Lam's (2012) study, in-depth interviews were conducted with 38 graduating students from a teacher training programme, in which their reasons for choosing to be teachers were discussed. Internal satisfaction was one of the major factors for participants to devote themselves to the teaching career. Participants in the study attributed this satisfaction to several reasons, such as their love for teaching, influencing the next generation, and enjoying being with kids and developing relationships with them, which is in line with the findings from prior literature that teachers generally are motivated by altruistic motivations (e.g. Sinclair, 2008).

However, Lam and Yan (2011) also continued to describe the teachers' stories when they interviewed them 2 years later. Eleven of the teachers attended another in-depth interview after 2 years of teaching upon the completion of their teacher training programme. Participants were asked to recall their reasons for becoming a teacher and then they were asked about (i) whether their beliefs had changed,

(ii) whether there were any changes in their career and why, and (iii) whether they were satisfied with their work experience as a teacher and if so, why. Beginning teachers in the study were classified into either idealistic types, who chose to teach because of personal interest in the nature of the job, or pragmatic types who were concerned about extrinsic rewards, such as salary. The analysis suggested that the school environment had a crucial role in teachers' professional development. As reported in their study, if they work in a suitable environment, where autonomy and innovation are encouraged in teaching and curriculum, and with a reasonable workload, the idealistic teachers will enjoy their job and work hard to improve their teaching. Interestingly, if they are allowed to work in such a supportive environment, the pragmatic teachers will gradually become more interested in teaching and motivated to give more effort to improve their teaching. In contrast, if teachers work in a destructive environment where they have to face heavy workloads, tedious administrative work, and managerial pressure, they will be likely to have negative emotions and burnout, and eventually switch to other schools or even quit the profession, regardless of the type of teacher. The studies concluded that school-based factors are crucial in sustaining teachers' passion for teaching, and heavy workload, inequity in teaching assignment allocation and restrained professional autonomy may limit the time teachers spend in meaningful work in teaching. The time teachers spend in other unrelated works will take away the time they could spend on supporting students, which creates frustration for teachers. Other studies also echo the same idea that an unfavourable working environment will negatively affect employees' motivation and engagement in their work (e.g. Pearson & Moomaw, 2006). However, the unfavourable situation of the teaching environment and the teaching profession currently seems to suggest an international tendency (Ballet, Kelchtermans, & Loughran, 2006) which is worthy of attention.

Teachers' Declining Mental Health and Dissatisfactions with the Teaching Profession

The unfavourable conditions of the teaching profession are not uncommon at the world level. Extensive literature and survey reports have suggested that the recruitment and retention of quality teachers over the world is a problem (Changying, 2007; Department for Education and Skills [DfES], 2005; Scott, Stone, & Dinham, 2001). Teachers' mental health and the pressures of teaching have also been documented across different countries. A recent survey has revealed that 64% of Hong Kong teachers feel highly pressurized and 84% of teachers feel exhausted regarding their work (Hong Kong Federation of Education Workers [HKFEW], 2016). Johnson et al. (2005) find teaching to be one of the six most stressful occupations in the UK, after comparing practitioners' mental health in 26 professions. A report released in 2017 suggests that teachers scored the highest numbers in terms of showing symptoms of depression, anxiety and panic attacks compared with the working population as a whole (Adams, 2018). Similarly in Singapore, teachers report the greatest number of mental health symptoms among six different sets of professionals (Chan, Lai, Ko, & Boey, 2000; Martin, Collie, & Frydenberg, 2017); in Spain, teacher stress has led to depression and it has emerged as a common problem for school teachers (Betoret, 2006). In the USA, from the figures in mid-2005, up to 25% of beginning teachers leave the teaching field before their third year, and almost 40% leave the profession within the first 5 years of teaching (National Center for Education Statistics, 2005); teacher shortages have continued to be a serious problem in the past 10 years in many countries such as the U.S. and the U.K. (Spring, 2017; Steinhardt, Smith Jaggars, Faulk, & Gloria, 2011). This endangers the quality of teaching in schools.

In Hong Kong, despite the relatively high salary of this profession, teaching seems to be losing its appeal and youngsters' interest in becoming a teacher is declining. Seventy-six percent of teachers report discouragement over whether the next generation will join the profession, and this is an increasing trend (Lai, Chan, Ko, & So, 2005; HKFEW, 2016). Specifically, long working hours, heavy workload (requiring 12–16 h on average to complete all the duties everyday), unrelated administrative duties (HKFEW, 2011), taking care of students with diverse education needs, and decreasing job security (e.g. Lai & Law, 2010; HKFEW, 2015, 2016; Tang & Yeung, 1999; Titus & Ora, 2005), have added much pressure to teachers. The growing misbehaviour problems in the classroom have intensified PRESSURE ON teachers, creating teacher exhaustion and burnout, which lowers the level of career commitment for many teachers (Choi & Tang, 2009; HKFEW, 2016). Teachers in Hong Kong are found to have a low level of job satisfaction, happiness and morale (Chan, 2013; HKFEW, 2015; Lau, Chan, Yuen, Myers, & Lee, 2008; Yeung & Liu, 2007).

Teacher suicides have given further warning signals to governments and policymakers about the mental health issues of teachers in the twenty-first century. In the U.K., the increasing suicide rate among teachers indicates that teaching is the most highly stressed occupation in the country (Office for National Statistics, 2017), with 139 cases reported in a 5-year period from 2011 to 2015. The situation in the U.S. reflects a general upward trend. A growth of 86% of teacher suicide cases were identified over a 9-year period from 2001 to 2010 (American Federation of Teachers, 2017). Suicide is also a growing problem for Hong Kong teachers (Ng, 2011). Over the past two years, cases happened just before the first school day of the new academic year, causing great distress to the education community and impacting on the whole of society. The general situation of teacher suicide shows that the negative emotions of teachers have become so serious that it forces teachers to embark on self-destructive behaviours.

In sum, the evidence suggests that teaching has become a high-stressed profession all over the world; while a relatively high percentage of teachers suffer from depression, its negative effects on teachers' commitment, quality of teaching, and morale could not be under-estimated (Sutton & Wheatley, 2003). The teaching profession, on the other hand, has demands for higher quality teaching concurrently and teachers are having a more significant role to play in schools for preparing the young generation for a globalised society (National Education Association, 2015). The following sections will explore the factors that engage teachers in the profession to shed light on the growing problems in the teaching profession.

Social Support Giving Benefits Teacher Development

Teacher's Satisfaction in Teaching—The Psychic Rewards of Teaching

The declining professional commitment among teachers is a common phenomenon in the teaching profession; however, positive cases of teacher development reported in the literature provide insights for understanding the situation from a different perspective. In the same set of studies reported by Choi and Tang (2009), Lam (2012) and Lam and Yan (2011), the interest to serve students was found to be crucial in driving teachers to continue their efforts and keep them in the teaching profession, including teachers at the prospective, beginning, mid-career and late-career stages. Choi and Tang's (2009) interview study based on the narratives of 23 teachers on their career life stories found that for most of the teachers, the 'love for students' was regarded as a mediator to relieve the weariness of their heavy workload felt at the background of successive reform proposals in education in the society, endowing them with a sense of purpose which drove their work. In Lam and Yan's (2011) study, if the school environment was unable to provide organisational support to the teacher participants in helping them generate the sense of rewarding experience from students, e.g. the engagement into teaching innovations to support student learning, even highly committed teachers would be dissatisfied and feel burned out, as they were deprived of the chances to generate the satisfaction incongruent with their personal goals. It was reported from Lam and Yan's study that two out of the 20 teacher participants decided to quit teaching, though they were highly committed to the teaching profession when they began teaching two years earlier. It implies that gaining satisfaction from teaching serves to overcome the negative 'hygiene factors' (Herzberg, 2005) of the teaching profession, such as long working hours, heavy workload, and decreasing job security, and this satisfaction is to be gained from their care towards students and their work on students which they perceive as the main part of the profession. Despite the unfavourable working conditions of teaching described in these studies, the study results inform us that the satisfactions teachers gain from actualising their mission of serving students become a protective factor that protects teachers from the commitment crisis as found among the teachers in the teaching profession. This motivator, i.e. the satisfaction gain from serving students, can even rekindle teachers' passion at a time that the teaching profession has suggested many issues that have disappointed teachers, to support them in moving along in their teaching career.

The close connection between teacher and students as a significant source of teacher satisfaction has been reported in the literature earlier (e.g. Hargreaves, 1994; Lortie, 1975; Nias, Southworth, & Yeomans, 1989). These studies suggest that teachers feel joy, pleasure and pride when they spend time with students in school events, observe students' growth, and connect with former students who visit them after graduation. For teachers, job satisfaction is derived from reaching students and helping students achieve (Lortie, 1975), which is 'self-generating' (Rosenholtz &

246 6 Social Support Giving and Teacher Development

Simpson, 1990). This kind of reward is also known as 'psychic rewards' of teaching (Lortie, 1975). The 'psychic rewards' particularly pointed to the kind of satisfaction teachers experience in the teaching profession; this satisfaction must be created by themselves by actively creating the conditions that produce the reward, i.e. by making efforts in teaching and building relationship with students.

Other sources of teacher satisfaction include knowing that students enjoy teacher's lessons and students show care to teachers, and teachers find that the students they develop relationships with are responsive, motivated and responsible (Chen, 2016). According to Lortie (1975), the psychic rewards of teaching are derived from teachers' service ethic which draws people into teaching, and from the structure of teaching where teachers could invest energies and concentrate in the classroom, and feel that they could make a difference to students (Nias et al., 1989). According to Nias (1996), the unique psychic rewards of teaching suggest three types of motives, namely, serving moral outcomes, engaging students, motivating students to learn, and the wish to benefit all students.

Studies conducted in different countries (O'Connor, 2008; Hargreaves, 2000; Veldman, van Tartwijk, Brekelmans, & Wubbels, 2013) confirmed consistent findings, suggesting that the psychic rewards of teaching can overcome teachers' negative emotions in teaching. Moreover, teachers who are committed to teaching are found to generate a relevant form of caring practice that enables them to gain satisfaction from teaching (see Chap. 5 for an example). This finding provides insights for us to understand the internal processes of teacher engagement in the profession.

Social Support Giving Benefits Teacher—Satisfaction, Reduced Distress, Positive Development

In Chap. 5, the expert teachers demonstrate a form of practice that suggests teachers' concerns regarding learner's affect, motivation and learning capabilities. They are enthusiastic teachers who enjoy psychic rewards, and their teaching performance is characterised by techniques of connecting to students emotionally and intellectually. These teachers provide a prototype of good teaching that shows the strategies to best utilise nurturance behaviours and care. Their practice is characterised by enthusiasm, energy and care, which demonstrate teachers' communication and interaction with students for their coping and dealing with academic matters, enhancing students' self-esteem, developing students' sense of belonging and competence, etc. This practice also enhances teachers' relationships with students, from which teachers gain satisfaction, and the outcomes of learning for students are positive. These teachers believe in themselves, their teaching suggests a clear purpose and it drives them to develop pedagogies that interest and engage learners. It is known that a strong sense of self-efficacy can help a person maintain greater aspiration and anticipate successful achievement (Gecas & Schwalbe, 1983). It is, therefore, reasonable to infer that if teachers behave as active agents in the dynamic environment of teaching, and that these teachers can contribute to the lives of their students by involving themselves closely in the learning and teaching context to support students, their perceived competence, which is called self-efficacy, would be expected to be high (Ouweneel, Le Blanc, & Schaufeli, 2013). In such a case, teacher's perceived competence in teaching may lead to the experience of higher positive emotions, and such positive emotions are known to exert a generating effect, which engenders a person with thoughts of exploration and creative behaviours (Benight & Bandura, 2004; Fredrickson, 1998). These teachers would become more innovative, motivated to learn, and eager to pursue their personal goals. It is not difficult to imagine that teachers who engage with their students positively and emotionally would be energetic teachers who strive to make improvement in teaching for the sake of achieving more effective teaching to engage their students even more positively, and the more these teachers do this, the more confident they would become in achieving excellence in their work.

The hypothesis that teachers could enhance their professional development, along the path of giving social support, feeling of competence, and higher motivation to advance in careers was tested and confirm in a study by Lam (2015). In her study, 41 primary school teachers in Hong Kong, who were senior teachers in a teacher leadership-training course, aged from 31 to 51 participated. Participant-teachers were asked to complete a questionnaire to report on four variables. They include (i) giving of social support to students, which means the degree to which the teachers provided support to their student in the past year; (ii) self-efficacy beliefs, which explain how much teachers believed in their ability to tackle typical problems that arose from their jobs as teachers, such as misbehaving students and interpersonal relationships with colleagues; (iii) job satisfaction, which identifies the degree to which teachers rated if they were satisfied with their job and coping with job-related stress; and (iv) job aspirations, which looks into teachers' motivation to advance in their careers regarding their willingness to be innovative and their awareness of opportunities. The relationships between these four variables were explored. The results of the study suggested that teachers' giving of social support was significantly associated with their self-efficacy. On the other hand, teachers' self-efficacy positively predicted both job satisfaction and job aspiration, respectively. The results of this study suggest that teachers giving social support to students works in enhancing teachers' self-efficacy in teaching, and that teacher's perceived competence (self-efficacy) enhances their job aspirations. The relationship between self-efficacy and the motivation to pursue advancement in careers has also been proven by an earlier study conducted by Tschannen-Moran, Woolfolk Hoy, and Hoy (1998), in a western society. This finding suggests an important line of research that has implications for people's development since not everyone has experienced a satisfying career. This is especially true for the teaching profession, as many teachers were found to have experienced frustration and burnout.

Teacher satisfaction in teaching and their engagement in their teaching career could be explained by the motives for people to carry out altruistic helping behaviours, as suggested in the social support literature. There are three motives for human beings to offer support to others, i.e. when they realise that helping acts can earn social rewards, for reducing one's own distress; and as a giving out of people's empathetic concern for someone in need and intention to benefit the well-being of the needy (Omoto, Malsch, & Barraza, 2009). As suggested, teacher's 'love for students' has stood out as a common reason to explain teachers' motivation in joining the teaching profession; teachers who join the teaching profession have strong intentions of making a difference on students' lives. This can be explained as a motive which is generated from humans' empathetic concerns, similar to the urge to give help to the others. The motive to support someone is considered a primary determinant of prosocial behaviours. In the teachers' case, the urge to give support to students engages teachers themselves in the profession. They are committed and dedicated to the satisfying experience gained from teaching, as explained earlier in this chapter by teachers' psychic of teaching. Teacher's passion for changing students' lives through teaching is also the reason which keeps teachers in the profession despite the challenges they face in the education environment; this represents another motive for social support giving. Helping behaviours, as prosocial behaviours, are found to reduce distress (Midlarsky, 1991), enhance health (Schwartz & Sendor, 1999), and enable a lower risk of mortality, and support giving to others associated with positive affect and satisfaction in one's life (Kahana, Bhatta, Lovegreen, Kahana, & Midlarsky, 2013). Giving support to students could, therefore, generate a healing effect to reduce teachers' stress, assuring teachers of the meaning of teaching and making them realise their self-worth, instead of distancing them from their work. Therefore, it may be the case that committed teachers are more engaged, as their enthusiasm creates the condition for more positive career development.

The nature of social support discussed in the health psychology literature provides insights to explain teacher behaviours. As discussed in Chaps. 4 and 5, the empathic concern of teachers and altruism involved in teaching can largely facilitate the relationship that is needed to produce favourable education outcomes for learners. Equally, the social support literature also hints to the nature of the teaching profession that requires an attitude similar to social support giving and the techniques and consideration of giving social support effectively, which could in turn help teachers to perform better in teaching, overcome challenges, and advance their career to a fulfilling one. The ideas and complications of why a significant number of teachers become burnt out or demoralised and cannot sustain their interest in the profession are explored in the following section.

Surviving the Demands and Becoming a Competent Teacher

The discussion above suggests two different scenarios which illustrate the occupational characteristics of teaching. On the one hand, teaching is stressful, and teachers are overburdened with negative emotions by the increasing demands of the profession; on the other hand, teaching is intrinsically meaningful, and the satisfaction teachers gain from teaching encourages them to stay committed and invest efforts to achieve this satisfaction (i.e. the psychic rewards of teaching), therefore they make advancement in their career development. A strand of inquiry that appears worthy of exploring is the factors that can help teachers to sustain their teaching commitment. This topic can shed light on understanding why teachers become burnt out and decide to leave the profession, and what the variables are that support teachers' sustained engagement in their teaching career. This part of discussion covers topics on the emotional work of teaching at the classroom and organisational levels, teacher's personality and teacher emotions.

Teaching as 'Emotional Work' Versus 'Emotional Labour'

Teaching is categorised as a 'high burnout' job in the literature (Cordes & Dougherty, 1993; Hebson, Earnshaw, & Marchington, 2007). It is regarded as a 'human-intensive' profession (Yilmaz, Altinkurt, Gunder, & Sen, 2015) which involves managing emotions in a complex emotional ecology (Zembylas, 2007). Teaching is, however, classified as a 'caring' profession (Brotheridge & Grandey, 2002), which makes it a breed apart from the ordinary service professions; it is placed in the same category as health care and social service work where a mission to offer support is identified.

Teachers are expected to play a variety of roles to guide and instruct students, in order to help students acquire positive attitudes, skills and knowledge, and prepare them to become highly motivated individuals who are interested in pursuing intrinsic goals in their adult life. Central to this role is the teacher's work in managing the classroom as well as interacting with students, which serve to facilitate learning effectively. In the literature, this part of work is known as 'emotional work' (Hargreaves, 2001) which makes it a breed apart from only seeing teaching as a technical job of knowledge delivery England, Farkas, Kilbourne, and Dou (1988) define emotional work as the "efforts made to understand others, to have empathy with their situation, to feel their feelings as part of one's own" (p. 91) (Isenbarger & Zembylas, 2006). The definition implies the meaning of the emotional work of teaching as the ways in which teachers manage to create emotional understanding in the discourse between teacher and students during classroom instruction, and to introduce emotional scaffoldings to enable students to learn with positive affect; in this way students can be more receptive to teacher's instruction (Isenbarger & Zembylas, 2006). Emotional scaffoldings mean guiding and making the other persons understand, by taking care of the well-being of the other persons in the communication, trying to make them understand and resolve their doubts so that they are motivated and eager to learn and participate.

The emotional aspect of teaching is driven by a motive of the teacher which is created by their internal feeling of empathic concerns for students non-selectively (Noddings, 2015). The emotional work of teaching happens in classroom instruction; teachers have to be truly engaged in their interactions with students and in the delivery of the lesson and to develop a clear purpose in the classroom for managing the emotional discourse with students. It also expects learners to contribute by taking part as learners with responsive and supportive behaviours. To name but a few, teachers try to consider students' perspectives and listen to student's concerns when they have to come up with a decision; teachers model appropriate attitude, disposition and manner so that students could adopt the same in solving their own problems in future; and teachers use humour when the class appears to be inactive or dispirited.

As discussed earlier, pioneering researchers on teachers' professional lives argued that teachers' personal teaching goals, commitment, and passion in teaching are the motivational resources for teachers in making progress and advancement in their career (e.g. Hargreaves, 1994; Lortie, 1975; Nias et al., 1989), which can be used to explain the delicate content of the emotional work of teaching. Isenbarger and Zembylas (2006) attempted to explain teaching as an emotional work by specifying the nature of a caring practice. This form of practice is generated by meaningful relationships, sustaining connections and responsiveness to learner needs (Noddings, 2015) instead of documented rules and the power of control. Noddings' (2013) framework of caring practice underscores teachers' skills of 'engrossment' and 'motivational displacement'; teachers put themselves into the position of students to feel about the cared for so that the lesson can proceed to cater for the interests and needs of students. As also discussed in Chap. 4, the instructional format of caring as suggested by Noddings (2013) composed of modelling, dialogue, practice, and confirmation, each illustrates for students a form of interaction that values respect, trustworthiness, autonomy and self-esteem. The practice of caring in classrooms requires teacher's efforts to build an atmosphere of trust that enables students to learn and explore in a supportive environment, and managing the emotional work of teaching is seen as a creative endeavour, an improvisation, an act of spontaneity, which maximise teachers' own potential, and help teachers to develop self-esteem (Goldstein & Lake, 2000) (similar to the teachers in Chap. 5). In addition to caring practice, other forms of practice were also suggested in the literature which emphasise the cultivation of positive affect and relatedness in the learning environment. These include pedagogies such as cultural responsive teaching which uses cultural knowledge and experiences of diverse students to form a caring school environment (Vavrus, 2008), the personal-centred approach which advocates empathy, unconditional positive regard (warmth), genuineness, non-directivity and encouragement of critical thinking (Cornelius-White, 2007; Rogers, 1983), and the emotional design of instruction (EDI) framework (Astleitner, 2000). These practices also illustrate the characteristics of social support in teachers' classroom practice and the teaching expertise, and they are discussed in Chaps. 4 and 5.

Both Day (2004) and Hargreaves (1998) echoed caring as the soul of teaching. They suggested that relationships with students are the key to defining good teaching; they specified that the active role of teachers in connecting with students has made teaching a meaningful activity. The expert teacher literature also concludes affect (i.e. feeling, and motivation of students) as a major domain of teacher expertise. Expert teachers are found to possess 'deep processing strategies' and a 'high level of engagement' in teaching (Berliner, 2001); their teaching is sophisticated, high-level emotional work, such as attending to individual learning progress and at the same time proceeding with a brisk movement of the whole class when they teach (Borko & Livingston, 1989). Chapter 5 also provides an empirical study of four expert teachers who demonstrate teacher caring behaviours. In sum, both theoretical and empirical evidences come to agree that teachers' emotional work in the classroom is underlined by teacher's commitment to every individual student's development, their social support behaviours, and their care about students' well-being. Because of this, teachers are willing to take teaching as emotional work but not mechanistic action, making the difference that learners are individuals whose needs and emotions have to be taken care of in the interactions that occur in the classroom.

As the emotional work of teaching is discussed as a professional part of teaching, other researchers conceptualise teaching as a performance of professional behaviours according to some expected, standardised rules. Instead of seeing teaching with an internalised, intrinsic motivation, this view elaborates a capitalist labour process known as 'emotional labour', which was originally proposed by Hochschild (1983). Emotional labour is used to describe "the management of feeling to create a publicly observable facial and bodily display" (Hochschild, 1983, p. 7) for organisational profit. According to this interpretation, employees' emotions and behaviours should be performed according to normalised performance standards, which have display rules (Muraven & Baumeister, 2000). Employees' work is thought to be emotional labour as they have to 'surface act' display rules in doing their jobs and exhibit professional behaviours (Morris & Feldman, 1996). The intention of masking truly felt emotions by performing standard emotions (such as a faked smile and a courteous response) has been found to have a damaging effect on employees though. This also implies that the person who serves should not need to care about their clients other than the service they provide at the surface. The difference of true emotion and performed emotions which creates emotional dissonance to employee's feelings is found to cause depersonalisation and burnout.

An increasing number of researchers have used an emotional labour perspective to study teacher stress and burnout in relation to teachers' delivery of instruction in the classroom, as teachers are bound by expectations of discharging their duties according to the expectation of schools to satisfy certain standards (Carson & Templin, 2007; Yilmaz et al., 2015). These studies have confirmed the positive relationship between teachers' emotional labour work and burnout, which supplements ideas in understanding teacher engagement in their teaching careers. A study by Yilmaz et al. (2015), for example, used the Emotional Labour Scale and Maslach Burnout Inventory on over 5000 teacher participants in Turkey. The findings of this study suggested that teachers who performed surface acting to hide their anger in a given teaching situation predicts increased levels of emotional exhaustion, as a burnout syndrome, while teachers who experienced more enjoyment in teaching in a given situation reported lower levels of emotional labour.

The following part further discusses teacher's work at the organisational level to suggest that the process of construction of teacher's self in the environment is a complicated, continuous construction process.

Emotional Work at the Organisational Level Constructs Teachers' Self and Agency

Apart from the emotional work teachers handle with students in the classroom when they teach and communicate, the effectiveness of teaching in relation to emotional work is also determined by organisational factors, and these factors are explained as transactional factors, which have posed the greatest challenges to teachers in managing teaching in schools. Transactional factors address the interaction of individual factors (teachers' personal beliefs and strategies) and the organisational factors (setting, school culture, decision-making power) (Chang, 2009), and it exactly pinpoints the challenges in teacher's emotional work, in the areas which are in conflict with teachers' caring practice and the vision to serve student development. The case study reported by Zembylas (2007) on primary teachers in the U.S. context suggests that an experienced teacher carried out a year-long integrated unit of study as a preferred pedagogy to create a learning community for students to experience authentic learning; however, it clashed with the school's emphasis on the testing of content knowledge. Lam's (2011a, 2011b) qualitative study illustrates a student-teacher attending block practice in a primary school in the setting of Hong Kong. In the same vein, the teacher implemented project learning with her classes despite the discouraging comments from the mentor teacher and the other teachers who thought that the approach was not effective for achieving the prescribed outcomes of learning. In both cases, the two teachers demonstrated their emotional work of teaching within the social norm, culture and power relationship in relation to the teachers' own teaching goal, which is regarded as a discursive practice (Zembylas, 2005) among these different values and expectations. This means that the experiences of these committed teachers were constructed by the interplay of power of the school (that comes from the control and authority that request teachers to behave) and resistance (that teachers would like to implement an approach which they found more relevant and effective) of the teachers, as a negotiation (Barnett & Hodson, 2001).

Teachers' effort in maintaining the expectations of different parties involved in the education process is also called the political dimension of teaching; it can be explained by the interaction that teachers are involved in between several multiple micro-worlds. According to Barnett and Hodson (2001), these micro-worlds include the curriculum, the subject knowledge epistemology, and a teacher's personal beliefs. The school curriculum is usually set by the government or central authority which requires teachers to refer to prescribed teaching and assessment strategies (e.g. those serving accountability requirements). The micro-world of subject epistemology is subject to the nature of academic discipline, such as the scientific inquiry of science. A teacher's personal belief system is another micro-world that affects how they plan lessons and manage teaching. The complex interaction of micro-worlds creates scenarios of negotiations that form an emotional ecological system (Zembylas, 2005) in the professional environment of teaching. In the negotiation process, teachers internalised the need to self-control negative feelings, and regulate their emotions, in such a way that they can communicate in acceptable and strategic ways that can enable their goals to be met. This is a process of constructing teachers' self in the teaching profession.

Yin and Lee (2012) named the process of regulating emotions for achieving one's own personal target in teaching as 'instrumentalising emotions'. They suggested seven strategies of teachers' emotional regulations representing teachers' emotional work in managing the political environment of teaching. These comprise the skills of pretending, restraining, refocusing, reframing, separating, releasing and outpouring. This supplements an important perspective for teachers about their knowledge of the emotional aspects of teaching, and may also imply that developing teachers' interest or teachers who have a clear vision for teaching are the most crucial factors in teacher training and development, as the teachers who processed understanding and knowledge of the emotional aspect of handling teaching have a stronger motivation to compromise the conflicts they find the teaching by the satisfaction they aim at from teaching.

Viewing teaching as emotional work or emotional labour gives insights to us in understanding the different pathways teachers go through in their teaching career, by way of how they manage teaching. If teachers find that they have to act out an appropriate behaviour in order to preserve a harmonious classroom, although they feel that their emotions are being suppressed, it may mean that these teachers have not truly come to understand that teaching is an emotional work and it is a form of caring practice. Teaching cannot be done by simply performing standardised procedures, as teaching involves communication and relationship building with students and colleagues in schools, which is analogous to a social support situation. This difference marks two contrasting views of teaching, i.e. technocratic-rationalist teachers versus professional-contextualist teachers, as suggested by Sachs (2003), categorising two types of teachers who form their identity with different conceptions, respectively, namely, a service-provider and a caring-mentor of teaching. The latter suggests a prototype of good teaching that has generally been agreed in the education literature over the centuries. As a classroom embodies intense human interactions, problem situations, and outcomes, teachers' spontaneous interaction in the classroom can build up relationships with students and promote their engagement into the learning environment cognitively and emotionally. At another level, teachers' actions in the classroom cannot be executed without considering a host of environmental and political factors, therefore teaching is a construction process for teachers to learn to regulate emotions and the skills of handling communications and interactions in the school environment. As encounters with students increase in time, simply suppressing emotions will create enormous negative emotions for teachers which eventually lead to burnout. The literature discussed in the last section also provides evidence to conclude that performing teaching as emotional labour (i.e. controlling emotions in teaching) will possibly be linked to burnout, while teachers who play the role of a caring mentor who performs 'emotional work' in the classroom were found to sustain the commitment in teaching and stay in the profession.

The literature arrives to the consensus that teachers who are committed to teaching are keen to manage students and the approach they take in relationship building and social support giving benefits their own development. Managing teaching as emotional work helps teachers to acquire the skills of teaching; it enables teachers to concentrate on the design of instructional methods, exploring and investigating pedagogical practices and handling the negotiation process of realising the personal values of teaching to achieve personal satisfaction in teaching, which benefits student learning and one's own professional development. The idea of reflective practice proposed by Schon (1983) echoes the concern of the approach of seeing teaching as emotional work in teachers' professional's practice. It specifies teachers' inquiry in a form of reflection-in-action, in "searching, hunting, inquiring, to find materials that will resolve the doubt" (Dewey, 1933, p. 12), and to settle and dispose of the perplexity one experiences in the practice of teaching (Kember, 2001). Such reflection makes the claim for the professionalism of teaching as more of an art than a science. As argued by Schon (1983), technical rationality (i.e. applying standard procedures in teaching), does not suffice for professionals to solve the problems they encounter in their profession, as the problems encountered in professional practice are often of an ill-defined nature. For example, a students' disruptive behaviour in the classroom may be subject to different reasons and has to be handled with the teachers' tactfulness, personal styles, values, and with reference to the bureaucratic instruction of the school organisation. Seeing teaching as emotional work enables teachers to conceptualise teaching in a professional frame of reference. Its importance lies in the framing of problems to look for the best suitable solution for a particular classroom situation (Lam, 2011a). Additionally, while reflective practice has an affective dimension, i.e. feeling about or doubts about the situations of teaching, teachers' passion for learners and their concerns about learners' feeling and emotions should be essential ingredients that drive teachers to implement effective practice. This means that reflection engages teachers to keep thinking about their interaction with learners in the learning context, which echoes the emotional work of teaching.

On the whole, good teaching is underpinned by teachers' commitment and genuine interest in supporting learners regarding their future development. When conducting teaching, teachers have to manage the interaction with students in the classroom while they have to consider the context of the education environment to ensure that the teacher's responsibilities are fulfilled and that teaching can be achieved meaningfully. Therefore, teacher's work is often regarded as emotional work as teaching requires not only the work of emotional scaffoldings with students, but their attitude and motivation for helping students to achieve, and their efforts in dealing with the political situation so that they can carry out the job of teaching meaningfully. Though, as will be discussed later in this chapter, the environmental factors might constrain teachers' exercise of the emotional work of teaching. Teachers' emotional work is enacted with feelings (passion for teaching) and professional teaching skills; teachers are 'passionate beings' (Hargreaves, 1998) who believe in themselves that the work they do can benefit students (Schaufeli & Salanova, 2007). Their work is perceived as 'sincere emotional giving' as suggested by Ashforth and Humphreys (1993). Committed and engaged teachers will engage in emotional work productively because teachers find that the work they accomplish benefits humankind, and they develop professional competence as they are engaged in teaching as a reflective practitioner; hence, they develop self-worth and satisfaction in teaching and that they continue to enhance the expertise of teaching. This psychological mechanism echoes the role of support giver in the social support literature. The satisfying condition creates a cyclical effect for teachers and it generates satisfaction and energies for teachers to continue teaching with strong motivation. Thus, these teachers are found to enjoy positive career development.

In addition to teachers' mission that can drive them to be successful teachers as discussed earlier in this chapter, there are other traits or attributes that can support teachers in handling the emotional work of teaching. The following two sections discuss character traits and teacher emotions which might explain why some teachers may be more engaged in teaching while some may be prone to burnout, and shed light on teacher development and teachers reflecting on their teaching and teaching career.

Personality Traits and Knowledge of Teacher Emotions that Facilitate Teaching

Personality and character traits may explain part of the reasons why some teachers stay in the teaching profession with longevity and strong commitment, while the others' commitment fades in time, and consequently give up their teaching career or become frustrated and burnt out. Evidence suggests that teachers possessing personality traits such as hardiness, gratitude, and forgiveness are found to be more resistant to stress and have better subjective well-being and mental health (Chan, 2013). Researchers also found that teachers who are hard driven and persistent (Mo, 1991), and who have a positive affectivity personality (Chiu & Kosinski, 1997) are less prone to burnout, as these teachers can focus on the positive sides of their self, events and environments. Furthermore, teachers who can conduct high-quality teaching in a classroom with emotional and behavioural problems are found to possess higher levels of agreeableness, conscientiousness, and openness in their personalities (Buttner, Pijl, Bijstra, & van den Bosch, 2015).

Research has proved that teachers with higher social and emotional competence are likely to exhibit more effective classroom management; they are highly self-aware people, who recognise and have control of their emotions, in order to motivate themselves as well as their students (Guerra, Modecki, & Cunningham, 2014; Jennings & Greenberg, 2009). Socio-emotional competence is an important trait for teachers as they perform emotional functioning in a myriad of tasks in the classroom and at the collegial level, as well as dealing with communication and negotiations with administrators in a social and political setting. Socio-emotional competence encompasses four trait dimensions that include self-awareness, self-management, relationship skills and responsible decision-making (Durlak et al., 2007). It is regarded as one of the keys to maintain teacher commitment and protect them from career frustration. Jennings and Greenberg (2009) explained how these characteristics applied in the classroom context. They mentioned that socially and emotionally competent teachers lay the focus of teaching on building supportive and encouraging relationships; they discover students' abilities and strengths and encourage motivation and cooperation among students. These teachers can create a classroom climate with low levels of conflict and classroom misbehaviors, and manage the classroom smoothly by resolving conflicts and seeking collaborative efforts for solving problems (Jennings, Sonowberg, Coccia, & Greenberg, 2011). The authors further mentioned that those who fail to handle social and emotional challenges may tend to use reactive and punitive responses, and in turn create serious disruptive classroom discipline problems, which often lead to teacher burnout. Teacher's socio-emotional competence and personality are found to determine teachers' overall mood in teaching (Abenavoli, Jennings, Greenberg, Harris, & Katz, 2013).

The emotional work of teaching creates joy and excitement; it also generates sweat and tears in teacher's experience. There are unsettling issues, unfulfilled expectations and relationship issues awaiting teachers to solve, and teachers are often required to make rapid-fire decisions inside and outside the classroom, therefore managing teaching often generates emotions. The classroom situation may generate positive or negative emotions; generally, positive emotions engender positive energies for teachers in handling classroom situations, and teacher's emotions may affect their cognition, motivation and problem solving (Sutton & Wheatley, 2003). Emotions are generated through conscious and/or unconscious judgments by an individual, through a personal psychological system (Chen, 2016; Zembylas & Schutz, 2009). For example, teachers may recall a negative experience they had with students in the past when they come across a similar situation at the present, the negative emotions they had before would cause teachers to think negatively should similar episodes arose. If teachers could alter their emotional state by referring to some pleasant experience with students in the past, the positive emotional state would help them categorise the situation positively, and teachers would be willing to solve students' problems with favourable results. Teacher's emotions would also determine the actions they take and the outcomes (Sutton & Wheatley, 2003). For example, when students submit their homework late, teachers may think that the students are 'nasty and irresponsible, but teacher may also think that they are 'unable to manage time and fear telling you in advance'. As in the latter case, teachers can create a positive effect as they might look into the reason for a late submission with the students concerned and encourage them to solve the issues that have caused the problem of late submission and learn from the case, while they may also use strategies to manage students' learning motivation and behaviour. This may, in turn, encourage the students and motivate them to study with greater efforts and lead to positive outcomes.

Teachers' unconscious emotions towards student behaviours in the classroom may trigger negative affect in students, which affect their relationships with students and create negative impact on management of the class. By studying teachers' countertransference (CT), which generally means the teachers' reaction arising from unresolved conflicts and the vulnerabilities of themselves projected on students' behaviour in the classroom (Robertson, 2001; Yeh & Hayes, 2011), researchers found that teachers' unconscious unresolved emotions in teaching may become a barrier to maintaining good teacher–student relationships, as teachers may lose empathy and understanding for students under this influence (Slater, Veach, & Li, 2013). A study by Slater et al. (2013) on 14 expert teachers' CT reported that expert teachers would 'proactively' enhance the relationships with their students in order to prevent or reduce CT.

Teachers derive positive feelings in teaching such as love, joy, satisfaction, pride and excitement; they also have negative emotions such as anger, frustration, anxiety and sadness (Oldham, 2010). Teacher's positive emotions have been discussed in the explanation of psychic reward of teaching in an earlier section. Positive emotions (e.g. the joy of teaching) stimulate teachers to work enthusiastically and select more ambitious goals in teaching (Locke & Latham, 1990). While these teachers gain satisfaction from interacting with and offering support to students, they are thought to be teachers who perform caring practice, and who have developed the skills to manage the detailed emotional work of teaching. Negative emotions are thought to obstruct goal attainment; it renders negativity in human relationships and inter-actions. Circumstances of negative emotions of teachers are reviewed in the work of Chang (2009), Chen (2016), and Sutton and Wheatley (2003). They suggested teachers may develop unpleasant emotions in situations such as a poor relationship with students, students' poor results due to laziness and inattention, and discomfort with having to make fast and uncertain decisions. The authors also suggested that negative emotions are also caused by teachers' worry about how to improve student achievement, pressure from parents, and fear of a competitive environment in which they have to compete against each other.

Regarding the causes of unpleasant emotions, teacher emotions arising from instructional practice most significantly affect teachers, especially when teachers are asked to change their instructional practice (Chen, 2016). Chang (2009) deduced from research evidence that while teachers' emotion of guilt is caused by teachers themselves (such as being unprepared for a lesson), teacher's emotion of anger is caused by others (inappropriate attitude of students), while frustration and anxiety are caused by circumstances when teachers have low control potential on these emotions such as the volume of non-educational workload, inequitable distribution of work, and teachers' limited professional autonomy (Lam & Yan, 2011). This explains the negative emotions that have been felt by teachers in the current educational environment.

The strategy of suppressing negative emotions such as anger may lead to uncontrollable emotional behaviour such as yelling at students, and this would harm the relationship with students and undermine the learning and teaching environment (Sutton & Wheatley, 2003). For teachers, the suppression of emotions renders self-monitoring and self-corrective actions during the period the emotion lasts. Similar to surface acting, it reduces cognitive resources and impairs memory for information (Richards & Gross, 2000; Wang & Groth, 2014). The hiding of stressful emotions may also lead to higher levels of stress and burnout (Carson, Baumgartner, Matthews, & Tsouloupas, 2010). The strategies of exercising tight control to stop students' misbehaviour would cause a distance between teacher and students and would result in low social engagement and academic engagement of students (Wentzel & Miele, 2009).

Poor emotional management would lead to teacher burnout, in such a situation that teachers can no longer maintain involvement in or commitment to work (Darling-Hammond, 2001; Montgomery & Rupp, 2005; Schaufeli, Leiter, & Maslach, 2009). The burnout syndrome entails the states of feeling emotionally over-extended (emotional exhaustion), displaying a detached attitude towards work and other persons in the workplace (depersonalisation), and having a low sense of self-efficacy or feeling of inefficiency (diminished accomplishment) (Brotheridge & Grandey, 2002). Since teaching involves detailed emotional work in the classroom, and teachers have to handle the challenges of the teaching environment, teachers have to be conscious about their own emotions and develop strategies to manage its consequence and understand how to regulate emotion in teaching. Staying away from handling emotional relationship with students and suppressing negative emotions are therefore not recommended; some passive emotional management strategies may not be the preferred tactics of managing emotions in teaching. The implications at the end of this chapter will further discuss this.

The Performativity Culture Risks the Caring Profession and Turns Teachers Away

The chapter so far has suggested a positive relationship between teachers' commitment in teaching and their career development; it has also investigated other variables that facilitate teachers in pursuing a meaningful teaching career. It has informed clearly that, to a large extent, teachers can take control of their own professional development by engaging themselves with commitment and interest in the teaching profession. This section suggests more specifically the emerging performativity culture in the twenty-first-century school environment, which is the area that may cause frustration to teachers, thus likely creating teacher burnout.

As suggested above, the political dimension of teachers' emotional work in the classroom is the most challenging part of teaching that may create negative emotions for teachers (Thomson, 2001). Since teachers have relatively less control over this part of work in their role, it is detrimental to teacher engagement in their teaching career.

The political work in school that affects teachers has been recently influenced by a typical form of culture known as performativity culture (Ball, 2003; Nicholl & McLellan, 2008; Troman, 2008). This culture prevails in societies in the twenty-first century which has been changing the core values of the teaching profession, having a serious influence on schools and teachers. Discussion in the past twenty years in education has focused on the influence of globalisation for bringing about new forms of management ideologies, which include managerialism and marketization. They have created a new discourse in education governance that focuses on accountability and auditing mechanisms. In such a context, education, as an area to serve human development, also has to renew its governance structure towards a set of new principles which are based on the competition of achievable outcomes. This new form of assessment that governs teacher is dictated by market accountability. Under this system, schools and teachers have to act upon institutionalised performance indicators. Schools, subject to external review mechanisms, have to prove to the public their quality, excellence and effectiveness (Ball, 2003), by measuring up to a system of judgements, classifications and targets, in the so-called performativity culture in schools. If this occurs, teachers are expected to perform in ways which show that they are 'being seen' to be doing something efficiently (Barty, Thomson, Blackmore, & Sachs, 2005; Blackmore, 2004) and that their work is monitored and evaluated by standard performance indicators.

The performance indicators are often discussed in the literature in relation to teacher's stress caused by education reform. They imply an increased control over the work of teachers through such monitoring systems to tally the outcomes of teachers' teaching performance in the classroom. The drawback of this system has been realised in empirical studies (Brotheridge & Grandey, 2002; Forrester, 2005; Hebson et al., 2007). A study by Hebson et al. (2007) reveals the divide between the teachers and the superintendent who comes from the school authority to review teachers' performance in the classroom, on how they view good teaching. The cases suggested that first of all the superintendent who executed the role of external reviewer failed to recognise teacher's good teaching behaviour which the teacher had intended to account for students who had special educational needs. The observer was looking for the behaviour espoused in the set of standard performance criteria across the broad spectrum of the education curriculum. Second, the observer who played the role of assessor also discouraged the teacher who had attempted to closely respond to individual needs of the students in her class; instead, the teacher was advised to work on the standard items and was told 'just do it' because 'a good teacher would just do it', without bothering to listen to the teachers' reflection.

Although the current education environment does not explicitly require teachers to change their practice to any standard approach, the performativity culture in school has gradually shaped teachers to perform in ways towards the technical competence of teaching prescribed according to appraisal requirements since the late twentieth century (Dorn, 1998). The caring aspects of teaching that teachers value may not be counted in the agenda of performativity assessment culture. As discussed earlier, the psychic rewards of teaching is the greatest satisfaction teachers gain from teaching, and the teacher/student relationship is the basis of learning and teaching where teachers find meaning to support their engagement in the challenging 'emotional work' of teaching, which leads to teachers' personal growth and career development. As performativity culture dominates current school system, a huge drawback for the education profession is foreseeable.

First of all, the performativity culture will gradually wear away the caring activities in teaching (Forrester, 2005) and replace it by the type of education which is similar to offering a commodity, whereby teachers can fulfill teaching by 'just doing it' according to the objective measurement rules. In such situations, good teaching means meeting the measurement objectives and it could be possible that teachers can teach to standard competence as expressed in 'items'; however, they are uninterested in teaching and not particularly interested in students' development; that means that teachers without a passion for teaching can be good performers. Second, the concern about performativity may mean the loss of authenticity in the interaction of teachers and students. Teachers would behave as mere labourers in the sense that teaching is to perform emotional display rules dictated by the job. Teachers are expected to interact with students in standard ways without taking care of teaching as an 'emotional work'. This way of simplifying teaching removes human nature from teaching, which makes teaching as a human activity become artificial and unethical. Third, conducting teaching in a uniform nature with minimal human feelings may constrain the development of both teachers and students, as the spontaneity, improvisation, and creativity involved in the interaction between learners and teachers will create outcomes that are beneficial to learners' intellectual and emotional development, and produce valuable scholarship in teaching to strength the academic field of education.

The changing expectation of the professional role has largely affected teachers and other stakeholders in the education community. Parents' choice of schools favours academic performance as the indicator of success for their children, which causes keen competition among schools (Woods, Bagley, & Glatter, 2005). This has formulated a consumerist perspective of viewing teachers as service providers, students as consumers and parents as clients (Wilkinson, 2007). The operation of the school is rebuilt upon a concept which is similar to business, with the performing schools measuring up to standards which are proved by the quantifiable hard data of success, and where the moral good that serve educational interest is marginalised (Blackmore, 2004). In order to become competitive, schools are subject to a uniform image building according to a global image; it destroys relationships and professional autonomy and the professionalism of teachers (Hargreaves & Fullan, 2012). In the long run, this will change the belief system in education, from the one previously valuing commitment, trust, and professional autonomy, towards a market-oriented, instrumental, standardised and narrow-focus conception.

Perhaps the increasing teacher stress and occupational burnout in the teaching profession are likely to be the result of more and more disagreements between teachers' personal goals and society's goals. It is especially true for teachers who are committed and who would want to serve this caring profession with integrity and morality, and those who enjoy the creative nature of teaching and would like to make a difference to students' lives. The predominant performativity ideology would be likely to damage the psychic rewards of teaching and lead to an approach to teaching that destroys the genuine interest of teachers to do well but cause an identity crisis to teachers for adapting to a mentality of 'performing' and 'being seen to be performing' (Mahoney, Menter, & Hextall, 2003). The virtue of teachers' social support giving that strengthens teacher and teacher development, and that benefits students, is going to be eroded by a performativity culture that discourages human interaction, which is a huge drawback teachers and educators seriously face.

Recommendations: Preparing and Supporting Teacher Development

The analysis in this chapter affirms that social support can be regarded as a trait of good teaching and it helps teachers to maintain a satisfying and fulfilling career. It also explains that teachers' passion for teaching generates productive energies so they can engage in the detailed, human-interaction intensive, emotional work of teaching. Furthermore, teachers have to acquire necessary character traits and understand emotion in dealing with their job successfully and meaningfully. The implications are discussed in this section in order to produce a number of suggestions regarding teacher training and development, in areas related to teacher's knowledge, professional disposition and capacities, and organisational support to promote teacher well-being.

Emotional Knowledge as Essential Knowledge for Teachers

As the analysis suggests, teacher's engagement into the emotional work of teaching is an important area of teacher expertise; teachers have to develop the knowledge of the political environment and develop skills of regulating one's own emotions in teaching. However, this perspective is not taken as seriously as academic knowledge and teaching skills in teacher preparation or in discussing teacher knowledge. Researchers over past decades have suggested terminologies to address the essential knowledge that teachers' need for teaching, such as pedagogical content knowledge (Shulman, 1986, 2000), pedagogical context knowledge (Barnett & Hodson, 2001), and technological pedagogical content knowledge (Mishra & Koehler, 2006). Each of these knowledge schemes emphasise a complex interaction among different body of knowledge that teachers use to conduct teaching effectively, including content (discipline or subject), pedagogy, context (different environmental factors in the classroom that affect the decision in teaching) and technology. The analysis of teacher motivation and traits in this chapter recommends that a key dimension of knowledge which has to be developed in teacher preparation is the emotional knowledge of teaching. This type of knowledge deals with several domains in the context of teaching (Denzin, 1994; Hargreaves, 2005; McCaughtry, 2004). According to Zembylas (2007), teachers have to acquire emotional knowledge of three domains. The individual domain deals with a teacher's personal beliefs about learning and teaching, knowledge and the learner; the relational domain deals with relationships with students and the learning environment; and the sociopolitical domain deals with the communication channels in schools and the extent of autonomy which is governed by the institutional and cultural context. Teachers may have to consider the possible conflicts between different domains when they carry out teaching. For example, in such situations as selecting a method to teach; creating an extra worksheet for a particular class; or deciding the use of instructional time for non-instructional matter, teachers have to think about the school rules and the consensus between colleagues to make a professional decision. While teachers in these situations would be struggling with complying with institutional uniformity versus fulfilling of a certain meaningful educational purpose in a special context; they have to consider what they have to do in order to accommodate the meaningful initiatives into the political environment, as well as the form of communication which may be necessary to help to take the proposals on board.

Teachers have to understand the emotions incurred in conflict negotiations between different domains as these happen. Knowledge of emotional ecology and the political environment are crucial to support teachers' work in the twenty-first century because of the increasingly diverse nature of the curriculum and the multiple values of education; understanding the political environment can also help teachers to problematize their role in schools. In such a way, teachers learn to manage the interaction among different stakeholders and knowledge authorities as part of the emotional work of teaching. This part of knowledge helps teachers develop proper strategies in dealing with situations and teachers' emotions and to avoid the reality shock and negative emotions that they may have caused for teachers. It also helps teachers to develop an approach to teaching that is professional oriented, meaningful and effective to support student learning. The emotional knowledge of teaching is especially important for teachers in the formative period and the beginning stages of teaching, as teachers' conceptions and epistemic beliefs are more resistant to change in later stage of a teachers' career (Patrick & Pintrich, 2001).

Strengthening Socio-emotional Capacity and Skills for Reflection

The challenges teachers face in the education environment, especially regarding the surrounding performative culture in the globalised economy, may demoralise teachers' commitment to teaching. Since teacher commitment is a drive to produce 'volitional functioning' (Ryan & Deci, 2000, 2011), which refers to the determination to work for achieving success; the commitment of teachers enable them to create psychological resources to overcome the challenges in teaching. The sense of commitment can also be seen as a push to teachers for achieving teaching expertise by continuous improvement to enhance teaching quality. In order to protect and sustain teacher's commitment in teaching and enable them to develop the capacities to manage the emotional work of teaching, training the emotional intelligence of teachers may be one of the important recommendations. Teachers' self-compassion is one of the important aspects to enhance teachers' capacity to manage the emotional work of teaching within the classroom and in the political environment of teaching. Self-compassion can be regarded as a quality trait which is predisposed to the intention of helping others, as self-compassion engenders understanding of oneself or the others who are in situations where suffering, failure, and feeling inadequate take place. Such situations are regarded as common in life (Goldstein, 2015). Self-compassion also comes from empathetic concern, which is the condition of offering social support to others (Neff, Rude, & Kirkpatrick, 2007). It is necessary for teachers to offer understanding and kindness to others or themselves at a time of failure, making mistakes, and facing challenges in life. As a character trait, self-compassion can be trained. It can be developed through intervention such as mindfulness programmes (Roeser & Eccles, 2015). Mindfulness has been defined as "paying attention in a particular way: on purpose, in the present moment, and non-judgmentally" (Kabat-Zinn, 1994, p. 4). Its practice aims to cultivate an individual's positive emotion toward oneself and other people (Salzberg, 1995). The success of this type of programme has been found in enhancing greater awareness of sensation, feelings and thoughts, awareness of one's action and reasons for the action, less judgment and reactivity, resulting in less occupational stress. Through the acquisition of these skills, teachers manage teaching more effectively, and the healthy being can sustain their interest in the profession.

Relationally, some educators and statutory authorities have suggested a new domain of development—professional dispositions (e.g. Hen & Goroshit, 2016; National Council for the Accreditation of Teacher Education, 2006; O'Connor, 2008; Schon, 1983), which can be explained as the intelligence to deal with unknown situations and problems. This kind of intelligence includes the abilities such as gathering information from different sources and in a non-judgmental manner, be emotionally regulated and resilient, and have an attitude of kindness and compassion during times of difficulty (Jennings & Greenberg, 2009). As students' learning is largely shaped by teachers, especially their social and emotional development (Eccles & Roeser, 1999; Hamre & Pianta, 2006), teachers' capacity to work with and support others may influence the quality of their students' learning (Edwards & Mackenzie, 2005). The training of teacher cognition that helps teachers to cope with and be resilient to social-emotional and cognitive challenges in the classroom (Roeser et al., 2013) is also a form of training for teachers through which teachers shape their professional identity as teachers. This will provide meaning to their teaching experiences engaging them for continuous growth in the profession.

The skills for reflective practice are recommended to be taught and put into wide practice in teacher education. As student teachers learn to master academic knowledge and theories in the school environment, their real life practice of teaching in schools is the resources of learning for themselves for improving and enhancing their management of the emotional work of teaching. In order to maintain good quality practice, practitioners have to acquire the skills before they can engage in high quality reflection-in-action. These skills refer to the use of problem-framing techniques to identify issues that bother teachers or trigger their thoughts, in areas where they would like to find a better way to deal with them. Teachers can use question protocols to identify teaching situations and to shed understanding in handling the situation, such as: 'What features do I observe when I am aware of the object?'; 'What are my assumptions when I make this judgement?' 'What procedures do I enact when I perform this skill?'; 'How do I frame the problem I am trying to solve?' (Lam, 2011a).

Reflection entails building new understanding to suit teachers' actions to current situations (Hatton & Smith, 1995); it can take different forms such as discussion, writing critical incidents, classroom observational analysis, mentoring, and action research.

Building Support Networks and Setting Shared Goals to Promote Meaningful Teaching

The discussion in the earlier section argues that the quality of teaching is supposed to be the core of education; as the OECD (2009) advocated, the implementation of any initiatives should involve teachers and other stakeholders in schools because these initiatives cannot generate any impact at the school level if they go against the views of educators. This vision can be taken on board in formulating policies for changing the performativity culture of school into a professional learning culture. If school development initiatives and teacher professional development policies can be developed based on sound rationales of education, the performance culture can be gradually replaced. Reform educators such as Levin (2010) also agree with this idea. Schools can organise ongoing teacher professional development activities by considering the professional life cycle of teachers to ensure professional development progressively for them. Regular forms of professional development, such as lesson study (Lewis, Perry, & Murata, 2006), can be more extensively organised into a main part of learning for teachers, which promotes teacher reflection and encourages teachers to create, transfer, and advance professional knowledge of teaching.

Lesson study adopts an action research model (Murata, 2011), and involves a group of teachers or individuals to plan a lesson. In a typical lesson study model, teachers then take turns to conduct the lesson in consecutive sessions in a different class. When a teacher conducts a session, the others would serve as observers. The core team holds post-lesson discussion after every lesson conducted by a teacher of the team, by exchanging views to improve the plan. The discussion creates opportunities for teachers to reflect collectively, as they share perspectives to solve problems in a 'community of learners' (Lieberman, 2009), through which teachers can sharpen their understanding about teaching. This form of knowledge, which is developed by a group of people who produce and use the knowledge, is called situated knowledge (Lave & Wenger, 1991, 2005), or practical knowledge (Elbaz, 1981). It is very useful to teachers as it is the knowledge that helps solve the problems emerging from one's own context. The emotional work of teaching involves the use of a form of knowledge called tacit knowledge (Eraut, 2000) Instead of learning from lectures, tacit knowledge is more appropriate to be learned by practice and reflection upon practice, through exchanges in a learning community supported by more experienced teachers (Dudley, 2013). Learning study in a community of learners can focus learners on a lesson topic in real-life practice and the exchange process helps teachers to grasp the knowledge in a context which is very relevant to real practice, furthermore, it can make individual's tacit knowledge (the knowledge not written in books but central to the execution of good practice) (Leonard & Sensiper, 1998) explicit and creates form of artefacts (e.g. articulated, shared ideas; and lesson plans) (Fernandez, Cannon, & Chokshi, 2003) that benefit learning for other teachers.

It would be appropriate if learning study activities can be facilitated by teachers who are keen on pedagogies, who are willing to serve as the learning leader of the team. The learning leader can design the lesson study events, such as prioritising themes for study to explore topics of common concerns. The emotional qualities of teaching reported in Chap. 5 can be referenced as the foci of lesson study, e.g. teacher immediacy, catering for diversities, and planning for group work. Lesson study can promote other means of learning such as blog writing and e-sharing platforms to create channels for exchange and open discussion on feelings and tips about teaching. Under specific circumstances, schools may also deploy external resources or partnership with neighbouring schools in the same district to enlarge the exchange circle for professional learning. The more opportunities created for reflection in real life teaching, the better for teachers to acquire teaching expertise, which contribute to teachers' acquisition of skills to handle the emotional work of teaching.

Promoting Opportunities to Enhance Teacher Self-efficacy

As teacher's satisfaction is largely derived from the psychic reward of teaching, i.e. interacting with students and seeing students' growth, a highly achievement-oriented education system could be a threat to teachers (Choi, 2003) as teachers would expect to enjoy the interaction with students as a major part of their profession rather than taking academic result as the prime or only goal of teaching. Since teachers' satisfaction is based on the rewarding experience they gain from giving scaffoldings to students and interacting with them, and giving social support to students are found to enhance their self-efficacy that also helps in advancing their profession. School leaders can promote this satisfaction in the organisational context.

First, schools could identify space in the timetabling setting and provide a regular structure for accommodating informal interaction between teachers and students. For example, a short period about 30 min can be scheduled additionally in the school timetable for teachers to meet with students. This space enables teachers to see the positive development of students and students to engage in informal conversations with teachers. It also offers students an opportunity to express appreciation to teachers. In many countries, the teacher's day is scheduled in the national calendar. Schools can make this day explicit by remarking it in the school calendar and finding ways to make it visible on the day, such as by putting up a banner in the school website. Furthermore, to yield satisfaction for teachers, as also mentioned by Hargreaves (1999), mechanisms such as alumni association and other network between students and graduates to sustain teacher relationship with graduates can be established to create opportunities for teachers to appreciate the satisfaction they have in seeing the development and growth of students.

In order to enhance teacher–student interaction, schools could focus the attention of teachers on their teaching development by creating space in learning and teaching matters. Schools could evaluate teachers' workload and job responsibility. One way of doing this is to reallocate resources to support teachers in relieving those administrative duties that are time-consuming. This can create space for teachers to handle matters with students, and sustain teachers' enthusiasm in teaching as teachers would appreciate the feelings of satisfaction engendered by having more time to give support to students.

Second, school leaders can share with teachers the ethos and the mission of the school, emphasising student development as the key interest of the school and articulating it in school policies. For example, feedback on teacher's performance in teacher appraisal should tie to teacher professional development events, where an emphasis should be placed on learning and teaching. This suggestion is also agreed with by other educators in the literature (e.g. Iwanicki, 1998; Ovando, 2001; Robinson, Lloyd, & Rowe, 2008). In addition, evaluation of teaching can be used as a means of identifying areas of professional development (Isoré, 2009), instead of focusing on a summative grade. Supervisors and senior teachers could make use of the annual review to reinforce an environment that places student development as their prime concern, enhancing teachers' key interests in learning and teaching, and recognising teachers who are highly motivated in teaching and influencing teachers who are less engaged in supporting students. Focusing the discussion in teacher appraisal on ways of improving teaching can also lessen teachers' pressure because of heavy accountability in organisations.

Organisational Support to Promote Teacher Well-being

To promote positive emotions and teacher well-being, organisational support should be planned in a holistic manner to enable employees to be satisfied with their job and retain their positions. As social support giving is found to be positively associated with teachers' self-efficacy, school managers can develop teachers' work environment to help enhance teachers' self-efficacy.

School managers can adopt teacher satisfaction and positive affect as goals in planning the overall policies for the school to promote teacher's active participation and engagement in their work. These two concepts are found to enhance teacher satisfaction and job efficacy (Zembylas, 2003). To enhance teacher satisfaction, school managers should focus on empowering teachers by assigning jobs that are relevant to them based on their strengths (Fernet, Senécal, Guay, Marsh, & Dowson, 2008). Creating an autonomy-supportive school environment can allow teachers to be productive and creative; such an environment can create a safe environment for teachers. School leaders should exercise flexibility, encourage teacher autonomy, and implant respect in the school culture so that teachers feel proud to be members of the teaching profession. School leaders should acknowledge teachers' thoughts and provide

Recommendations: Preparing and Supporting Teacher Development

teachers with competence feedback (Deci, Eghrari, Patrick, & Leone, 1994) as a common norm in the school, therefore, teachers are willing to share and discuss and learn from others. To enable teachers to learn from each other, school leaders can arrange senior teachers and more experienced teacher mentors to share their experience with junior teachers, in innovative ways that cultivate teamwork and team spirit. For example, school leaders can design a shared-job policy to allow teachers to pair up and learn the jobs that teachers are interested in, even though they have yet to have any experience in doing it. In order to develop a working culture which is pleasant and engaging, common rooms and space for group discussion and luncheon are useful as they can encourage teachers and students to share and discuss academic, learning and teaching matters, and have conversations and share some leisure time together.

To enhance teachers' emotional well-being, school leaders should recognise that teacher emotion is not only an individual experience but also a collective matter of interest (Nias, 1996). Creating a supportive school environment for staff members is the most crucial factor. In school, support should be provided for novice teachers' to enhance their self-efficacy since they are at the stage of establishing teacher's identity in the classroom and in the profession (Day & Gu, 2007). Support systems such as mentoring can be developed in schools to help teachers engage in productive interactions and meaningful dialogues regarding student learning. It provides opportunities for teachers' reappraisal and formation of adaptive responses to work stress (Kahn, Schneider, & Jenkins-Henkelman, 2006), and can motivate them to further develop in the profession. School supervisors should present as warm and caring leaders, among other personality traits and management strategies. Caring leaders have been found to be positively related to the job satisfaction of teachers (Teven, 2007). Developing collegial support in school is crucial as positive relationships with colleagues can serve as an emotional resource to cope with external issues. This is also beneficial for professional development. This idea is also echoed by Day and Gu (2009). Moreover, efforts by the school leaders to maintain a trusting teacher–administrator relationship is essential; it can enhance teachers' feelings of connectedness to the school. School leaders' work with parents and teachers is crucial as the coordinated communication among teachers and parents can be targeted in consensual ways. It helps to cultivate the spirit of a working partnership among the school parties and the parents and creates a united force to support members of the team. This coordinating effort is deemed important as relationships with parents are identified as one of the most challenging elements of emotional work for teachers in the job of teaching.

Further Research

The chapter comes up with a few ideas for further research. Previous studies on teacher–student relationships suggest the type of social support which matters most to teachers is emotional support (such as teachers giving encouragement to students and assuring students about their confidence in doing their work). In many studies, the effect of 'love for students' on teachers is related to positive emotions such as joy and satisfaction. It appears that the nature of the type of social support that teachers give to their students, and how such support should be offered, is a clear topic for study to know about the emotional work of teaching. At present, research on the emotional work of teaching is scant, while this theme has emerged as a crucial one in teacher development research and educational theories (Batson, Ahmad, Lishner, & Tsang, 2016; Gallant, 2013; Isenbarger & Zembylas, 2006; Lam, 2011b; Tsang, 1998, 2011). Teachers' emotional work is a potential topic that calls for more classroom research on teachers, as identified in this chapter. Its findings may address the issues explored in this chapter such as teachers' commitment, caring practice, communication skills, teacher knowledge, and emotion, which underlie the expertise of teachers. Since the scope of studying the emotional work of teaching is very broad; in embarking on this topic, it may be useful for researchers to adopt the focuses generated from social support research. The focuses such as different approaches of support and types of support can be used to construct framework for understanding teacher's emotional work. The results of studying teachers' emotional work may further suggest content to guide teacher education programmes, which has a potential contribution to make to teacher education. Such studies could also have implications for identifying the scales of measuring social support in teaching, which is a potential area demanding further studies. The variation of styles of support giving to high and low ability students has also emerged as a topic that has important implications for teaching, such as which types of support would work better on a specific group of students (e.g. the types of help that suit high achievers vs. low achievers), and to inform practice. More in-depth school-based studies regarding teacher development policies and practice of how leaders lead teachers in the twenty-first century teaching environment to promote the forms of learning have also become an area of noticeable interest.

Conclusion

Teacher development is an important process of growth for teachers; however, with the teacher burnout issue and the dominant values of society of the twenty-first century, teacher development has become an increasingly worrying issue around the world. Positioning teachers as social support givers who maintain a strong commitment in supporting student learning upon teachers' empathetic concerns, the analysis of literature in this chapter affirms that 'love for students' is a common reason for teachers joining the teaching profession, and it is also the critical condition that maintains teachers' development in the teaching profession despite the challenges of the teaching job itself and in the educational environment. The chapter consolidates the evidence that teachers' social support giving to students is positively associated with their work-related self-efficacy, job satisfaction, and job aspiration. They also have to manage the discursive process of teaching within the social environment so as to

Conclusion

carry out teachers' goals and missions. This chapter also discusses the attributes that can facilitate good teaching practice such as the emotional work of teaching, teacher personality traits and teacher emotions. These topics suggest the need for enhancing teachers' psychological well-being. It also specifies the need for developing teacher's knowledge and the strategies in handling the challenging political environment in the workplace which is caused by the value conflicts of various stakeholders in different micro-systems. As a whole, the discussion implies important content of learning to prepare teachers for the day-to-day teaching in schools and the challenges in the profession, which can be adopted as the content of teacher education programmes.

The content regarding teachers' emotional work in the classroom is highly relevant to teachers' caring practice and the features of social support practice teachers demonstrate in teaching as discussed in Chaps. 4 and 5, suggesting that teaching is not only a series of techniques but a matter of caring for learners' affect in the social environment as well as the scaffoldings given to learners to engage them emotionally and help them learn and achieve cognitively.

The chapter highlights the negative impact of the performativity culture prevalent in the twenty-first century and makes a number of suggestions for creating supportive conditions to support teacher's development and growth in the profession. The chapter also conveys the important message that teacher's love for teaching is an essential quality for good teaching. Further research suggests a few research agendas to identify teachers support giving strategies to give more insights into the emotional work of teaching.

The chapter comprises a substantial component of the book regarding the benefits of social support giving to support providers, in the position of teachers. The analysis suggests that teachers' social support giving to students underlies the emotional work of teaching, and it is positively related to teachers' personal and professional development and contributes positively to their well-being. As social support in the context of learning and teaching is seen to be beneficial to learners and teachers, as discussed in the previous chapters, it is important that the environment should promote social support giving. Then teacher development is seen to be essential and teacher education to train and develop the social support traits of teachers in managing classroom teaching appears to be crucial as discussed in the implications taken from the chapter. Figure 6.1 summarises teachers' social support giving to students as explored in this chapter and the effects on such support for students as explored in Chap. 4; it depicts the positive outcomes on both the side of teachers and students, generally leading to teachers' career progress and students' positive educational outcomes.

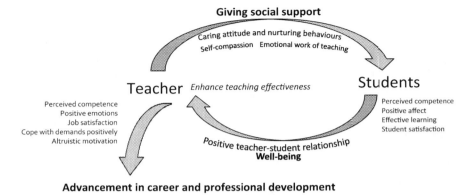

Fig. 6.1 The benefits of social support giving on teachers and the effects on students

References

Abenavoli, R. M., Jennings, P. A., Greenberg, M. T., Harris, A. R., & Katz, D. A. (2013). The protective effects of mindfulness against burnout among educators. *Psychology of Education Review, 37*(2), 57–69.
Adams, R. (2018). Why teachers in England are suffering from so much stress. *The Guardian*. Retrieved from https://www.theguardian.com/education/2018/jan/11/teachers-england-suffering-from-so-much-stress-explainer.
American Federation of Teachers. (2017). Retrieved from https://www.aft.org/news/survey-shows-educators-are-feeling-stressed-out.
Ashforth, B. E., & Humphrey, R. H. (1993). Emotional labor in service roles: The influence of identity. *Academy of Management Review, 18*(1), 88–115.
Astleitner, H. (2000). Designing emotionally sound instruction: The FEASP-approach. *Instructional Science, 28*(3), 169–198.
Ball, S. J. (2003). The teacher's soul and the terrors of performativity. *Journal of Education Policy, 18*(2), 215–228.
Ballet, K., Kelchtermans, G., & Loughran, J. (2006). Beyond intensification towards a scholarship of practice: Analysing changes in teachers' work lives. *Teachers and Teaching, 12*(2), 209–229.
Barnett, J., & Hodson, D. (2001). Pedagogical context knowledge: Toward a fuller understanding of what good science teachers know. *Science Education, 85*(4), 426–453.
Barty, K., Thomson, P., Blackmore, J., & Sachs, J. (2005). Unpacking the issues: Researching the shortage of school principals in two states in Australia. *The Australian Educational Researcher, 32*(3), 1–18.
Batson, C. D., Ahmad, N., Lishner, D. A., & Tsang, J. (2016). Empathy and altruism. Oxford handbook of hypo-egoic phenomena: *Theory and Research on the Quiet Ego*, 161–174.
Benight, C. C., & Bandura, A. (2004). Social cognitive theory of posttraumatic recovery: The role of perceived self-efficacy. *Behaviour Research and Therapy, 42*(10), 1129–1148.
Berliner, D. C. (2001). Learning about and learning from expert teachers. *International Journal of Educational Research, 35*(5), 463–482.
Betoret, F. D. (2006). Stressors, self-efficacy, coping resources, and burnout among secondary school teachers in Spain. *Educational Psychology, 26*(4), 519–539.
Blackmore, J. (2004). Leading as emotional management work in high risk times: The counterintuitive impulses of performativity and passion. *School Leadership & Management, 24*(4), 439–459.

References

Borko, H., & Livingston, C. (1989). Cognition and improvisation: Differences in mathematics instruction by expert and novice teachers. *American Educational Research Journal, 26*(4), 473–498.

Brotheridge, C. M., & Grandey, A. A. (2002). Emotional labor and burnout: Comparing two perspectives of "people work". *Journal of Vocational Behavior, 60*(1), 17–39.

Buttner, S., Pijl, S. J., Bijstra, J., & van den Bosch, E. (2015). Personality traits of expert teachers of students with behavioural problems: A review and classification of the literature. *The Australian Educational Researcher, 42*(4), 461–481.

Carson, R. L., Baumgartner, J. J., Matthews, R. A., & Tsouloupas, C. N. (2010). Emotional exhaustion, absenteeism, and turnover intentions in childcare teachers: Examining the impact of physical activity behaviors. *Journal of Health Psychology, 15*(6), 905–914.

Carson, R. L., & Templin, T. J. (2007, April). *Emotional regulation and teacher burnout: Who says that the management of emotional expression doesn't matter*. In American Education Research Association Annual Convention, Chicago.

Chan, D. W. (2013). Subjective well-being of Hong Kong Chinese teachers: The contribution of gratitude, forgiveness, and the orientations to happiness. *Teaching and Teacher Education, 33*, 22–30.

Chan, K. B., Lai, G., Ko, Y. C., & Boey, K. W. (2000). Work stress among six professional groups: The Singapore experience. *Social Science and Medicine, 50*(10), 1415–1432.

Chang, M. L. (2009). *Teacher emotional management in the classroom: Appraisals, regulation, and coping with emotions*. In Annual Meeting of the American Educational Research Association, San Diego, CA.

Changying, W. (2007). Analysis of teacher attrition. *Chinese Education & Society, 40*(5), 6–10.

Chen, J. (2016). Understanding teacher emotions: The development of a teacher emotion inventory. *Teaching and Teacher Education, 55*, 68–77.

Chiu, R. K., & Kosinski, F. A. (1997). Relationships between dispositional traits and self-reported job satisfaction and distress: An investigation of nurses and teachers in Hong Kong. *Journal of Managerial Psychology, 12*(2), 71–84.

Choi, P. K. (2003). Introduction: Education policy in Hong Kong. *Journal of Education Policy, 18*, 637–639.

Choi, P. L., & Tang, S. Y. F. (2009). Teacher commitment trends: Cases of Hong Kong teachers from 1997 to 2007. *Teaching & Teacher Education, 25*, 767–777.

Cordes, C. L., & Dougherty, T. W. (1993). A review and an integration of research on job burnout. *Academy of Management Review, 18*(4), 621–656.

Cornelius-White, J. (2007). Learner-centered teacher-student relationships are effective: A meta-analysis. *Review of Educational Research, 77*(1), 113–143.

Darling-Hammond, L. (2001). The challenge of staffing our schools. *Educational Leadership, 58*(8), 12–17.

Day, C. (2004). The passion of successful leadership. School *Leadership & Management, 24*(4), 425–437.

Day, C., & Gu, Q. (2007). Variations in the conditions for teachers' professional learning and development: Sustaining commitment and effectiveness over a career. *Oxford Review of Education, 33*(4), 423–443.

Day, C., & Gu, Q. (2009). Veteran teachers: Commitment, resilience and quality retention. *Teachers and Teaching: Theory and Practice, 15*(4), 441–457.

Deci, E. L., Eghrari, H., Patrick, B. C., & Leone, D. R. (1994). Facilitating internalization: The self-determination theory perspective. *Journal of Personality, 62*(1), 119–142.

Denson, T. (2009). Socrates, (469–399 BC). Retrieved from http://www.automotive-technology.co.uk/?p=165.

Denzin, N. K. (1994). *On understanding emotion*. Transaction Publishers.

Department for Education and Skills. (2005). *Statistics of education: School workforce in England* (2004th ed.). London: DfES.

Dewey, J. (1933). *How we think: A restatement of the relation of reflective thinking to the educative process*. DC: Heath and Company.

Dorn, S. (1998). The political legacy of school accountability systems. *Education Policy Analysis Archives, 6*(1), 2–32.

Dudley, P. (2013). Teacher learning in Lesson Study: What interaction-level discourse analysis revealed about how teachers utilised imagination, tacit knowledge of teaching and fresh evidence of pupils learning, to develop practice knowledge and so enhance their pupils' learning. *Teaching and Teacher Education, 34,* 107–121.

Durlak, J. A., Dymnicki, A. B., Taylor, R. D., Weissberg, R. P., Schellinger, K. B., Dubois, D., ... & O'brien, M. U. (2007). *Collaborative for Academic, Social, and Emotional Learning (CASEL)*.

Eccles, J. S., & Roeser, R. (1999). School and community influences on human development. In M. Bornstein & M. Lamb (Eds.), *Developmental psychology: An advanced textbook* (4th ed., pp. 503–554). Mahwah, NJ: Lawrence Erlbaum.

Edwards, A., & Mackenzie, L. (2005). Steps towards participation: The social support of learning trajectories. *International Journal of Lifelong Education, 24*(4), 287–302.

Elbaz, F. (1981). The teacher's "practical knowledge": Report of a case study. *Curriculum inquiry, 11*(1), 43–71.

England, P., Farkas, G., Kilbourne, B. S., & Dou, T. (1988). Explaining occupational sex segregation and wages: Findings from a model with fixed effects. *American Sociological Review*, 544–558.

Eraut, M. (2000). Non-formal learning and tacit knowledge in professional work. *British Journal of Educational Psychology, 70*(1), 113–136.

Fernandez, C., Cannon, J., & Chokshi, S. (2003). A US–Japan lesson study collaboration reveals critical lenses for examining practice. *Teaching and Teacher Education, 19*(2), 171–185.

Fernet, C., Senécal, C., Guay, F., Marsh, H., & Dowson, M. (2008). The work tasks motivation scale for teachers (WTMST). *Journal of Career Assessment, 16*(2), 256–279.

Forrester, G. (2005). All in a day's work: Primary teachers 'performing' and 'caring'. *Gender and Education, 17*(3), 271–287.

Fredrickson, B. L. (1998). What good are positive emotions? *Review of General Psychology, 2,* 300–319.

Gallant, A. (2013). Self-conscious emotion: How two teachers explore the emotional work of teaching. In N. Melissa et al. (Eds.), *Emotion and school: Understanding how the hidden curriculum influences relationships, leadership, teaching, and learning* (pp. 163–181). Emerald Group Publishing Limited.

Gecas, V., & Schwalbe, M. L. (1983). Beyond the looking glass self: Social structure and efficacy-based self-esteem. *Social Psychology Quarterly, 46,* 77–88.

Goldstein, E. (2015). *Uncovering happiness: Overcoming depression with mindfulness and self-compassion*. New York: Simon & Schuster.

Goldstein, L. S., & Lake, V. E. (2000). "Love, love, and more love for children": Exploring preservice teachers' understandings of caring. *Teaching and Teacher Education, 16*(8), 861–872.

Guerra, N., Modecki, K., & Cunningham, W., (2014). Developing social-emotional skills for the labor market: The practice model. *World Bank Policy Research Working Paper No. 7123*. Retrieved from: https://ssrn.com/abstract=2530772 Gwegwe, Ngcwele (2016). *A checklist for every parent*. Retrieved from Smashwords http://gabrielatardea-development.blogspot.hk/2010/01/educational-quotes-by-famous.html.

Hatton, N., & Smith, D. (1995). Reflection in teacher education: Towards definition and implementation. *Teaching and Teacher Education, 11*(1), 33–49.

Hamre, B. K., & Pianta, R. C. (2006). Student-teacher relationships. In G. G. Bear & K. M. Minke (Eds.), *Children's needs III: Development, prevention, and intervention* (pp. 59–71). Washington, DC, US: National Association of School Psychologists.

Hargreaves, A. (1994). *Changing teachers, changing times: Teachers' work and culture in the postmodern age*. New York: Teachers College Press.

References

273

Hargreaves, A. (1999). The psychic rewards (and annoyances) of teaching. In M. Hammersley (Ed.), *Researching school experience: Ethnographic studies of teaching and learning* (pp. 85–104). London & New York: Falmer Press.

Hargreaves, A. (2000). Mixed emotions: Teachers' perceptions of their interactions with students. *Teaching and Teacher Education, 16*(8), 811–826.

Hargreaves, A. (2001). Emotional geographies of teaching. *Teachers College Record, 103*(6), 1056–1080.

Hargreaves, A. (2005). The emotions of teaching and educational change. In A. Hargreaves (Ed.), *Extending educational change: International handbook of educational change* (pp. 278–295). Springer: Dordrecht.

Hargreaves, A., & Fullan, M. (2012). *Professional capital: Transforming teaching in every school.* Teachers College Press.

Hebson, G., Earnshaw, J., & Marchington, L. (2007). Too emotional to be capable? The changing nature of emotion work in definitions of 'capable teaching'. *Journal of Education Policy, 22*(6), 675–694.

Hen, M., & Goroshit, M. (2016). Social–emotional competencies among teachers: An examination of interrelationships. *Cogent Education, 3*(1), 1151996.

Herzberg, F. (2005). Motivation-hygiene theory. In J. B. Miner (Eds.), *Organizational behavior one: Essential theories of motivation and leadership* (pp. 61–74). New York: ME Sharpe Inc.

Hochschild, A. R. (1983). *The managed heart: Commercialization of human feeling.* Berkeley, CA: University of California Press.

Hong Kong Federation of Education Workers. (2011). *Teachers' administrative work and happiness.* Retrieved February 4, 2013 from http://www.hkfew.org.hk/upload/article/20120105/20111115A.pdf (in Chinese).

Hong Kong Federation of Education Workers. (2015, May). [Teacher well-being questionnaire]. Retrieved from https://hkfew.org.hk/UPFILE/ArticleFile/201552117534113.pdf.

Hong Kong Federation of Education Workers. (2016, June). [Teacher well-being questionnaire]. Retrieved from https://hkfew.org.hk/ckfinder/userfiles/files/%E3%80%8C%E6%95%99%E5%B8%AB%E8%BA%AB%E5%BF%83%E5%81%A5%E5%BA%B7%E3%80%8D%E5%95%8F%E5%8D%B7%E8%AA%BF%E6%9F%A5.pdf.

Isenbarger, L., & Zembylas, M. (2006). The emotional labour of caring in teaching. *Teaching and Teacher Education, 22*(1), 120–134.

Isoré, M. (2009). Teacher evaluation: Current practices in OECD countries and a literature review. *OECD Education Working Papers, No. 23.* OECD Publishing (NJ1).

Iwanicki, E. F. (1998). Evaluation in supervision. In G. R. Firth & E. F. Pajak (Eds.), *Handbook of research on school supervision* (pp. 138–175). New York: Simon & Schuster.

Jennings, P. A., & Greenberg, M. T. (2009). The prosocial classroom: Teacher social and emotional competence in relation to student and classroom outcomes. *Review of Educational Research, 79*(1), 491–525.

Jennings, P. A., Snowberg, K. E., Coccia, M. A., & Greenberg, M. T. (2011). Improving classroom learning environments by cultivating awareness and resilience in education (CARE): Results of two pilot studies. *The Journal of Classroom Interaction, 46*(1), 37–48.

Johnson, S., Cooper, C., Cartwright, S., Donald, I., Taylor, P., & Millet, C. (2005). The experience of work-related stress across occupations. *Journal of Managerial Psychology, 20*(2), 178–187.

Kabat-Zinn, J. (1994). *Wherever you go, there you are: Mindfulness meditation in everyday life.* New York: Hyperion.

Kahana, E., Bhatta, T., Lovegreen, L. D., Kahana, B., & Midlarsky, E. (2013). Altruism, helping, and volunteering: Pathways to well-being in late life. *Journal of aging and health, 25*(1), 159–187.

Kahn, J. H., Schneider, K. T., Jenkins-Henkelman, T. M., & Moyle, L. L. (2006). Emotional social support and job burnout among high-school teachers: Is it all due to dispositional affectivity? *Journal of Organizational Behavior, 27*(6), 793–807.

Kember, D. (2001). *Reflective teaching and learning in the health professions.* Oxford: Blackwell Science.

Lai, K. C., Chan, K. W., Ko, K. W., & So, K. S. (2005). Teaching as a career: A perspective from Hong Kong senior secondary students. *Journal of Education for Teaching, 31*(3), 153–168.

Lai, K. C., & Law, K. Y. (2010). *Primary and secondary school teacher workload study report.* Hong Kong: Hong Kong Institute of Education. Retrieved from http://www.ied.edu.hk/upload_main/main/file/100909_report.pdf.

Lam, B. H. (2011a). Teacher as researcher and teacher development. In S. N. Phillipson & B. H. Lam (Eds.), *Learning and teaching in the Chinese classroom* (pp. 231–264). Hong Kong: HKU Press.

Lam, B. H. (2011b). A reflective account of a pre-service teacher's effort to implement progressive curriculum in field practice. *Schools: Studies in Education, 8*(1), 22–39.

Lam, B. H. (2012). Why do they want to become teachers? A study on prospective teachers' motivation to teach in Hong Kong. *The Asian Pacific Education Researcher, 21*(2), 307–314.

Lam, B. H. (2015). There is no fear in love—The giving of social support to students enhances teachers' career development. In R. Osbourne (Ed.), *Job satisfaction: Determinants, workplace implications and impacts on psychological well-being* (pp. 73–96). Hauppauge, NY: Nova Science Publishers.

Lam, B. H., & Yan, H. F. (2011). Beginning teachers' job satisfaction: The impact of school-based factors. *Teacher Development, 15*(3), 333–348.

Lau, P. S. Y., Chan, R. M. C., Yuen, M., Myers, J. E., & Lee, Q. A. Y. (2008). Wellness of teachers: A neglected issue in teacher development. In J. C. K. Lee & L. P. Shiu (Eds.), *Developing teachers and developing schools in changing contexts* (pp. 101–116). Hong Kong: The Chinese University Press.

Lave, J., & Wenger, E. (1991). *Situated learning: Legitimate peripheral participation.* Cambridge: Cambridge University Press.

Lave, J., & Wenger, E. (2005). Practice, person, social world. In H. Daniel (Ed.). *An introduction to Vygotsky* (pp. 149–156). London & New York: Routledge.

Lee, T. H. (2000). *Education in traditional China: A history* (Vol. 13). Boston: Brill.

Leonard, D., & Sensiper, S. (1998). The role of tacit knowledge in group innovation. *California Management Review, 40*(3), 112–132.

Levin, B. (2010). Governments and education reform: Some lessons from the last 50 years. *Journal of Education Policy, 25*(6), 739–747.

Lewis, C., Perry, R., & Murata, A. (2006). How should research contribute to instructional improvement? The case of lesson study. *Educational Researcher, 35*(3), 3–14.

Lieberman, J. (2009). Reinventing teacher professional norms and identities: The role of lesson study and learning communities. *Professional Development in Education, 35*(1), 83–99.

Locke, E. A., & Latham, G. P. (1990). *A theory of goal setting & task performance.* Englewood Cliffs, NJ, US: Prentice-Hall Inc.

Lortie, D. (1975). *Schoolteacher: A sociological analysis.* Chicago: University of Chicago.

Mahoney, P., Menter, I., & Hextall, I. (2003). *Edu-business: Are teachers working in a new world.* In Annual Meeting of the American Educational Research Association, Chicago (April).

Martin, A. J., Collie, R. J., & Frydenberg, E. (2017). Social and emotional learning: Lessons learned and opportunities going forward. In E. Fridenberg, A., Martin, & R. Collie (Eds.), *Social and emotional learning in Australia and the Asia-Pacific* (pp. 459–471). Singapore: Springer.

McCaughtry, N. (2004). The emotional dimensions of a teacher's pedagogical content knowledge: Influences on content, curriculum, and pedagogy. *Journal of Teaching in Physical Education, 23*(1), 30–47.

Midlarsky, E. (1991). Helping as coping. In M. S. Clark (Ed.), *Review of personality and social psychology* (Vol. 12, pp. 238–264). Prosocial behavior. Thousand Oaks, CA, US: Sage Publications, Inc.

Mishra, P., & Koehler, M. J. (2006). Technological pedagogical content knowledge: A framework for teacher knowledge. *Teachers College Record, 108*(6), 1017.

Mo, K. W. (1991). Teacher burnout: Relations with stress, personality, and social support. *Education Journal, 19*(1), 3–11.

References

Montgomery, C., & Rupp, A. A. (2005). A meta-analysis for exploring the diverse causes and effects of stress in teachers. *Canadian Journal of Education/Revue Canadienne de l'Education, 28*(3), 458–486.

Morris, J. A., & Feldman, D. C. (1996). The dimensions, antecedents, and consequences of emotional labor. *Academy of Management Review, 21*(4), 986–1010.

Murata, A. (2011). Introduction: Conceptual overview of lesson study. In *Lesson study research and practice in mathematics education* (pp. 1–12). Springer Netherlands.

Muraven, M., & Baumeister, R. F. (2000). Self-regulation and depletion of limited resources: Does self-control resemble a muscle? *Psychological Bulletin, 126*(2), 247.

National Center for Education Statistics. (2005). *Schools and staffing survey (SASS) and teacher follow-up survey (TFS)*. Data File. Washington, DC: U.S. Department of Education. Retrieved from http://nces.ed.gov/surveys/SASS.

National Council for the Accreditation of Teacher Education. (2006). *Professional standards for the accreditation of schools, colleges, and departments of education*. Retrieved from http://www.ncate.org/documents/standards/unit_stnds_2006.pdf.

National Education Association. (2015). *Preparing 21st century students for a global society*. Retrieved from http://www.nea.org/assets/docs/A-Guide-to-Four-Cs.pdf.

Neff, K. D., Rude, S. S., & Kirkpatrick, K. L. (2007). An examination of self-compassion in relation to positive psychological functioning and personality traits. *Journal of Research in Personality, 41*(4), 908–916.

Ng, K. C. (2011, August 29). Stressed teachers suffer in silence. South China Morning Post.

Ngcwele, N. (2016). *A checklist for every parent*. Retrieved from Smashwords: http://gabrielatardea-development.blogspot.hk/2010/01/educational-quotes-by-famous.html.

Nias, J. (1996). Thinking about feeling: The emotions in teaching. *Cambridge Journal of Education, 26*(3), 293–306.

Nias, J., Southworth, G., & Yeomans, R. (1989). *Staff relationships in the primary school: A study of organizational cultures*. Mansell.

Nicholl, B., & McLellan, R. (2008). 'We're all in this game whether we like it or not to get a number of As to Cs'. Design and technology teachers' struggles to implement creativity and performativity policies. *British Educational Research Journal, 34*(5), 585–600.

Noddings, N. (2013). *Caring: A relational approach to ethics and moral education* (2nd ed.). California: University of California Press.

Noddings, N. (2015). *The challenge to care in schools* (2nd ed.). Teachers College Press.

O'Connor, K. E. (2008). "You choose to care": Teachers, emotions and professional identity. *Teaching and Teacher Education, 24*(1), 117–126.

OECD. (2009). *Making reform happen in education*. (Paper prepared for the Education Committee, EDU/EDPC(2009)20). Paris: OECD.

Office for National Statistics (2017). *UK Perspectives 2016: In continuation of Regional and Country Profiles*. London: Dandy Booksellers.

Oldham, J. (2010). Positive and negative emotions. *Journal of Psychiatric Practice, 16*(2), 71.

Omoto, A. M., Malsch, A. M., & Barraza, J. A. (2009). Compassionate acts: Motivations for and correlates of volunteerism among old adults. In B. Fehr, S. Sprecher, & L. G. Underwood (Eds.), *The science of compassionate love: Theory, research, and applications* (pp. 257–282). Malden, MA: Wiley-Blackwell.

Ouweneel, E., Le Blanc, P. M., & Schaufeli, W. B. (2013). Do-it-yourself: An online positive psychology intervention to promote positive emotions, self-efficacy, and engagement at work. *Career Development International, 18*(2), 173–195.

Ovando, M. N. (2001). Teachers' perceptions of a learner-centered teacher evaluation system. *Journal of Personnel Evaluation in Education, 15*(3), 213–231.

Patrick, H., & Pintrich, P. R. (2001). Conceptual change in teachers' intuitive conceptions of learning, motivation, and instruction: The role of motivational and epistemological beliefs. In T. Bruce & R. J. Sternberg (Eds.), *Understanding and teaching the intuitive mind: Student and teacher learning* (pp. 117–143). London: Lawrence Erlbaum Associates.

Pearson, L. C., & Moomaw, W. (2006). Continuing validation of the teaching autonomy scale. *The Journal of Educational Research, 100*(1), 44–51.

Richards, J. M., & Gross, J. J. (2000). Emotion regulation and memory: The cognitive costs of keeping one's cool. *Journal of Personality and Social Psychology, 79*(3), 410–424.

Robertson, D. R. (2001). Beyond learner-centeredness: Close encounters of the systemocentric kind. *Journal of Faculty Development, 18*(1), 7–13.

Robinson, V. M., Lloyd, C. A., & Rowe, K. J. (2008). The impact of leadership on student outcomes: An analysis of the differential effects of leadership types. *Educational Administration Quarterly, 44*(5), 635–674.

Roeser, R. W., & Eccles, J. S. (2015). Mindfulness and compassion in human development: Introduction to the special section. *Developmental Psychology, 51*(1), 1.

Roeser, R. W., Schonert-Reichl, K. A., Jha, A., Cullen, M., Wallace, L., Wilensky, R., ... & Harrison, J. (2013). Mindfulness training and reductions in teacher stress and burnout: Results from two randomized, waitlist-control field trials. *Journal of Educational Psychology, 105*(3), 787–804.

Rogers, C. R. (1983). *Freedom to learn for the 80's*. Columbus: Charles E. Merrill Publishing Company.

Rosenholtz, S. J., & Simpson, C. (1990). Workplace conditions and the rise and fall of teachers' commitment. *Sociology of Education, 64*(4), 241–257.

Ryan, R. M., & Deci, E. L. (2000). Intrinsic and extrinsic motivations: Classic definitions and new directions. *Contemporary Educational Psychology, 25*(1), 54–67.

Ryan, R. M., & Deci, E. L. (2011). A self-determination theory perspective on social, institutional, cultural, and economic supports for autonomy and their importance for well-being. In *Human autonomy in cross-cultural context* (pp. 45–64). Springer: Dordrecht.

Sachs, J. (2003). *The activist teaching profession*. Buckingham: Open University Press.

Salzberg, S. (1995). *Loving-kindness: The revolutionary art of happiness*. Boston: Shambhala.

Schaufeli, W. B., Leiter, M. P., & Maslach, C. (2009). Burnout: 35 years of research and practice. *Career Development International, 14*(3), 204–220.

Schaufeli, W., & Salanova, M. (2007). Work engagement: What do we know? *Managing social and ethical issues in organizations, 135,* 177. Retrieved from http://www.psihologietm.ro/OHPworkshop/schaufeli_work_engagement_1.pdf.

Schon, D. A. (1983). *The reflective practitioner: How professionals think in action*. New York: Basic Books.

Schwartz, C. E., & Sendor, R. M. (1999). Helping others helps oneself: Response shift effects in peer support. *Social Science and Medicine, 48*(11), 1563–1575.

Scott, C., Stone, B., & Dinham, S. (2001). I love teaching but.... international patterns of teacher discontent. *Education Policy Analysis Archives, 9*(28), 1–7.

Shulman, L. S. (1986). Those who understand: Knowledge growth in teaching. *Educational Researcher, 15*(2), 4–14.

Shulman, L. S. (2000). Teacher development: Roles of domain expertise and pedagogical knowledge. *Journal of Applied Developmental Psychology, 21*(1), 129–135.

Sinclair, C. (2008). Initial and changing student teacher motivation and commitment to teaching. *Asia-Pacific Journal of Teacher Education, 36*(2), 79–104.

Slater, R., Veach, P. M., & Li, Z. (2013). Recognizing and managing countertransference in the college classroom: An exploration of expert teachers' inner experiences. *Innovative Higher Education, 38*(1), 3–17.

Spring, J. (2017). *American education*. Routledge.

Steinhardt, M. A., Smith Jaggars, S. E., Faulk, K. E., & Gloria, C. T. (2011). Chronic work stress and depressive symptoms: Assessing the mediating role of teacher burnout. *Stress and Health, 27*(5), 420–429.

Sutton, R. E., & Wheatley, K. F. (2003). Teachers' emotions and teaching: A review of the literature and directions for future research. *Educational Psychology Review, 15*(4), 327–358.

Tang, T. O., & Yeung, A. S. (1999). *Hong Kong teachers' sources of stress, burnout, and job satisfaction*. Paper presented at the International Conference on Teacher Education, Hong Kong.

References

Teven, J. J. (2007). Teacher temperament: Correlates with teacher caring, burnout, and organizational outcomes. *Communication Education, 56*(3), 382–400.

Thomson, P. (2001). How principals lose 'face': A disciplinary tale of educational administration and managerialism. *Discourse, 22*(1), 1–28.

Titus, L., & Ora, K. (2005). Teacher education. In M. Bray & R. Koo (Eds.), *Education and society in Hong Kong and Macao* (pp. 73–85). Netherlands: Springer.

Troman, G. (2008). Primary teacher identity, commitment and career in performative school cultures. *British Educational Research Journal, 34*(5), 619–633.

Tsang, K. K. (2011). Emotional labor of teaching. *Educational Research, 2*(8), 1312–1316.

Tsang, N. M. (1998). Re-examining reflection—A common issue of professional concern in social work, teacher and nursing education. *Journal of Interprofessional Care, 12*(1), 21–31.

Tschannen-Moran, M., Woolfolk, Hoy A., & Hoy, W. K. (1998). Teacher efficacy: Its meaning and measure. *Review of Educational Research, 68*, 202–248.

Vavrus, M. (2008). Culturally responsive teaching. *21st Century Education: A Reference Handbook, 2*, 49–57. Retrieved from https://static1.squarespace.com/static/55a68b71e4b075daf6b2aa0b/t/55a7322ae4b0a573ba71de46/1437020714535/CulturallyResponsiveTeaching.pdf.

Veldman, I., van Tartwijk, J., Brekelmans, M., & Wubbels, T. (2013). Job satisfaction and teacher–student relationships across the teaching career: Four case studies. *Teaching and Teacher Education, 32*, 55–65.

Wang, K. L., & Groth, M. (2014). Buffering the negative effects of employee surface acting: The moderating role of employee–customer relationship strength and personalized services. *Journal of Applied Psychology, 99*(2), 341.

Wentzel, K. R., & Miele, D. B. (2009). Promoting self-determined school engagement: Motivation, learning, and well-being. In K. R. Wentzel & D. B. Miele (Eds.), *Handbook of motivation at school* (pp. 185–210). Routledge.

Wilkinson, G. (2007). Civic professionalism: Teacher education and professional ideals and values in a commercialised education world. *Journal of Education for Teaching, 33*(3), 379–395.

Woods, P., Bagley, C., & Glatter, R. (2005). *School choice and competition: Markets in the public interest?* Routledge.

Yeh, Y., & Hayes, J. A. (2011). How does disclosing countertransference affect perceptions of the therapist and the session? *Psychotherapy, 48*(4), 322–329.

Yeung, A. S., & Liu, W. P. (2007). *Workload and psychological wellbeing of Hong Kong teachers.* Paper presented at the Australian Association for Research in Education, Fremantle.

Yilmaz, K., Altinkurt, Y., Guner, M., & Sen, B. (2015). The relationship between teachers' emotional labor and burnout level. *Eurasian Journal of Educational Research, 59*, 75–90.

Yin, H. B., & Lee, J. C. K. (2012). Be passionate, but be rational as well: Emotional rules for Chinese teachers' work. *Teaching and Teacher Education, 28*(1), 56–65.

Zembylas, M. (2003). Emotions and teacher identity: A post-structural perspective. *Teachers and Teaching, 9*(3), 213–238.

Zembylas, M. (2005). Beyond teacher cognition and teacher beliefs: The value of the ethnography of emotions in teaching. *International Journal of Qualitative Studies in Education, 18*(4), 465–487.

Zembylas, M. (2007). Emotional ecology: The intersection of emotional knowledge and pedagogical content knowledge in teaching. *Teaching and Teacher Education, 23*(4), 355–367.

Zembylas, M., & Schutz, P. A. (2009). Research on teachers' emotions in education: Findings, practical implications and future agenda. In P. Schutz & M. Zembylas (Eds.), *Advances in teacher emotion research* (pp. 367–377). Springer: Boston, MA.

Zeng, P. (2005). *Teacher evaluation in Chinese elementary schools: An historical account.* Scholars Archive: Brigham Young University.

Chapter 7
Constructing a Supportive Environment for Student Learning and Teacher Development

Abstract This chapter provides the conclusion to the book. It presents the key concepts and investigation results explored in Chaps. 2–6, followed by the key recommendations, a statement of the contribution of the book and future research directions and limitation. The chapter begins with a discussion of the philosophical beliefs encountered in the classical literature, acknowledging social support as a positive virtue that can help one enjoy a well-lived life. It further discusses the decline of social network systems, and the social values that continue to undermine the healthy development of youngsters in our twenty-first century, knowledge-based society. The rising trend of poor mental health worldwide is outlined, which supplies the background to suggest a renewed interest of social support in education. A synthesised report of the key content of the book is presented. It begins with the description of various social support assumptions and their functions, and the research issues related to social support. It further describes teachers' social support and other social support resources in the classroom as reviewed in the book. Based on the review of social support across the fields of health psychology and education, a meta-theory is derived suggesting that social bonds, relationships and a supportive environment are crucial factors to support learning in schools. The results of studies on expert teachers' social support behaviour are reported. Social support is realised as an important and crucial trait that enhances teacher's teaching expertise, and the triad of teaching expertise is recommended as a potential topic for further investigation regarding teaching expertise. The results of studies of social support givers in the role of teacher are discussed. It suggests that social support giving is positively associated with teachers' self-efficacy, and that teachers' self-efficacy can drive their career advancement and overcome the pressure teachers may experience in teaching. The results suggest that 'love for students' is a trait of good teachers, and social support as the behaviour driven by the love for students helps teachers develop teaching expertise, and also leads to teachers' better career development. Recommendations derived from the book are then discussed. They suggest the core values for establishing a supportive social environment to support student learning,

---

The original version of this chapter was revised: Belated corrections have been incorporated. The correction to this chapter is available at https://doi.org/10.1007/978-981-13-3577-8_8

© Springer Nature Singapore Pte Ltd. 2019
B. LAM, *Social Support, Well-being, and Teacher Development*,
https://doi.org/10.1007/978-981-13-3577-8_7

280   7 Constructing a Supportive Environment for Student …

and proposes directions for teacher training and professional development, and ways to enhance teacher-efficacy in the organisational context. On the basis of its content, this chapter discusses the contributions the book makes to the academic community, makes suggestions for further investigation and discusses the book's limitations.

Social Support—Human's Innate Ability to Connect

Humans are designed by evolution to be group-living animals, bestowed with instruments that allow them to flourish within social situations (Caporeal, 1997), along with an innate need to affiliate with their fellow humans (Galea et al., 2002). When deprived of healthy relationships, humans tend to demonstrate various behavioural symptoms, including depression (Barrera, 1986), aggression (Anderson & Bushman, 2002) and even suicidal tendencies (Gliatto & Rai, 1999) that may disadvantage and constrain one's development. It is within this background that the concept of 'social support' gained prominence in health psychology, and later, psychology in general, which studies the link between psychological processes and health.

The classical literature also suggests the beneficial effect of social support to echo the importance of social relationships. Artistotle (384 BC—322 BC), in his *Nicomachean Ethics*, stated that the pursuit of pleasure and wealth is not what a 'human' life should aim for; he proposed Eudaimonia (well-being) as the proper goal of human life that can be achieved by becoming involved in the cultivation of virtue (Fowers, 2012). A virtue is a character trait. Aristotle believed that virtue is a positive trait that makes its possessor a good human being. He also believed that human nature contains all the positive virtues; by practicing them one can succeed in one's own purpose (Borchet, 2006) and achieve happiness. This kind of happiness does not equal activities that are merely pleasure-producing, but related to work that may lead to wellness and good for people (Ryan & Deci, 2001), such as maintaining good social relationships. It can help one develop a well-lived life—a good life (Hursthouse, 2001). This explains why human beings are eager to provide voluntary help to one another, such as mentoring junior colleagues and giving extra help to students. The effect of receiving and giving support is powerful both for the taker and the giver. Artistotle agreed that humans are social and moral beings who enjoy sharing, giving and taking, and taking care of others; they treasure the reciprocal feeling of friendship, and demonstrate civic virtues of living together (Vetlesen & Nortvedt, 2000, as cited in Jørgensen & Nafstad, 2005). This philosophical assumption is in some way consistent with Confucian (551 BC–479 BC) philosophy, suggesting that the life of an ideal person, also called sage (聖人) (Lee, 2000), is committed to the search for personal moral perfection (Lam, 2011a); socially, the sage collects friends and 'through these friends he promotes humanity' (the Analects, as cited in Lee, 2000, p. 10).

While social support is suggested as a spontaneous human behaviour that is universal to the livelihood of human beings, the twenty-first century has shown a farther distance existing between people due to the globalisation of the economy. The description of some of the societal issues will serve as the backdrop to explain the motive for writing this book.

Societal Background and Problems in the Education Environment

In the world around us a competitive global economy is shaped by a 'process in which traditional boundaries separating individuals and societies gradually and increasingly recede' (Okasha, 2005, p. 1). It increases interdependency of different countries and creates opportunities for economic advancement; however, it also creates drawbacks that affect the life of school-aged students, the youth, and teachers in every society. This background acts as the backdrop to this book.

At the outset, the global economy of the twenty-first-century society affects the younger generation regarding their personal values and state of well-being. Evidence proves that in the global culture, materialism is spreading among adolescents across nations (Twenge & Kasser, 2013), and it leads people to seek materialistic values instead of the pursuit of higher values (Larson, 2002) such as the virtues of life. Such materialism creates symptoms of anxiety and distress among people (Kasser & Ahuvia, 2002), poor social relationships (Kasser & Ryan, 2001) and less academic competence (King & Datu, 2017).

Consumerism beliefs lower people's social engagement, and correlate with negative emotion, aggressiveness, mistrust and reduced feelings of personal responsibility (Bauer, Wilkie, Kim, & Bodenhausen, 2012). Materialistic individuals also tend to prefer greater distance from other people and be more hesitant to give help (Bauer et al., 2012; Vohs, Mead, & Goode, 2006). While culture is often regarded as a coping resource to support the development of self-esteem, the fading of local cultures undermines the psychological protective effects of social identities as individuals (Arnett, 2002). As globalisation is in progress, people are increasingly disconnected from one another, as they witness changes to the social support system (Sharma & Sharma, 2010). As society emphasises personal achievement (Gottfredson & Hirschi, 1990), it has resulted in a loss of social cohesion.

The decline in mental health worldwide recently has alerted researchers to the negative health conditions in society. One in every four people in the world is suffering from or has had the experience of mental disorders, and approximately 450 million people suffered from these conditions in 2001 (World Health Organization [WHO], 2001), and a further upward trend is expected. Depression is presently one of the most common mental disorders and also a main cause of disability across the world. Currently, it affects an estimated 300 million people worldwide (WHO, 2017). Declining mental health levels also trigger suicide cases—every 40 s a person dies by suicide and there are many more unknown attempts. The situation is so alarming that suicide has become the second leading cause of death globally among young people aged 15–29 (WHO, 2014), who should have been entitled to a fruitful adolescence and young adulthood.

As achievement is regarded as a common goal in life in a materialistic world, academic pressure has overwhelmed students over the world (Arun & Chavan, 2009; Cheung & Chiu, 2016). In the case of Hong Kong, for example, the mentality of 'winning at the starting line' is common (Hong Kong Institute of Asia-Pacific Studies,

2016). School sees examination results as the benchmark for success. The education system is not the only one to blame; as social relationships weaken, youngsters nowadays engage heavily in the Internet, where they have control of viewing what they like and freely 'unfriend' people they dislike. This gradually leads to a decline in interpersonal skills and resilience (Cheung & Chiu, 2016). Together with their over-protective parents' shelter, students find it difficult to learn how to solve their own problems in real life and they lack social support and skills to cope with stress properly. Hence, once the young people fail in school work, they feel useless. Although the authority has attempted to employ a 'no-loser' principle (Education Commission, 2000, p. 9), a number of students see themselves as losers (Bray, 2017) and suicide becomes their last resort to escape from the stress.

The education environment has also caused frustration for teachers. Though many of the education reforms in different countries are planned to fit the next generation for the knowledge-based society (e.g. Curriculum Development Council, 2014), nowadays, because of the competition brought by a globalised economy, schools and teachers are under pressure to gain examination results (Barbara, 2004). As the schools are governed by a strong accountability and auditing system, teachers are expected to meet up with standard performance indicators, making themselves 'being seen' to be meeting the required standards (Blackmore, 2004), hence examination results and documentation of performance have caused huge workloads for teachers. This performative culture (Ball, 2003) has turned education to an auditing business, which is the reason why students are trained to sit for examinations as they are part of the performance to be shown under this accountability system, for local and international benchmarking and comparison. For teachers, the mental health issues are worrying as they become a worldwide phenomenon (Betoret, 2006). Since the twenty-first century teaching has become one of the most stressful occupations in many countries (Adams, 2018; Martin, Collie, & Frydenberg, 2017). The increasing suicide rate as well as the recruitment and retention of quality teachers (Wang, 2007; Department for Education and Skills [DfES], 2005; Snyder, Tan, & Hoffman, 2006; Scott, Stone, & Dinham, 2001) results in a demoralised teaching profession.

The current situation of the societies as described above suggest the declining psychological well-being results from diminished social cohesion with local communities (McKenzie, Whitley, & Weich, 2002). Social support, which studies the psychological processes related to health by helping others (Taylor, 2007, 2011), and as a means to healthy functioning in the social environment (Durkheim, 2013), emerges as a universal cure for social dysfunction. Since young children and adolescents have to meet more demands in preparing their future life in societies nowadays, social support of teachers in schools appears to be essential for guiding students to cope with their future adult life. It is expected that teachers, taking the role of support givers, may gain insights from social support studies, and learn to stay motivated in playing the role of support givers in an environment surrounded by challenges in the current education environment.

Synthesis of the Investigation Results

Although it has been mentioned that teachers' caring and nurturance behaviour are important in teaching, this role has yet to be properly discussed or has not been explicitly addressed in the literature. Not only has this role been important, but also it has been gradually taken over by the increasing demands of examination-oriented training and the competition from achievement outcomes over the past two decades. Seeing that the study of social support is essentially related to human's intrinsic needs, and that education is based on human development, an investigation of social support is an attempt to connect some of the ideas in social support research to shed light on education.

This book has made an attempt to identify the knowledge of social support mainly in health psychology and explored the use of this concept in education, to draw implications for theory and practice. Since an investigation into the connection of social support across the two disciplines has not been conducted by other authors, the book itself is a study without a predetermined framework at the beginning. The author decided to conduct a thorough review of social support research to generate understanding so its connections to the education setting could be proposed. Apart from the chapters on introduction and conclusion, the book content ends up with the following content structure:

1. Social support and well-being, as the two concepts give the theoretical background of and indicate directions for its application in the field of education. The research approaches, and research outcomes of social support from the health psychology are explored; and well-being is found as the outcome and purpose of social support. This part makes suggestions on directions for social support research and a comprehensive understanding about social support research (Chaps. 2–3).
2. The theoretical link between social support and education, and social support sources in the education setting. An empirical study on expert teachers' behaviour is introduced to illustrate teachers' social support behaviour in teaching from a micro perspective (Chaps. 4–5).
3. The benefits that social support has for support providers, in the case of teachers, to explain the motives of social support giving to students, and whether teacher's social support provided to students has any relationship with their job aspiration and career development. As evidences confirm that teachers' support to students benefits both the students and the teacher themselves, other variables that facilitate teachers to provide social support are explored (Chap. 6).

The results revealed in the book have identified a meta-theory that take its root in social support research and educational theories and empirical studies. This meta-theory can act as the underpinning for learning and teaching to guide teachers' widened role of teaching in schools. The book also investigates the connections of support receivers and givers in the positions of learners and teachers in the classroom respectively. From the perspective of support receivers, it identifies from teachers' classroom practice and teachers' social support behaviours a form of teaching expertise that benefits learner in both psychological well-being and cognitive learning. From the perspective of support givers, it explores the benefits of social support giving on teachers who provide social support for students, and identifies the genuine interest of learners that underlies the kind of social support pedagogies teachers develop in the classroom; and proposes that this intrinsic interest in teaching actually benefits teacher development and career advancement.

About naming the book. Social Support is the main subject of the book, while well-being is the object for social support; the two words come together to suggest that social support can help people to achieve well-being, which is the key message of the book. In the book, social support in instructional practice is found to produce educational outcomes that contribute to students' well-being. The investigation has tentatively identified a form of teaching which demonstrates teachers' emotional work in the classroom. Such practice outlines the differences between a caring mentor of teaching and a knowledge imparter, with the former being effective in contributing to the well-being of young students; it is recommended as a model of practice that represents some form of teaching expertise. Teacher Development can be regarded as the area which the investigative results of the book serve—it studies the benefits of social support givers, as in the role of teachers, and it discovers that teachers' social support giving not only benefits student learning but also teachers' own professional development and career advancement. Therefore, a substantial part of the book reveals the results of developing the knowledge, traits and skills, to prepare teachers for carrying out social support practice in teaching. Hence, the book is titled 'Social Support, Well-being, and Teacher Development'.

The content of the book links the concept of social support to teaching, learning and teacher development, and the results point to the well-being of students and teachers.

In the following sections, this chapter aims to give a synthesised discussion of the results of the investigations that have been carried out, its recommendations, and the contributions that the book makes, followed by suggestions for future research directions. Instead of writing a summary of the book, the key content is discussed analytically based on a horizontal organisation. Readers may refer to the chapter outlines in Chap. 1 for a snapshot of the chapter content in its vertical organisation.

Social Support Research and Implications

The review of the mainstream research on social support is a key component of the book in its attempt to apply the findings to education. The result itself has given direction to researchers in academic disciplines such as health psychology, sociology, organisational studies and professional fields such as health care, social welfare and teaching. Some of the key concerns are reviewed in this integrated analysis.

Social support research has developed into several traditions. The most popular type being stress and buffering. It is an approach that studies social support functions

Synthesis of the Investigation Results

to relieve stress and enhance coping strategies, therefore feeling less stressed. Other approaches aim to gain understanding of individuals' self-perception and beliefs about the support around them, support gain in one's social network and relationships with the other people, to make implications for intervention programmes, policy and practice in different focuses. For example, the social constructivist and symbolic interaction list models, social capital and relationship perspectives explain a person's sense of supportiveness which is caused by one's perception, his/her interaction with people in the environment, and the network he/she maintains. The array of social support traditions and approaches also implies that embarking on social support research requires a detailed plan in order to ensure validity. The review conducted in the book provides some useful examples of how social support research can be constructed based on different research approaches. For example, in studying support actions that enhance people's well-being in stressful situations by improving their coping strategy, stress must be measured, whereas in studying people's social cognition, measuring stress is not necessary. The discussion of social support in the book also discusses the relevant instruments used in specific research focuses and their limitations.

The measurement of outcomes of social support is found to be highly relevant to higher order psychological concepts, such as well-being. Measures such as self-efficacy, self-esteem and motivation are common measurements that are also commonly used in educational research in measuring student outcomes. The investigation of social support research also ended up with the compilation of sample instruments that cover common measurements including various types of support measurements such as interpersonal support evaluation, subjective appraisal, stress and mental health and instruments that study networks such as an interview schedule for assessing psychosocial functioning and networks.

As for approaches and methods of study, most designed measures are in quantitative self-report questionnaire format. The potential constraint of the personal mood that could affect the recall of memory may undermine the validity of these results. Also there are other limitations to collecting data regarding support as it is so wide-ranging in daily life and some support is not visible. The review suggests utilising multiple measurements and focusing more attention on collecting observational data to supplement single self-report types. The review of social support research in this book has resulted to the formulation of a theoretical framework which emphasises the potent effect of social relationships on young learners. This framework has laid a strong theoretical foundation for educational studies which guide the work of education practitioners. For example, it implies the important roles teachers play in enhancing social bonds among students and in guiding students to act with reasoning and moral standards when interacting with each other in the classroom. As the current society is dominated by a diminishing sense of social cohesion (Sharma & Sharma, 2010), competitiveness (Barbara, 2004) and a performative culture ideology (Ball, 2003), an approach to education that promotes social support can also help in developing society in the long run. Accommodating the ideas from the social support research literature to education by making changes in learning and teaching in the classroom may directly benefit learners and teachers, whose mental health are found deteriorating (O'Brennan, Pas, & Bradshaw, 2017; Yeung & Liu, 2007).

Social Support Assumptions, Its Practice and Educational Outcomes

As explained, the book intends to focus on social support to generate ideas for further investigation in teaching and learning. The first question for the book is 'what is social support?' The book begins with identifying the theoretical assumptions of social support in health psychology which is the discipline from which this topic originates, and other supplementary ideas in the areas of sociology and psychology. The results regarding the meaning of social support are then linked with the education theories to form a cluster of theories and concepts to serve as underpinnings for the book in exploring social support in education.

The investigation into social support has resulted in five key assumptions in viewing social support and these assumptions have implications for the role of teachers in the environment of teaching. First, social support helps to buffer stress and improve coping actions (stress and coping) and to adjust to challenging situations that people encounter in life (Thiots, 2011). It is a give-and-take situation which resembles teachers and students in the classroom and school. Second, social support deals with a person's perception of availability of support, which predicts positive or negative outcomes and satisfaction with one's life (social constructionist and symbolic interaction list). Warm teacher–student interaction and a supportive school environment would make a difference in shaping students' social cognition, via positive development of self-concept and identity in the social environment. Third, social support, as the result of high quality relationships, can help a person to monitor behaviour that may have a positive effect on them such as resilience and interpersonal skills (good-quality relationships). This can be similarly applied to students if they are able to develop good relationships with people around them. Teachers and students are partly responsible for forming good relationships for school-aged children and adolescents in the ecological environment (Bronfenbrenner, 2005), as students are involved in a process of reciprocal interaction. Educational theories such as attachment (Bowlby, 1988), attachment neuroscience (Coan, 2008) and broaden-and-built (Lewis, 1993; Fredrickson, 1998; Fredrickson & Branigan, 2001, Fredrickson, 2004) have pointed out the importance of secure attachment and positive emotions. According to these theories, human connectedness can drive human beings to adopt action tendencies (such as exploring new information and engaging in social interactions), which can build cognitive resources and enduring personal bonds. The constructivist learning theory also proposes that social interaction can benefit human cognitive development (Vygotsky, 1978). The social support perspective gives emphasis to the emotional aspect of such interaction.

Synthesis of the Investigation Results

Fourth, people receive social support from both the 'close ties' and 'weak ties' (Lin, 2017) in their social network and network sites, leading to greater control of situations and beneficial outcomes in different life events (social capital). The teacher could be a critical person in a young person's social ties, while student peers are exchange partners who may play an important role in learning (Slavin, 2014). Finally, social support giving is found to have the benefits of reducing distress and enhancing self-worth, helping support givers to create a sense of competence and satisfaction. The analysis of social support and relevant educational theories suggest that satisfying social bonds and social ties are crucial to human development. As students are involved in the school as a community, teachers and peers are important resources to support learning in school. Its benefit is greater than academic study and is crucial to one's development. The motives and benefits of social support givers provide a potential area of investigation of teachers, as social support givers for students in the educational context.

A further review of social support was made in the field of education, and the results demonstrate the positive emotional and cognitive outcomes that social support has on students. To note a few, teacher's *emotional support* such as caring and empathy has a modelling effect on students that help produce prosocial behaviours and liking relationships in the classroom. Teachers' emotional support also means investing more detailed efforts in the choice of teaching strategies, hence learners' intrinsic interest is promoted and therefore higher academic achievement is accomplished. Students with emotional support are found to have lower engagement anxiety (Wang & Eccles, 2012) who are more willing to learn and to take a mastery approach in learning (Furrer & Skinner, 2003). Teachers' *warm relationships* as perceived by students are found to help students to buffer stress and enhance their self-esteem. It can help improve behaviours and is directly associated with students' adjustment (Reddy, Rhodes, & Mulhall, 2003). *Peer emotional support* is associated with prosocial behaviours such as exchanging resources and peer tutoring (Brutus & Donia, 2010). Peer support is found to enhance cognitive strategies, self-regulated learning strategies, socio-emotional competencies and the attributes of prosocial behaviours such as interest in study and a cooperative attitude (review in Russell, 2012; Suldo et al., 2008).

Teachers' expectation is conceived as social support resource as it consistently predicts student learning outcomes, achievement motivation, social adjustment and well-being (Verschueren, Doumen, & Buyse, 2012). For example, expectation on the structure of learning in the classroom predicts student engagement. At the same time, teachers' autonomy support is emphasised by researchers who studied autonomous motivation (Self-Determination Theory), expectation of teachers, such as the requirement of learning for learners, should be given with autonomy support (Deci & Ryan, 2008; Jang, Reeve, & Deci, 2010) to avoid exercising excess control over students. It is important to note that school environmental characteristics have a crucial role to play in determining student learning outcomes (Russell, 2012). They can facilitate or defeat teachers' work in the classroom in aspects such as values and goals towards learning. This underlies the core concern in the role of teachers in enhancing students' self-esteem, developing students' self-concept and providing an environment where students can relate to each other in building close social bonds.

Social support was originally studied in a non-school context, namely, in health psychology, which initially examined its effect on physical health such as patients' mortality rates (Frasure-Smith et al., 2000). However, it has become involved in psychological outcomes, suggesting that similar outcomes should be addressed in educational research in learning and teaching, gearing towards 'well-being'.

Deriving a Theory of Social Support to Guide Teaching Based on the review of social support literature, well-being is found to be the key outcome that social support addresses. Well-being is underpinned by the assumption that every person should be developed in accordance with their own abilities, resources and opportunities; even when people are facing psychological, emotional and social difficulties, they should be able to adapt and self-manage in the situation (Huber et al., 2001) and live healthily. The main ideas of well-being being discussed include the eudaimonic concept of well-being, which states that human beings should accept and live with their true selves (Waterman, 1993). This concept is elaborated in the self-determination theory, which educators have started to promote in the twenty-first century. It refers to one's autonomy (volition in one's behaviour regulation, i.e. intrinsic interest in one's engagement), competence (self-efficacy in different situations) and relatedness (being loved and connected to others) (Ryan & Deci, 2000), as the nutrients of well-being. In order to experience happiness, Seligman (2002, p. 263) suggests that one should develop their own 'signature strengths'. While 'everyone can accomplish' is an expectation for everyone, 'perceived support' and 'actual support received' human experience in the social environment determine one's life satisfaction in subtle ways. Positive support can increase human psychological resources as expressed in such areas as enhanced self-esteem, sense of belonging, self-efficacy and identity, which can help people to adjust, integrate and advance in one's life time or at the time of a stressful event. These non-cognitive outcome measures are used to measure the outcomes or effects of social support across the field of health care and education.

A resource list of prototypical pedagogies has also been developed in the review on relevant teaching methods. These pedagogies generally emphasise the sensitisation of human senses for learning which include feeling, thinking, deliberation, reflection, cooperative learning and scaffoldings and continuous feedback. Individual differences are highly valued in these pedagogies. These pedagogies include, for example, affective pedagogy (a taxonomy of affective learning) (Anderson et al., 2001), caring practice (Noddings, 2003), cultural responsive teaching (Vavrus, 2008), cooperative learning (Johnson, Johnson, & Smith, 1991; Slavin, 2014), nurture groups (Boxall, 2002), circle time (Mosley, 2005) and circle of friends (Goldstein, 2013) and the restorative justice approach (Morrison, 2002), with the last three mainly used in classrooms with special educational needs students.

While discussion about pedagogies is often focused on efficiency and cognitive aspects (Gillies, 2014), such as the concerns of cooperative and formative assessment of cognitive learning, the discussion of teaching methods in the book attempts to strengthen the discussion of these approaches on psychological well-being and the connection of non-cognitive and cognitive outcomes.

Synthesis of the Investigation Results 289

The integration of the theoretical and empirical literature in the field of healthy psychology and education has resulted in a theoretical framework, which is called a meta-theory in the book. It can be used to guide learning and teaching. In sum, the theory derived is based on the results of investigation reported in the book emphasising social bonds and relatedness as essential to the healthy functioning of human beings, which ultimately leads to well-being, i.e. to create satisfying social bonds and relationship in the social environment. The experience of human relationship of a person determines the emotional well-being and engagement behaviour of a person in learning. Social disengagement and deviated behaviours might result from the person's experience with other people and the world; positive interaction, i.e. social support and satisfying social experience, can help learners change their behaviour in healthier ways as good quality social interaction creates satisfaction, belongingness and higher level satisfaction that support one's growth. Social support also contributes to the intellect, in the situation where children and adolescents are involved in constructivist learning in which scaffoldings are enabled and provided. This meta-theory implies that the classroom and school are critical social environments for the development of children and young adolescents, in which context-based social support is fundamental to effective learning.

Effective Social Support and Variables of Studying Social Support in Education

Effective social support measures and conditions that facilitate effective social support are investigated in the book. It aims to provide parameters to guide social support giving, across different contexts and other variables. This has resulted in suggestions on effective social support conditions. For example, social support is not always welcome and some form of support is more acceptable, such as invisible support, than others (de Grood & Wallace, 2011), such as support from in-group members (Haslam, Reicher & Levine, 2012), similar others and those whom the person has a good relationship with (Carlson, Watts, & Maniacci, 2006), and that people may expect different types of support from their social network (Malecki & Demaray, 2003). Other variables that determine effective social support include a person's own past experience, personality, gender role taking, social norm and the size and intimacy of their social network.

With regard to effective support in education, the review suggests that gender differences and grade level are the two main variables for consideration. It is reported that girls' and boys' attention to social support are different. Girls care more about emotional support while boys care more about instrumental support and whether teachers are being fair (Suldo et al., 2008). This gender difference is in line with the findings in social support research in health psychology that males in general prefer active problem-solving strategies for tackling problems directly, whereas females tend to employ emotional coping when dealing with stress (Brannon, 2011; Matud,

2004). As for grade level, primary school students are more prone to emotional support, while teachers' social support is found prominent from the early years to mid-adolescence (Wentzel et al., 2010). The linkage between teacher support and student engagement has been found to be more robust for secondary school students than for elementary school students (Klem & Connell, 2004), as adolescents face more challenges in the current education environment. The preliminary evidence identified from the literature regarding effective support suggests that social support is valued by young children to adolescents, especially teachers' emotional support and instructional support, though further research is needed and this will be discussed in later sections.

The Practice of Social Support Teaching and the Triad of Teaching Expertise

The book also reports an empirical study of four expert teachers' social support behaviour in the classroom in the context of a secondary school in Hong Kong. The affective traits, such as caring, empathy, socio-emotional competence (Jennings & Greenberg, 2009) and behaviours such as autonomy-supportive teaching behaviour (Reeves, Deci, & Ryan, 2004) and a democratic interaction list approach of classroom management (Djigic & Stojiljkovic, 2011) have been discussed in the literature as the traits and approaches that can motivate learners and engage them in learning. However, it is not clear how the affective aspects of teaching can be linked to student learning outcomes. Since expert teachers have been found to possess an affective domain of teaching (Asad & Hassan, 2013; Hattie, 1999, 2003), a study on social support behaviour of expert teachers may further elaborate how social support is practiced in the classroom.

The findings of the empirical study resulted in some common characteristics in the instructional format used by the teachers. These teachers adopted a learner-centred approach in teaching, employing authentic and experiential learning activities focusing on promoting students' personal reflection, thinking and application. The four teachers showed that they were emotionally supportive throughout the lesson. They had high expectations of students even though the students were average to low-ability students. They tended to focus on tackling the critical features of the topic and guiding students to master relevant content and skills to learn the topic. These features were captured in the teachers' efforts in turning student learning into a series of moments where the students were prompted to engage in metacognition, which can be described as 'dialogic discourse'.

In sum, this approach involves learners in reflecting upon the work they have done or the ideas they have investigated throughout the process of learning (regulation of cognition), and engaging learners in a series of inquiries and problem-solving tasks so that learners will be able to proceed with learning with an appropriately selected method and they can master the topic of study (knowledge of cognition) (Ambrose,

Synthesis of the Investigation Results

Bridges, DiPietro, Lovett, & Norman, 2010). This whole approach to teaching is to help leaner's develop metacognitive learning so that they can become self-regulated learners. In the dialogic discourse, teachers involved themselves as knowledgeable and caring facilitators who attempted to engineer a process of learning that promoted students' intrinsic motivation of learning. It has the advantage of reducing students' learning anxiety and enhancing student participation in a class of average to low-ability students. The teachers maintained a very friendly manner and interactive communication pattern with stimulating language to encourage and invite students to take part by calling students' names or seeking voluntary responses. Students were given hints if they made an incomplete answer, or they were advised to obtain the answer by uptake of feedback during the dialogic discourse in the classroom openly. The analysis suggests that these teachers were also keen to select the methods and strategies that could help students to acquire learning of the topic effectively. They delivered specific content in user-friendly ways as they predicted the difficulties students might have in learning the topic. This situation can be explained by the teaching episodes in the study, e.g. in a Chinese Language lesson, a teacher asked students to do an origami exercise and then write step-by-step instructions for doing the same origami in a composition format to help learners become involved in the details of writing descriptions.

The approach of dialogic discourse used by the teachers is explained as the out-come of a triad of teaching expertise performed by teachers. In pedagogical terms, the triad of teaching expertise can be delineated into three areas. The first is suggested as teachers' commitment to teaching which can be shown in teacher's genuine interest in learners. This emotional trait of teaching enables teachers to give detailed attention to learners and be motivated to design pedagogies to help students learn. The second is teachers' communication skills for interacting with learners. These communication skills are found to be crucial throughout the lessons in focusing student attention, building relationships with and among students, and facilitating a conversation with students for the purpose of facilitating learning of the academic content. Thirdly, a structure of learning and teachers' attention to the steps in guiding students in mastering knowledge and developing skills for inquiring about knowledge is also identified.

This explains that teachers' communication skills are actually a useful tool and crucial for facilitating the use of metacognitive learning. These communication skills are subsumed in teachers' efforts to try to manage the discourse that helps learners learn and clarify learning in a sustained and continuous mode. Teachers have to play the role of facilitators. They have to genuinely care for students and take note of the learning progress of learners, so that they can continuously 'assess' students' performance and communicate with students about their mistakes and areas for improvement, and eventually help them to become interested, eager to learn and able to reflect on their learning. This approach of teaching is found to work very well for junior secondary school students in the empirical study reported in the book. In fact, the dialogic discourse is an important format of teaching as continued criticism has argued that teaching has been treated as a purely skill-based business (e.g. Hegarty, 2000). Also, in real situations, teachers who join the teaching force seem to be quite willing to adopt traditional, non-interactive teaching methods and such methods have, therefore, become predominant in schools (Lam, 2011b).

The investigation of social support behaviour of teachers ends up with the conceptualisation known as the triad of teaching expertise. The use of an interactive and dialogic approach to teaching can eliminate the use of a skills-based approach of teaching, as the amalgamated nature of teaching expertise enables teachers to experiment with teaching based on the use and application of different elements at the same time, such as understanding of the subject matter, finding out what is the best approach to learning for learners, and paying attention to guide students to master knowledge.

The investigation of the four teachers suggests that the expert teachers have a vision for education. Instead of serving short-sighted success in examinations, these teachers maintain a long-term goal in their work with students, i.e. to help learners develop true understanding of the knowledge they learn in school and develop a genuine interest in learning. They are concerned about students' well-being. Instead of making the questions and answers in the dialogic discourse as a control mechanism of imposing rules and controls, the teachers' approach to teaching is aligned with an 'autonomous supportive' teaching style (Deci & Ryan, 2008; Vansteenkiste, Niemiec, & Soenens, 2010). It is found that these teachers are interested in creating resources and support for students to enable them to acquire learning independently. They demonstrate the use of different types of social support in managing the dialogic discourse (e.g. emotional support, self-esteem support and instructional support).

The method of teaching identified from the investigation of the four teachers echoes the assumptions of social support research. These teachers consider the classroom as a social environment and see teaching as a socially situated practice that relies heavily on frequent human interactions (Hargreaves, 2000), giving support to each student while enhancing their abilities to become independent and motivated learners. Hence, even average to low-ability students are willing to participate because of the teachers' emotional and instructional support that gives students confidence, and because of the students' high-level engagement in the classroom the class is itself well managed. The analysis of the four teachers' teaching behaviour also implies that teaching should be a lively, interactive process between the teacher and the learners. This process should be unique according to the interest of learners. Therefore, it is not the skills per se that are important but the persons in the environment.

Teachers as Support Givers—Teacher Commitment Drives Career Development

The review of literature in the first part of the book explains the reasons for giving support. It is suggested that giving support carries the same benefit as receiving support in that it enhances well-being (Piliavin & Siegl, 2007) and health (Schwartz & Sendor, 1999). The kinship theory and reciprocal altruism theory explains that help-givers' offer of help to close kin is intended to be returned with the practical benefit of being helped back later on (Trivers, 1971). The motives of giving help are generated from different psychological statuses of well-being. One is in the situations purely generated from empathic concerns (Furrow, King, & White, 2004), i.e. when one feels that someone is in need, he or she intends to benefit the well-being of the needy; other situations such as helping others in order to reduce their (the help-givers') own distress (Batson & Shaw, 1991, cited in Omoto, Malsch, & Barraza, 2009); and one feels competence, involvement and usefulness (Caprara & Steca, 2005) when helping others. These reasons may explain the virtue of human beings regarding voluntary help to each other in a social environment as discussed at the beginning of this chapter. The area studying social support givers is one that research is lacking in. Given the current background of teacher burnout and mental health issues, studying teachers in the position of social support givers is relevant. It may yield important outcomes regarding teachers' motivation and career development. This topic is therefore investigated in the later part of the book; it is in line with the earlier part of investigation in the book that addresses some promising social support practices that could bring about positive educational outcomes for students.

The investigation has yielded some important findings. First, among voluminous studies, 'love for students' has stood out as a common reason to explain teachers' motivation for joining the teaching profession, which is also the reason that keeps teachers in the profession despite the challenges they face in the education environment, across cultures and over time. It is found that 'psychic reward of teaching', which means teachers' feeling of joy, pleasure and pride when they spend time with students in different events and circumstances (e.g. Hargreaves, 1994; Lortie, 1975; Nias, Southworth, & Yeomans, 1989), is the most satisfying experience of being a teacher. Teachers of all stages respond that this satisfaction is the most rewarding experience of teaching (Choi & Tang, 2009; Day & Gu, 2007, 2009), which helps them overcome their distress and the growing demands of the teaching profession. The review of empirical literature has also proved that, even highly committed teachers would be dissatisfied and feel burned out, if they are deprived of the chances to generate the satisfaction in congruent with their personal goals (Lam & Yan, 2011); however, love for students has also been found to be the only reason for staying in the profession for many teachers when challenges are posed for teachers by the education reform (Choi & Tang, 2009).

Another significant source of literature identifies the fact that teachers' giving of social support is significantly associated with their self-efficacy, and teachers' self-efficacy positively predicts both job satisfaction and job aspiration respectively (Lam, 2015). These findings are compared with the social support literature and they consistently arrive at theoretical assumptions that by giving social support to students, teachers could see themselves as more competent and feel more able to achieve their own goals, and they could overcome anxiety from teaching, in which state they are more likely to avoid the narrowing effect (Benight & Bandura, 2004) caused by the difficulties and challenges in the job and become more motivated to learn and advance in pursuing their teaching careers (Fredrickson, 2004).

Attempting to drawing connections in the investigation results, teachers' care for learners as explored in the book has been mapped with the review results on teachers' love for students in the context of investigating teachers' motives for giving support and its associated benefits in teachers' own development. It is found that teachers' emotional work of teaching (Isenbarger & Zembylas, 2006), as a form of practice focused on emotional scaffolding when a teacher delivers teaching, cannot be achieved without the drive from teachers' 'genuine interest in learners'—the empathic concerns of teachers for students. For example the teachers can not only assure students about what they have answered right but also hint about an important part of the answer they have not dealt with or have mistaken, as can be shown in the dialogic discourse of the four teachers reported in the book (Chap. 5),. The review of literature also explains that the practice of emotional work of teaching is the long-term goal of helping students master knowledge while they care about learners' diversity and progress. For example, teachers are used to putting themselves into 'motivational displacement' (Noddings, 2013) in teaching, to consider the needs of students and try to achieve the goal of learning for students affectively and meaningfully. The analysis contrasts the emotional work of teaching with teachers performing standard emotional rules or acting to suppress emotions and feelings, as in the case of 'emotional labour' (Tsang, 2011). The discussion in the book leads to a conclusive conceptualisation of the situation whereby the connection of teachers' love for students is translated into social support behaviour in teaching and can be transcended to teachers' teaching expertise (as found in the theoretical literature and the study on the four teachers). Teachers' performance of a form of detailed communication and scaffoldings (dialogic discourse and the triad of teaching expertise) suggests preliminary evidence to state/assert that the difference between emotional work and emotional labour lies in the differences between a caring mentor versus a service provider (Sachs, 2003); the former plays the role of emotional scaffolders (Zembylas, 2003). The investigation also further proves that teachers who are committed to teaching would present teaching in a form of practice that assimilates social support giving practices. This form of practice characterises teachers' emotional work of teaching in the classroom such as the teaching practices of the four teachers in the empirical study. Teachers who adopted this approach in teaching are more resilient because of their involvement in solving the problems in the context of teaching and that they have a clear understanding of the position to take when managing students and interacting with them, as can be shown in the description of the four teachers in Chap. 5.

Furthermore, the review of literature suggests that teachers' emotional work is enacted beyond the classroom level, to the level of negotiation at the organisational level and through this process teachers construct their agency (Yin & Lee, 2012). The adjustment of teachers in facing diverse learners and coping with their needs and internal struggles in the greater environment provides a lot of challenges for teachers in reality, causing emotional exhaustion and burnout to some of the teachers, which has affected the morale of the teaching profession. As the results of the book suggest, social support for students certainly does not mean simply giving care to students and being nice to them but giving care to learners similar to the empathic concerns

Synthesis of the Investigation Results

of teachers' intention to contribute to their well-being. The episodes of the dialogic discourse suggested in the empirical study of the four expert teachers illustrate how social support is carried out in classroom teaching. It can be tentatively concluded that social support, as a means of helping learners, can actually be managed in teachers' practice of teaching. As a crucial part of teachers' expertise in teaching, it can produce the outcomes of a high-level expertise in teaching. The dialogic discourse reflects such practice and further study may follow up to investigate its potential in teacher training, in order to prepare teachers to develop the skills and expertise in classroom practice.

The investigation related to teacher development has also covered the discussions of how teachers can sustain and advance in the stressful profession, by exploring other variables suggested in the literature that help teachers develop the capacities to manage teaching, such as teachers' knowledge about their own emotions and teacher personality traits. The literature points to the importance of teachers' well-being as teachers' reactions arise from unresolved conflicts when their vulnerabilities are projected on students' behaviour in the classroom (Ursano, Kartheiser, & Ursano, 2007), and the importance of socio-emotional competence (Kontos & Wilcox-Herzog, 1997). The implications of these suggestions will be discussed in the following sections.

Recommendations for School and Classroom Environment

The meta-theory derived from the book implies that the nature and quality of interaction with other human beings can create psychological resources (e.g. identity, self-esteem, motivation) and energies (e.g. engaging behaviours in learning and production) so that students can advance and achieve. It can also alter people's previous negative psychological state of being and create healthier experiences for them. Therefore, it might be useful for schools, which are coordinating units, to steer the direction of education in the school environment, to promote social values. A set of values based on the underpinnings of social support are suggested, which could help students to learn to become a social being, namely, *positive social relationships, personal growth, community spirit and justice.* A summary of the values governing the school environment is illustrated in Fig. 7.1.

Positive social relationship can create relatedness that can increase students' belongingness and strengthen students' support networks. It creates satisfying emotional experiences. Particularly, as implied from the empirical evidences, students from early years to adolescence need teachers' emotional support, and school teachers actually have a strong social and moral role to play apart from their academic role in schools. Yet, students' need in their transitional years to secondary school and girls and boys who experience puberty may have to be taken care of as they are facing adjustment issues; furthermore, understanding should be equally paid in recognising the background that learners bring to the classroom regarding their personal familial circumstances. On the whole, a positive relationship is a strong means of increasing

Fig. 7.1 The supportive classroom environment framework: social support has beneficial effects on psychological functioning which leads to well-being

their confidence in facing transition and buffering stress. References to intervention programmes such as peer learning and Circle Time, might be helpful in encouraging students' social life and building the social connections.

For *personal growth*, the ultimate purpose of school education can be conceptualised as a process which leads individuals to grow, and become assimilated to the ultimate purpose of social support. Well-being can be regarded as the outcome expected for education. This growth also implies giving opportunities to students to develop their own 'signature strengths' (Seligman, 2002, p. 263). It is therefore important to help students develop community spirit, as it offers students the opportunities to enjoy the satisfaction of contributing to others to earn social recognition and gain support from others. As for *justice*, a fair classroom system gives everyone the recognition and opportunities to advance. If an environment can consistently give the same rate of support and encouragement to individuals, it can give individuals the autonomy to pursue the interest that fits them, and this is believed to be able to accelerate learners' performance (Chory-Assad, 2002; Latham & Pinder, 2005). A supportive classroom environment would certainly trigger students' volitional actions, therefore it can help students to pursue and achieve the goals.

Inspired by the studies about the important role of school leadership, clear goals driven by social support values can help students perceive the school environment positively and receive equally important attention and respect in the classroom with sustainable and long-term effects. More importantly, consistent values across different levels of the school work to encourage the attributes of prosocial learning behaviour that are also essential. School leaders should work hand in hand with teachers and parents in creating a supportive environment that upholds values and develops norms to govern the school environment. Immediate changes are needed to shift the attention from assessment and examination to promoting learning and the training of independent learners, as learning and teaching for examinations create anxiety in learning and pressure for learning and teaching.

Recommendations for Teacher Development

The investigations in the book suggest a few areas of teacher professional development for education providers to consider when planning the future direction of teacher training, to cater for the development of societies towards the needs of the future. First, teachers' commitment does matter in pursuing a teaching career. As social support giving to students is found to have a positive link with teachers' self-efficacy that is directly associated with career development, teacher candidates who are interested in teaching should consider if they have an intrinsic interest in teaching. This can be generally assessed by whether one has a genuine interest in learners and in interacting with them. Choosing the right candidates for the teaching profession is equally important, and teacher commitment should be considered a serious criteria for selecting prospective teachers as this helps them carry out the emotional work of teaching in the complicated teaching environment.

The overall results addressed in the book have strongly implied the need for strengthening teacher education in a number of areas. In addition to other areas of teaching, teacher education programmes should focus on character traits development specific to the profession of teaching, in emotional domains such as self-compassion and socio-emotional competence. They can help teachers develop empathy and positive emotions; therefore they are more likely to develop a professional disposition in handling students and be more resilient in facing challenging situations.

Second, pedagogically, the triad of teaching expertise can be considered as the focus of training. It focuses on the developing teachers' genuine interest in learners and in teaching, immediacy communication skills and the facilitation of learners in metacognitive learning. This expertise can be cultivated and developed by adopting the teacher-as-researcher as a model for early training in their career (Patrick & Pintrich, 2001). Action research can help neophyte teachers adopt a formulated inquiry structure, by involving them in a cyclical reflection process of reflect, observe and act. Since reflection is the key element in action research (Graham & Phelps, 2003), prospective teachers and in-service teachers can learn 'problem-framing' and consider answers to teaching episodes whereby the teachers feel improvement may be needed, to help them develop the skills for handling challenging classroom situations. In this way, teachers can pay more attention to the persons and interaction in teaching. Instead of the tricks and skills of teaching methods, they can develop sensitivity to the issues in learning and the teaching context (Smith, 2001). Furthermore, action research might help teachers to manage the situation and their internal negotiations in their role, and seek proper resolutions of problems arising from the political environment. This can make them more competent in performing teaching and at the same time can enhance their passion for teaching, so that they are better prepared for the 'emotional work' in the classroom.

Specifically, the skills of teaching for metacognitive learning are largely determined by teachers' work on lesson planning such as in analysing the knowledge to be taught and considering the activities that help learners self-regulate learning, such as self-explaining (Aleven & Koedinger, 2002), modelling and application (Azevedo, 2005; Walberg & Paik, 2000), as well as teachers' delivery in the classroom. It may be appropriate that teachers can be engaged in cooperative lesson planning, classroom observation, video-analysis and discussion in a community of practice (Kiemer, Gröschner, Pehmer, & Seidel, 2015) to sharpen the triad of teaching expertise, based on shared comments and the evaluation of teaching in an open dialogue.

Third, organisational support is crucial for developing teachers. Since the investigation revealed that students are the source of teacher satisfaction, and giving support to students is most satisfying for teachers, schools should seek ways to promote teacher-student relationships and accommodate teacher-student interactions at the organisational level, e.g. creating time in the school timetable for student-teacher meetings and consultations, setting up channels for teachers to maintain continuous communication with student graduates who had been taught by the teachers, and recognising learning and teaching as the core mission of the school.

As the investigation suggests that social support giving to students is positively associated with teachers' efficacy, school leaders can make teachers' work environment more facilitative for teachers' work-related self-efficacy (Zembylas, 2003). For example, school leaders could assign jobs to teachers based on their strengths (Fernet, Senécal, Guay, Marsh, & Dowson, 2008). They should also look into workload issues in order not to harm teachers' self-efficacy. In order to enhance competence, schools can develop mentorship programmes to allow more experienced teachers to mentor novice teachers so that the inexperienced teachers could garner guidance in their teaching. This inter-teacher social support is also helpful for teachers to buffer stress and recover their confidence in teaching. Those who are assigned as mentors would also benefit by helping their less experienced mentees as social support givers; hence these more experienced teachers would develop images of themselves as capable professionals who feel satisfied with contributions to the growth of newer teachers. Being able to deliver specific feedback to teachers could help teachers develop self-efficacy (King & Newman, 2000) as it enables teachers to make improvements. As a whole, more aspiring teachers tend to be more productive (Reeve, 2009), therefore schools gain substantially from supporting teachers to gain work-related self-efficacy.

School leaders should encourage teacher autonomy and make teachers proud to be members of the teaching profession. School leaders should acknowledge teachers' thoughts and provide teachers with competence feedback (Deci, Eghrari, Patrick, & Leone, 1994) as a common norm of the school so that teachers are willing to share, discuss and learn from others. School leaders should pay attention to teachers' emotions and provide emotional support to colleagues to recognise teacher emotion as a collective matter of interest (Nias, 1996). Moreover, maintaining a trustful teacher–administrator relationship is essential; it can enhance teachers' feeling of connectedness to the school. In order to develop a pleasant and engaging working culture, common rooms and space for group discussion and luncheon are useful as

Recommendations for Teacher Development

they can encourage teachers and students to share and discuss academic, learning and teaching matters, have conversations and share some leisure time together.

Given that environmental support is the most important support source that determines teaching, the current performative culture may destroy teachers' commitment and create negative emotions in teachers, and this situation will strongly affect student learning and create mental health issues for both teachers and students. Schools should realise the prime goal of education is student development in an all-round manner, especially recognising and supporting teachers' work in social support giving. This final suggestion also highlights the intention of the book to propose social support as an essential guide to support teachers to realise the satisfaction in and meaning of teaching so that it can benefit students to appreciate the real joy of learning and prepare them for taking appropriate roles in a future society. Figure 7.2 summarises the investigation findings of the book and the connections between different parts.

Contributions of the Book

The most significant contribution of the book is that it has developed a strong theoretical perspective of viewing learning, teaching and teacher development based on social support, a research component originating from the field of health psychology. This perspective provides a frame of reference to view the outcomes of education as well-being, conceptualises interpersonal relationships as a global facilitator of enhancing the processes of achieving positive education outcomes, and generates a number of theoretical implications and practical suggestions in the field of education, such as the meta-theory of education established on the grounds of social bonds and social relationships, the nature and content of teacher expertise, teacher's self-generating rewards gain from social support giving that can support their career development positively, and organisational support for teachers based on self-efficacy development, to note a few.

The social support perspective, presented as a meta-theory, views education as the nature of experience of human beings, which is defined as intrinsically influenced by the nature and quality of interaction with other human beings to determine a healthy state of being. This evidence-based perspective underscores social relationships, social support and human relatedness as the conditions for effective learning, providing inferences and examples to enable a comprehensive understanding of social support resources, practice and insights in the field of education. The theories and practice of social support discussed in the book can provide content and materials to supplement the meaning of learner-centred education that has appeared to be ambiguous and controversial in the education literature (Sriprakash, 2013), yet is promoted as the best practice for adoption worldwide (UNESCO, 2008). By using the frame of reference of social support, the book has provided readers with a synthesised cluster of educational theories, concepts, exemplary models and prototypical practices that illustrate social support in learning and teaching, giving concrete ideas to

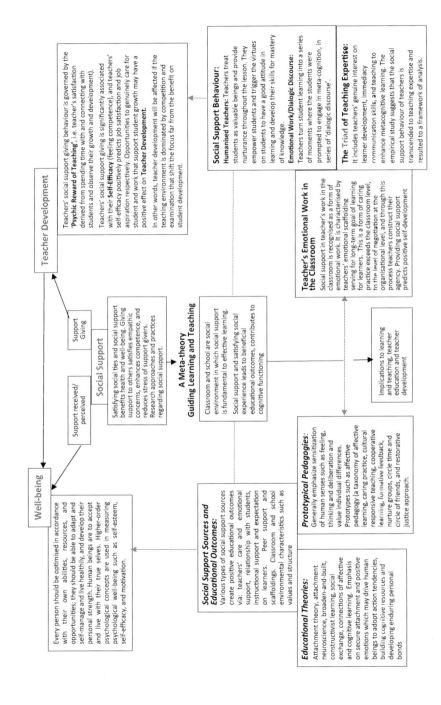

Contributions of the Book

◀**Fig. 7.2** Overall Summary: Social Support, Well-being, Teacher Development. *Social Support* benefits support receivers and support givers on **Well-being**. A **Meta-theory** is derived based on an analysis of **Social Support Sources** and their **Educational Outcomes** in the classroom context, **Educational Theories** and **Prototypical pedagogies**, it links to well-being. The study on teacher's **Social Support Behaviour** has generated a framework known as the **Triad of Teaching Expertise**, this expertise can be used to guide the practice of teaching, and it is potentially related to the practice of teaching as **Emotional Work**. This practice is recognised as a recommended approach of teaching that demonstrates the characteristics of a caring mentor of teaching. Finally, teacher's social support giving behaviour is found to be governed by teachers' genuine concerns in helping students as **Psychic Reward of Teaching** (i.e. empathic concerns of social support givers that may lead to satisfaction), it leads to enhanced self-efficacy, this sense of competence is also found to drive **Teacher Development** and career advancement. **Implications** are made to learning and teaching, and teacher development, particular attention is given in the suggestions for teacher's professional training and development in the school context, addressing issues in the current educational environment

teachers in guiding their classroom practice, and giving an analytic reference source to researchers for academic purposes.

The exploration of social support in teaching also contributes to the academic dialogue regarding the preferential status of cognitive learning over affective learning, by providing empirically based inferences and theoretical claims on the importance of affective traits such as caring, empathy, affect and emotional support. It suggests that affective traits and teachers' action of social support do not only help learners become more motivated and engaged, they are also essential as part of the ingredients in forming a high-level teacher expertise that serves both emotional and cognitive learning. Notably, evidence taken from the book have found that teachers' social support for learners leads to enhanced motivation, self-esteem and social goals, interest in learning and cognitive strategies. The discussion in the book has problematized the meaning of emotional support by referring to its research traditions, and studied its beneficial effects in the literature, relating it to teaching practice and the development of teaching expertise through an integrated discussion in the book. Correspondingly, by using social support as a construct to conceptualise teacher behaviour, it attempts to elucidate a few concepts related to classroom teaching, namely, the 'emotional work of teaching', 'the triad of teaching expertise' (commitment, communication skills and skills for promoting metacognitive learning) and 'dialogic discourse'. They can be regarded as evidence that represents professional teachers' teaching expertise, giving insights to the evolving field of study on expert teaching (Turner, 2013). The discovery of the wholeness of the teachers' 'triad of teaching expertise' further argues against the training of teachers frequently focuses on teaching styles and methods, suggesting important contents for professional teacher training. The book also makes recommendations for creating a supportive school environment based on a set of suggested values including identity, self-concept, self-esteem, self-efficacy and students' intrinsic motivation for learning. The set of values are also suggested as appropriate outcome measures for learning to identify students' well-being. Furthermore, with the analysis of social support practice in the classroom, the implications drawn from the book strongly defend the knowledge of teaching to be built upon reflective practice, providing arguments to strengthen the education discipline and the form of scholarship educators and teachers should practice such as action research, practitioner-based practice and lesson study.

One of the highlights of the book is the investigation of the benefits of providing support for support givers, in the case of teachers giving support to students. It ended up with stimulating results that imply teachers' love for students is a major determinant of teacher satisfaction that can drive their career advancement and overcome the pressure teachers may experience in teaching. It suggests that the study of the 'social support giver' is a relatively undeveloped area of research in education and has the potential to make significant contributions to the field. Conclusively, based on the investigation results on social support in learning, teaching and teachers' motive for teaching, the book has suggested a number of important implications for teacher education and professional development. It proposes that greater attention should be given to cultivating teachers' self-efficacy and intrinsic motivation in teaching by creating more opportunities for teachers to interact with students as it is the most satisfying experience that teachers encounter. It also suggests strengthening the professional disposition of teachers, including emotional knowledge of teaching in teacher training, and developing the capacities of teachers to be teacher-researchers, addressing some important content to strengthen current teacher education curriculum content and teacher development approaches, and proposing directions and methods for teacher training and development.

The discussion of social support sources at various levels in the educational environment can give insights and solutions to problems to policy makers, school administrators and leaders and teachers, in their work at the frontline. The book also provides a comprehensive commentary outlining the problems of education in schools in the twenty-first century, such as the predominant performative culture and materialistic and consumerist cultures, which have weakened social relationships in societies and created mental health issues for students, teachers and people over the globe. At the time the book is published, it is realised that the discourse on educational change has been more articulated with advocacies being made at both school management and voices from teachers including working with changes in schools (Rebora, 2017), managing changes (Cohen, 2017), responding to changes (Sacks, 2017) and making changes possible (Thiers, 2017), to name but a few. Social support, as a concept promoted in the book, can be a norm for use to improve education and the livelihood of people in societies throughout the world.

As to researchers and practitioners who are interested in social support research in the field of health psychology and related fields, this book provides the most updated review on the topic which can facilitate research and practice. The cross-disciplinary exploration in the book has enabled the integration of theories and produced knowledge that extends outside the boundary of specified fields to provide solutions to problems. The discussion of the nature of knowledge creation in the book thus provides an exemplar for investigating methods and knowledge in other fields.

Further Research Directions

The use of a social support perspective to systematically measure educational processes and outcomes is still not common in educational research, while the existing literature partly refers to common topics such as student-teacher relationships and teacher's emotional support without giving specific explanations of such terms. Therefore, the topic of study on social support has great potential for further research in the field of education, especially if it may provide content for the curriculum of teacher training in the future. Studies on types of support, and the impact of various social support types on student learning in self-esteem, motivation and social goals are helpful to identify outcomes and effects of social support. Specific investigations on social support outcomes such as effects on students' self-regulated learning and cognitive learning strategies are also important topics to suggest the long-term effect of social support on learners. Gaining from the insights from the social support literature in health psychology, studies to identify the suitability of support and effective support measures in teaching can also be formulated, such as visible and invisible support, relationship closeness to support givers, gender and culture, etc. Furthermore, peer support is also a potential research topic, the findings of which may contribute to the pedagogical research literature such as cooperative learning and peer learning. With regard to the triad of teaching expertise, further studies on teachers' use of the traits of social support, skills of communication and the skills to enhance metacognitive learning can yield further understanding of the potential expertise that has been identified from the study. It may be useful to identify if other approaches of teaching of expert teachers may also demonstrate such skills, however present in forms other than dialogic discourse.

The school environment is found to determine the effectiveness of social support. While research to identify school environment support to student engagement is currently a popular topic, it may be useful if the scope of study on the teachers' role can be developed to strengthen the applicability of engagement studies, and to inform the role of teachers in the professional practice of teaching. At present, studies on social support are focused on children and young adolescents in primary schools, therefore, research into secondary school students and university students may enable understanding for students across different age groups. Furthermore, the evaluation focusing on learning and teaching pedagogies regarding social support could also refer to the aspects related to students' non-cognitive attributes, apart from academic results, with reference to the meta-theory the book suggests.

Classroom-based observational studies on teacher–student interaction should be given more attention as they can inform about the skills and techniques of handling emotional work in the classroom. Research to look into the effect of social support for high achievers and low achievers, and students with special education needs may provide important implications to guide practice, yet they are still undeveloped in the literature. The variation of styles of support given to high and low-ability students has also emerged to be a topic that has important implications for teaching, such as which types of support would work better for a specific group of students (e.g. the types of help that suit high achievers versus low achievers), and to inform practice.

With regard to teacher development, the nature of the type of social support that teachers give to their students, and how such support should be offered, emerge as a potential topic for study. Such work can strengthen research on the emotional work of teaching which is currently scant in the literature, and the results can provide ideas to guide social support practice among practitioners. More in-depth school-based studies regarding teacher development policies and practice of how school leaders lead teachers in the twenty-first century's teaching environment to promote the forms of learning is also an area of noticeable interest. The comparison of experienced and inexperienced teachers' support may also be a useful topic to generate ideas to understand teacher development.

Regarding methodology, quantitative study and qualitative study instruments are recommended to elaborate the features of social support and the outcomes for students, and teachers' personal thoughts in teaching. They may end up with protocols and thought processes to guide teacher development in aspects such as empathic concerns and support giving strategies in specific classroom situations. The renewal of measurement scales for social support research would certainly be useful to stimulate research on social support in different professional fields and discipline areas, since the changes of the means of interaction among people and types of support relationship in the social network have been tremendous over the past few decades. Comparative research across cultures might provide salient findings to address differences of support relationships. Studies of social support givers, including teachers and other professionals have the potential to contribute to various fields such as career development.

There are several notable limitations to this book resulting from the content that is largely derived from the literature of existing data reports and research findings, instead of data developed to address the particular focus of the book. Some of the topics that are thoroughly researched in social support literature in the health care and psychology literature, such as effective social support, have yet to be developed in the field of education. While they are discovered to be areas of research as addressed above, the link of such topic is not correspondingly drawn between the fields. Though efforts have been made to capture a wide range of up-to-date sources, due to the extensive research literature on social support and the diverse research constructs used in the educational literature related to this topic, and the fact that the development of social support research varies between the fields of health psychology and education, the review has limitations in capturing the salient features between the studies as content analysis is the main strategy for drawing the content for review and comparison. Furthermore, the discussion of education is mainly focused on primary and secondary school students, which may limit the extent of the literature review, though this may yield a meaningful result of school-aged student analysis. While the ideas suggested in the book establish some promising premises that warrant further investigations and can provide insights for the field of education, they are subject to the refinement of empirical testing and confirmation in dynamic educational environment and different cultural backgrounds.

Overall Conclusion

The quality of teaching and student learning outcomes are two topical issues which have interested different stakeholders in the twenty-first century. There are numerous schemes for ensuring quality and improving teaching practices in schools which are prevalent at the world level, such as the advocacy of changing the traditional transmission teaching methods to ones that promote active discovery and social learning. However, the success of teaching innovations and education reform policies are often based on narrowly defined conceptions as suggested in the discourse of society at large, such as how much these methods can help students achieve better grades. This viewpoint has generated a lot of pressure for learners and teachers, bringing about negative consequences for their health and well-being as a noticeable phenomenon in the last two decades.

The theoretical framework of social support in education has been expounded in the book to emphasise that human flourishing can be facilitated by human relatedness and the perception of supportiveness from the social environment. The book also identifies teachers' empathic concerns for learners and teachers' commitment to teaching which can create self-generating energies to support teachers' volitional actions in teaching. As a result, these teachers have experienced more enjoyable trajectories of professional development in their career. Furthermore, the triad of teaching expertise resulting from the book features teachers' expertise in managing the emotional work of the classroom; this expertise suggests the wholeness of teachers' empathic concerns, communication skills and their metacognitive teaching skills as the formulation of professional skills and knowledge in conducting teaching. This finding also argues for the important notion of teacher professional development, placing the emphasis of teacher training on the underlying trait and commitment for the profession.

As a whole, the book provides comprehensive theories, exemplary methods and recommendations to strengthen the position of teachers in carrying out the role of a caring mentor in teaching. It describes the current needs of society to revitalise the profession of teaching, by the insights drawn from the theoretical perspective of social support. Hopefully the discussion of social support, well-being and teacher development in this book can shed light on the future directions of education to seek improvement in the near future.

References

Adams, R. (2018). Why teachers in England are suffering from so much stress. *The Guardian*. Retrieved from https://www.theguardian.com/education/2018/jan/11/teachersengland-suffering-from-so-muchstress-explainer.

Aleven, V. A., & Koedinger, K. R. (2002). An effective metacognitive strategy: Learning by doing and explaining with a computer-based Cognitive Tutor. *Cognitive Science, 26*(2), 147–179.

Ambrose, M. L. (2002). Contemporary justice research: A new look at familiar questions. *Organizational Behavior and Human Decision Processes, 89*(1), 803–812.

Ambrose, S. A., Bridges, M. W., DiPietro, M., Lovett, M. C., & Norman, M. K. (2010). *How learning works: Seven research-based principles for smart teaching*. USA: Wiley.

Anderson, C. A., & Bushman, B. J. (2002). Human aggression. *Annual Review of Psychology, 53*, 27–51.

Anderson, L. W., Krathwohl, D. R., Airasian, P. W., Cruikshank, K. A., Mayer, R. E., Pintrich, P. R., ... & Wittrock, M. C. (2001). *A taxonomy for learning, teaching, and assessing: A revision of Bloom's taxonomy of educational objectives, abridged edition*. White Plains, NY: Longman.

Arnett, J. J. (2002). The psychology of globalization. *American Psychologist, 57*(10), 774–783.

Arun, P., & Chavan, B. (2009). Stress and suicidal ideas in adolescent students in Chandigarh. *Indian Journal of Medical Sciences, 63*(7), 281.

Asad, E. M. M., & Hassan, R. B. (2013). The characteristics of an ideal technical teacher in this modern Era. *International Journal of Social Science and Humanities Research, 1*(1), 1–6.

Azevedo, R. (2005). Using hypermedia as a metacognitive tool for enhancing student learning? The role of self-regulated learning. *Educational Psychologist, 40*(4), 199–209.

Ball, S. J. (2003). The teacher's soul and the terrors of performativity. *Journal of Education Policy, 18*(2), 215–228.

Barbara, L. M. (2004). The learner-centered psychological principles: A framework for balancing academic achievement and social-emotional learning outcomes. In E. Z. Joseph, R. W. Roger, C. W. Margaret, & J. W. Herbert (Eds.), *Building academic success on social and emotional learning: What does the research say?* (pp. 23–39). New York: Teachers College Press.

Barrera, M. (1986). Distinctions between social support concepts, measures, and models. *American Journal of Community Psychology, 14*(4), 413–445.

Bauer, M. A., Wilkie, J. E., Kim, J. K., & Bodenhausen, G. V. (2012). Cuing consumerism: Situational materialism undermines personal and social well-being. *Psychological Science, 23*(5), 517–523.

Benight, C. C., & Bandura, A. (2004). Social cognitive theory of posttraumatic recovery: The role of perceived self-efficacy. *Behaviour Research and Therapy, 42*(10), 1129–1148.

Betoret, F. D. (2006). Stressors, self-efficacy, coping resources, and burnout among secondary school teachers in Spain. *Educational Psychology, 26*(4), 519–539.

Blackmore, J. (2004). Leading as emotional management work in high risk times: The counterintuitive impulses of performativity and passion. *School Leadership & Management, 24*(4), 439–459.

Bowlby, J. (1988). *A secure base: Parent–child attachment and healthy human development*. New York: Basic Books.

Boxall, M. (2002). *Nurture groups in school: Principles & practice*. Sage.

Brannon, L. (2011). *Gender: Psychological Perspectives* (6th ed.). Boston: Allyn & Bacon.

Bray, M. (2017). Benefits and tensions of shadow education: Comparative perspectives on the roles and impact of private supplementary tutoring in the lives of Hong Kong students. *Journal of International and Comparative Education, JICE*, 18–30.

Brutus, S., & Donia, M. B. (2010). Improving the effectiveness of students in groups with a centralized peer evaluation system. *Academy of Management Learning & Education, 9*(4), 652–662.

Caporeal, L. R. (1997). The evolution of truly social cognition: The core configuration model. *Personality and Social Psychology Review, 1*(4), 276–298.

Caprara, G. V., & Steca, P. (2005). Self–efficacy beliefs as determinants of prosocial behavior conducive to life satisfaction across ages. *Journal of Social and Clinical Psychology, 24*(2), 191–217.

Carlson, J., Watts, R., & Maniacci, M. (2006). *Adlerian therapy*. Washington, DC: American Psychological Association.

Cheung, E. & Chiu, P. (2016, March 12). Students at breaking point: Hong Kong announces emergency measures after 22 suicides since the start of the academic year. *The South China Morning Post*. Retrieved from http://www.scmp.com/news/hong-kong/health-environment/article/1923465/students-breaking-point-hong-kong-announces.

References

Choi, P. L., & Tang, S. Y. F. (2009). Teacher commitment trends: Cases of Hong Kong teachers from 1997 to 2007. *Teaching and Teacher Education, 25*(5), 767–777.

Chory-Assad, R. M. (2002). Classroom justice: Perceptions of fairness as a predictor of student motivation, learning, and aggression. *Communication Quarterly, 50*(1), 58–77.

Coan, J. A. (2008). Toward a neuroscience of attachment. In J. Cassidy & P. R. Shaver (Eds.), *Handbook of attachment: Theory, research, and clinical applications* (2nd ed., pp. 241–265). New York: The Guilford Press.

Cohen, D. B. (2017). Managing change—before it drives you out of teaching. *Educational Leadership: Gearing up for Change, 74*, 34–38. Retrieved from http://www.ascd.org/publications/educational-leadership/jun17/vol74/num09/Managing-Change%E2%80%94Before-It-Drives-You-Out-of-Teaching.aspx.

Curriculum Development Council (2014). *Basic Education Curriculum Guide—To Sustain, Deepen and Focus on Learning to Learn (Primary 1—6)*. Retrieved from http://www.edb.gov.hk/attachment/en/curriculum-development/doc-reports/guide-basic-edu-curriculum/BECG_2014_en.pdf.

Day, C., & Gu, Q. (2007). Variations in the conditions for teachers' professional learning and development: Sustaining commitment and effectiveness over a career. *Oxford Review of Education, 33*(4), 423–443.

Day, C., & Gu, Q. (2009). Veteran teachers: Commitment, resilience and quality retention. *Teachers and Teaching: Theory and Practice, 15*(4), 441–457.

de Grood, J. A., & Wallace, J. E. (2011). In sickness and in health: An exploration of spousal support and occupational similarity. *Work & Stress, 25*(3), 272–287.

Deci, E. L., Eghrari, H., Patrick, B. C., & Leone, D. R. (1994). Facilitating internalization: The self-determination theory perspective. *Journal of Personality, 62*(1), 119–142.

Deci, E. L., & Ryan, R. M. (2008). Self-determination theory: A macrotheory of human motivation, development, and health. *Canadian Psychology/Psychologie Canadienne, 49*(3), 182–185.

Demaray, M. K., & Malecki, C. K. (2003). Perceptions of the frequency and importance of social support by students classified as victims, bullies, and bully/victims in an urban middle school. *School Psychology Review, 32*(3), 471–490.

Department for Education and Skills. (2005). *Departmental Report 2005*. Retrieved from https://assets.publishing.service.gov.uk/government/uploads/system/uploads/attachment_data/file/272106/6522.pdf.

Djigic, G., & Stojiljkovic, S. (2011). Classroom management styles, classroom climate and school achievement. *Procedia-Social and Behavioral Sciences, 29*, 819–828.

Durkheim, E. (2013). *Durkheim: The rules of sociological method: And selected texts on sociology and its method*. UK: Palgrave Macmillan.

Education Commission. (2000). *Review of education system reform proposals*. Retrieved from http://www.e-c.edu.hk/doc/en/publications_and_related_documents/consultation_documents/e_ABR.pdf.

Fernet, C., Senécal, C., Guay, F., Marsh, H., & Dowson, M. (2008). The work tasks motivation scale for teachers (WTMST). *Journal of Career Assessment, 16*(2), 256–279.

Fowers, B. J. (2012). Placing virtue and the human good in psychology. *Journal of Theoretical and Philosophical Psychology, 32*(1), 1–9.

Frasure-Smith, N., Lespérance, F., Gravel, G., Masson, A., Juneau, M., Talajic, M., et al. (2000). Social support, depression, and mortality during the first year after myocardial infarction. *Circulation, 101*(16), 1919–1924.

Fredrickson, B. L. (1998). What good are positive emotions? *Review of General Psychology, 2*, 300–319.

Fredrickson, B. L. (2004). The broaden-and-build theory of positive emotions. *Philosophical Transactions of the Royal Society B: Biological Sciences, 359*(1449), 1367.

Fredrickson, B. L., & Branigan, C. (2001). Positive emotions. In T. J. Mayne & G. A. Bonnano (Eds.), *Emotion: Current issues and future directions* (pp. 123–151). New York: Guilford Press.

Furrer, C., & Skinner, E. (2003). Sense of relatedness as a factor in children's academic engagement and performance. *Journal of Educational Psychology, 95*(1), 148–162.

Furrow, J. L., King, P. E., & White, K. (2004). Religion and positive youth development: Identity, meaning, and prosocial concerns. *Applied Developmental Science, 8*(1), 17–26.

Galea, S., Ahern, J., Resnick, H., Kilpatrick, D., Bucuvalas, M., Gold, J., et al. (2002). Psychological sequelae of the September 11 terrorist attacks in New York City. *New England Journal of Medicine, 346,* 982–987.

Gillies, R. M. (2014). Cooperative learning: Developments in research. *International Journal of Educational Psychology, 3*(2), 125–140.

Gliatto, M. F., & Rai, A. K. (1999). Evaluation and treatment of patients with suicidal ideation. *American Family Physician, 59*(6), 1500–1506.

Goldstein, H. (2013). *Circle of Friends. In Encyclopedia of Autism Spectrum Disorders* (pp. 641–645). New York: Springer.

Gottfredson, M. R., & Hirschi, T. (1990). *A general theory of crime.* Stanford: Stanford University Press.

Graham, A., & Phelps, R. (2003). 'Being a teacher': Developing teacher identity and enhancing practice through metacognitive and reflective learning processes. *Australian Journal of Teacher Education, 27*(2), 2.

Hargreaves, A. (1994). *Changing teachers, changing times: Teachers' work and culture in the postmodern age.* New York: Teachers College Press.

Hargreaves, A. (2000). Mixed emotions: Teachers' perceptions of their interactions with students. *Teaching and Teacher Education, 16*(8), 811–826.

Haslam, S. A., Reicher, S. D., & Levine, M. (2012). When other people are heaven, when other people are hell: How social identity determines the nature and impact of social support. In J. Jetten, C. Haslam, & S. A., Haslam (Eds.), *The social cure: Identity, health and well-being* (pp. 157–174). London, New York: Psychology Press.

Hattie, J. (1999, August 2). *Influences on student learning.* Inaugural Lecture: Professor of Education, University of Auckland.

Hattie, J. (2003, October). *Teachers make a difference: What is the research evidence?* Paper presented at the Australian Council for Educational Research Annual Conference on Building Teacher Quality, Melbourne.

Hegarty, S. (2000). Teaching as a knowledge-based activity. *Oxford Review of Education, 26*(3–4), 451–465.

Hong Kong Institute of Asia-Pacific Studies (2016). *Survey findings on views on "winning at the starting line" in Hong Kong.* Retrieved from http://www.cuhk.edu.hk/hkiaps/tellab/pdf/telepress/16/SP_Press_Release_20160808.pdf.

Huber, M., Knottnerus, J. A., Green, L., van der Horst, H., Jadad, A. R., Kromhout, D., … & Schnabel, P. (2011). How should we define health?. *BMJ: British Medical Journal (Online), 343.* http://dx.doi.org/10.1136/bmj.d4163.

Hursthouse, R. (2001). *On Virtue Ethics.* Oxford: Oxford University Press.

Isenbarger, L., & Zembylas, M. (2006). The emotional labour of caring in teaching. *Teaching and Teacher Education, 22*(1), 120–134.

Jang, H., Reeve, J., & Deci, E. L. (2010). Engaging students in learning activities: It is not autonomy support or structure but autonomy support and structure. *Journal of Educational Psychology, 102*(3), 588–600.

Jennings, P. A., & Greenberg, M. T. (2009). The prosocial classroom: Teacher social and emotional competence in relation to student and classroom outcomes. *Review of Educational Research, 79*(1), 491–525.

Johnson, D. W., Johnson, R. T., & Smith, K. A. (1991). Cooperative Learning: Increasing College Faculty Instructional Productivity. ASHE-ERIC Higher Education Report No.4. *School of Education and Human Development, The.* Washington, DC: George Washington University.

Jørgensen, I. S., & Nafstad, H. E. (2005). Positive psychology: Historical, philosophical, and epistemological perspectives. *Tidsskr Nor Psykol, 42*(10), 885–896.

References

Kasser, T., & Ahuvia, A. (2002). Materialistic values and well-being in business students. *European Journal of Social Psychology, 32*(1), 137–146.

Kasser, T., & Ryan, R. M. (2001). Be careful what you wish for: Optimal functioning and the relative attainment of intrinsic and extrinsic goals. In P. Schmuck, Peter & K. M. Sheldon (Eds.), *Life goals and well-being: Towards a positive psychology of human striving* (pp. 116–131). Ashland, OH, US: Hogrefe & Huber Publishers.

Kiemer, K., Gröschner, A., Pehmer, A. K., & Seidel, T. (2015). Effects of a classroom discourse intervention on teachers' practice and students' motivation to learn mathematics and science. *Learning and Instruction, 35,* 94–103.

King, R. B., & Datu, J. A. D. (2017). Materialism does not pay: Materialistic students have lower motivation, engagement, and achievement. *Contemporary Educational Psychology, 49,* 289–301.

King, M. B., & Newmann, F. M. (2000). Will teacher learning advance school goals? *Phi Delta Kappan, 81*(8), 576.

Klem, A. M., & Connell, J. P. (2004). Relationships matter: Linking teacher support to student engagement and achievement. *Journal of School Health, 74*(7), 262–273.

Kontos, S., & Wilcox-Herzog, A. (1997). Teachers' interactions with children: Why are they so important? *Research in Review. Young Children, 52*(2), 4–12.

Lam, B. H. (2011a). Constructivist Perspectives on Learning. In S. N. Pillipson & B. H. Lam (Eds.), *Learning and teaching in the Chinese classroom—responding to individual needs.* Hong Kong: Hong Kong University Press.

Lam, B. H. (2011b). A Reflective account of a pre-service teacher's effort to implement progressive curriculum in field practice Schools. *Studies Education, 8*(1), 22–39.

Lam, B. H. (2015). There is no fear in love—the giving of social support to students enhances teachers' career development. In R. Osbourne (Ed.), *Job satisfaction: Determinants, workplace implications and impacts on psychological well-being* (pp. 73–96). Hauppauge, NY: Nova Science Publishers.

Lam, B. H., & Yan, H. F. (2011). Beginning teachers' job satisfaction: The impact of school-based factors. *Teacher Development, 15*(3), 333–348.

Larson, R. W. (2002). Globalization, societal change, and new technologies: What they mean for the future of adolescence. *Journal of Research on Adolescence, 12*(1), 1–30.

Latham, G. P., & Pinder, C. C. (2005). Work motivation theory and research at the dawn of the twenty-first century. *Annual Review of Psychology, 56*(1), 485–516.

Lee, T. H. C. (2000). *Education in traditional China: A history.* Boston: Brill.

Lewis, M. (1993). Self-conscious emotions: Embarrassment, pride, shame, and guilt. In M. Lewis & J. M. Haviland (Eds.), *Handbook of emotions* (pp. 563–573). New York: Guilford Press.

Lin, N. (2017). *Building a network theory of social capital. In Social capital* (pp. 3–28). UK: Routledge.

Lortie, D. (1975). *School teacher: A sociological analysis.* Chicago: University of Chicago.

Martin, A. J., Collie, R. J., & Frydenberg, E. (2017). Social and emotional learning: Lessons learned and opportunities going forward. In E. Frydenbert, A., Martin, & R. Collie (Eds.), *Social and Emotional Learning in Australia and the Asia-Pacific* (pp. 459–471). Singapore: Springer.

Matud, M. P. (2004). Gender differences in stress and coping styles. *Personality and Individual Differences, 37*(7), 1401–1415.

McKenzie, K., Whitley, R., & Weich, S. (2002). Social capital and mental health. *The British Journal of Psychiatry, 181*(4), 280–283.

Morrison, B. (2002). *Bullying and victimisation in schools: A restorative justice approach. Australian Institute of Criminology: trends & issues in crime and criminal justice,* 219. Retrieved from http://www.aic.gov.au.

Mosley, J. (2005). *Circle time for young children.* UK: Routledge.

Nias, J. (1996). Thinking about feeling: The emotions in teaching. *Cambridge Journal of Education, 26*(3), 293–306.

Nias, J., Southworth, G., & Yeomans, R. (1989). *Staff relationships in the primary school: A study of organizational cultures.* Mansell.

Noddings, N. (2003). *Happiness and education*. Cambridge, UK: Cambridge University Press.

Noddings, N. (2013). *Caring: A relational approach to ethics and moral education*. Berkeley and Los Angeles, California: University of California Press.

O' Brennan, L., Pas, E., & Bradshaw, C. (2017). Multilevel examination of burnout among high school staff: Importance of staff and school factors. *School Psychology Review, 46*(2), 165–176.

Okasha, A. (2005). Globalization and mental health: A WPA perspective. *World Psychiatry, 4*(1), 1–2.

Omoto, A. M., Malsch, A. M., & Barraza, J. A. (2009). Compassionate acts: Motivations for and correlates of volunteerism among older adults. In B. Fehr, S., Sprecher, & L., G., Underwood (Eds.), *The science of compassionate love: Theory, research, and applications* (pp. 257–282). Singapore: Blackwell Publishing Ltd.

Patrick, H., & Pintrich, P. R. (2001). Conceptual change in teachers' intuitive conceptions of learning, motivation, and instruction: The role of motivational and epistemological beliefs. In B. Torff & R. J., Sternberg (Eds.), *Understanding and teaching the intuitive mind: Student and teacher learning* (pp. 117–143). Mahwah, New Jersey: Lawrence Erlbaum Associates, Publishers.

Piliavin, J. A., & Siegl, E. (2007). Health benefits of volunteering in the Wisconsin longitudinal study. *Journal of Health and Social Behavior, 48*(4), 450–464.

Rebora, A. (2017). Perspectives/ Working with change in schools. *Educational Leadership: Gearing up for Change, 74*, 5. Retrieved from http://www.ascd.org/publications/educational-leadership/jun17/vol74/num09/Working-With-Change-in-Schools.aspx.

Reddy, R., Rhodes, J. E., & Mulhall, P. (2003). The influence of teacher support on student adjustment in the middle school years: A latent growth curve study. *Development and Psychopathology, 15*(1), 119–138.

Reeve, J. (2009). Why teachers adopt a controlling motivating style toward students and how they can become more autonomy supportive. *Educational Psychologist, 44*(3), 159–175.

Reeve, J., Deci, E. L., & Ryan, R. M. (2004). Self-determination theory: A dialectical framework for understanding socio-cultural influences on student motivation. *Big theories revisited, 4*, 31–60.

Russell, S. L. (2012). *Individual-and classroom-level social support and classroom behavior in middle school*. Ph.D. dissertation. University of Maryland, College Park, ProQuest Dissertations Publishing.

Ryan, R. M., & Deci, E. L. (2000). Self-determination theory and the facilitation of intrinsic motivation, social development, and well-being. *American Psychologist, 55*(1), 68–78.

Ryan, R. M., & Deci, E. L. (2001). On happiness and human potentials: A review of research on hedonic and eudaimonic well-being. *Annual Review of Psychology, 52*(1), 141–166.

Sachs, J. (2003). *The activist teaching profession*. Buckingham: Open University Press.

Sacks, A. (2017). Empowering teaches to respond to change. *Educational Leadership: Gearing up for Change, 74*, 40–45. Retrieved from http://www.ascd.org/publications/educational-leadership/jun17/vol74/num09/Empowering-Teachers-to-Respond-to-Change.aspx.

Schwartz, C. E., & Sendor, R. M. (1999). Helping others helps oneself: response shift effects in peer support. *Social Science & Medicine, 48*(11), 1563–1575.

Scott, C., Stone, B., & Dinham, S. (2001). International patterns of teacher discontent. *Education Policy Analysis Archives, 9*(28), 1–16.

Seligman, M. E. (2002). Positive psychology, positive prevention, and positive therapy. *Handbook of Positive Psychology, 2*, 3–12.

Sharma, S., & Sharma, M. (2010). Globalization, threatened identities, coping and well-being. *Psychological Studies, 55*(4), 313–322.

Slavin, R. E. (2014). Cooperative Learning and Academic Achievement: Why Does Groupwork Work? *Anales de Psicología/Annals of Psychology, 30*(3), 785–791.

Smith, M. K. (2001). *Donald Schon: learning, reflection and change*. Retrieved from http://infed.org/mobi/donald-schon-learning-reflection-change/.

Snyder, T. D., Tan, A. G., and Hoffman, C. M. (2006). *Digest of Education Statistics 2005* (NCES 2006–030). U.S. Department of Education, National Center for Education Statistics. Washington, DC: U.S. Government Printing Office.

References

Sriprakash, A. (2013). New learner subjects? Reforming the rural child for a modern India. *Discourse: Studies in the Cultural Politics of Education, 34*(3), 325–337.

Suldo, S. M., Shaffer, E. J., & Riley, K. N. (2008). A social-cognitive-behavioral model of academic predictors of adolescents' life satisfaction. *School Psychology Quarterly, 23*(1), 56–69.

Taylor, S. E. (2007). Social support. In H. S. Friedman & R. C. Silver (Eds.), *Foundations of health psychology* (pp. 145–171). Oxford: Oxford University Press.

Taylor, S. E. (2011). Social support: A review. In S. F., Howard (Ed.), *The handbook of health psychology* (pp. 189–214). Oxford: Oxford University Press.

Thiers, N. (2017) Making progress possible: A conversation with Michael Fullan. *Educational Leadership: Gearing up for Change, 74*, 8–14. Retrieved from http://www.ascd.org/publications/educational-leadership/jun17/vol74/num09/Making-Progress-Possible@-A-Conversation-with-Michael-Fullan.aspx.

Thoits, P. A. (2011). Mechanisms linking social ties and support to physical and mental health. *Journal of Health and Social Behavior, 52*(2), 145–161.

Trivers, R. L. (1971). The evolution of reciprocal altruism. *The Quarterly Review of Biology, 46*(1), 35–57.

Tsang, K. K. (2011). Emotional labor of teaching. *Educational Research, 2*(8), 1312–1316.

Turner, R. B. (2013). *Expert teaching: Knowledge and pedagogy to lead the profession*. UK: Routledge.

Twenge, J. M., & Kasser, T. (2013). Generational changes in materialism and work centrality, 1976–2007: Associations with temporal changes in societal insecurity and materialistic role modeling. *Personality and Social Psychology Bulletin, 39*(7), 883–897.

UNESCO (2008). First collection of good practices for quality education. Paris: UNESCO. Retrieved at: http://unesdoc.unesco.org/images/0016/001627/162766e.pdf.

Ursano, A. M., Kartheiser, P. H., & Ursano, R. J. (2007). The teaching alliance: A perspective on the good teacher and effective learning. *Psychiatry: Interpersonal and Biological Processes, 70*(3), 187–194.

Vansteenkiste, M., Niemiec, C. P., & Soenens, B. (2010). The development of the five mini-theories of self-determination theory: An historical overview, emerging trends, and future directions. In T. C., Urdan & S. A., Karabenick (Eds.), *The decade ahead: Theoretical perspectives on motivation and achievement* (pp. 105–165). Emerald Group Publishing Limited.

Vavrus, M. (2008). Culturally responsive teaching. 21st Century Education: *A Reference Handbook, 2*, 49–57. Retrieved from https://static1.squarespace.com/static/55a68b71e4b075daf6b2aa0b/t/55a7322ae4b0a573ba71de46/1437020714535/CulturallyResponsiveTeaching.pdf.

Verschueren, K., Doumen, S., & Buyse, E. (2012). Relationships with mother, teacher, and peers: Unique and joint effects on young children's self-concept. *Attachment & Human Development, 14*(3), 233–248.

Vohs, K. D., Mead, N. L., & Goode, M. R. (2006). The psychological consequences of money. *Science, 314*(5802), 1154–1156.

Vygotsky, L. (1978). Interaction between learning and development. *Readings on the Development of Children, 23*(3), 34–41.

Walberg, H. J., & Paik, S. J. (2000). Effective Educational Practices. Educational Practices Series–3. Brussels: International Academy of Education.

Wang, Y. (2007). Analysis of teacher attrition. *Chinese Education & Society, 40*(5), 6–10.

Wang, M. T., & Eccles, J. S. (2012). Social support matters: Longitudinal effects of social support on three dimensions of school engagement from middle to high school. *Child Development, 83*(3), 877–895.

Waterman, A. S. (1993). Two conceptions of happiness: Contrasts of personal expressiveness (eudaimonia) and hedonic enjoyment. *Journal of Personality and Social Psychology, 64*(4), 678–691.

Wentzel, K. R., Battle, A., Russell, S. L., & Looney, L. B. (2010). Social supports from teachers and peers as predictors of academic and social motivation. *Contemporary Educational Psychology, 35*(3), 193–202.

World Health Organization (2001 October). *Mental disorders affect one in four people* (World health report). Retrieved from http://www.who.int/whr/2001/media_centre/press_release/en/.

World Health Organization (2014). *Preventing suicide: A global imperative*. Retrieved from http://apps.who.int/iris/bitstream/10665/131056/1/9789241564779_eng.pdf?ua=1&ua=1.

World Health Organization (2017 April). *Mental disorders fact sheet*. Retrieved from http://www.who.int/mediacentre/factsheets/fs396/en/.

Yeung, A. S., & Liu, W. P. (2007). *Workload and psychological wellbeing of Hong Kong teachers*. Fremantle: Paper presented at the the Australian Association for Research in Education.

Yin, H. B., & Lee, J. C. K. (2012). Be passionate, but be rational as well: Emotional rules for Chinese teachers' work. *Teaching and Teacher Education, 28*(1), 56–65.

Zembylas, M. (2003). Emotions and teacher identity: A poststructural perspective. *Teachers and Teaching, 9*(3), 213–238.

Correction to: Social Support, Well-being, and Teacher Development

Correction to:
B. LAM, *Social Support, Well-being, and Teacher Development*, https://doi.org/10.1007/978-981-13-3577-8

The original version of this book was revised: Author-provided text corrections have been incorporated.

In preface: I cannot thank him enough for his support to write for me as he knows me only at a distance; his foreword has added substantial strength to the book. A very special thanks should go to Prof. Dave Coniam for writing the other Foreword II and his valuable guidance to me during the course of writing this monograph. I have found this project more rewarding than I could have ever imagined as I learned under his mentorship. I would like to deeply thank Prof. Richard Ryan for writing the recommendation for the book. Through the investigations in this book, I have learnt much from Prof. Ryan's scholarship, and through my communication with him when inviting him to write the recommendation, I am truly benefit from his encouragement. I am sure that this feeling of support would last my academic career and lifetime.

To read as: I cannot thank him enough for his support to write for me as he knows me only at a distance. A very special thanks should go to Prof. Dave Coniam for writing the other Foreword II and his valuable guidance to me during the course of writing this monograph. I have found this project more rewarding than I could have ever imagined as I learned under his mentorship. I would like to deeply thank Prof. Richard Ryan for writing the recommendation for the book and his encouragement.

The updated version of these chapters can be found at
https://doi.org/10.1007/978-981-13-3577-8_1
https://doi.org/10.1007/978-981-13-3577-8_4
https://doi.org/10.1007/978-981-13-3577-8_7

© Springer Nature Singapore Pte Ltd. 2019
B. LAM, *Social Support, Well-being, and Teacher Development*,
https://doi.org/10.1007/978-981-13-3577-8_8

C2 Correction to: Social Support, Well-being, and Teacher Development

In chapter 1: some might feel the competition of time and would want to minimise emotional work because of the heavy syllabus they have to cover in class (Lam, 2011a, 2011b, 2011c).

To read as: some might feel the competition of time and would want to minimise emotional work because of the heavy syllabus they have to cover in class (Lam, 2011a, 2011b).

Driven by the wish for 'becoming the dragon' (Chinese idiom) which prevails in Chinese societies, as a result of the degenerated Confucian heritage culture (Lam, 2011a, 2011b, 2011c),

To read as: Driven by the wish for 'becoming the dragon' (Chinese idiom) which prevails in Chinese societies, as a result of the degenerated Confucian heritage culture (Lam, 2011a, 2011b),

Lam, B. H. (2011b). A reflective account of a preservice teacher's effort to implement a progressive curriculum in field practice. Schools, 8(1), 22–39

Lam, B. H. (2011c). The contexts of teaching in the 21st century. In S. N. Phillipson & B. H. Lam (Eds.), Learning and teaching in the Chinese classroom (pp. 1–30). Hong Kong: Hong Kong University Press.

To read as: Lam, B. H. (2011b). The contexts of teaching in the 21st century. In S. N. Phillipson & B. H. Lam (Eds.), Learning and teaching in the Chinese classroom (pp. 1–30). Hong Kong: Hong Kong University Press.

In chapter 4: While it provides teachers with a new approach to handling class ethos and improving class cohesion (Barrett & Randall),

To read as: While it provides teachers with a new approach to handling class ethos and improving class cohesion (Barrett & Randall, 2004),

The impact of teachers' emotional support in increasing students' academic achievement can partly be explained by the skills students adopt through teachers' emotional work of scaffolding, and partly because of the positive attitude of teachers who WHO may have a positive influence on students.

To read as: The impact of teachers' emotional support in increasing students' academic achievement can partly be explained by the skills students adopt through teachers' emotional work of scaffolding, and partly because of the positive attitude of teachers who may have a positive influence on students.

These researchers proposed structure and autonomy support as inseparable in teaching to produce effective learning outcomes.

To read as: These researchers proposed autonomy support and structure as inseparable in teaching to produce effective learning outcomes.

In chapter 7: Third, organisational support is crucial for developing teachers. Since the investigation revealed that students are the source of teacher satisfaction, and giving support to students is most satisfying for teachers, schools should seek ways to promote teacher—student relationships and accommodate teacher—student interactions at the organisational level, e.g. creating time in the school timetable for student—teacher meetings and consultations,

To read as: Third, organisational support is crucial for developing teachers. Since the investigation revealed that students are the source of teacher satisfaction, and giving support to students is most satisfying for teachers, schools should seek

Correction to: Social Support, Well-being, and Teacher Development

ways to promote teacher-student relationships and accommodate teacher-student interactions at the organisational level, e.g. creating time in the school timetable for student-teacher meetings and consultations,

The use of a social support perspective to systematically measure educational processes and outcomes is still not common in educational research, while the existing literature partly refers to common topics such as student—teacher relationships and teacher's emotional support without giving specific explanations of such terms.

To read as: The use of a social support perspective to systematically measure educational processes and outcomes is still not common in educational research, while the existing literature partly refers to common topics such as student-teacher relationships and teacher's emotional support without giving specific explanations of such terms.

Regarding methodology, qualitative study and qualitative study instruments are recommended to elaborate the features of social support and the outcomes for students, and teachers' personal thoughts in teaching.

To read as: Regarding methodology, quantitative study and qualitative study instruments are recommended to elaborate the features of social support and the outcomes for students, and teachers' personal thoughts in teaching.

The erratum book has been updated with the changes.

Printed in the United States
By Bookmasters